Lecture Notes in Computer Science　　10028

Commenced Publication in 1973
Founding and Former Series Editors:
Gerhard Goos, Juris Hartmanis, and Jan van Leeuwen

More information about this series at http://www.springer.com/series/7408

Roderick Bloem · Eli Arbel (Eds.)

Hardware and Software: Verification and Testing

12th International
Haifa Verification Conference, HVC 2016
Haifa, Israel, November 14–17, 2016
Proceedings

 Springer

Editors
Roderick Bloem
IAIK
Graz University of Technology
Graz
Austria

Eli Arbel
IBM Research Labs
Haifa
Israel

ISSN 0302-9743   ISSN 1611-3349 (electronic)
Lecture Notes in Computer Science
ISBN 978-3-319-49051-9   ISBN 978-3-319-49052-6 (eBook)
DOI 10.1007/978-3-319-49052-6

Library of Congress Control Number: 2016956611

LNCS Sublibrary: SL2 – Programming and Software Engineering

Printed on acid-free paper

This Springer imprint is published by Springer Nature
The registered company is Springer International Publishing AG
The registered company address is: Gewerbestrasse 11, 6330 Cham, Switzerland

Preface

This volume contains the proceedings of the 12th Haifa Verification Conference (HVC 2016). The conference was hosted by IBM Research Haifa Laboratory and took place during November 14–17, 2016. It was the 12th event in this series of annual conferences dedicated to advancing the state of the art and state of the practice in verification and testing. The conference provided a forum for researchers and practitioners from academia and industry to share their work, exchange ideas, and discuss the future directions of testing and verification for hardware, software, and complex hybrid systems.

Overall, HVC 2016 attracted 26 submissions in response to the call for papers. Each submission was assigned to at least three members of the Program Committee and in some cases additional reviews were solicited from external experts. The Program Committee selected 13 papers for presentation. In addition to the contributed papers, the program included four invited talks, by Swarat Chaudhuri (Rice University), Markulf Kohlweiss (Microsoft Research), Rajeev Ranjan (Cadence), and Andreas Veneris (University of Toronto). On the last day of the conference, the HVC award was presented to Marta Kwiatkowska (University of Oxford), Gethin Norman (University of Glasgow), and Dave Parker (University of Birmingham), for the invention, development and maintenance of the PRISM probabilistic model checker. A special session about verification and testing challenges of autonomous systems was held on the first day of the conference. Thanks to Yoav Hollander (Foretellix LTD) for presenting in this session. On November 13, one day before the conference, we held a tutorial day with tutorials by Sanjit A. Seshia (University of California, Berkeley) on formal inductive synthesis, by Hari Mony (IBM) on sequential equivalence checking for hardware design and verification, by Amir Rahat (Optima Design Automation) on design reliability, and by Cristian Cadar (Imperial College) on dynamic symbolic execution and the KLEE infrastructure.

We would like to extend our appreciation and sincere thanks to the local organization team from IBM Research Haifa Laboratory: Tali Rabetti, the publicity chair, Revivit Yankovich, the local coordinator, Yair Harry, the Web master, and the Organizing Committee, which consisted of Laurent Fournier, Sharon Keidar-Barner, Moshe Levinger, Michael Vinov, Karen Yorav, and Avi Ziv. We would also like to thank the tutorial chair Natasha Sharygina (University of Lugano), and the HVC Award Committee, consisting of Armin Biere (Johannes Kepler University), Hana Chockler (King's College London), Kerstin Eder (University of Bristol), Andrey Rybalchenko (Microsoft Research), Ofer Strichman (Technion), and particularly its energetic chair, Leonardo Mariani (University of Milano Bicocca).

HVC 2016 received sponsorships from IBM, Cadence Design Systems, Mellanox Technologies, Mentor Graphics, Qualcomm, and Intel. (Thanks!)

Submission and evaluation of papers, as well as the preparation of this proceedings volume, were handled by the EasyChair conference management system. (Thanks, Andrei!)

It was a pleasure to organize this conference with so many old friends!

Graz   Eli Arbel
September 2016   Roderick Bloem

Organization

Program Committee

Eli Arbel	IBM Research, Israel
Domagoj Babic	Google, USA
Aviv Barkai	Intel Corporation, Israel
Nikolaj Bjorner	Microsoft Research, USA
Roderick Bloem	Graz University of Technology, Austria
Hana Chockler	King's College London, UK
Rayna Dimitrova	MPI-SWS, Germany
Adrian Evans	iRoC Technologies, France
Franco Fummi	University of Verona, Italy
Raviv Gal	IBM Research, Israel
Warren Hunt	University of Texas, USA
Barbara Jobstmann	EPFL and Cadence Design Systems, Switzerland
Laura Kovacs	Vienna University of Technology, Austria
João Lourenço	NOVA LINCS – Universidade Nova de Lisboa, Portugal
Annalisa Massini	Sapienza University of Rome, Italy
Hari Mony	IBM Corporation, USA
Nir Piterman	University of Leicester, UK
Pavithra Prabhakar	Kansas State University, USA
Sandip Ray	NXP Semiconductors, USA
Orna Raz	HRL, IBM Research, Israel
Martina Seidl	Johannes Kepler University Linz, Asutria
Sanjit A. Seshia	UC Berkeley, USA
A. Prasad Sistla	University of Illinois at Chicago, USA
Ufuk Topcu	University of Texas at Austin, USA
Eran Yahav	Technion, Israel

Additional Reviewers

Arechiga, Nikos	Krakovski, Roi	Sadigh, Dorsa
Dreossi, Tommaso	Lal, Ratan	Salvo, Ivano
Fremont, Daniel J.	Mari, Federico	Soto, Miriam Garcia
Gao, Sicun	Rabe, Markus N.	Veneris, Andreas
Junges, Sebastian	Rabetti, Tali	

Abstracts

Current Trends and Future Direction in Eco-system of Hardware Formal Verification: A Technical and Business Perspective

Rajeev K. Ranjan

Cadence, San Jose, USA

Hardware formal verification is increasingly being adopted in the modern SoC design and verification flow for architectural specification and verification through RTL development and debugging through SoC integration – all the way up to post-silicon debugging. The productivity and quality benefits of adopting this technology for a gamut of verification tasks are well established. In this talk, we will cover the current trends and future directions in this area that is shaped by the technical feasibility of the solutions and the business RoI seen by different stakeholders V- chip companies, design/verification engineers, formal EDA vendors, and formal solution development engineers.

Guiding Formal Methods with Discovered Knowledge

Swarat Chaudhuri

Rice University, Houston, USA

Systems for automated formal reasoning about programs depend on human specification at multiple levels. Users of such a system must write full specifications of the tasks that they want performed. The designer of the system is expected to formalize the domain-specific language in which tasks are described, and specify the domain-dependent heuristics that guide automated reasoning. The assumption of specifications reflects a common expectation in formal methods research: that humans hold deep knowledge about problem domains and instances. In practice, this expectation can be violated and lead to hard-to-use or brittle tools. In this talk, we describe a new class of formal methods that address this difficulty through automatic discovery of knowledge from corpora of pre-existing code, execution traces, and proofs.

The starting point of this work is the observation that a human who describes or solves a reasoning task does not do so in a vacuum, but using insights established through prior experiences of their own or others. The thesis is that such insights can be algorithmically learned from datasets of existing formal artifacts, and can lead to systems for automated reasoning that demand less human intervention than traditional tools. The talk will describe multiple instantiations of this thesis, including a statistical notion of program correctness, a program synthesis algorithm guided by a "neural" model of program syntax and semantics, and an approach to program verification that uses pre-existing formal proofs.

Bug Wars: Automation Awakens

Andreas Veneris

Department of Electrical and Computer Engineering, and Department of
Computer Science, University of Toronto, Toronto, Canada

Verification is the undisputed bottleneck in the design cycle consuming two thirds of the total chip development effort. This is in part because of the complexity of modern designs, the impact of geographical dispersed teams integrating new components with third-party/legacy IP under tight time-to-market goals, the evolving role of verification engineers to not only discover bugs but also aid correct them and the ever-evolving nature of the task itself. Today verification has stretched itself beyond its traditional boundaries into validation as most of silicon re-spins are not due to physical defects but because of functional errors not discovered or fixed earlier in the design cycle. Although parts of verification have been automated the core issue driving this gap remains debugging as it consumes more than half of the overall effort being a predominantly manual task.

In this talk, we revisit automation efforts in functional debug from late 1980s, when it was first introduced, to recent formal advances placing it into context as we recount new directions. In more detail, we will first outline early methodologies stemming from test and fault diagnosis to more recent techniques based on Boolean satisfiability. We will examine different angles of the debug problem and respective solutions for its various manifestations in the verification cycle. This will allow us to appraise theoretical and practical parallels in the foundations of those two tasks. As we evaluate the progress in debug automation, we will point out emerging deficiencies of existing methodologies more notably during regression verification. To that end, we will present novel techniques in debugging triage where statistical solutions, a radical departure from existing debug efforts, need complement traditional simulation/formal methods to not only take into account the design response but also the human factor. We will conclude with a mantra that research in debugging in the past 30 years points to a direction where verification and test prove once again to be fields deeply intertwined, and we will provide guidance for methodologies in silicon debug rooted on existing functional debug procedures.

miTLS: Can Cryptography, Formal Methods, and Applied Security be Friends?

Markulf Kohlweiss

Microsoft Research, Cambridge, UK

TLS was designed as a transparent channel abstraction to allow developers with no cryptographic expertise to protect their application against attackers that may control some clients, some servers, and may have the capability to tamper with network connections. However, the security guarantees of TLS fall short of those of a secure channel, leading to a variety of attacks. The Triple Handshake attack exploits combinations of RSA and Diffie-Hellman key exchange, session resumption, and renegotiation to bypass many recent countermeasures.

At the same time we study the provable security of TLS, as it is implemented and deployed. To capture the details of the standard and its main extensions, we rely on miTLS, a verified reference implementation of the protocol. miTLS inter-operates with mainstream browsers and servers for many protocol versions, configurations, and ciphersuites; and it provides application-level, provable security for some. This leads to the strange case of how something provable secure can be insecure.

In this talk I will play Dr Jekyll and Mr Hyde by playing off our CRYPTO proof and our S&P attack against each other.

Contents

SAT-Based Combinational and Sequential Dependency Computation

Mathias Soeken[1]([✉]), Pascal Raiola[2], Baruch Sterin[3], Bernd Becker[2],
Giovanni De Micheli[1], and Matthias Sauer[2]

[1] EPFL, Lausanne, Switzerland
mathias.soeken@epfl.ch
[2] University of Freiburg, Freiburg im Breisgau, Germany
[3] UC Berkeley, Berkeley, CA, USA

Abstract. We present an algorithm for computing both functional dependency and unateness of combinational and sequential Boolean functions represented as logic networks. The algorithm uses SAT-based techniques from *Combinational Equivalence Checking* (CEC) and *Automatic Test Pattern Generation* (ATPG) to compute the dependency matrix of multi-output Boolean functions. Additionally, the classical dependency definitions are extended to sequential functions and a fast approximation is presented to efficiently yield a sequential dependency matrix. Extensive experiments show the applicability of the methods and the improved robustness compared to existing approaches.

1 Introduction

In this paper we present an algorithm to compute the *dependency matrix* $D(f)$ for a given combinational or sequential multi-output function f. For every input-output pair, the combinational dependency matrix indicates whether the output depends on the input, and whether the output is positive or negative unate in that input [21].

Several algorithms in logic design use the dependency matrix as a *signature* [23] to speed up computation, e.g., Boolean matching [14], functional verification [11,12], or reverse engineering [29]. Although most of these algorithms make implicit use of the dependency matrix, the name has been used in this paper for the first time. The name is inspired by the output format of functional dependence and unateness properties in the state-of-the-art academic logic synthesis tool ABC [4]. Functional dependency is also related to *transparent logic* [19,24]. Given a set of inputs X_d and a set of outputs Y_d, the problem is to find a set of inputs X_c that is disjoint from X_d and that distinguishes the output values at Y_d for different input assignments to X_d. In contrast, we consider functional dependence without constraints for all input-output pairs.

Existing algorithms for computing the dependency matrix are based on Binary Decision Diagrams (BDDs, [5]) and have been implemented in ABC [4]. It is important to point out that the term *functional dependence* is used

© Springer International Publishing AG 2016
R. Bloem and E. Arbel (Eds.): HVC 2016, LNCS 10028, pp. 1–17, 2016.
DOI: 10.1007/978-3-319-49052-6_1

to describe a different property in a related context: In [12,13,16], the authors refer to functional dependence as the question whether given a set of Boolean functions $\{f_1, \ldots, f_n\}$, there exists an f_i, that can be written as $h(f_1, \ldots, f_{i-1}, f_{i+1}, \ldots, f_n)$. In other words, functional dependence is defined as a Boolean function w.r.t. to a set of Boolean functions. In contrast, we consider the functional dependence of a Boolean function w.r.t. a single variable as functional dependence.

Our algorithm uses techniques from *Combinational Equivalence Checking* (CEC, e.g., [22]) and *Automatic Test Pattern Generation* (ATPG, e.g., [15,26, 27]). We employ efficient incremental SAT-based solving techniques and extract incidental information from solved instances to reduce runtime consumption on complex functions.

We furthermore present an extension of the combinational dependency definition to sequential functions. We account the sequential counterpart of a functional dependence relation to an input-output pair if the given relation constantly holds after some finite number of steps. As an example, some output f may be always positive unate in some input x after a certain number of iteration steps of the circuit. In this case, we call f sequential positive unate in x, even if this relation is not guaranteed in the first steps.

An established method to prove properties on sequential circuits is bounded model checking (BMC) as first introduced in [1], used, e.g., in [8,25]. In BMC a circuit is modelled iteratively for k steps as a combinational circuit. With approaches such as k-induction [18] and Craig interpolation [20] BMC becomes a complete model checking method. However, as such complete methods are rather computationally expensive, we rely on an iterative approximation to compute the sequential dependency matrix solely based on the combinational dependency matrix. By iteratively analyzing the combinational dependency until a fixed point is derived, we can accurately conclude structural dependency and unateness.

In an extensive experimental evaluation we demonstrate the applicability of our methods to various combinational and sequential benchmark sets. Within reasonable amounts of computing time we are able to accurately compute the combinational dependency matrix as well as an approximation of our sequential dependency matrix with a small number of iterations. We further show the robustness of our proposed algorithm compared to a previous state-of-the-art algorithm that times out or suffers from memory explosion on complex functions. Finally, we present a case study in which the dependency matrix is used as a signature in reverse engineering to effectively reduce the search space and improve the performance of the underlying application.

The rest of the paper is organized as follows. Section 2 presents the fundamentals of the work. In Sect. 3 we introduce our SAT-based approach to compute the dependency matrix of combinational circuits, and extend it in Sect. 4 to sequential circuits. The experimental results are presented in Sect. 5 and Sect. 6 concludes the work.

2   Background

2.1   Functional Dependencies

A Boolean function $f(x_1, \ldots, x_n)$ is *functionally dependent* in x_i if $f_{\bar{x}_i} \neq f_{x_i}$ where the *co-factors* f_{x_i} or $f_{\bar{x}_i}$ are obtained by setting x_i to 1 or 0 in f, respectively. We call f_{x_i} the positive co-factor and $f_{\bar{x}_i}$ the negative co-factor. The function f is said to be *positive unate* in x_i, if

$$f_{\bar{x}_i} \leq f_{x_i} \tag{1}$$

and *negative unate* in x_i, if

$$f_{\bar{x}_i} \geq f_{x_i}, \tag{2}$$

where the comparisons '$\leq$' and '$\geq$' are applied to the binary strings that represent the truth tables of $f_{\bar{x}_i}$ and f_{x_i}. f is said to be unate in x_i if it is either positive or negative unate in x_i. Clearly, a function f is both positive and negative unate in x_i, if f does not depend on x_i. Hence, we call f *strictly* positive (negative) unate in x_i, if f is positive (negative) unate in x_i *and* depends on x_i. If f is neither positive nor negative unate in x_i, we say that f is *binate* in x_i.

Example 1. The functions $x_1 \wedge x_2$ and $x_1 \vee x_2$ are positive unate in both x_1 and x_2. The function $x_1 \rightarrow x_2$ is negative unate in x_1 and positive unate in x_2. The function $x_1 \oplus x_2$ is binate in both variables.

Let $f : \mathbb{B}^n \rightarrow \mathbb{B}^m$ be a multi-output Boolean function where each output is represented by a Boolean function $f_j(x_1, \ldots, x_n)$. The *dependency matrix* $D(f)$ is an $m \times n$ matrix with entries $d_{j,i}$ where

$$d_{j,i} = \begin{cases} \text{p} & \text{if } f_j \text{ is strictly positive unate in } x_i, \\ \text{n} & \text{if } f_j \text{ is strictly negative unate in } x_i, \\ \text{d} & \text{if } f_j \text{ depends on, but is not unate in } x_i, \\ \bullet & \text{otherwise.} \end{cases} \tag{3}$$

Example 2. Let $f : \mathbb{B}^5 \rightarrow \mathbb{B}^3$ with $f_1 = x_1 \wedge x_2$, $f_2 = x_3 \rightarrow x_5$, and $f_3 = x_1 \oplus x_2 \oplus x_5$. Then

$$D(f) = \begin{bmatrix} \text{p} & \text{p} & \bullet & \bullet & \bullet \\ \bullet & \bullet & \text{n} & \bullet & \text{p} \\ \text{d} & \text{d} & \bullet & \bullet & \text{d} \end{bmatrix}.$$

2.2   Boolean Satisfiability

In our algorithm we translate decision problems into instances of the SAT problem [3]. SAT is the problem of deciding whether a function f, has an assignment x for which $f(x) = 1$. Such an assignment is called a *satisfying assignment*. If f has a satisfying assignment it is said to be *satisfiable*. Otherwise, f is said to be *unsatisfiable*.

In general, SAT is NP-complete [6,17]. SAT solvers are algorithms that can solve SAT problems and, while worst-case exponential, are nonetheless very efficient for many practical problems. SAT solvers also return a satisfying assignment if the instance is satisfiable. Most of the state-of-the-art SAT solvers are conflict-driven and employ clause-learning techniques [10]. In *incremental* SAT one asks whether f is satisfiable under the assumption of some variable assignments. These assignments are only temporarily assumed, making it possible to reuse the SAT instance and learned information when solving a sequence of similar SAT problems. In the remainder of the paper, we refer to instances of SAT as if they were calls to an incremental SAT solver. SAT?(f, α) is true if f is satisfiable under the assumptions α, and UNSAT?(f, α) is true if f is unsatisfiable under the assumptions α.

3   SAT-Based Dependency Computation

This section presents the SAT-based algorithm to compute the functional dependencies of a function. We first describe the encoding into SAT, then an implementation of the algorithm, and finally possible optimizations.

3.1   SAT Encoding

We encode the test for functional dependence and unateness as an instance of the SAT problem using the following theorem.

Theorem 1. *Let* $f(x_1, \ldots, x_n)$ *be a Boolean function. Then*

1. *f is functionally dependent in x_i, if and only if $f_{\bar{x}_i} \oplus f_{x_i}$ is satisfiable,*
2. *f is positive unate in x_i, if and only if $f_{\bar{x}_i} \wedge \bar{f}_{x_i}$ is unsatisfiable, and*
3. *f is negative unate in x_i, if and only if $f_{x_i} \wedge \bar{f}_{\bar{x}_i}$ is unsatisfiable.*

Proof. We only show the direction of "if"; the "only if" direction follows immediately from the definition of functional dependency and unateness.

1. Let x be a satisfying assignment to $f_{\bar{x}_i} \oplus f_{x_i}$. Then, we have $f_{\bar{x}_i}(x) \neq f_{x_i}(x)$.
2. Assume the function was satisfiable and let x be a satisfying assignment. Then $f_{\bar{x}_i}(x) = 1$ while $f_{x_i}(x) = 0$ which contradicts Eq. (1).
3. Analogously to (2).   □

In the implementation, we make use of the following immediate consequence of the theorem.

Corollary 1. *f is functionally independent in x_i, if and only if $f_{\bar{x}_i} \oplus f_{x_i}$ is unsatisfiable.*

In the following we consider multi-output functions $f : \mathbb{B}^n \to \mathbb{B}^m$, where each output is a function f_j. In order to compute the full dependency matrix which contains the dependency for each input-output pair, we transform the problem to a sequence of SAT instances as illustrated by the generic miter in Fig. 1. The

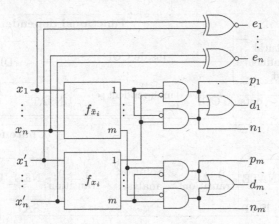

Fig. 1. Generic miter to encode functional dependency as SAT instance

two boxes represent two copies of f. The upper copy, with inputs $x_1, \ldots, x_n$, is used as the negative co-factor, while the lower copy, with inputs $x'_1, \ldots, x'_n$, is used as the positive co-factor of f. The groups of three gates on the lower right hand side realize the XOR operation which connect the outputs of the two copies. The signals of the AND gates are exposed as outputs and will be used to encode the unateness problems. The XNOR gates in the upper right of the figure are used to force all but one of the inputs, to have equal values.

Let $\Pi(f_j)$ be the characteristic Boolean function which is obtained by encoding the miter in Fig. 1 for the function f_j using encodings such as Tseytin [32] or EMS [9]. Also let $E_i = \{x_i = 0, \ x'_i = 1\} \cup \{e_k = 1 \mid k \neq i\}$ be assignments that lead to a correct interpretation of the miter for input x_i, i.e., x_i is set to 0, x'_i is set to 1 and all the other inputs need to have the same value. We define three problems on top of the incremental SAT interface:

$$\text{DEP}(f_j, x_i) = \text{SAT?}(\Pi(f_j), E_i \cup \{d_j = 1\}) \tag{4}$$

$$\text{POS\_UNATE}(f_j, x_i) = \text{UNSAT?}(\Pi(f_j), E_i \cup \{p_j = 1\}) \tag{5}$$

$$\text{NEG\_UNATE}(f_j, x_i) = \text{UNSAT?}(\Pi(f_j), E_i \cup \{n_j = 1\}) \tag{6}$$

Then the problems described in Theorem 1 and Corollary 1 can be solved as follows. The function f_j functionally depends on x_i, if $\text{DEP}(f_j, x_i)$ holds. And the function f_j is positive (negative) unate in x_i, if $\text{POS\_UNATE}(f_j, x_i)$ ($\text{NEG\_UNATE}(f_j, x_i)$) holds.

3.2 Algorithm

Figure 2 displays the general flow of the algorithm. For each pair of an input $x = x_i$ and an output $y = f_j$ the algorithm starts with a simple structural dependency check. If x is outside of y's structural cone of influence, it can be concluded that y is independent of x. This is a very efficient check. Otherwise,

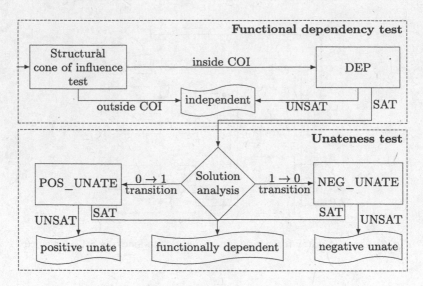

Fig. 2. Functional dependency and unateness computation flow

the algorithm proceeds with a functional dependency check $\mathrm{DEP}(y, x)$ as defined in Eq. (4). We omit the arguments from the boxes.

If the instance is unsatisfiable, y is independent from x as no assignment exists that results in different logic values for y under the side constraint of $y_{\bar{x}} \oplus y_x$. In case the instance is satisfiable, x and y are at least functionally dependent. Additionally, the SAT solver returns a satisfying assignment which is analyzed for the logic value of y. In case $y_{\bar{x}}$ is 1 (and therefore y_x is 0), y cannot be positive unate in x as a counter example for Eq. (1) is found. Likewise, negative unateness can be falsified if $y_{\bar{x}}$ is 0. Note that one of the two cases must hold as the original instance requires a difference between $y_{\bar{x}}$ and y_x.

In a last step, the algorithm specifically checks for unateness with an additional call to the SAT solver, unless it has been ruled out previously. If this SAT call is unsatisfiable, unateness can be concluded, otherwise the algorithm returns functional dependence.

3.3 Optimizations

As discussed above, we use incremental SAT solving because many of the calls to the SAT solver are very similar. Hence, instead of encoding a miter-like structure as illustrated in Fig. 1 for each input-output pair in an individual instance, we encode the complete output cone of a target input x_i in a single instance to profit from incremental SAT solving. We enforce the co-factors of x_i as unit clauses in this instance. As we target combinational circuits, the direction of the co-factors does not influence the satisfiability of the instance. Hence, we can restrict the search space by enforcing x_i to logic 1 and x_i' to logic 0 without loss of generality. Furthermore, XOR gates are encoded for output pairs to enforce them to differ using assumptions in the SAT solver.

On the output side, we iteratively run through each output in x's cone of influence and enforce a difference between $f_{\bar{x}_i}$ and f_{x_i} using an assumption. If the resulting instance is UNSAT we can conclude independence. Otherwise, the input-output pair is at least functionally dependent. By observing the direction of the difference at the output, we consider the pair either as a candidate for positive or negative unateness and run the respective check as described earlier.[1]

Additionally, we perform a forward looking logic analysis of each satisfiable SAT instance to extract incidental information for future solver calls. In our experiments we found quite often, that the difference not only propagates to the target output, but also to multiple other outputs. Hence, we check the logic values of all following outputs as well. Additionally, an output may incidentally show differences in both directions and hence unateness can be ruled out without additional SAT calls.

The described SAT instances are very similar to detecting a stuck-at-1 fault at the input x. Hence, we employ encoding based speed-up techniques that are known from solving such ATPG problems. By adding D-chains [31] that add redundant information to the instance, the SAT solver can propagate the differences more easily. Additionally, we tuned the SAT solver's internal settings towards the characteristics of the circuit-based SAT instances which are dominated by a large number of rather simple SAT calls. For instance, we do not use preprocessing techniques on the SAT instances.

4   Sequential Functional Dependency

While the prior definitions and algorithms are specified for combinational circuits, we also investigate the definition of dependency in sequential circuits.

To translate the properties from Sect. 2.1 to sequential circuits, we use a similar approach as used in (un)bounded model checking: An output y_j is called *sequential functionally dependent* in an input x_i if and only if there exists a number $k \in \mathbb{N}$, such that $f_j^{(k)}$ is functionally dependent in x_i, where $f_j^{(k)}$ represents the Boolean function of the output modelled over k steps.

For $f_j^{(1)}$ the sequential circuit can be treated as a combinational one. For $f_j^{(k)}$ with $k > 1$, the definition of sequential dependence follows the combinational one if the sequential circuit is considered as an iterative logic array with an unlimited number of time frames. Hence, such a definition allows to extend combinational dependency in a natural way to sequential dependency.

In contrast to the complexity of the combinational dependency computation of a single input-output pair (which is NP-complete since it is an ATPG problem), sequential dependency computation is identical to invariant checking which can be expressed by an unbounded model checking approach and is PSPACE-complete.

---

[1] We also performed a structural check for each input-output pair if there potentially exists an inverting path between them. If this is not the case, the additionally SAT-call to check for unateness may be skipped. However, the performance impact was insignificant and hence we did not employ this optimization.

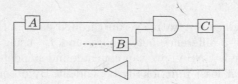

Fig. 3. Example circuit

Sequential independence is defined as the contrary of sequential dependence. An output y_j is called (strictly) *sequential positive/negative unate* in x_i, if there exists a k_0, such that for every number $k \in \mathbb{N}$ with $k > k_0$, $f_j^{(k)}$ is (strictly) positive/negative unate in x_i.

Example 3. Let $f^{(k)}$ be the Boolean function corresponding to the flip flop C in the circuit in Fig. 3 in the kth step. Then C is alternating strictly positive and negative unate in A. Thus, C is neither sequential positive nor negative unate in A. However, C is sequential dependent in A.

4.1   Approximative Algorithm

We use the methods from Sect. 3 to compute the combinational dependency matrix $D(f)$ for $f^{(0)}$ and then initialize the sequential dependency Matrix $D^s(f)$ as $D(f)$. For clarity, to refer to an entry of the dependency matrix with output y_j and input x_i we write d_{y_j,x_i} instead of $d_{j,i}$. Respective entries of the sequential dependency matrix are denoted as $d_{j,i}^s$.

For each output $y = f_j$ and input x we check, if there exist x_k and y_l, such that

- x_k and y_l correspond to the same flip flop φ,
- $d_{y,x_k}^s \neq \bullet$ and
- $d_{y_l,x}^s \neq \bullet$.

The path-dependence of y in x over φ is defined with the equation

$$\text{pd}_\varphi(y,x) = \begin{cases} p & \text{if } d_{y,x_k}, d_{y_l,x} \text{ unate and } d_{y,x_k} = d_{y_l,x}, \\ n & \text{if } d_{y,x_k}, d_{y_l,x} \text{ unate and } d_{y,x_k} \neq d_{y_l,x}, \\ d & \text{otherwise.} \end{cases} \tag{7}$$

If $\text{pd}_\varphi(y,x) \neq d_{y,x}^s$, we may need to update the dependence value of the sequential dependency matrix $d_{y,x}^s$:

$$d_{y,x}^s \leftarrow \begin{cases} \text{pd}_\varphi(y,x) & \text{if } \text{pd}_\varphi(y,x) = d_{y,x}^s \lor d_{y,x}^s = \bullet, \\ d & \text{otherwise.} \end{cases} \tag{8}$$

Now we choose different y_l, x_k, y and/or x and start from the top until we reach a fixed point. Our algorithm focuses on positive unateness (p) and negative unateness (n), in contrast to strict positive unateness ($\mathbf{p}$) and strict negative unateness ($\mathbf{n}$).

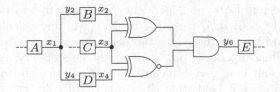

Fig. 4. Example circuit (2)

According to the definitions in the previous section, all dependencies marked as seq. positive unate (p), seq. negative unate (n) or seq. independent ($\bullet$) by our approximation are correctly classified as we will show in Sect. 4.2.

However, the dependencies marked as seq. functionally dependent (d) may be inaccurate as $d^s_{j,i} = d$ is an over-approximation. Hence, the algorithm allows an accurate classification for three dependency conditions, while avoiding the computational complexity of a completely accurate algorithm (that still can be applied if completeness is needed).

To see that $d^s_{j,i} = d$ does not generally imply sequential dependence, see Fig. 4, where $d^s_{6,2} = d$, $d^s_{2,1} = p$, $d^s_{6,4} = d$ and $d^s_{4,1} = p$. Therefore $d^s_{6,1} = d$, but because of the partly inverse reconvergence, y_6 is sequentially independent in x_1.

If the XNOR-Gate in Fig. 4 was replaced by an XOR-Gate, y_6 would be sequentially dependent in x_1, while no values of its combinational dependency matrix would differ from the combinational dependency matrix of the original circuit. Since these two circuits have the same combinational dependency matrix, but different sequential dependency matrices, it is not possible to build an exact algorithm for sequential dependency, solely based on the combinational dependency matrix.

4.2 Proof of Correctness for p, n and $\bullet$

The correctness of the classification of an input-output pair as either p, n or $\bullet$ can be shown as follows:

p: Proof by contradiction: For the correctness of the return value p, let the algorithm return p for output (or flip flop) y and input (or flip flop) x, but y is not sequential positive unate in x. Then there exists an (arbitrary high) $k \in \mathbb{N}$, such that $f^{(k)}$, the Boolean function of y, is not positive unate in x. Following from the definition of unateness (cf. Sect. 2.1), there exists an input sequence $\hat{x}$, such that $f^{(k)}_{\overline{x}}(\hat{x}) = 1$ and $f^{(k)}_x(\hat{x}) = 0$. For clarity, we use the abbreviations $x^{[\overline{x}]} = 0$, $y^{[\overline{x}]} = 1$ and $x^{[x]} = 1$, $y^{[x]} = 0$ where $[\overline{x}]$ and $[x]$ indicate the logic value for the respective case. There must exist a path from x to y, where the path follows $x = p_0, p_1, \ldots, p_{m-1}, p_m = y$, all p_i with $0 < i < m$ represent flip flops and $\forall i \leq m : p_i^{[\overline{x}]} \neq p_i^{[x]}$.

For any $i < m$, p_{i+1} combinationally depends on p_i, therefore the entry in the combinational dependency matrix for p_{i+1} on p_i (d_{p_{i+1},p_i}) is not $\bullet$, thus d, p or n. As seen in Eq. 8, no dependency value gets overwritten by $\bullet$, which leads to $d^s_{p_{i+1},p_i} \in \{\mathsf{d}, n, p\}$ for all i. If $d^s_{p_{i+1},p_i}$ in any calculation step was d, $d^s_{p_{i+1},p_i}$ would be d in the sequential dependency matrix, as d can not get overwritten. Then, by Eq. 7, $\mathrm{pd}_\varphi(x,y)$ would be step-wise calculated as d, which would result in $d^s_{y,x} = \mathsf{d}$ in contradiction to the algorithm returning p. Thus, for any $i < m$, it holds that $d^s_{p_{i+1},p_i} \in \{n, p\}$.

Let $I_{\mathrm{Same}} = \{i < m : p_i^{[\overline{x}]} = p_{i+1}^{[\overline{x}]}\}$ and $I_{\mathrm{Diff}} = \{i < m : p_i^{[\overline{x}]} \neq p_{i+1}^{[\overline{x}]}\}$, then I_{Diff} contains an odd number of elements, because $p_0^{[\overline{x}]} \neq p_m^{[\overline{x}]}$. For any $i \in I_{\mathrm{Same}}$, it holds that $d^s_{p_{i+1},p_i} \neq n$ resp. $d^s_{p_{i+1},p_i} = p$ in every calculation step and similarly for any $i \in I_{\mathrm{Diff}}$, always $d^s_{p_{i+1},p_i} = n$. The calculated dependency pd for the given path along $p_0, \dots, p_m$ will then be calculated based on an odd number of n and otherwise only p, which will by Eq. 7 result in path dependence n. Therefore, by Eq. 8, the algorithm does not return p, a contradiction.

n: The proof of the correctness of the return value n is analogous to the proof of the correctness of p. The major difference is that I_{Diff} contains an even number of elements. This will force a path calculation to result in p, making impossible, that the algorithm returns n.

$\bullet$: Proof by contradiction: For the correctness of the return value $\bullet$, let the algorithm return $\bullet$ for output y and input x, but y is not sequential independent in x, i.e. sequential dependent in x. Following from a similar argument as for p, there must exist a path, which follows $x = p_0, p_1, \dots, p_{m-1}, p_m = y$, all p_i with $0 < i < m$ represent flip flops and $\forall i \leq m : p_i^{[\overline{x}]} \neq p_i^{[x]}$. By Eq. 8, every $d^s_{p_{i+1},p_i}$ in any calculation step is not $\bullet$. Then $\mathrm{pd}_\varphi(x,y)$ would by Eq. 7 be step-wise calculated not as $\bullet$, which would by Eq. 8 result in $d^s_{p_{i+1},p_i} \neq \bullet$ in the sequential dependency matrix, in contradiction to the algorithm returning $\bullet$. $\square$

5   Experimental Results

We implemented the proposed approach in C++ on top of the ATPG framework PHAETON [26] and the SAT solver *antom* [28]. All experiments were carried out on a single core of an Intel Xeon machine running at 3.3 GHz, 64 GB main memory running Linux 3.13. For the evaluations, we used combinational arithmetic benchmarks from EPFL[2] as well as sequential benchmarks from the ITC'99 [7] benchmark suite and industrial benchmarks provided by NXP (starting with 'b' and 'p' followed by a number, respectively). Finally, we applied the method to the OpenCore benchmarks from the IWLS'05 [2] family. In order to keep the section compact, we skipped the benchmarks that had either negligible runtime or that could not be solved within a timeout of 2 h.

---

[2] lsi.epfl.ch/benchmarks.

Table 1. Combinational experiments

Circuit	IO	Dependencies				Statistics			Runtimes	
		Struct.	Func.	Pos.	Neg.	Incidental	Instances	Solves	Unateness	Total
adder	256129	0	16512	256	0	16512	256	17024	4.07	4.40
bar	135128	0	896	16384	0	777	135	33670	1.08	17.70
divisor	128128	0	12220	66	2082	13026	128	9519	4502.32	4871.53
log2	3232	0	1022	0	2	979	32	686	3746.98	3750.90
max	512130	32512	32512	1024	512	15271	512	82241	37.13	110.24
sin	2425	0	577	22	0	441	24	472	17.86	31.23
square	64128	0	6041	68	3	5956	64	3926	447.34	450.51
b14	277299	11	21803	705	68	18403	277	22368	20.74	27.71
b15	485519	19504	40704	3338	292	33017	485	57931	77.33	231.29
b17	14511511	44054	135906	11271	1225	109432	1451	177747	234.55	637.20
b18	33073293	1084	331223	22367	2250	266523	3307	326342	439.45	690.52
b20	522512	5298	51508	1212	370	42795	522	52742	120.06	232.61
b21	522512	5310	51508	1238	136	42171	522	53808	94.69	203.93
b22	735725	5313	78254	1740	359	65388	735	76254	163.15	280.46
p35k_s	28612229	0	140676	10802	10697	123321	2861	147727	628.73	1090.66
p45k_s	37392550	409	24910	13638	860	14256	3739	62307	20.84	59.95
p78k_s	31483484	377	52338	6032	0	48970	3148	50197	47.34	73.73
p81k_s	40293952	1380	387839	11724	18737	324849	4029	308638	419.38	897.82
p100k_s	55575489	756	77829	24347	3406	51415	5557	147954	4959.58	5236.16
des_area	367192	0	11328	288	0	9756	367	5623	2.78	6.16
spi	272273	16256	4205	982	117	1977	272	24649	1.54	10.03
systemcdes	312255	592	2341	590	8	1580	312	4222	0.61	1.57
wb_dma	747748	1195	10880	2364	842	6674	747	19879	2.25	4.54
tv80	372391	9452	15265	1917	218	11906	372	28468	9.71	21.49
systemcaes	928799	14613	17158	939	44	13273	928	29743	7.43	19.21
ac97_ctrl	22532247	10	7940	7083	831	5315	2253	25510	0.87	2.67
pci_bridge32	35173559	9906	59360	12179	2512	38839	3517	108600	57.35	106.20
aes_core	788659	0	7290	541	29	6285	788	5636	2.17	4.43
wb_conmax	18992186	1976	46132	23968	16346	37884	1899	125420	39.40	98.11
des_perf	90418872	0	29344	7448	0	18627	9041	51718	16.63	68.60

All times are in seconds.

5.1   Combinational Dependency

Table 1 lists the results of the evaluation. The first three columns list the name of the circuit as well as the number of inputs and outputs. The following four columns list the identified dependencies. The number of only structural dependencies (that are found to be independent) are given first followed by the number of dependent classifications (excluding unateness) and finally the number of positive or negative unate classifications, respectively. The next three columns list statistics of the proposed SAT-based approach: The number of functional dependencies that were found incidentally followed by the number of generated SAT instances and calls to the SAT solver. The final two columns list the runtime for unateness checking and the total runtime in seconds.

As can be seen, our approach is able to completely compute the dependency matrix on a wide range of mid-sized circuits taken from various academic and industrial benchmark circuits within a maximum computation time of 2 h (7200 s).

Interestingly, the number of input-output pairs that are positive unate are roughly an order of magnitude higher than those that are negative unate. This is most prominent for the barrelshifter circuit 'bar' from the EPFL benchmarks that contains mostly positive unate pairs but no negative one.

The effect of the optimizations described in Sect. 3.3 can be witnessed by the high number of dependencies identified incidentally as well the high ratio between the number of instances as well as the calls to the SAT solvers. Hence, these methods effectively keep the runtimes in check.

5.2   Comparison to Existing Approach

We compared our approach to the BDD-based implementation in ABC [4] where identical circuit definitions readable for both tools were available. We listed the results in Table 2.

The proposed SAT-based approach shows superior performance for the rather complex benchmark sets of the EPFL as well as the ITC'99 benchmarks where the approach does not suffer from excessive memory usage. For complex functions, the BDD-based approach did not terminate due to insufficient memory requirements.

For the EPFL benchmarks, the BDD-based approach did not terminate due to a timeout which we set to 7200 s. 7 of the 10 arithmetic EPFL benchmarks can be solved using the SAT-based approach, and for 6 of them the SAT-based

Table 2. Comparison to the BDD-based approach from ABC [4]

		Runtimes		ABC [4]	
Circuit	In/Out	Unate.	Total	Unate.	Total
adder	256/129	4.07	4.40	0.01	0.54
bar	135/128	1.08	17.70	18.96	19.05
divisor	128/128	4502.32	4871.53	TO	TO
log2	32/32	3746.98	3750.90	TO	TO
max	512/130	37.13	110.24	TO	TO
sin	24/25	17.86	31.23	0.15	866.99
square	64/128	447.34	450.51	TO	TO
b14	277/299	20.74	27.71	74.17	120.07
b15	485/519	77.33	231.29	199.45	368.25
b17	1451/1511	234.55	637.20	MO	MO
b18	3307/3293	439.45	690.52	MO	MO
b20	522/512	120.06	232.61	MO	MO
b21	522/512	94.69	203.93	MO	MO
b22	735/725	163.15	280.46	MO	MO

All times are in seconds; MO: memory out; TO: timeout (≥7200 s).

approach found the solution faster. The three remaining benchmarks cannot be solved within 7200 s by both approaches. It is worth noting that for benchmarks that are rather small or structurally simple (such as the adder) the BDD-based approach performs faster than the SAT-based approach.

5.3 Sequential Dependency

Table 3 shows the results of the sequential dependency computation algorithm as presented in Sect. 4 that was executed on the sequential versions of the benchmark circuits from the previous experiment where possible. At first, the name of the circuit, the number of flip flops as well as the number of inputs and outputs are given. Following, as in the previous section we list the different dependencies as well as the number of iterations through the combinational dependency matrix. Finally, the runtimes for the generation of the combinational dependency matrix, the extension to the sequential matrix as well as the total runtime (all in seconds) are given.

As can be seen, the sequential algorithm needs only a few iterations to conclude the sequential dependency for all benchmarks. Hence, the overall impact on the runtime is limited and for most of the circuits less than the runtime of the combinational method. When comparing the results of the dependencies, one

Table 3. Sequential experiments

Circuit	FFs	IO	Sequential dependencies					Runtime SAT-based		
			Struct.	Func.	Pos.	Neg.	Iterations	Comb.	Sequential	Total
b14	245	3254	62	60702	108	1	3	27.71	0.06	27.77
b15	449	3670	18112	161327	282	4	3	231.29	0.40	231.69
h17	1414	3797	3020	1680385	217	0	3	637.20	17.27	654.47
b18	3270	3723	0	10575260	87	2	3	690.52	362.10	1052.62
b20	490	3222	0	246240	38	2	3	232.61	0.85	233.46
b21	490	3222	0	246240	38	2	2	203.93	0.57	204.50
b22	703	3222	0	487257	59	3	3	280.46	5.21	285.68
p35k_s	2173	68856	0	243835	10786	10712	3	1090.66	2.39	1093.05
p45k_s	2331	1408219	90	1826005	1093874	3253	5	59.95	208.98	268.94
p78k_s	2977	171507	0	616075	26788	0	5	73.73	28.76	102.50
p81k_s	3877	15275	1566	2974664	6693	8024	3	897.82	85.70	983.51
p100k_s	5395	16294	92	4797360	1091341	5894	5	5236.16	301.64	5537.80
des_area	128	23964	0	70464	0	0	3	6.16	0.03	6.19
spi	229	4344	27456	21010	1050	11	3	10.03	0.05	10.08
systemcdes	190	12265	0	47603	3202	2	4	1.57	0.04	1.61
wb_dma	533	214215	0	128209	1268	79	4	4.54	0.89	5.43
tv80	359	1332	0	132696	59	2	3	21.49	0.23	21.72
systemcaes	670	258129	0	716373	1	0	3	19.21	2.32	21.53
ac97_ctrl	2199	5448	5	132290	155065	658	3	2.67	7.11	9.79
pci_bridge32	3358	159201	20030	3825065	12332	155	3	106.20	138.70	244.90
aes_core	530	258129	0	285777	390	4	3	4.43	2.00	6.43
wb_conmax	770	11291416	0	647425	13152	512	3	98.11	5.39	103.50
des_perf	8808	23364	0	13852506	116088	0	3	68.60	1129.18	1197.78

can note that the number of functional dependencies increases at the cost of the other classifications. This is expected as many structural dependencies get functional when considering multiple timeframes. Additionally, the requirements for sequential positive as well as sequential negative unateness are much harder to meet than their combinational counterparts and hence such classifications tend to be changed to a functional dependency.

5.4   Application to Reverse Engineering

We show the applicability of functional dependency and unateness information in a small case study of reverse engineering. We consider the *Permutation-Independent Subset Equivalence Checking* (SPIEC) problem [29]: Given a block $f_b : \mathbb{B}^n \to \mathbb{B}^m$ and a component $f_c : \mathbb{B}^r \to \mathbb{B}^s$ with $n \geq r$ and $m \geq s$, SPIEC asks whether there exists a mapping from all primary inputs and primary outputs of f_c to primary inputs and primary outputs in f_b such that the block realizes the same function as the component w.r.t. this mapping.

The algorithm presented in [29] solves this problem by finding subgraph isomorphisms of simulation graphs for the block and the component. A simulation graph has input vertices, output vertices, and vertices for some characteristic simulation vectors. A subgraph isomorphism in these graphs provides a candidate mapping that can be verified using combinational equivalence checking [22]. Subgraph isomorphism is translated into a constraint satisfaction problem according to [30] while additionally considering application-specific information extracted from the circuits, e.g., functional dependency and unateness properties.

The constraint satisfaction implementation starts by creating a domain for each vertex in the component's simulation graph. The domain is a set of possible candidate vertices in the block's simulation graph. Filtering methods then try to reduce the size of the domains such that eventually either (i) some domain is empty and therefore no matching exists, or (ii) all domains contain a single element from which the mapping can directly be extracted. If the filtering techniques cannot advance to any of these two cases, one has to start branching using a backtracking algorithm. The aim is to avoid backtracking, which can be achieved by effective filtering methods.

In our experiment we considered the impact of the dependency matrix by comparing three different scenarios: (i) no information is provided, (ii) the dependency matrix is provided for the component which allows the use of structural dependency information as a signature, and (iii) the dependency matrix is provided for both the block and the component allowing the use of functional dependency and unateness properties as signatures for filtering. We measure the quality by comparing the accumulated domain sizes after all filtering methods are exhausted right before backtracking is initiated.

Table 4 shows the results of our experiments. The circuits for blocks (c1–c10) and components (adder, multi, shift,[3] and subtract) are the same that were

---

[3] In [29] shift-left and shift-right are considered separately. Since these operations are equivalent under permutation, the measured numbers in the experiment also do not differ.

Table 4. Reverse engineering experiment

	adder	multi	shift	subtract
c1-8	0/0/0	730/661/609	44/44/44	0/0/0
c2-8	890/770/482	1753/706/612	1217/595/578	860/639/428
c3-8	489/24/24	797/455/425	577/256/240	0/0/0
c4-8	712/0/0	1280/0/0	1024/421/421	26/26/26
c5-8	690/462/24	1405/423/401	1089/44/44	26/26/26
c6-8	1234/1140/273	1820/0/0	1600/930/930	719/989/422
c7-8	141/25/25	796/0/0	576/401/401	27/27/27
c8-8	368/0/0	576/0/0	427/44/44	0/0/0
c9-8	1291/984/24	1885/566/476	1665/645/636	951/881/388
c10-8	131/24/24	1596/0/0	456/253/253	0/0/0

evaluated in [29] in their 8-bit variant. Each cell in the matrix represents the application of SPIEC to the block and component of the respective row and column, respectively. Each cell shows three numbers. These numbers are the accumulated domain sizes of primary inputs and outputs for each of the three considered scenarios. The cell is shaded gray if the component is contained in the block. As can be seen in the table, the dependency matrix has a strong influence on the results since the domain sizes can be significantly reduced, often resulting in a matching that provides a solution. For example, in the case of c9 and the adder a mapping has been found only if the dependency matrices for both the block and the component are provided. In the case of c4 and the adder one needs to compute at least the component's dependency matrix to conclude that it is not contained in that block without backtracking.

6   Conclusions

We presented a SAT-based algorithm to compute functional dependence properties of combinational as well as sequential Boolean functions. We inspect which outputs in a multi-output function are functionally dependent on which inputs. Furthermore, the algorithms checks whether the input-output pair is unate if it is dependent, which is a stronger property. Furthermore, incremental encoding techniques known from ATPG problems are employed to speed up the algorithm. Additionally, we extended the classical dependency classifications to sequential circuits and presented an iterative approximative algorithm to compute such sequential dependencies.

In extensive experimental studies on different benchmarks suites we detailed the robustness of the algorithms especially for hard combinational as well as sequential benchmarks. Additionally, our methods show better performance compared to previously presented BDD-based approaches with which many of the instances cannot be solved due to memory limitations or timeouts.

Acknowledgments. The authors wish to thank Robert Brayton and Alan Mishchenko for many helpful discussions. This research was partially financed by H2020-ERC-2014-ADG 669354 CyberCare and the Baden-Württemberg Stiftung gGmbH Stuttgart within the scope of its IT security research programme.

References

1. Biere, A., Cimatti, A., Clarke, E.M., Fujita, M., Zhu, Y.: Symbolic model checking using SAT procedures instead of BDDs. In: Design Automation Conference, pp. 317–320 (1999)
2. Albrecht, C.: IWLS 2005 benchmarks. In: International Workshop for Logic Synthesis (IWLS) (2005). http://www.iwls.org
3. Biere, A., Heule, M.J.H., van Maaren, H., Walsh, T. (eds.): Handbook of Satisfiability, Frontiers in Artificial Intelligence and Applications, vol. 185. IOS Press, Amsterdam (2009)
4. Brayton, R., Mishchenko, A.: ABC: an academic industrial-strength verification tool. In: Touili, T., Cook, B., Jackson, P. (eds.) CAV 2010. LNCS, vol. 6174, pp. 24–40. Springer, Heidelberg (2010). doi:10.1007/978-3-642-14295-6_5
5. Bryant, R.E.: Graph-based algorithms for Boolean function manipulation. IEEE Trans. Comput. **35**(8), 677–691 (1986)
6. Cook, S.A.: The complexity of theorem-proving procedures. In: Symposium on Theory of Computing, pp. 151–158 (1971)
7. Corno, F., Reorda, M., Squillero, G.: RT-level ITC'99 benchmarks and first ATPG results. IEEE Des. Test Comput. **17**(3), 44–53 (2000)
8. Saab, D.G., Abraham, J.A., Vedula, V.M.: Formal verification using bounded model checking: SAT versus sequential ATPG engines. In: VLSI Design, pp. 243–248 (2003)
9. Een, N., Mishchenko, A., Sörensson, N.: Applying logic synthesis for speeding up SAT. In: Marques-Silva, J., Sakallah, K.A. (eds.) SAT 2007. LNCS, vol. 4501, pp. 272–286. Springer, Heidelberg (2007). doi:10.1007/978-3-540-72788-0_26
10. Eén, N., Sörensson, N.: An extensible SAT-solver. In: Giunchiglia, E., Tacchella, A. (eds.) SAT 2003. LNCS, vol. 2919, pp. 502–518. Springer, Heidelberg (2004). doi:10.1007/978-3-540-24605-3_37
11. van Eijk, C.A.J., Jess, J.A.G.: Exploiting functional dependencies in finite state machine verification. In: European Design and Test Conference, pp. 9–14 (1996)
12. Jiang, J.-H.R., Brayton, R.K.: Functional dependency for verification reduction. In: Alur, R., Peled, D.A. (eds.) CAV 2004. LNCS, vol. 3114, pp. 268–280. Springer, Heidelberg (2004). doi:10.1007/978-3-540-27813-9_21
13. Jiang, J.R., Lee, C., Mishchenko, A., Huang, C.: To SAT or not to SAT: scalable exploration of functional dependency. IEEE Trans. Comput. **59**(4), 457–467 (2010)
14. Katebi, H., Markov, I.L.: Large-scale Boolean matching. In: Design, Automation and Test in Europe, pp. 771–776 (2010)
15. Larrabee, T.: Test pattern generation using Boolean satisfiability. IEEE Trans. CAD Integr. Circuits Syst. **11**(1), 4–15 (1992)
16. Lee, C., Jiang, J.R., Huang, C., Mishchenko, A.: Scalable exploration of functional dependency by interpolation and incremental SAT solving. In: International Conference on Computer-Aided Design, pp. 227–233 (2007)
17. Levin, L.A.: Universal sequential search problems. Probl. Inf. Transm. **9**(3), 115–116 (1973)

18. Sheeran, M., Singh, S., Stålmarck, G.: Checking safety properties using induction and a SAT-solver. In: Hunt, W.A., Johnson, S.D. (eds.) FMCAD 2000. LNCS, vol. 1954, pp. 127–144. Springer, Heidelberg (2000). doi:10.1007/3-540-40922-X_8
19. Marhöfer, M.: An approach to modular test generation based on the transparency of modules. In: IEEE CompEuro 1987, pp. 403–406 (1987)
20. McMillan, K.L.: Interpolation and SAT-based model checking. In: Hunt, W.A., Somenzi, F. (eds.) CAV 2003. LNCS, vol. 2725, pp. 1–13. Springer, Heidelberg (2003). doi:10.1007/978-3-540-45069-6_1
21. McNaughton, R.: Unate truth functions. IRE Trans. Electron. Comput. **10**(1), 1–6 (1961)
22. Mishchenko, A., Chatterjee, S., Brayton, R.K., Eén, N.: Improvements to combinational equivalence checking. In: International Conference on Computer-Aided Design, pp. 836–843 (2006)
23. Mohnke, J., Molitor, P., Malik, S.: Limits of using signatures for permutation independent Boolean comparison. Form. Methods Syst. Des. **21**(2), 167–191 (2002)
24. Murray, B.T., Hayes, J.P.: Test propagation through modules and circuits. In: International Test Conference, pp. 748–757 (1991)
25. Reimer, S., Sauer, M., Schubert, T., Becker, B.: Using MaxBMC for pareto-optimal circuit initialization. In: Conference on Design, Automation and Test in Europe, pp. 1–6, March 2014
26. Sauer, M., Becker, B., Polian, I.: PHAETON: a SAT-based framework for timing-aware path sensitization. IEEE Trans. Comput. **PP**(99), 1 (2015)
27. Sauer, M., Reimer, S., Polian, I., Schubert, T., Becker, B.: Provably optimal test cube generation using quantified Boolean formula solving. In: ASP Design Automation Conference, pp. 533–539 (2013)
28. Schubert, T., Reimer, S.: antom (2013). https://projects.informatik.uni-freiburg.de/projects/antom
29. Soeken, M., Sterin, B., Drechsler, R., Brayton, R.K.: Reverse engineering with simulation graphs. In: Formal Methods in Computer-Aided Design, pp. 152–159 (2015)
30. Solnon, C.: AllDifferent-based filtering for subgraph isomorphism. Artif. Intell. **174**(12–13), 850–864 (2010)
31. Stephan, P., Brayton, R.K., Sangiovanni-Vincentelli, A.L.: Combinational test generation using satisfiability. IEEE Trans. CAD Integr. Circuits Syst. **15**(9), 1167–1176 (1996)
32. Tseytin, G.: On the complexity of derivation in propositional calculus. In: Studies in Constructive Mathematics and Mathematical Logic (1968)

Multi-core SCC-Based LTL Model Checking

Vincent Bloemen$^{(\boxtimes)}$ and Jaco van de Pol

Formal Methods and Tools, University of Twente, Enschede, The Netherlands
{v.bloemen,j.c.vandepol}@utwente.nl

Abstract. We investigate and improve the scalability of multi-core LTL model checking. Our algorithm, based on parallel DFS-like SCC decomposition, is able to efficiently decompose large SCCs on-the-fly, which is a difficult problem to solve in parallel.

To validate the algorithm we performed experiments on a 64-core machine. We used an extensive set of well-known benchmark collections obtained from the BEEM database and the Model Checking Contest. We show that the algorithm is competitive with the current state-of-the-art model checking algorithms. For larger models we observe that our algorithm outperforms the competitors. We investigate how graph characteristics relate to and pose limitations on the achieved speedups.

1 Introduction

The automata theoretic approach to LTL model checking involves taking the synchronized product of the negated property and the state space of the system. The resulting product is checked for emptiness by searching for an *accepting cycle*, i.e. a reachable cycle that satisfies the accepting condition [35]. If an accepting cycle is found the system is able to perform behavior that is not allowed by the original property, hence we say that a counterexample has been found.

In order to fully utilize modern hardware systems, the design of parallel algorithms has become an urgent issue. Model checking is a particularly demanding task (in both memory and time), which makes it a well-suited candidate for parallelization. *On-the-fly* model checking makes it possible to find a counterexample while only having to search through part of the state space. However, the on-the-fly restriction makes it especially difficult to design a correct and efficient parallel algorithm. In practice, this causes the algorithms to rely on *depth-first search (DFS)* exploration [32].

General Idea of the Algorithm. We present a multi-core solution for finding accepting cycles on-the-fly. It improves recent work [30] by communicating partially found *strongly connected components (SCCs)* [2]. The general idea of our algorithm is best explained using the example from Fig. 1. In Fig. 1a, two threads (or workers), which we call 'red' and 'blue', start their search from the initial state, a. Here, state f is an accepting state, and the goal is to find a reachable cycle that contains an accepting state. We assume that the workers have no prior

© Springer International Publishing AG 2016
R. Bloem and E. Arbel (Eds.): HVC 2016, LNCS 10028, pp. 18–33, 2016.
DOI: 10.1007/978-3-319-49052-6_2

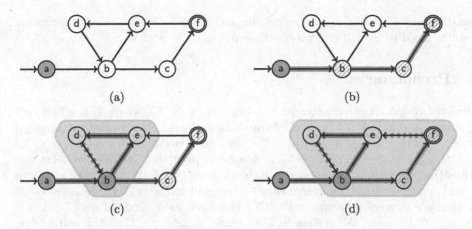

Fig. 1. Example where two workers cooperate to find a counterexample. (Color figure online)

knowledge of any other state (on-the-fly). Using a successor function suc(), the successor states of a can be computed (thus, suc(a)={b}).

In Fig. 1b we observe a situation where the red worker has explored the path a → b → c → f. Suppose that the red worker halts and the blue worker starts exploring the path a → b → e → d and observes suc(d)={b} (Fig. 1c). The blue worker then finds a cycle that contains the states {b,d,e} and stores this information globally.

Now consider what happens in Fig. 1d. Here, the red worker continues its search and explores the edge f → e. Since the states {b,d,e} are part of a known cycle, and the red worker has explored the path b → c → f → e, we can thus implicitly assume that states c and f are part of the same SCC and form {b,c,d,e,f}. Remarkably, the algorithm can detect an accepting cycle while neither the red nor the blue worker explored the cycle f → e → d → b → c → f.

We make the following contributions in this paper.

- We provide an SCC-based on-the-fly LTL model checking algorithm by extending on previous work [2] and the work from Renault et al. [30].
- We empirically compare our algorithm with state-of-the-art algorithms (all implemented in the same toolset), using an extensive set of well-known benchmark models. We show that our algorithm is competitive and even outperforms the competitors for larger models.
- We observe and discuss relations between the algorithms and scalability for models containing large SCCs.

In order to carry out the necessary experiments, we have extended the LTSMIN toolset [17] to connect with the Spot v2.0 library [7] for generating Büchi Automata.

Overview. The remainder of the paper is structured as follows. In Sect. 2 we provide preliminaries on model checking. Section 3 discusses related work on parallel model checking. We present our algorithm in Sect. 4. The experiments are discussed in Sect. 5 and we conclude our work in Sect. 6.

2   Preliminaries

Directed Graph. A directed graph is a tuple $G := \langle V, E \rangle$, where V is a finite set of states, and $E \subseteq V \times V$ is a set of transitions. We denote a transition (or edge) $\langle v, w \rangle \in E$ by $v \to w$. A *path* $v_0 \to^* v_n$ is a sequence of states $v_0, \ldots, v_n \in V^*$ s.t. $\forall_{0 \le i < n} : v_i \to v_{i+1}$, $v_0 \to^+ v_n$ denotes a path that contains at least one transition. A *cycle* is a non-empty path where $v_0 = v_n$. We say that two states v and w are *strongly connected* iff $v \to^* w$ and $w \to^* v$, written as $v \leftrightarrow w$. A *strongly connected component (SCC)* is defined as a maximal set $C \subseteq V$ s.t. $\forall v, w \in C : v \leftrightarrow w$. We call an SCC C *trivial* if $\exists v \in V : C = \{v\}$ and $v \not\to v$. We call C a *partial SCC* if all states in C are strongly connected, but C is not necessarily maximal.

Automaton Graph. The synchronized product of the negated LTL property and the state space of the system is usually represented with an *automaton graph*. There are different ways to represent an automaton graph. In practice, two common ways to describe an automaton graph is by using a *Büchi Automaton (BA)* or a *Transition-based Generalized Büchi Automaton (TGBA)*.

Definition 1 (BA). *A BA is a tuple $\mathcal{B} := \langle V, E, A, v_0 \rangle$, where V is a finite set of states, $E \subseteq V \times V$ is a set of transitions, $A \subseteq V$ is the set of accepting states, and $v_0 \in V$ is the initial state. An accepting cycle C on $\mathcal{B}$ is defined as a cycle, reachable from v_0, where $C \cap A \neq \emptyset$.*

Definition 2 (TGBA). *A TGBA is a tuple $\mathcal{K} := \langle V, \delta, F, v_0 \rangle$, where V is a finite set of states, $\delta \subseteq V \times 2^F \times V$ is a set of transitions where each transition is labeled by a subset of acceptance marks, F is a finite set of acceptance marks, and $v_0 \in V$ is the initial state. An accepting cycle C on $\mathcal{K}$ is defined as a cycle $\langle w_0, a_0, w_1 \rangle, \ldots, \langle w_n, a_n, w_0 \rangle$, reachable from v_0, where $a_0 \cup \ldots \cup a_n = F$. Any BA can be represented with a TGBA using the same number or fewer states and transitions* [13].

For the remainder of the paper, unless stated otherwise, we consider the automaton graph to be represented as a *BA*. We make the assumption that an automaton graph is computed *on-the-fly*. This implies that an algorithm initially only has access to the initial state v_0, and can compute successor states: $\text{suc}(v) := \{w \in V \mid v \to w\}$.

3   Related Work

Sequential algorithms for explicit-state on-the-fly LTL model checking can be distinguished in two classes, *Nested DFS (NDFS)* and *SCC-based* algorithms.

For an excellent overview on *sequential* NDFS and SCC-based algorithms, we would like to refer the reader to the work of Schwoon and Esparza [32]. Both NDFS- and SCC-based algorithms can perform in linear time complexity on the number of edges in the graph.

NDFS Based Algorithms. NDFS, originally proposed by Courcoubetis et al. [3], performs two interleaved searches. An outer DFS to find accepting states and an inner DFS that checks for cycles around accepting states. Since its inception, several improvements have been made [11,15,32].

Multi-core NDFS. A number of multi-core variants on NDFS have been designed that scale on parallel hardware in practice [8,9,20,21]. These algorithms are based on *swarm verification* [14]. The idea is that all workers initially start from the initial state, but the list of successor states is permuted for each worker. This way, distinct workers will explore different parts of the graph with a high probability.

We consider CNDFS [8] to be the state-of-the-art NDFS-based algorithm. Independent NDFS-like instances are launched and global information is shared between the workers during (and after) the backtrack procedure. The algorithm performs in linear time.

We note that NDFS-based algorithms are explicitly based on using BA acceptance. To the best of our knowledge, no parallel NDFS-like algorithm exists for checking TGBAs.

SCC-Based Algorithms. SCC-based model checking consists of finding SCCs and detecting if the accepting criteria is met in one of these components. Tarjan's algorithm [34] is generally favored for the SCC detection procedure due to its linear time complexity and ability to perform on-the-fly. Couvreur [4], and Gelden-huys and Valmari [12] proposed modifications to more quickly recognize accepting cycles. Notably, an SCC-based model checking algorithm can be used to check for emptiness on *generalized* Büchi automata [5,32].

Multi-core SCC-Based Algorithms. There are a number of parallel algorithms that can detect SCCs in an explicitly given graph, e.g. [10,16,25,31,33]. However, none of these are applicable in the on-the-fly context since they require knowledge about a state's predecessors and/or depend on random access to the state space. There has been a lot of recent activity in finding SCCs on-the-fly. This pursuit has resulted in three new algorithms [2,23,29,30].

The algorithm by Lowe [23] is based on spawning multiple *synchronized* instances of Tarjan's algorithm. Here, each state may only be visited by one worker and a work-stealing-like procedure is used to handle conflicts that arise. Experimental evaluation shows that Lowe's algorithm performs well if the graph contains many small SCCs, but this seems to deteriorate quickly when the SCC sizes grow. Lowe's algorithm has a quadratic worst-case complexity.

The algorithm by Renault et al. [29,30] is also based on spawning multiple instances of Tarjan's (and/or Dijkstra's [6]) algorithm, but here a state may be visited by multiple workers. The approach is based on swarmed verification, where individual searches globally communicate fully explored SCCs – which are avoided by other workers from then on. To improve LTL checking, acceptance conditions are globally updated per partial SCC whenever a worker detects a cycle, making it possible to find a counterexample in a similar fashion as we present in Fig. 1. We consider this algorithm the current state-of-the-art of SCC-based parallel on-the-fly model checking and it performs in quasi-linear time complexity.

In this paper, we applied the UFSCC algorithm by Bloemen et al. [2] for LTL model checking. We discuss the algorithm extensively in Sect. 4 and show how this improves the scalability for graphs containing large SCCs.

4   Multi-core SCC Algorithm for LTL Model Checking

The main idea of the UFSCC algorithm is that it globally communicates *partially found SCCs* while maintaining a quasi-linear time complexity. This means that when a worker has locally found a cycle, it merges all states on that cycle in a global structure (implemented with concurrent union-find). In order to make efficient use of this information, the structure also tracks which workers have visited the partial SCCs to support a more lenient form of detecting back-edges. The structure also tracks which states have been fully explored and allows workers to concurrently select states that still require exploration.

A collection of disjoint sets is used for globally tracking partially discovered SCCs. This collection, $\pi : V \rightarrow 2^V$, satisfies the following invariant: $\forall v, w \in V :$ $w \in \pi(v) \Leftrightarrow \pi(v) = \pi(w)$. In other words, the set for a specific state can be obtained from any member of the set. This also implies that every state must belong to exactly one set. A Unite function is used to combine two disjoint sets, while maintaining the invariant. As an example, let $\pi(v) := \{v\}$ and $\pi(w) := \{w, x\}$ (note $\pi(w) = \pi(x)$) , then Unite(π, v, w) combines $\pi(v)$ and $\pi(w)$, resulting in $\pi(v) = \pi(w) = \pi(x) = \{v, w, x\}$ while not modifying any other mappings. These properties follow directly from an implementation with union-find.

The Algorithm. The algorithm can be found in Fig. 2. We assume that every line is executed atomically[1]. Each worker p has its own local search stack, R_p. The global collection π and global sets Dead and Done are initialized in Lines 2–3. Dead implies that an *SCC* is fully explored and Done implies that a *state* is fully explored. Every worker starts exploring from the initial state v_0. Disregarding Line 7 for the moment, Lines 8–15 describe the procedure to fully explore a state. For every successor w of v' there are three cases to be distinguished:

1. $w \in$ Dead (Line 9): State w is part of an already completed SCC, it may be ignored since no new information can be obtained.

---

[1] In practice this is not exactly true, however all necessary conditions are preserved by using a fine-grained locking structure.

```
1  ∀ p ∈ [1...P] : Rₚ := ∅
2  ∀ v : π(v) := {v}
3  Dead := Done := ∅
4  UFSCC₁(v₀) || ... || UFSCCₚ(v₀)
5  procedure UFSCCₚ(v)
6  ·  Rₚ.push(v)
7  ·  while v' := π(v) \ Done do
8  ·  ·  for each w ∈ Random(suc(v')) do
9  ·  ·  ·  if w ∈ Dead then continue
10 ·  ·  ·  else if ∄w' ∈ Rₚ : w ∈ π(w') then UFSCCₚ(w)
11 ·  ·  ·  else while π(v) ≠ π(w) do
12 ·  ·  ·  ·  ·  r := Rₚ.pop()
13 ·  ·  ·  ·  ·  s := Rₚ.top()
14 ·  ·  ·  ·  ·  Unite(π, r, s)
15 ·  ·  ·  if π(v) ∩ Acc ≠ ∅ then report CE
16 ·  ·  Done := Done ∪ {v'}
17 ·  if π(v) ⊄ Dead then Dead := Dead ∪ π(v)
18 ·  if v = Rₚ.top() then Rₚ.pop()
```

Fig. 2. Multi-core UFSCC algorithm for LTL model checking of BAs.

2. $w \notin \mathsf{Dead} \land \nexists w' \in R_p: w \in \pi(w')$ (Line 10): State w is not part of the local search stack and it is also not in a partial SCC that contains a state from the local search stack (assuming that π correctly tracks partially found SCCs). Since the current worker has not visited w before, nor any state in $\pi(w)$, it regards w as an undiscovered state and recursively explores it.

3. $w \notin \mathsf{Dead} \land \exists w' \in R_p: w \in \pi(w')$ (Lines 11–15): Here, the worker's stack does contain a state w' that is in the same partial SCC as w (the stack may also contain w itself). This forms a cycle and thus all states on said cycle are united. We assume that partial SCCs adhere to the strong connectivity property and that the search stack sufficiently maintains a DFS order.[2]

In case a cycle is detected, Line 15 checks whether the partial SCC contains an accepting state. If this is true, we can be sure that an accepting cycle is found.

We now discuss lines 7 and 16. We maintain a mechanism to globally mark states as being fully explored. A state v is fully explored if all its outgoing transitions direct to states in already completed SCCs (the successor is part of the Dead set) or to states in the same partial SCC, $\pi(v)$. In both these cases, no new information can be obtained from the successors. At Line 16, state v' is fully explored and is marked as such. Fully explored states are included in the Done set and are disregarded for exploration. Line 7 picks a state out of $\pi(v)$ for exploration that is not fully explored. This is possible since all states in $\pi(v)$ are strongly connected, thus no condition is violated. In case every state in $\pi(v)$

---

[2] With sufficiently maintaining a DFS order we mean that for any two successive states v and w on the local search stack, we have $v \rightarrow^+ w$; i.e. we do not require a direct edge from v to w, but w must be reachable from v.

is marked Done, the while loop ends and we conclude that the entire (partial) SCC has been fully explored and can be marked as complete. This is achieved by merging $\pi(v)$ with the Dead set at Line 17.

For a proof of correctness, we refer the reader to Bloemen et al. [2].

Global Data Structure. The underlying global data structure satisfies the following conditions:

- Provide means to check if the current worker has previously visited a state inside the partial SCC (successor cases 2 and 3).
- Provide means to globally mark states as being fully explored, and a selection mechanism for states in a partial SCC that have not yet been fully explored.

The union-find structure uses parent pointers that direct to the representative or *root* of the set. The structure is extended to track worker IDs in the partial SCCs. The worker ID is added to the root of the set when the worker enters a (locally) new state. The set of worker IDs is updated during the Unite operations. This ensures that if a worker ID is set for a particular state, it remains being set if the partial SCC containing that state gets updated.

In order to mark states as being fully explored (inside a partial SCC), the structure is extended with a cyclic list which is depicted in Fig. 3 for a partial SCC. It tracks states that have not yet been marked Done, which we call Busy states, (depicted white) and removes Done (depicted gray) states from this list. Workers can then use the list pointers to find remaining Busy states of the partial SCC. At a certain point in time, the list becomes empty, i.e. every state in the partial SCC is marked Done. We thus conclude that all states in the partial SCC have been fully explored, which implies that the entire SCC has been fully explored and can be marked as being complete.

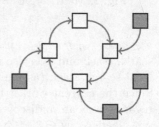

Fig. 3. Cyclic list structure.

Figure 4 depicts a consequence of using the abovementioned cyclic list for selecting states to fully explore. A worker starts from state a with the edge $a \rightarrow c$. It could then detect that state c is already marked Done and the worker picks a new state, d. From state d, the worker resumes its exploration. State e might also be marked Done, and the worker continues searching from state h.

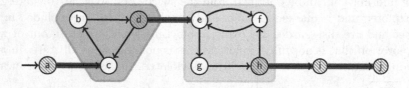

Fig. 4. Example showing a possible state traversal for one worker.

Note that this search order maintains the depth-first search order sufficiently for detecting cycles (See foot note 2).

For more details regarding the implementation of the algorithm and global data structure we refer the reader to Bloemen et al. [2].

Finding Accepting Cycles on TGBAs. The algorithm is extended to track acceptance marks in each SCC. A counterexample is then found when every acceptance mark is present in an SCC. In the algorithm from Fig. 2 this implies storing a set of acceptance marks alongside the partial SCCs and update this set with every Unite operation. In the implementation this is achieved by ensuring that the root of the union-find structure contains the most up-to-date acceptance set. If the acceptance set of the root contains all acceptance marks, a counterexample has been detected.

In summary, for each node we maintain a pointer towards the union-find root, and pointers to the successors in the list. For the root nodes we maitain a set of bits for the involved workers, and in case TGBAs are used also a set of bits for the acceptance marks that have been found.

5   Experiments

Experimental Setup. All experiments were performed on a machine with 4 AMD Opteron™ 6376 processors, each with 16 cores, forming a total of 64 cores. There is a total of 512 GB memory available.

Implementation. The extended UFSCC algorithm is implemented in the LTSMIN toolset [17]. We furthermore extended LTSMIN to use the Spot v2.0 library [7] for generating Büchi automata (both BA and TGBA) from LTL formulas.

We compare the UFSCC algorithm (implemented for BA and TGBA acceptance) with (sequential) NDFS [3], CNDFS [8] and the SCC-based algorithm by Renault et al. [29] which we further refer to as Renault. We attempt to minimize performance differences caused by effects other than those resulting from the algorithmic differences, hence each algorithm is implemented in the LTSMIN toolset. All multi-core algorithms make use of LTSMIN's internal shared hash tables [22], and the same randomized successor distribution method is used throughout. The shared hash table is initialized to store up to 2^{28} states.

Models and Formulas. We used models and LTL formulas from three existing benchmark sets and describe these as follows.

- BEEM-orig[3]: This consists of the complete collection of original (DVE) models and formulas from the BEEM database [26]. Additionally, a number of realistic formulas were added for several parameterized models (see Blahoudek et al. [1] for details), forming a total of over 807 formulas.

---

[3] Available at http://fi.muni.cz/~xstrejc/publications/spin2014.tar.gz.

- BEEM-gen[4]: These are the same models and LTL formulas as used by Renault et al. [29,30]. The (DVE) models are a subset of the BEEM database [26] such that every type of model from the classification of Pelánek [27] is represented. A total of 3,268 randomly generated formulas were selected such that the number of states, transitions and number of SCCs were high in the synchronized cross products.
- MCC[5]: We used a selection of the 2015 Model Checking Contest problems [19]. This consists of Petri net instances (specified in PNML) of both academic and industrial models, forming a total of 928 models. For each model, 48 different LTL formulas were provided that check for fireability (propositions on firing a transition) and cardinality (comparing the number of tokens in places), forming a total of $928 \times 48 = 44,544$ experiments. We performed an initial selection using UFSCC with 64 cores and selected instances taking between one second and one minute to check.[6] This resulted in 1,107 experiments.

We combined all datasets for the experiments, totaling 5,128 experiments and 2,950 contain a counterexample. Each configuration was performed at least 5 times and we computed all results by using the averages. The algorithms were not always able to successfully perform an experiment in the maximum allowed time of 10 min. When comparing two configurations, we only consider experiments where both algorithms performed successfully and within the time limit.

All results and means to reproduce the results are publicly available online at https://github.com/utwente-fmt/LTL-HVC16. We compare UFSCC with respectively NDFS, CNDFS, and Renault (all performed on BAs) in the upcoming sections. Some additional experiments follow and the results are summarized in Tables 1 and 2. In the context of validation, we are pleased to note that we won in the LTL category of the 2016 Model Checking Contest [18], where we employed the UFSCC algorithm.

5.1   Comparison with NDFS

We first compare the results of UFSCC with the sequential NDFS algorithm. Figure 5 shows the speedup of UFSCC (using 64 workers) compared to NDFS. Here, the point $(x = 10, y = 20)$ implies that the NDFS algorithm took 10 s to complete and UFSCC is 20× faster (thus taking only 0.5 s). We first consider the experiments that do not contain counterexamples (Fig. 5a).

The colored marks depict the 'origins' of the models. When relating this to time and speedup, the different classes are dispersed similarly, though the BEEM-gen models are more clustered.

Generally, UFSCC performs at least 10× faster than NDFS. In Table 1 we observe that the average[7] speedup is 14.16. For larger models (where NDFS

---

[4] Available at https://www.lrde.epita.fr/~renault/benchs/TACAS-2015/results.html.

[5] Available at http://mcc.lip6.fr/2015/.

[6] The reason for this selection is to avoid unrealistic computation times, since the scalability measurements require a run of a sequential algorithm as well.

[7] When we discuss averages over the experiments, we always take the geometric mean.

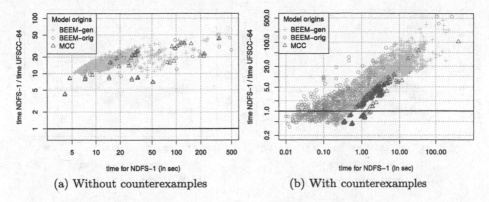

(a) Without counterexamples   (b) With counterexamples

Fig. 5. Time comparison of UFSCC using 64 workers with sequential NDFS. (Color figure online)

requires more time), the speedup increases. We observed that the improvement in time to model check closely relates to the size of the model. This effect is also visible in Table 1, where the speedup grows from 13.24 to 24.35 when comparing the smallest and largest class of models.

The results are a bit different for experiments that do contain counterexamples (Fig. 5b). Here, UFSCC is actually slower than NDFS for some 'smaller' instances (where NDFS completes within 1 s). This is explained by the extra setup time required for UFSCC, combined with an additional bookkeeping on the data structures, which becomes purposeless in trivial cases.

For increasingly larger models, the speedup for UFSCC improves rapidly. This speedup becomes superlinear (more than 64× faster using 64 workers), which is explained by the fact that multiple workers are more likely to find a counterexample due to randomization [8,28].

When relating the results to the origins of the models, we more clearly observe differences. NDFS performs (on average) the fastest on the BEEM-orig experiments, and the slowest on the MCC experiments. For all benchmarks with counterexamples, UFSCC performs on average 4.87 times faster than NDFS. Note that when taking the subset of models where NDFS takes more than 10 s, UFSCC is 30 times faster.

5.2 Comparison with CNDFS

We compare the results of UFSCC with CNDFS, where both algorithms use 64 workers. Results for models without counterexamples are depicted in Fig. 6a.

In most cases, the performance of UFSCC and CNDFS is comparable, and the time difference rarely exceeds a factor of 2. The figure classifies the experiments by the number of transitions in the model. From this classification it becomes clear that UFSCC's relative performance improves for larger models. In Table 1 we find that the relative speedup of UFSCC versus CNDFS increases from 0.95 to 1.31. One can also observe in this table that UFSCC slightly outperforms CNDFS in graphs containing large SCCs.

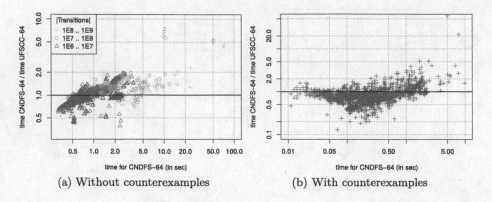

(a) Without counterexamples   (b) With counterexamples

Fig. 6. Time comparison of UFSCC with CNDFS, both using 64 workers.

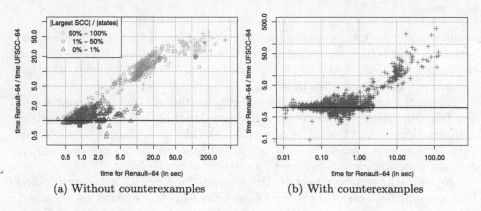

(a) Without counterexamples   (b) With counterexamples

Fig. 7. Time comparison of UFSCC with Renault, both using 64 workers.

For models with counterexamples (Fig. 6b) CNDFS clearly performs better for most of the models. On average, UFSCC is 0.79 times as fast as CNDFS. However, the techniques do complement each other since UFSCC outperforms CNDFS in 14 % of the instances, in particular the experiments where CNDFS performs slowest.

5.3 Comparison with Renault

We compare the results of UFSCC with Renault, where both algorithms use 64 workers. Recall that both algorithms are SCC-based. Figure 7a depicts the results for experiments without counterexamples.

We observe a clear distinction when relating the results with the SCC characteristics. A significant speedup is observed for all models containing a largest SCC that consists of at least 1 % of the total state space. This is explained by the fact that Renault does not communicate partially found SCCs searches as explained in Sect. 3, whereas UFSCC does achieve this.

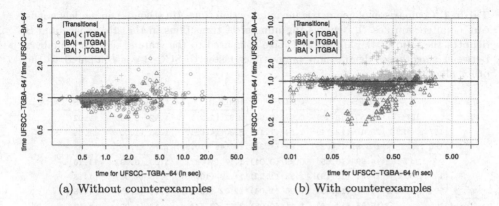

(a) Without counterexamples   (b) With counterexamples

Fig. 8. Time comparison of UFSCC using BAs with its TGBA variant, both using 64 workers. Here, |Transitions| compares (a) the total number of transitions in the complete cross-product and (b) the average number of uniquely explored transitions by the algorithms.

From Table 1 we notice that UFSCC's speedup increases for larger models (19.58× speedup for the largest class of models), this can be mainly explained by the differences in SCC sizes.

For models with counterexamples (Fig. 7b), we observe that Renault performs similar to UFSCC for most of the models. This is to be expected since accepting cycles are detected in the same manner. However, the same effect concerning SCC sizes as in Fig. 7a seems present. We further analyzed some of the experiments where Renault performs relatively poor and indeed found that these instances contain large SCCs.

5.4   Experiments Using TGBA

One can consider classifying LTL formulas by using the temporal hierarchy of Manna and Pnueli [24]. For one of these classes, called *persistence*, each SCC in the automaton of the formula either fully consists of accepting states or non-accepting states. This class of problems can be reduced to a simple DFS [36]. In the dual, called *recurrence*, the automaton for the formula contains both accepting and non-accepting cycles in the same SCCs, making it necessary to perform an accepting cycle search. The combination of multiple recurrence and persistence formulas is described as a *reactive* formula, and can benefit from TGBA-acceptance by using a different accepting mark for each formula.

We made a comparison with two versions of UFSCC, where one is implemented for checking on BAs and the other for TGBAs. We found that only a few instances could be classified as persistence.

While the results do differ per model, the TGBA and BA implementations perform equally well on average in Fig. 8a and b. Also, in Fig. 8a one can observe that in most cases the size of the cross-product is equal for the BA and TGBA versions. A consequence is that a TGBA should not provide any benefit over a BA in these cases.

Table 1. Comparison of geometric mean execution times (in seconds) on models **without** counterexamples. **T** denotes the number of transitions in the state space and **S** denotes the ratio of the largest SCC size compared to the state space. The numbers between parentheses denote how many times faster UFSCC-BA is compared to the other algorithm.

		NDFS	CNDFS	Renault	UFSCC-TGBA	UFSCC-BA
T	0 .. 1E7	13.55 (13.24)	0.97 (0.95)	2.32 (2.27)	1.02 (0.99)	1.02
	1E7 .. 1E8	25.47 (18.71)	1.54 (1.13)	6.30 (4.63)	1.36 (1.00)	1.36
	1E8 .. INF	183.37 (24.35)	9.89 (1.31)	147.44 (19.58)	7.76 (1.03)	7.53
S	0% .. 1%	14.99 (13.65)	0.99 (0.91)	1.17 (1.06)	1.09 (0.99)	1.10
	1% .. 50%	18.33 (16.19)	1.38 (1.22)	11.83 (10.46)	1.13 (1.00)	1.13
	50% .. 100%	15.77 (13.69)	1.20 (1.04)	12.02 (10.44)	1.15 (1.00)	1.15
Total		15.95 (14.16)	1.11 (0.98)	3.01 (2.67)	1.12 (1.00)	1.13

Table 2. Comparison of geometric mean execution times (in seconds) on models **with** counterexamples. The numbers between parentheses denote how many times faster UFSCC-BA is compared to the other.

	NDFS	CNDFS	Renault	UFSCC-TGBA	UFSCC-BA
Total	1.52 (4.87)	0.25 (0.79)	0.37 (1.17)	0.31 (1.00)	0.31

Perhaps surprisingly, TGBAs do not benefit model checking in the experiments that we performed. Even when the TGBA version does provide a smaller cross-product, the algorithms still perform similarly. This may be explained by the additional overhead and bookkeeping for tracking acceptance sets.

5.5   Additional Results

We compare the relative maximal SCC size with the classification of transitions according to UFSCC, i.e. the number of *dead*, *visited* and *new* transitions (see Sect. 4).

The results for all experiments without counterexamples are summarized in Fig. 9. Here, the small, medium, and large SCC size cases relate to the respective three SCC classes in Table 1. The main observation is that models with large SCCs contain a high number of interconnectivity. In the 'large' class, 57.5 % of all explored transi-

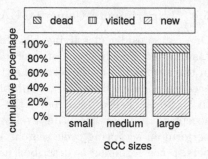

Fig. 9. Successor distribution for UFSCC using 64 workers.

tions direct to already visited states (either locally visited or part of a globally known partial SCC).

Ideally, a multi-core algorithm should perfectly divide all states and transitions equally over all workers with minimal overhead. In practice, we observe that some transitions are explored by multiple workers. For UFSCC, with 64 workers, we analyzed the ratio of all explored transitions (cumulative for all workers) compared to the number of uniquely found transitions. For models without counterexamples this ratio is 141.0 %, meaning that the 64 workers perform a combined total of 41.0 % redundant explorations. Notably, for models that contain 1E7..1E8 transitions, the ratio drops to 118.8 % and 116.2 % for the largest class of models. SCC sizes do not seem to influence the re-exploration ratio.

The ratio for models with counterexamples is 182.8 %. This higher ratio is explained by the fact that only a small part of the state space is explored, which leaves few opportunities for branching the searches.

We observed that while large SCCs are generally highly interconnected in practice, the work is divided effectively since the re-exploration ratio is limited.

6 Conclusion

We showed that the UFSCC algorithm is well-suited for multi-core on-the-fly LTL model checking. The algorithm improves on related work by globally communicating partially detected SCCs, causing it to achieve good speedups on models with large SCCs. We also showed that the algorithm scales better compared to existing work when the state space increases.

Although we have considerably improved the scalability of LTL model checking, there is still room for improvement. For large models we observe a 25× speedup with 64 cores. We consider maintaining the concurrent union-find structure to be the main bottleneck. A combination with work-stealing queues or synchronizing the search instances may prove beneficial. Other directions are to extend this work to support partial-order reduction and fairness checking.

Acknowledgements. We thank Alfons Laarman for his aid with the implementation and Jeroen Meijer for his work on the Petri net benchmarks. We also thank Alexandre Duret-Lutz, Marcus Gerhold and the anonymous reviewers for their helpful comments. This work is supported by the 3TU.BSR project.

References

1. Blahoudek, F., Duret-Lutz, A., Křetínský, M., Strejček, J.: Is there a best Büchi automaton for explicit model checking? In: Proceedings of the 2014 International SPIN Symposium on Model Checking of Software, SPIN 2014, pp. 68–76. ACM (2014)
2. Bloemen, V., Laarman, A., van de Pol, J.: Multi-core on-the-fly SCC decomposition. In: Proceedings of the 21st ACM SIGPLAN Symposium on Principles and Practice of Parallel Programming, PPoPP 2016, pp. 8:1–8:12. ACM (2016)
3. Courcoubetis, C., Vardi, M., Wolper, P., Yannakakis, M.: Memory-efficient algorithms for the verification of temporal properties. In: Kurshan, R. (ed.) Computer-Aided Verification, pp. 129–142. Springer US, New York (1993)
4. Couvreur, J.-M.: On-the-fly verification of linear temporal logic. In: Wing, J.M., Woodcock, J., Davies, J. (eds.) FM 1999. LNCS, vol. 1708, pp. 253–271. Springer, Heidelberg (1999). doi:10.1007/3-540-48119-2_16

5. Couvreur, J.-M., Duret-Lutz, A., Poitrenaud, D.: On-the-fly emptiness checks for generalized Büchi automata. In: Godefroid, P. (ed.) SPIN 2005. LNCS, vol. 3639, pp. 169–184. Springer, Heidelberg (2005). doi:10.1007/11537328_15
6. Dijkstra, E.W.: Finding the maximum strong components in a directed graph. In: Dijkstra, E.W. (ed.) Selected Writings on Computing: A personal Perspective. Texts and Monographs in Computer Science, pp. 22–30. Springer, New York (1982)
7. Duret-Lutz, A., Lewkowicz, A., Fauchille, A., Michaud, T., Renault, É., Xu, L.: Spot 2.0 — a framework for LTL and ω-automata manipulation. In: Artho, C., Legay, A., Peled, D. (eds.) ATVA 2016. LNCS, vol. 9938, pp. 122–129. Springer, Heidelberg (2016). doi:10.1007/978-3-319-46520-3_8
8. Evangelista, S., Laarman, A., Petrucci, L., van de Pol, J.: Improved multi-core nested depth-first search. In: Chakraborty, S., Mukund, M. (eds.) Automated Technology for Verification and Analysis. LNCS, vol. 7561, pp. 269–283. Springer, Heidelberg (2012)
9. Evangelista, S., Petrucci, L., Youcef, S.: Parallel nested depth-first searches for LTL model checking. In: Bultan, T., Hsiung, P.-A. (eds.) ATVA 2011. LNCS, vol. 6996, pp. 381–396. Springer, Heidelberg (2011). doi:10.1007/978-3-642-24372-1_27
10. Fleischer, L.K., Hendrickson, B., Pınar, A.: On identifying strongly connected components in parallel. In: Rolim, J. (ed.) IPDPS 2000. LNCS, vol. 1800, pp. 505–511. Springer, Heidelberg (2000). doi:10.1007/3-540-45591-4_68
11. Gaiser, A., Schwoon, S.: Comparison of Algorithms for Checking Emptiness on Büchi Automata. CoRR abs/0910.3766 (2009)
12. Geldenhuys, J., Valmari, A.: Tarjan's algorithm makes on-the-fly LTL verification more efficient. In: Jensen, K., Podelski, A. (eds.) Tools and Algorithms for the Construction and Analysis of Systems. LNCS, vol. 2988, pp. 205–219. Springer, Heidelberg (2004)
13. Giannakopoulou, D., Lerda, F.: From states to transitions: improving translation of LTL formulae to Büchi automata. In: Peled, D.A., Vardi, M.Y. (eds.) FORTE 2002. LNCS, vol. 2529, pp. 308–326. Springer, Heidelberg (2002). doi:10.1007/3-540-36135-9_20
14. Holzmann, G., Joshi, R., Groce, A.: Swarm verification techniques. IEEE Trans. Softw. Eng. **37**(6), 845–857 (2011)
15. Holzmann, G., Peled, D., Yannakakis, M.: On nested depth first search. In: Proceedings of the Second SPIN Workshop, vol. 32, pp. 81–89 (1996)
16. Hong, S., Rodia, N., Olukotun, K.: On fast parallel detection of strongly connected components (SCC) in small-world graphs. In: 2013 International Conference High Performance Computing, Networking, Storage and Analysis (SC), pp. 1–11 (2013)
17. Kant, G., Laarman, A., Meijer, J., Pol, J., Blom, S., Dijk, T.: LTSmin: high-performance language-independent model checking. In: Baier, C., Tinelli, C. (eds.) TACAS 2015. LNCS, vol. 9035, pp. 692–707. Springer, Heidelberg (2015). doi:10.1007/978-3-662-46681-0_61
18. Kordon, F., Garavel, H., Hillah, L.M., Hulin-Hubard, F., Chiardo, G., Hamez, A., Jezequel, L., Miner, A., Meijer, J., Paviot-Adet, E., Racordon, D., Rodriguez, C., Rohr, C., Srba, J., Thierry-Mieg, Y., Trinh, G., Wolf, K.: Complete Results for the 2016 Edition of the Model Checking Contest (2016)
19. Kordon, F., Garavel, H., Hillah, L.M., Hulin-Hubard, F., Linard, A., Beccuti, M., Hamez, A., Lopez-Bobeda, E., Jezequel, L., Meijer, J., Paviot-Adet, E., Rodriguez, C., Rohr, C., Srba, J., Thierry-Mieg, Y., Wolf, K.: Complete Results for the 2015 Edition of the Model Checking Contest (2015)

20. Laarman, A., Langerak, R., Pol, J., Weber, M., Wijs, A.: Multi-core nested depth-first search. In: Bultan, T., Hsiung, P.-A. (eds.) ATVA 2011. LNCS, vol. 6996, pp. 321–335. Springer, Heidelberg (2011). doi:10.1007/978-3-642-24372-1_23

21. Laarman, A., van de Pol, J.: Variations on multi-core nested depth-first search. In: Barnat, J., Heljanko, K. (eds.) PDMC 2011. EPTCS, vol. 72, pp. 13–28 (2011)

22. Laarman, A., Pol, J., Weber, M.: Multi-core LTSMIN: marrying modularity and scalability. In: Bobaru, M., Havelund, K., Holzmann, G.J., Joshi, R. (eds.) NFM 2011. LNCS, vol. 6617, pp. 506–511. Springer, Heidelberg (2011). doi:10.1007/978-3-642-20398-5_40

23. Lowe, G.: Concurrent depth-first search algorithms based on Tarjan's algorithm. Int. J. Softw. Tools Technol. Transf. **18**(2), 1–19 (2015)

24. Manna, Z., Pnueli, A.: A hierarchy of temporal properties. In: Proceedings of the Sixth Annual ACM Symposium on Principles of Distributed Computing, PODC 1987, p. 205. ACM (1987)

25. Orzan, S.: On Distributed Verification and Verified Distribution. Ph.D. thesis (2004)

26. Pelánek, R.: BEEM: benchmarks for explicit model checkers. In: Bošnački, D., Edelkamp, S. (eds.) SPIN 2007. LNCS, vol. 4595, pp. 263–267. Springer, Heidelberg (2007). doi:10.1007/978-3-540-73370-6_17

27. Pelánek, R.: Properties of state spaces and their applications. Int. J. Softw. Tools Technol. Transf. **10**(5), 443–454 (2008)

28. Rao, V.N., Kumar, V.: Superlinear speedup in parallel state-space search. In: Nori, K.V., Kumar, S. (eds.) Foundations of Software Technology and Theoretical Computer Science. LNCS, vol. 338, pp. 161–174. Springer, Heidelberg (1988)

29. Renault, E., Duret-Lutz, A., Kordon, F., Poitrenaud, D.: Parallel explicit model checking for generalized Büchi automata. In: Baier, C., Tinelli, C. (eds.) TACAS 2015. LNCS, vol. 9035, pp. 613–627. Springer, Heidelberg (2015). doi:10.1007/978-3-662-46681-0_56

30. Renault, E., Duret-Lutz, A., Kordon, F., Poitrenaud, D.: Variations on parallel explicit emptiness checks for generalized Büchi automata. Int. J. Softw. Tools Technol. Transf. 1–21 (2016). http://link.springer.com/journal/10009/onlineFirst/page/1

31. Schudy, W.: Finding strongly connected components in parallel using O(log2n) reachability queries. In: Proceedings of the Twentieth Annual Symposium on Parallelism in Algorithms and Architectures, SPAA 2008, pp. 146–151. ACM (2008)

32. Schwoon, S., Esparza, J.: A note on on-the-fly verification algorithms. In: Halbwachs, N., Zuck, L.D. (eds.) TACAS 2005. LNCS, vol. 3440, pp. 174–190. Springer, Heidelberg (2005). doi:10.1007/978-3-540-31980-1_12

33. Slota, G.M., Rajamanickam, S., Madduri, K.: BFS and coloring-based parallel algorithms for strongly connected components and related problems. In: 2014 IEEE 28th International Parallel and Distributed Processing Symposium, pp. 550–559 (2014)

34. Tarjan, R.E.: Depth-first search and linear graph algorithms. SIAM J. Comput. **1**(2), 146–160 (1972)

35. Vardi, M.Y., Wolper, P.: An automata-theoretic approach to automatic program verification. In: Proceedings of the First Symposium on Logic in Computer Science, pp. 322–331. IEEE Computer Society (1986)

36. Černá, I., Pelánek, R.: Relating hierarchy of temporal properties to model checking. In: Rovan, B., Vojtáš, P. (eds.) MFCS 2003. LNCS, vol. 2747, pp. 318–327. Springer, Heidelberg (2003). doi:10.1007/978-3-540-45138-9_26

Gating Aware Error Injection

Eli Arbel[1]([✉]), Erez Barak[2], Bodo Hoppe[3], Shlomit Koyfman[1], Udo Krautz[3], and Shiri Moran[1]

[1] IBM Research Lab, Haifa, Israel
{arbel,shlomitk,shirim}@il.ibm.com
[2] IBM Systems, Haifa, Israel
ebarak@il.ibm.com
[3] IBM Systems, Boeblingen, Germany
{bohopp,krautz}@de.ibm.com

Abstract. Error injection is one of the most commonly used techniques for estimating the reliability of a given hardware design. While error injection in dynamic simulation is widely used in the industry, other methods exist as well, e.g. hardware error injection and fault-tolerance analysis using formal verification. As covering the entire space of all possible fault injections is impractical, nearly all workload-based error injection methods (e.g. simulation or emulation techniques) use a statistical approach for error injection, i.e. they only inject a fraction of all possible faults. As a result, the statistical fault injection approach is much more efficient in characterizing the overall reliability of the design than in finding particular reliability-related bugs. On the other hand, the formal-based approach guarantees full coverage of the design space, including under all possible faults, granted the formal analysis can be completed. However, performing formal verification on design hierarchies with error detection and recovery logic is usually unfeasible. To address the challenge of effectively finding reliability-related bugs on large industrial designs, this paper proposes a novel approach which is aimed at finding a particular kind of design bugs related to gating conditions which correspond to error detection logic. We present an automated method for identifying those gating conditions and generating a gating-aware fault injection module. Experimental results on a real microprocessor arithmetical unit demonstrates the effectiveness of our method in finding real design bugs using relatively small amount of error injection tests.

1 Introduction

Reliability has become one of the major concerns in modern VLSI design. Various applications require high design reliability, ranging from chips embedded in automotive and avionic systems to general purpose microprocessors deployed in mass-scale or required to provide long periods of availability while performing mission- and business-critical computations [5,9,17,25]. As a consequence,

This work has been partially supported by the EU's H2020 RIA IMMORTAL (www.h2020-immortal.eu).

R. Bloem and E. Arbel (Eds.): HVC 2016, LNCS 10028, pp. 34–48, 2016.
DOI: 10.1007/978-3-319-49052-6_3

data integrity in the digital level introduces various challenges for logic designers and verification engineers. A substantial amount of effort may be required for properly designing and verifying a highly reliable chip.

Design reliability may be influenced by different factors. Needless to say, functional correctness is a prime factor affecting reliability. Hence, a large amount of effort is devoted to verifying the functional correctness of a given design before it is taped-out and delivered [11]. However, even a totally bug-free design is still susceptible to failures occurring during its normal operation. These failures may originate from various sources, for example, aging effects which essentially degrade the silicon reliability and negatively affect signal and data integrity [3]. Additionally, a prominent source for design failures is related to soft-errors, which are attributed to various phenomena in the environment which may change the design behavior. Soft errors can occur due to the emission of alpha particles from the silicon and packaging materials [16]. An even more dominant source for soft-errors in current technology nodes are particles arriving to earth from outer-space [21]. Generally speaking, those particles may carry enough energy to cause an electrical disturbance in the design which may eventually lead to a bit-flip in one of the design signals or memory elements. Such bit-flips are hazardous to data integrity if not mitigated and may lead to machine hangs or - even worse - to a silent data corruption [10].

In order to ensure a reliable operation of a given design in the presence of the various environmental effects, i.e. soft-errors, various design techniques are employed. Assuming the single event upset (SEU) and single event transient (SET) models [19], a common approach is to introduce redundancy in the logic which enables detecting bit-flips, allowing for automatic design level recovery while maintaining data integrity. Examples for commonly used error detection and correction techniques include parity protection, double/triple modular redundancy, CRC and residue checking [2,13]. These protection methods are implemented in hardware and intended to operate during the normal execution of the hardware. As such, these structures need to be verified to ensure they are implemented correctly and provide the required fault coverage while not compromising mainline functionality.

Several approaches for verifying error detection and correction logic exist. One of the most commonly used approaches is to perform error injection. In this approach faults are deliberately introduced during the verification process, usually using simulation-based methods. In general, the goal here is to observe that the design can gracefully recover from various faulty scenarios or at least detect the presence of faults and notify the upper layers of the system (e.g. firmware or software). Numerous error injection techniques have been suggested by researchers, including proton beam experiments [6], error injection using emulation [22] and simulation based error injection [14]. In most cases these techniques rely on *statistical fault injection*, i.e. the error location and time is randomly chosen during the error injection process. In order to increase the error injection efficiency, a stuck-at fault model can be used as a way to overcome various fault masking effects and increase the overall fault coverage [24].

Another approach for verifying reliability aspects is based on formal verification. Several works have proposed to use model checking to analyze the reliability of the design w.r.t soft and hard errors. The works described in [12,15,23] run formal verification on the entire design aiming at checking safety reliability properties. While this approach may unlock reliability related problems, its main disadvantage comes from the limited capacity of formal verification. The authors of [1] describe a method which alleviates the formal verification capacity issue by verifying protection structures locally. This method is helpful in identifying that a certain area of the logic is protected by a certain protection scheme, however, it may miss bugs related to control and gating conditions derived from a higher level context.

While the verification of an individual reliability mechanism, like parity protection, is fairly easy, the verification of such mechanisms from a higher level perspective, like a logic unit or a processor core, is much more complex. This is because power and other non-functional requirements necessitates gating the result of these checks. In particular, clock gating is used in high performance designs to turn off reliability checks when certain parts of the logic are not used. These gates, however, create a significant verification challenge because it is necessary to consider much larger parts of the logic to verify the reliability feature and to consider all gating conditions. To the best of our knowledge, existing error injection methods do not explicitly address the challenges related to gating conditions of error detection logic, thus making them less efficient in discovering gating-related bugs. In this paper we present a novel approach for performing error injection while considering existing gating conditions and steering the injection efforts accordingly. In the heart of this approach lies a methodology which uses structural analysis to find all error detection signals and their corresponding gating conditions automatically. Given a design RTL, our method extracts existing error detection structures in the design and performs functional analysis using formal methods to extract any related gating conditions of these structures. Based on this analysis, we synthesize an injection module which controls the location and time in which an error injection should occur in correspondence with the existing gating logic. This module is then incorporated into the verification environment and executed against standard functional verification tests.

The main benefit of our suggested approach is that the error injection occurs on particular memory elements and at particular cycles in which a certain problem is likely to occur, thus maximizing the probability of discovering reliability-related bugs in a given test. In addition, due to the local spatial and temporal nature of the error injection, the debuggability of failures discovered by our method is relatively simple, compared to other error injection methods which are based on stuck-at faults models. Finally, the error injection module created by our method is synthesized automatically and can seamlessly be incorporated in existing simulation and formal verification environments.

The rest of the paper is structured as follows. In Sect. 2 we provide required preliminaries for the paper. Section 3 provides a comprehensive description of the suggested methodology together with implementation details of its various steps. A discussion about the applicability of this methodology to both simulation-based and formal verification methods is also provided. Experimental results and conclusions are given in Sects. 4 and 5, respectively.

2 Preliminaries

In this section we briefly describe some of the concepts used in the paper. A *netlist* $C = \langle V, E \rangle$ is a graph representation of the logic which consists of gates (V) and wires (E). A netlist may describe a combinatorial circuit, in which case V consists of Boolean gates only (AND, OR, XOR etc.), or it can describe a sequential circuit where V also includes sequential elements. We use the term *latch* to describe a memory element (e.g. flip flop). The edges E of the graph represent wires and can be classified as internal (gate to gate), primary inputs or primary outputs. The *single-event-upset (SEU)* model assumes a single bit flip can occur in one memory element (e.g. one flip-flop) at one clock cycle.

An *error checker* c is a latch which *fires*, or outputs the logical value 1, in case of an error. Otherwise, the value of the checker is 0, indicating that no error has occurred. An *error detection signal* is a Boolean expression affecting a checker that becomes True if and only if an error has occurred. Each error detection signal has a corresponding *gating condition*. A *blocking* gating condition will prevent the error detection signal from affecting the checker. The input of a checker is a set of error detection signals and their gating conditions. The error checker will fire if at least one of the error detection signals is active and its corresponding gating condition is not blocking. Formally, let $\{c_1, \ldots c_n\}$ denote error detection signals, with gating conditions $\{g_1, \ldots g_n\}$, and let I denote the checker's input. Then

$$I = \bigvee_{1 \leq i \leq n} (c_i \wedge g_i)$$

A latch is *potentially protected* by an error checker if a single bit flip inside the latch will activate an error detection signal of the checker. It is *protected* if any bit-flip that may affect the functionality of the relevant circuit will result in the checker firing. For the sake of simplicity, we will sometimes refer to a *gating condition of a latch* instead of referring to the gating condition of the error signal that will become active when the latch flips.

For example, in Fig. 1 a bit-flip in each of the encircled latches will result in an erroneous parity check of the error signal $e1$, but if the gating condition is blocking (c_enable is low) then the checker will not fire. Thus, all the encircled latches are potentially protected by the checker. Error injection is the process of simulating the presence of faults following a given fault model (e.g. bit flips), in order to verify the behavior of the design in such scenarios. Finally, a *unit* is a sub component of a chip that usually defines a particular hardware functionality and for which a dedicated verification environment exists. Examples of such units are the load-store unit and the arithmetical operation unit.

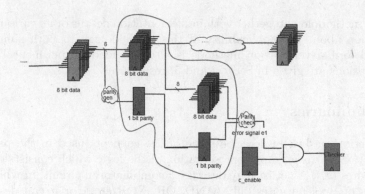

Fig. 1. Potentially protected latches

3   Gating Aware Error Injection Methodology

3.1   Approach

We attempt to detect the tricky scenario in which a specific latch is potentially protected, but due to *over gating* of the relevant error detection signal a bit flip in the latch will not cause the error checker to fire and will propagate to the interface and cause silent data corruption. This scenario can be very difficult to catch with existing reliability verification methodologies.

However, using static analysis this scenario can be tackled. If the error detection signal protecting a given latch is gated then the latch value should not propagate to the interface and should not affect the functionality of the unit. Now assume there is an oracle that tells us which are the potentially protected latches and for each such latch what is the relevant gate on the error detection signal. *Inverting* the value of a single potentially protected latch, each time the relevant gate is blocking, should not affect the normal functionality. For example, in Fig. 1 an inverted value of one of the encircled latches should not affect the normal operation of the unit when the corresponding error detection signal is gated, namely c_enable is low. If, however, the latch is over gated, then there exists a scenario in which inverting the value of this latch will result in a wrong value propagating to the interface and affecting the functionality of the design. An exhaustive functional verification flow should detect such a scenario. The inverse is also true. Namely, if an exhaustive functional verification flow has detected no fails when inverting the value of a latch as above, then this latch is indeed protected.

Two infinite execution sequences S and S' are equivalent if in each and every cycle they agree on the values of the interface. The proof of the following lemma is straightforward.

Lemma 1. *Let L be a potentially protected latch and let g be the gating condition of the latch. Let S be a legal execution scenario and let S^{I_L} be the scenario obtained from S by inverting the value of L in any cycle g is blocking. If for all legal execution scenarios S, the scenario S^{I_L} is equivalent to S, then L is indeed protected.*

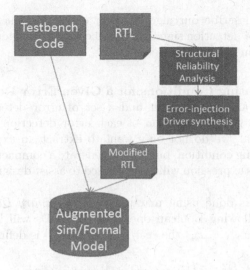

Fig. 2. High-level flow of our proposed methodology

Our gating aware methodology is based on the above Lemma. Following is an overview of the methodology (consider Fig. 2):

1. A static analysis algorithm which finds potentially protected latches and their gating conditions is executed on the design RTL.
2. A driver that randomly chooses a latch from the list provided by the previous stage and corrupts it whenever it is gated is synthesized. This driver is then automatically integrated with RTL which is also being automatically modified to support error injection by the synthesized driver.
3. The modified RTL is then merged with the standard simulation testbench (e.g. for unit level verification) or the formal verification environment, depending on the type of verification the methodology is being used with.
4. Verification is commenced.

Step 1 is described in Subsect. 3.2; Step 2 is described in Subsect. 3.3 and Step 3 is described in Subsects. 3.4 and 3.5.

3.2 Static Analysis Algorithm

As mentioned, our methodology uses a static analysis algorithm which identifies error detection signals and the following information per signal:

1. The list of latches potentially protected by it
2. The relevant gating condition

The identification of the error detection signal and the potentially protected latches can be done for parity based error detection signals as described in [1]; this is extendable to other types of error detection logic, e.g. CRC and residue.

In this section we describe our algorithm for extracting the gating condition between a given error detection signal and its checker. This algorithm is oblivious to the error detection mechanism being used.

Extracting the Gating Conditions for a Given Error Detection Signal. Given an input to an error checker and a set of error detection signals, we need to extract the gating condition of each error detection signal. For each error detection signal, we do not only want to extract an expression logically equivalent to its gating condition, but also to generate a compact human readable expression, since this expression will later be used to assist designers in debugging the fails.

This extraction is done using manipulation on *Binary Decision Diagrams (BDDs)* [4]. The following Boolean operators on BDDs will be used. Given a Boolean function $f(x_1, \ldots, x_n)$ the *restrict* operator [7] is defined as follows:

$$f|_{x_i} = f(x_1, \ldots, x_{i-1}, 1, x_{i+1}, \ldots x_n)$$

similarly

$$f|_{\neg x_i} = f(x_1, \ldots, x_{i-1}, 0, x_{i+1}, \ldots x_n)$$

The restrict operation is extended from variables to any function g as follows [8,18]. Let $f(\bar{x})$, $g(\bar{x})$ be Boolean functions.

$$f|_{g(\bar{x})} = \begin{cases} f(\bar{x}) & \text{if } g(\bar{x}) = 1 \\ \text{arbitrary} & \text{otherwise} \end{cases}$$

When applying the restrict operations on functions, there is freedom to deviate from f when $g(\bar{x}) = 0$ and herein lies the opportunity to optimization and reduction in the size of the BDD. The last operator we will use is the *Existential quantification* applied on variables and defined as follows.

$$\exists x_i f(x_1 \ldots x_n) = f|_{x_i} \vee f|_{\neg x_i}$$

Let e be a checker's input net, let p be an error detection signal for which we want to extract the gating condition and let $c_1, \ldots c_n$ be other error detection signals. The nets of e, p and each c_i are given. Formally, e can be written as

$$e = (p \wedge g) \vee f$$

where g and f are Boolean functions, g is the gating condition we seek, and f represents the other (than p) error detection signals along with their gating[1]. The algorithm to extract g is as follows.

---

[1] We assume that e can be written as above with a single appearance of p. Intuitively, this assumption implies that if p implies an erroneous condition then $\neg p$ does not imply one; clearly, this is a very reasonable assumption. If this fails to hold for some reason we skip this error detection net.

1. **BDD construction.** Construct a BDD from e in which p and each c_i are terminal vertices.
2. **Extracting** $g \vee f$. Let $e_p \doteq e|_p$.
3. **Extracting** f. Let $e_{\neg p} = e|_{\neg p}$.
4. **Extracting** g. Let $h' = e_p|_{\neg(e_{\neg p})}$.
5. **Syntactic optimization.** Let $h'' = \exists c_n(\exists c_{n-1}(\ldots(\exists c_1(h))\ldots))$.
6. **Final gating computation**

$$h = \begin{cases} h' & \text{if } h'' \equiv 1 \\ h'' & \text{otherwise} \end{cases}$$

Claim. For all practical purpose $h \equiv g$. Moreover, in a vast majority of the cases the expression h will be over the minimal set of variables.

Proof. Clearly, $e_p \equiv (g \vee f)$ and $e_{\neg p} \equiv f$. In fact, using a state of the art BDD package one could expect to have $e_p = (g \vee f)$ and $e_{\neg p} = f$. Intuitively, in step 4 above we have the expressions $e_p = g \vee f$ and $e_{\neg p} = f$ and we want to "eliminate" f from $g \vee f$ and be left with g. However, this is not so trivial since f is not a terminal vertex, and might have common terminal vertices with g. The desired outcome is to have $h' = g$. It is not hard to see that, using a state of the art BDD package, this is also the most likely outcome. However, following carefully the definition of the restrict extension, there are three more outcomes which we must address. These are: $h' = g \wedge \neg f$, $h' = g \vee f$ and $h' = (g \wedge \neg f) \vee f$. To understand why these outcomes do not pose a problem, we have to recall that f represents an erroneous state that would not occur in the normal execution, and that when it occurs the checker will fire and a recovery action will be initiated. Hence, during a verification test it is very unlikely that f will be high; but if it is high then the checker will fire and this test will be aborted, since the interface corruption is prevented by a recovery action. Hence, for all practical purposes, we may assume that f is equivalent to *False*, and we are done with the first part of the claim.

Consider the second part. There are two possible redundant components in h': the "$\vee f$" component and the "$\wedge \neg f$" component. The semantic of f is the conjunctions of the error detection signals $c_1, \ldots c_n$ with possible gating conditions. Hence, existentially quantifying these c_i would result in h' being equivalent to 1 if the "$\vee f$" component is indeed present; in this case we will be left with the original h'. However, even though theoretically this "$\vee f$" component could exist, practically it is highly unlikely, in any reasonable BDD package, given that the restrict operations optimizes the "arbitrary" part to minimize BDD. Now consider the "$\wedge \neg f$" component; recalling again the semantic of f, existential quantification of these c_is would eliminate $\wedge \neg f$ from the final h.

3.3   Driver Synthesis

The error injection is done by synthesizing a driver that performs the actual corruption of latches based on the provided knowledge of latches and their gating conditions. Hence, as a preliminary step we execute the algorithm described in

```
el_opcode_qCorrupt <=   (corrupted_index=5600) and
        not E1_DISPATCH_Q;

f2_result_qCorrupt <=   (corrupted_index=5601) and
        not (f2_issue_valid_q AND (NOT f2_cold_kill_q) );
```

Fig. 3. Synthesized code example

the previous subsection, upon completion of which we receive a set of latches and corresponding gating conditions. Let CorruptionPull = $\{L_1, \ldots, L_n\}$ be the set of latches, and for each latch L_i let G_{L_i} be the corresponding gating condition. In the first cycle of the test a latch from the corruption pool is randomly chosen and throughout the test the value of this latch (and only of this latch) is inverted each time the relevant gating condition is blocking the relevant checker from firing. The values of the other latches, as well as the value of the chosen latch in cycles the gating condition is not blocking, remains untouched.

The above is implemented by a synthesized driver that will then be integrated into the verification flow. For each latch L_i, a new signal L_iCorrupt is synthesized; this signal is high in cycle i if and only if this latch was the one randomly chosen and G_{L_i} is blocking in cycle i. Figure 3 presents synthesized example of two such signals; *corrupted_index* is the latch determining which latch to corrupt - it is randomized in the first cycle of the test and is kept constant. Then, each latch L_i from the corruption pool is being inverted if and only if L_iCorrupt is high; otherwise its value remains untouched. In addition, in order to assist fails' debugging, new signals are introduced. For example, the signal CorruptedInCycle holding the conjunction of all the L_iCorrupt is synthesized. Following this signal and using advanced trace viewer options, the designer can track the signal that was corrupted and the cycles in which the signal was corrupted.

3.4   Driver Integration - Dynamic Simulation Approach

We integrate the above driver in a unit verification environment, using the standard environment testbench for dynamic simulation. The unit which we used for this case study performs arithmetic operations in the next IBM mainframe. The above testbench is generated using deep hardware knowledge and dedicated tools which ensure exhaustive coverage per instruction. During the project cycle the testbench is frequently enhanced based on the analysis of previous runs to increase coverage. This integration enables low cost error injection and reliability verification in the sense that it is not required to construct a new dynamic simulation verification environment or a new testbench.

After the DUT is stable and detecting new functional bugs becomes rare, the driver is integrated into the simulation environment. This stability is achieved after around 2/3 of the project cycles. The driver introduces a variety of new tests - the Cartesian product of the standard tests and the latches from the corruption pool. The fails we are after are the usual testbench functional fails, with one exception: if a checker fires and a recovery process is initiated, the test is aborted. Since redundant checks may exist, another checker having a different gating condition may fire, after we corrupt a latch. Since in a normal operation checkers should not fire, this abortion is justified.

3.5   Driver Integration - Formal Verification Approach

We integrate our driver also in the unit level formal verification environment. This is done in order to achieve higher coverage on a per instruction basis, compared to simulation and also to generate shorter, easier to debug traces when fails are detected. We assume an environment that specifies all the constraints and rules to properly stimulate the DUT's interface already exists. We furthermore assume a set of properties that specifies the proper output behavior already exists as well.

We extended our testbench to cover the fault detection output more precisely. In particular we modify the property about the fault detection signals of the DUT. Previously we checked that no fault was detected when running the testbench without any error injection. A driver that always injects a fault would require a modification of the above property. Using the modified property we want to prove that outputs behave as expected if no fault is detected, or to find a counter-example showing that some outputs don't behave as expected while no fault is signaled.

The gating aware driver is synthesized automatically and compiled into the testbench together with the standard interface driver and the modified set of properties. The formal analysis considers all possible injections at once but the result trace would contain a single injection only.

4   Experimental Results

4.1   Dynamic Simulation

We will present two types of experimental results. First, a qualitative measure of the results will be presented: a few failed traces will be analyzed in order to demonstrate the quality of the findings of the new methodology and to show it would have been very difficult to detect these fails with other methods. Then, a quantitative measure will be presented, making a quantity comparison between relevant existing verification methodologies and our new methodology. This will show that the new methodology is very effective.

We start with analyzing a few of the failed traces detected by our new methodology. The fails are presented in Table 1. They were produced with the methodology described in Subsect. 3.4. Namely, each of these fails is a result of a test from the dynamic simulation testbench that failed when a randomly chosen latch was corrupted whenever it was gated. The gate related data in the table refers to the gating condition of the latch that was corrupted in the relevant test. All tests below were executed for additional 100 cycles after the failed cycle. A few points come up when looking at the table:

Table 1. A few failed traces detected by the gating aware methodology

Test number	Test length (in cycles)	First non gated cycle	Number of gated cycles	Maximal window of Gated cycles	Non gated cycles
1	23, 726	91	23, 212(98 %)	2, 864	6
2	626	83	602(96 %)	314	2
3	1, 002	125	922(92 %)	732	42
4	478	127	468(98 %)	232	2
5	6, 948	123	4, 128(59 %)	674	740
6	2, 562	451	1, 878(73 %)	398	250
7	1, 248	945	1, 246(98 %)	946	2
8	1, 320	81	1, 178(89 %)	342	8
9	1, 556	111	1, 230(79 %)	396	38

– There is a decent variety of failed tests; they vary in length (from less than 500 cycles and up to almost 24 k cycles), in the percentage of cycles in which the relevant error detection signal is gated (from 59 % to 98 %) and in the maximal window size with non-gated cycles (from 2 and up to 740).
– In all the tests the relevant error detection signal is gated in a vast majority of the cycles; moreover, it is gated for more than 95 % of the cycles in 45 % of the tests. This implies that the gating mechanism is essential in our systems and how crucial it is to verify that we are not over gating.
– It is interesting to mention that in 1/3 of the fails the gate was off (non-blocking) only for a single full clock cycle each time (a full clock cycle contains 2 ticks.)
– Clearly, finding these fails by just randomizing the corrupted cycle would be equivalent to finding a needle in a haystack. Moreover, these fails would also be very hard to detect using the *stuck at* [24] error injection method in which the randomly chosen latch is being stuck high or low throughout the entire test. In all tests the relevant gate is not blocking for some cycles before the corruption that caused the fail. Hence, in a stuck at error injection method it is almost certain the relevant error detection signal will be active in a non gated cycle and as a result the checker will fire (initiating a recovery process) and the test will be aborted prior to the failed cycle.

As mentioned earlier, we tested our new methodology by integrating it into existing functional verification methodology of a unit of the next IBM main-frame core. We now show that our methodology is an efficient and effective enhancement to the existing reliability verification methodology as well as to the existing functional verification methodology it is integrated with. We show that the additional required computation power is minor and that the amount of the new detected coverage bugs is significant.

Considering the functional verification flow our new method is integrated with, the addition of computation cycles is around 1 %: our new methodology consumes 3 % of the tests in the period it is executed. As mentioned in Subsect. 3.4, the new methodology is executed for about 33 % of the life time of the project. Clearly, this is a minor overhead. And each and every test we are performing here increases coverage since this specific reliability coverage has never been targeted in the unit functional verification efforts.

Considering the existing error injection methodology [24], it is worth mentioning that while our methodology is only targeting coverage bugs the existing methodology addresses a variety of reliability issues in addition to coverage, such as verification of proper recovery process. Also, while our methodology is executed on a sub component of the core, the other methodology is executed on the core.

The existing error injection methodology is an order of magnitude larger than our methodology, executed on the arithmetic operation unit, almost in all aspects: size, number of tests and the test length (in cycles). This makes sense, since our methodology was integrated with the functional verification of a unit while the error injection methodology is executed on the entire core. However, the number of design bugs we found in our test case is the **same** order of magnitude as the number of coverage bugs detected by the existing methodology for the entire core. Hence, when our methodology will be integrated into all units of the core, one would expect an order of magnitude more coverage than with the existing methodology.

To summarize, our methodology, integrated with the existing functional unit verification, requires a small amount of additional resources, compared both to the unit functional verification and to existing error injection methodology. Yet, the additional number of coverage bugs is significant and moreover these bugs are very difficult to detect with other methods. This implies that our methodology provides an efficient and significant coverage enhancement.

4.2 Formal Verification

Similar to the dynamic simulation we integrate our approach into the formal verification unit environment. This is done without any alteration of the original environment targeting arithmetical correctness and interface protocol properties. Our experiments consider scenarios in which one instruction is executed in the unit's pipeline at a time. This enables easier debug and shorter runtime for our proofs. We compare the runtime for proving the correctness of arithmetic instructions in two cases: with injecting faults into gated checkers and without doing so. We show that the runtime in the former case is not significantly increased unless much more complex reliability logic gets into the cone of influence of our properties, e.g. for instructions that are additionally protected by residue [20] checks. Residue checks compute several multiplications, causing a large increase in runtime or memory consumption for our FV tool. Note that the differences in runtime and memory consumption can also be attributed to different heuristics chosen by our FV tool (Table 2).

Table 2. Comparison of proofs for arithmetic only vs arithmetic w/ Injection

Instruction	Arithmetic only		Arithmetic w/ Injection	
	Runtime (s)	Memory (MB)	Runtime (s)	Memory (MB)
vtp	2946.65	934.65	2068.95	946.90
kdb	2001.61	2206.63	10420.12	1308.19
lxer	395.64	1991.49	968.62	9688.33
rrxtr	2773.44	2312.71	1241.25	3285.54

5   Conclusion and Future Work

We have presented a new method for reliability coverage verification. This method has several advantages: it detects reliability coverage holes that are very difficult to detect with other methods; its overhead is small; and finally, it is executed on the standard verification environment (either dynamic simulation or formal). We have tested the new methodology on a unit of the next IBM mainframe that implements arithmetic operations and the results were satisfactory.

This method can be further expanded, and along with structural identification of protected latches [1], provide a complete scalable method for reliability coverage verification. Using structural identification, potentially protected latches can be identified; this implies the set of latches for which no protection exist. However, a latch that is potentially protected could have various gating conditions on the way to the checkers. In this work we only consider the gating condition between the error detecting signal to the checker. The natural extension would be to use similar techniques to verify all the gating conditions in each path from a potentially protected latch to the relevant checker.

References

1. Arbel, E., Koyfman, S., Kudva, P., Moran, S.: Automated detection and verification of parity-protected memory elements. In: International Conference on Computer-Aided Design (ICCAD 2014), pp. 1–8. IEEE (2014)
2. Avirneni, N.D.P., Somani, A.: Low overhead soft error mitigation techniques for high-performance and aggressive designs. IEEE Trans. Comput. **61**(4), 488–501 (2012)
3. Borkar, S.: Designing reliable systems from unreliable components: the challenges of transistor variability and degradation. IEEE Micro **25**(6), 10–16 (2005)
4. Bryant, R.E.: Graph-based algorithms for boolean function manipulation. IEEE Trans. Comput. **35**(8), 677–691 (1986)
5. Chang, Y.C., Huang, L.R., Liu, H.C., Yang, C.J., Chiu, C.T.: Assessing automotive functional safety microprocessor with ISO 26262 hardware requirements. In: 2014 International Symposium on VLSI Design, Automation and Test (VLSI-DAT), pp. 1–4, April 2014

6. Cher, C.Y., Muller, K.P., Haring, R.A., Satterfield, D.L., Musta, T.E., Gooding, T.M., Davis, K.D., Dombrowa, M.B., Kopcsay, G.V., Senger, R.M., Sugawara, Y., Sugavanam, K.: Soft error resiliency characterization and improvement on IBM BlueGene/Q processor using accelerated proton irradiation. In: 2014 International Test Conference, pp. 1–6, October 2014

7. Clarke, E.M., Grumberg, O., Peled, D.A.: Model Checking. MIT Press, Cambridge (2001)

8. Clarke, E.M., Kurshan, R.P. (eds.): Computer-Aided Verification. Proceedings of a DIMACS Workshop. 1990, New Brunswick, New Jersey, USA. DIMACS Series in Discrete Mathematics and Theoretical Computer Science 18–21 June 1990, vol. 3. DIMACS/AMS (1991)

9. Constantinescu, C.: Impact of deep submicron technology on dependability of VLSI circuits. In: Proceedings of International Conference on Dependable Systems and Networks, DSN 2002, pp. 205–209 (2002)

10. Fiala, D., Mueller, F., Engelmann, C., Riesen, R., Ferreira, K., Brightwell, R.: Detection and correction of silent data corruption for large-scale high-performance computing. In: 2012 International Conference for High Performance Computing, Networking, Storage and Analysis (SC), pp. 1–12, November 2012

11. Foster, H.D: Trends in functional verification: a 2014 industry study. In: Proceedings of 52nd Annual Design Automation Conference, San Francisco, CA, USA, 7–11 June 2015, pp. 48:1–48:6 (2015)

12. Frehse, S., Fey, G., Arbel, E., Yorav, K., Drechsler, R.: Complete and effective robustness checking by means of interpolation. In: FMCAD, pp. 82–90 (2012)

13. Gaisler, J.: A portable and fault-tolerant microprocessor based on the SPARC V8 architecture. In: Proceedings of International Conference on Dependable Systems and Networks, DSN 2002, pp. 409–415 (2002)

14. Kooli, M., Di Natale, G.: A survey on simulation-based fault injection tools for complex systems. In: 2014 9th IEEE International Conference On Design Technology of Integrated Systems in Nanoscale Era (DTIS), pp. 1–6, May 2014

15. Krautz, U., Pflanz, M., Jacobi, C., Tast, H.W., Weber, K., Vierhaus, H.T.: Evaluating coverage of error detection logic for soft errors using formal methods. In: Proceedings of Conference on Design, Automation, Test in Europe: Proceedings, DATE 2006, vol. 3001, pp. 176–181. European Design and Automation Association, Leuven, Belgium (2011)

16. Lantz, L.: Soft errors induced by alpha particles. IEEE Trans. Reliab. 45(2), 174–179 (1996)

17. Mack, M.J., Sauer, W.M., Swaney, S.B., Mealey, B.G.: IBM POWER6 reliability. IBM J. Res. Dev. 51(6), 763–774 (2007)

18. McMillan, K.L.: Symbolic Model Checking. Kluwer, Dordrecht (1993)

19. Mukherjee, S.: Architecture Design for Soft Errors. Morgan Kaufmann Publishers Inc., San Francisco (2008)

20. Nicolaidis, M.: Design techniques for soft-error mitigation. In: 2010 IEEE International Conference on IC Design and Technology (ICICDT), pp. 208–214. IEEE (2010)

21. O'Gorman, T.J.: The effect of cosmic rays on the soft error rate of a dram at ground level. IEEE Trans. Electron Devices 41(4), 553–557 (1994)

22. Ramachandran, P., Kudva, P., Kellington, J.W., Schumann, J., Sanda, P.: Statistical fault injection. In: Proceedings of 38th Annual IEEE/IFIP International Conference on Dependable Systems and Networks, DSN 2008, Anchorage, Alaska, USA, 24–27 June 2008, pp. 122–127 (2008)

23. Seshia, S.A., Li, W., Mitra, S.: Verification-guided soft error resilience. In: DATE, pp. 1442–1447 (2007)
24. Thompto, B.W., Hoppe, B.: Verification for fault tolerance of the IBM system z microprocessor. In: Proceedings of 47th Design Automation Conference, DAC 2010, Anaheim, California, USA, 13–18 July 2010, pp. 525–530 (2010)
25. Wang, F., Agrawal, V.D.: Soft error considerations for computer web servers. In: 2010 42nd Southeastern Symposium on System Theory (SSST), pp. 269–274, March 2010

ddNF: An Efficient Data Structure
for Header Spaces

Nikolaj Bjørner[1]([⊠]), Garvit Juniwal[2], Ratul Mahajan[1], Sanjit A. Seshia[2],
and George Varghese[3]

[1] Microsoft Research, Redmond, USA
nbjorner@microsoft.com
[2] University of California, Berkeley, USA
[3] University of California, Los Angeles, USA

Abstract. Network Verification is emerging as a critical enabler to manage large complex networks. In order to scale to data-center networks found in Microsoft Azure we developed a new data structure called ddNF, *disjoint difference Normal Form*, that serves as an efficient container for a small set of equivalence classes over header spaces. Our experiments show that ddNFs outperform representations proposed in previous work, in particular representations based on BDDs, and is especially suited for *incremental* verification. The advantage is observed empirically; in the worst case ddNFs are exponentially inferior than using BDDs to represent equivalence classes. We analyze main characteristics of ddNFs to explain the advantages we are observing.

1   Introduction

Just as design rule checkers statically verify hardware circuits and type checkers flag type violations in a program before execution, the emerging field of network verification seeks to proactively catch network bugs before they occur in practice by reading router tables and configuration files and checking for properties such as reachability, isolation, and loops. When compared to hardware design automation and software analysis, formal tooling around networks, is at an infant state. Networks are commonly managed using tools developed by network vendors using proprietary formats. Bare bones network tools, such as traceroute, may be the only and best option for debugging networks. Modern large scale public cloud services crave more powerful tools, including static analysis tools that can answer reachability properties in large networks.

This challenge has been recognized relatively recently: The seminal work of Xie [16] focused on reachability in IP networks and Anteater [10] provided a more abstract framework using a SAT solver to compute reachability bugs, and Header Space Analysis (HSA) [7] used a compact representation to compute all reachable headers. Later, Veriflow [8] and NetPlumber [6] found a way to do faster, incremental verification, and Network Optimized Datalog [9] implemented efficient header space verification in an expressive Datalog framework, thereby

S.A. Seshia—UC Berkeley authors supported in part by the NSF ExCAPE project (CCF-1139138).

© Springer International Publishing AG 2016
R. Bloem and E. Arbel (Eds.): HVC 2016, LNCS 10028, pp. 49–64, 2016.
DOI: 10.1007/978-3-319-49052-6_4

allowing higher level properties called beliefs [9] to be expressed. Properties verified include more complex path predicates (e.g., traffic between two hosts flows through a middlebox) and differential reachability (e.g., is reachability same in all load balanced paths).

Yang and Lam [17] made a crucial observation that most headers are treated the same when analyzing any given network. It is therefore much more efficient to find the relatively small set of equivalence classes of headers and then perform reachability queries based on these classes instead of integrating header computation while checking reachability. Yang and Lam base their equivalence class computation on BDDs, which succinctly represent sets of headers. Each equivalence class is a BDD (covering a disjoint set). Whenever inserting a new set, their algorithm requires examining all previous sets and performing BDD operations. While elegant and easy to implement, the overall quadratic number of BDD calls and the fact that BDDs require an overhead per bit struck us as an over fit for the networking domain.

In this paper we introduce the ddNF (disjoint difference Normal Form) data-structure and algorithms that handles the partition of headers in a particularly efficient way. In essence, our new ddNF data structure pre-computes a compressed representation of the relevant header spaces instead of the "run-time" compression employed by say HSA [7] while answering reachability queries. This transformation turns large graphs into small tractable sizes for quantitative analyses and allows faster incremental verification than the BDD based approach used in [17].

2   An Overview of ddNFs

We first provide a quick overview of ddNFs. Consider a very tiny network as an example with 3 data centers A, B, and C in Fig. 1. Assume that the set of prefixes represented by B is $0\star$ and the set of prefixes of C is $1\star$. There are two routers: the leftmost router forwards every packet to its rightmost port $p1$, and the rightmost router splits traffic to B and C via the ports $p2$ and $p3$ respectively.

To compute the reachability from data center A, regular header space methods such as HSA [7] will start with the wild-card expression $\star\star$ (which represents all packets with two bits) which flows to the second router. This set of packets "splits" into two pieces. The first piece is the packets representing $1\star$ which flow down to C. The upper piece is the set of packets covered by the rule $\star$. But since the router does longest match semantics, this rule only applies to packets that do not match $1\star$, in other words to $\star\star - 1\star$. While this is indeed $0\star$ in this simple example, Header Space methods [7] keep headers in this difference of cubes representation and (to avoid state explosion) only lazily extract solutions when a symbolic packet reaches a destination.

While lazy differencing keeps the size of the header space representation manageable, it does require an intersection of an incoming header space with each set of matching rules at a router, an expensive operation that grows with the number of bits in each header and the number of matching rules. Yang and

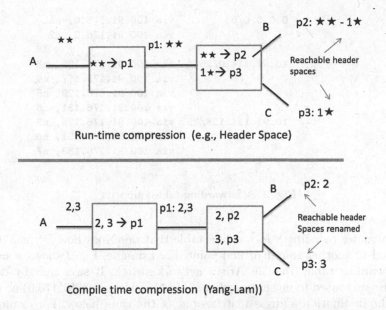

Fig. 1. Run-time vs. pre-computed header space compression

Lam [17] suggest a different technique that we refer to as pre-computed compression that has some analogies with first computing labels for each set of headers as in MPLS [13]. The idea (shown at the bottom of Fig. 1 is to rewrite each header expression in a matching rule as a union of disjoint header expressions (called "atomic predicates" in [17]) which are then replaced by integers.

For example, ✶✶ is the union of 1✶ and 0✶, which we represent by the integers 2 and 3 respectively (we avoided integer 1 to avoid confusion with the bit value 1) and the forwarding table is rewritten as shown. Now the same process is used to compute reachability, but this time we use lists of integers instead of wild-card matching and intersection. While it is unclear that this method works for all reachability queries, it does work very fast for basic reachability, yielding 1-2 orders of speedup compared to even the fastest run-time methods [7].

Yang and Lam [17] calculate the pre-computed set of forward equivalence classes (atomic predicates on headers) using BDDs. We use a dedicated data structure called a ddNF that we found experimentally outperforms BDDs on our benchmarks. Similar to BDDs, ddNFs are also generalized tries, but *in contrast to BDDs that branch on one bit at a time, ddNFs branch based on a subsumption relation between entire wild-card expressions.* Our approach comes with another twist: the ddNF data-structure simply indexes a partition all wild-card expressions and does not rely on aggregating these expressions for output ports as in [17].

3   Firewalls, Routers and Ternary Bit-Vectors

We model an IP router as a set of rules. Firewalls are modeled as special routers that route packets either onward or to a sink that drops packets.

```
 1      0.0.0.0/0          via 100.91.176.0, n1
 2                         via 100.91.176.2, n2
 3
 4      10.91.114.0/25     via 100.91.176.125, n3
 5                         via 100.91.176.127, n4
 6                         via 100.91.176.129, n5
 7                         via 100.91.176.131, n6
 8      10.91.114.128/25   via 100.91.176.125, n3
 9                         via 100.91.176.131, n6
10                         via 100.91.176.133, n7
11      ...
```

Fig. 2. A forwarding table snippet.

Each router contains a forwarding table that describes how IP packets are forwarded to another router or end-point. For example, Fig. 2 shows a snippet of a forwarding table from an Arista network switch: It says that by default addresses are routed to either neighbor n_1 (with address 100.91.176.0) or to n_2, unless the destination address matches one of the rules below. For example, if the first 25 bits of the address match the same 25 bits of 10.91.114.0, then the packet is forwarded to either n_3, n_4, n_5 or n_6.

Ternary bit-vectors (TBVs)[1] succinctly encode matching conditions using 1, 0 and $\star$ (the latter denoting "don't care"). A TBV models a range of IP addresses by concatenating the bytes corresponding to each integer separated by dots, and then adding don't-cares for the last $32 - n$ bits if the prefix is of the form A/n. Thus, 10.91.114.0/25 corresponds to the TBV 00001010 01011011 01110010 0$\star\star\star\star\star\star\star$ and 10.91.114.128/25 corresponds to the TBV 00001010 01011011 01110010 1$\star\star\star\star\star\star\star$; note that these TBVs are *incompatible* in that there is a bit position where one has a 1 while the other has a 0. We use $tbv, tbv_1, \ldots$ to denote ternary bit-vectors in $\{1, 0, \star\}^k$ of the same fixed length k. For example 10$\star\star$00 is a TBV of length $k = 6$.

Ternary bit-vectors denote a set of (concrete) bit-vectors. For example 10$\star\star$00 denotes the set $\{100000, 100100, 101000, 101100\}$. We use ternary bit-vectors and the sets they denote interchangeably. For example, we write $1 \star 0 \subset \star\star 0$.

Definition 1 (Routers). *A router, $\mathcal{R}$, is an ordered list of rules $\rho_1, \rho_2, \rho_3, \ldots, \rho_n$ where $\rho_j = \langle tbv_j, p_j \rangle$ is a pair comprising a ternary bit-vector tbv_j and an output port p_j. The rules have the following semantics: a packet header h, which is a bit-vector, matches rule $\rho_j = \langle tbv_j, p_j \rangle$ (and is forwarded to ports p_j) if each of the vectors $tbv_1, \ldots, tbv_{j-1}$ contain a conflicting bit (a 0 where h has a 1, or vice versa), whereas tbv_j has no such conflicting bit.*

The *matching condition* for rule $\rho_j = \langle tbv_j, p_j \rangle$ is the Boolean function representing the set of bit-vectors $tbv_j \backslash \{tbv_1, tbv_2, \ldots, tbv_{j-1}\}$. We denote this Boolean function by MC_j. Note that our definition of a router does not let the router rewrite headers.

---

[1] Also called "cubes" in the VLSI CAD literature.

We note that router matching conditions have a special syntactic form, which we formally define below.

Definition 2 (Difference of Cubes). *A difference of cubes (DOC) is an expression of the form* $tbv \backslash \{tbv_1, tbv_2, \ldots, tbv_m\}$ *for ternary bit-vectors* tbv, tbv_1, tbv_2, $\ldots$, tbv_m.

For example, the DOC $1 \star\star \backslash \{110, 101\}$ encodes the set $\{111, 100\}$.

A network consists of a set of connected routers. That is, a network, $\mathcal{N}w$, is a set of routers $\{\mathcal{R}_1, \mathcal{R}_2, \ldots, \mathcal{R}_n\}$ along with, for each router $\mathcal{R}_i$, a map $\mathcal{L}_i$ from output ports of $\mathcal{R}_i$ to adjacent ("next hop") routers. In real networks, routers send traffic to non-routers that are end-points of traffic flow. It is a bit simpler, though, to pretend that end-points are routers that either have no incoming or no outgoing links.

A *predicate* is a Boolean function over the header bits. We adapt the definition of *atomic predicate* from Yang and Lam [17] as below.

Definition 3 (Atomic Predicates). *Given a network, a set of predicates* P_1, $\ldots$, P_n *are atomic if they are mutually disjoint, their union is equivalent to true, and in a given network* $\mathcal{N}w$, *every matching condition in any router rule for is equivalent to a union of predicates from* $\{P_1, \ldots, P_n\}$.

Note that for every set of routers there is a coarsest set of atomic predicates.

4 Pre-computed Compression via ddNFs

We wish to perform pre-computed compression by rewriting each router rule (as in [17]) using a set of integers that represent the disjoint matching conditions in order to speed up reachability checking. Instead of using BDDs to enumerate mutually disjoint matching conditions, we propose a new data structure called a ddNF that we show is more efficient for the networking domain.

As recognized in Veriflow [8] and NetPlumber [6] efficiency is important to enable *real-time incremental analysis* as router rule changes occur at high speed (for instance, to accommodate rapid virtual machine migration). For these environments, ddNFs reduce the phase of creating disjoint matching conditions from tens of seconds to a few milliseconds. Further, if rules change, but reuse existing prefixes (for example, a route change), then the ddNF requires no updates. However, in [17] because rules are aggregated on ports before computing disjoint reasons, a routing change that switches a prefixes to a new port can cause label changes.

4.1 Representing Disjoint Sets of Bit-Vectors as DdNFs

Given a set of routers and rules from each router, we seek to enumerate all overlapping segments, such that each rule can be written as a set of mutually disjoint matching conditions potentially shared with other rules. For example, if one rule matches on $10\star\star$ and a different rule matches on $1\star0\star$, then the first set is decomposed into two disjoint sets: $100\star, 10\star\star\backslash\{100\star\}$, and the second set is decomposed into $100\star, 1\star0\star\backslash\{100\star\}$. The three sets are mutually disjoint. Any member of the set $100\star$ (the members are $1001, 1000$) matches both rules, whereas members of $1\star0\star\backslash\{100\star\}$ (the members are $1101, 1100$) match only the second rule.

The *disjoint decomposed normal form*, ddNF, data structure is used to create and maintain a disjoint decomposition from DOCs. Recall that DOCs such as $100\star, 1\star0\star\backslash\{100\star\}$ are differences of (sets of) ternary bit vectors.

Definition 4 (ddNF). *A ddNF is a directed acyclic graph (DAG) data structure, represented as a four-tuple*

$$\langle \mathcal{N}, E, \ell, root \rangle$$

where $\mathcal{N}$ is a set of nodes, $E \subseteq \mathcal{N} \times \mathcal{N}$ are edges, and ℓ is a labeling function mapping every node to a ternary bit-vector, and $root \in \mathcal{N}$ is a designated root node such that all nodes are reachable from it and $\ell(root) = \underbrace{\star\star\star\star}_{k}$. In addition, the ddNF data structure must satisfy the following properties:

- *Whenever $E(n, m)$ for two nodes $n, m \in \mathcal{N}$, then $\ell(m) \subset \ell(n)$.*
- *Conversely, if $n, m \in \mathcal{N}$ and $\ell(m) \subset \ell(n)$, then either $E(n, m)$ or there is a node, $m' \in \mathcal{N}$, such that $\ell(m) \subset \ell(m') \subset \ell(n)$.*
- *No two nodes are labeled by the same ternary bit-vector.*
- *The range of ℓ (i.e., the set of ternary bit-vectors labeling all nodes in $\mathcal{N}$) is closed under intersection.*   □

Fig. 3 shows an example ddNF.

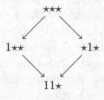

Fig. 3. Example ddNF. The root (top most node) denotes the DOC $\star\star\star\backslash\{1\star\star, \star1\star\}$, the left-most node $1\star\star\backslash\{11\star\}$, right-most node $\star1\star\backslash\{11\star\}$, and the bottom node denotes $11\star$.

The conditions for a ddNF ensure that the data structure is canonical up to isomorphism. Thus, we have

Proposition 1 (ddNFs are unique up to isomorphism). *Given a set S of ternary bit-vectors closed under intersection and containing the ternary bit-vector comprising of all $\star$ there is a unique ddNF labeled by S.*

Proof Sketch: Take the bit-vectors from S, then create the root node from the all-$\star$ bit-vector and for each of the other TBVs create an associated node. Two nodes are connected if their labels are strict subsets and there is no intermediary node labeled by a TBV that is subset-wise between them.   □

We can reconstruct a DOC from a ddNF node n in the following way:

$$doc(n) = \ell(n) \backslash \{\ell(m) \mid m \in children(n)\}$$

In this way, each node represents a set disjoint from all other nodes. Conversely, we can retrieve the set of nodes that denote a difference of cube $tbv_0 \backslash \{tbv_1, \ldots, tbv_m\}$ expression by taking

$$DC(n_0) \backslash (DC(n_1) \cup \ldots \cup DC(n_m))$$

assuming the ddNF has nodes labeled $\ell(n_0) = tbv_0, \ldots, \ell(n_m) = tbv_m$, and the downward closure $DC(n)$ is defined recursively as

$$DC(n) = \{n\} \cup \bigcup \{DC(m) \mid m \in \mathcal{N}, (n,m) \in E\}$$

Note that not all nodes are necessarily representing non-empty sets. This is the case when the set of TBVs labeling children covers the TBV of the parent. Checking non-emptiness of a node amounts to checking satisfiability of the formula

$$fml(tbv) \wedge \bigwedge_i \neg fml(tbv_i)$$

where

$$fml(tbv) = \bigwedge_{i \mid tbv[i]=1} p_i \wedge \bigwedge_{i \mid tbv[i]=0} \neg p_i$$

It is however often easy to quickly determine non-emptiness in a greedy way by creating a sample bit-vector that is contained in the positive component, but different from negative components by swapping the first bit where the positive has a $\star$ and the negative has a non-$\star$ value.

4.2   Inserting into and Using ddNFs

We will now describe how to update and query the ddNF data structure described in the previous section. The main operation is insertion of ternary bit-vectors. Insertion of a ternary bit-vector t can be described as follows: First of all, we insert a node n labeled by new ternary bit-vector t above the nodes closest to the *root* node that are strict subsets of t. In these positions, the new node n inherits the parents the less general node. Second, if t has a non-empty intersection with a node n', that is neither a subset or a super-set of t, then we have to create a node corresponding to $\ell(n') \cap t$ and insert this to the ddNF and ensure that t is inserted above this new node. Algorithm 1 shows pseudo-code that implements the informally described insertion algorithm. Figures 4 and 5 show two main uses of the algorithm.

The effect of inserting ternary bit-vectors into a ddNF is characterized by the following proposition:

Algorithm 1. Insert(n,r): Insertion of node n labeled by ternary bit-vector t under a ddNF node r

---

Input: n - node labeled by ternary bit-vector t
Input: r - node in ddNF
Output: a node in the ddNF labeled by t
1 **if** $\ell(r) = t$ **then**
2 | **return** r;
3 **end if**
4 $inserted \leftarrow \bot$;
5 **foreach** $(r, child) \in E$ **do**
6 | **if** $t \subseteq \ell(child)$ **then**
7 | | $inserted \leftarrow \top$;
8 | | $n \leftarrow \text{Insert}(n, child)$;
9 | **end if**
10 **end foreach**
11 **if** $inserted$ **then**
12 | **return** n;
13 **end if**
14 **foreach** $(r, child) \in E$ **do**
15 | **if** $\ell(child) \subset t$ **then**
16 | | $E \leftarrow \{(n, child)\} \cup E \setminus \{(r, child)\}$
17 | **end if**
18 **end foreach**
19 $E \leftarrow E \cup \{(r, n)\}$;
20 **foreach** $(r, child) \in E, t' = \ell(child)$ **do**
21 | **if** $t \nsubseteq t' \ \wedge \ t \cap t' \neq \emptyset$ **then**
22 | | $m \leftarrow fresh\ node\ labeled\ by\ t \cap t'$;
23 | | $\text{Insert}(m, r)$; // Ensure $child$ and n share m as common descendant
24 | **end if**
25 **end foreach**
26 **return** n

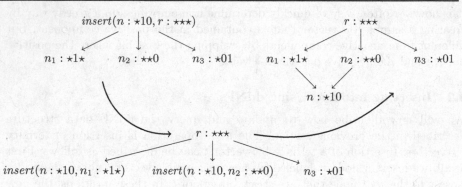

Fig. 4. Insertion below children. In the top left we insert node n labeled by $\star 10$ into a root r, which is labeled by $\star\star\star$. Both nodes n_1 and n_2 generalize n, while n_3 is disjoint from n. Insertion therefore proceeds as in the bottom of the figure by recursively inserting n into n_1 and n_2. After insertion completes, we obtain the ddNF given top right.

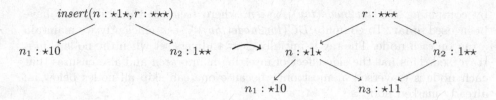

Fig. 5. Insertion with subsumption. When inserting $n : \star 1 \star$ into r we detect that n is more general than n_1, so n is inserted above n_1. On the other hand, n and n_2 are compatible, but neither generalize the other, so we create a fresh node n_3 labeled by the intersection $\star 11$ and it is inserted in a way that is illustrated in Fig. 4.

Proposition 2 (Disjoint Decomposition). *The resulting ddNF obtained after inserting the ternary bit-vectors $tbv_1, tbv_2, \ldots, tbv_n$ has one node corresponding to every possible distinct non-empty set obtained by intersecting some k of the n TBVs while excluding the remaining $n - k$.*

Another way of viewing the above result is that the ddNF has precisely one node for every disjoint region in the Venn-diagram of the sets denoted by the inserted TBVs. This property follows from the conditions in Definition 4.

Algorithm 2 shows the extraction of a ddNF from a set of routers. It also extracts a map from TBVs to labels in the extracted ddNF.

Algorithm 2. Extract a ddNF for a set of routers

Input: *Routers* a set of routers with routing rules from TBVs to ports
Output: A ddNF representing the TBVs used in *Routers*
Output: *tbv2node* a map from TBVs to labels
1 $ddNF \leftarrow$ a ddNF with a single root node;
2 $tbv2node \leftarrow [\star \cdots \star \mapsto root]$;
3 **foreach** $R \in Routers$ **do**
4   **foreach** $\langle tbv, p \rangle \in R$ **do**
5          $n \leftarrow$ Fresh node labeled by tbv;
6          $n \leftarrow$ Insert$(n, root)$;
7          $tbv2node[tbv] \leftarrow n$;
8   **end foreach**
9 **end foreach**
10 **return** $ddNF, tbv2node$

Algorithm 3 shows how we reach our goal for pre-computed header space compression to convert each router to a small lookup table from labels to output ports. The algorithm uses the ddNF extracted from Algorithm 2. It traverses the rules, using the ddNF to extract a set of labels corresponding to each rule. It assumes that the rules are prioritized on a first-applicable basis, such that earlier rules have precedence over later rules. Thus, labels used for earlier rules cannot be used for later rules. The algorithm subtracts previously used labels by computing $DC(tbv2node(tbv)) \setminus seen$, where $seen$ are the nodes that have been used so far. To compute $DC(tbv2node(tbv)) \setminus seen$ efficiently we maintain a tag on each node. The tag is initially clear and gets set when the node is first traversed. This has the side-effect of inserting it into $seen$ and also ensures that each node is traversed at most once because one can skip all nodes below an already marked node.

Algorithm 3. Convert each router R into a map R' from labels to output ports.

Input: *Routers* a set of routers with routing rules from TBVs to ports
Input: a ddNF for the TBVs used in *Routers*
Input: a map *tbv2node* from TBVs to nodes in the ddNF
Output: *Routers'* a set of routers whose routing rules map labels to ports

```
1  Routers' ← ∅;
2  foreach R ∈ Routers do
3  │    R' ← the empty map from ddNF nodes to ports;
4  │    foreach ⟨tbv, p⟩ ∈ R in order of appearance do
5  │    │    seen ← ∅
6  │    │    labels ← DC(tbv2node[tbv]) \ seen
7  │    │    foreach ℓ ∈ labels do
8  │    │    │    R'[ℓ] ← p
9  │    │    end foreach
10 │    │    seen ← seen ∪ DC(tbv2node[tbv])
11 │    end foreach
12 │    Routers' ← Routers' ∪ {R'}
13 end foreach
14 return Routers'
```

We can further optimize the labeling obtained from Algorithm 3 by using a post-processing pruning step. Define the equivalence relation $\simeq$ between two labels as follows:

$$\ell \simeq \ell' := \bigwedge_{R' \in Routers'} R'[\ell] = R'[\ell']$$

That is, two labels are equivalent if the forwarding behavior is the same for each router. We can then remove all but one equivalence class representative from each $\simeq$ class and still compute reachability. In [14], we extended this reduction by taking a transitive congruence closure. We describe this approach in more detail in Sect. 5.

Finally, when we check reachability for a set of headers (given by a DOC), we compute the set of labels associated with the DOC and check reachability for each of the labels.

4.3 Comparing ddNFs with BDDs

First of all let us notice that the conversion of a set of TBVs into ddNF can be exponential.

Example 1. Suppose we have a routing table with the following rules:

1	`1.*.*`	via port1
2	`*.1.*`	via port2
3	`*.*.1`	via port3

The rules use the ternary bit-vectors $1\star\star, \star 1\star, \star\star 1$. They decompose into 8 disjoint subsets and the corresponding ddNF is shown in Fig. 6.

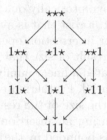

Fig. 6. Maximal ddNF

As we will later observe, the structure of real routing tables makes this worst case very unlikely; ddNFs perform very well in practice.

Yang and Lam [17] use BDDs [4] to represent header spaces and leverage BDD operations to compute a coarsest partition refinement, such that every set in the resulting partition has the same forwarding behavior across all routers. Algorithm 4 sketches how the approach from [17] creates one predicate per output port that summarizes the set of headers that are forwarded to the given port. Recall that we assume that a router is an ordered list of rules of the form $\langle tbv, p \rangle$, where *tbv* is a matching condition and p is the name of an output port. The result of Algorithm 4 is a disjoint partition of sets over the header space of a router.

Algorithm 4. Extracting predicates for a router

---

1 $Ps \leftarrow [p \mapsto \emptyset \mid p \in Ports]$
2 $seen \leftarrow \emptyset$
3 **foreach** $\langle tbv, p \rangle \in Router$ *in order of appearance* **do**
4 | $Ps[p] \leftarrow Ps[p] \cup (tbv \setminus seen)$
5 | $seen \leftarrow tbv \cup seen$
6 **end foreach**
7 $Ps[sink] \leftarrow Ps[sink] \cup \overline{seen}$

The partitions created for each router are then combined into a maximally coarse partition as follows: Let $Ps_1, \ldots, Ps_n$ be the partitions extracted from routers $1, \ldots, n$. Then the final partition can be computed using Algorithm 5.

Algorithm 5. Partition refinement

---
1 $\mathcal{R} \leftarrow \{\top\}$
2 **foreach** $i = 1, \ldots, n; p \in Ports$ **do**
3 $\quad | \quad \mathcal{R} \leftarrow \{P \cap R, \overline{P} \cap R \mid P = Ps_i[p], R \in \mathcal{R}\} \setminus \{\emptyset\}$
4 **end foreach**
5 **return** $\mathcal{R}$

This algorithm requires an asymptotically quadratic number of BDD operations during partition refinement, a cost that is avoided with ddNFs.

First, note that each union or intersection operation (line 4 in Algorithm 4, line 5 in Algorithm 5) creates a result of size that is potentially the sum of the size of the arguments. When iterated a linear number of times, this may produce potentially quadratic space overhead. Furthermore, the number of operations in Algorithm 5 is also quadratic in the size of the result. The ddNF data-structure may likewise increase in size during an insertion. However, the overall space overhead of the ddNF structure is bounded by the number of disjoint partitions, and the number of operations for an insertion is bounded by the bit-width of the header space multiplied by the number of resulting classes (the longest path of a ddNF is at most the bit-width of the header space). There is an important constant factor that differentiates BDDs and ddNFs as well: The ternary bit-vectors in the ddNF tree can be represented using machine words. A ternary bit can be represented using two bits in the usual way: 01 for true, 10 for false, 11 for $\star$ and 00 for undefined. The intersection of two TBVs is defined if it does not contain a sequence of 00s. Then if a machine has word size w (which is typically 64 these days) one can represent a k-bit ternary bit using $\lceil 2 \cdot k/w \rceil$ words. BDDs, in contrast allocate a separate node per bit, each node has a field for the current variable and pointers to left and right children. Typical implementations use also fields for reference counts. As we show in the next section, the evaluation also shows that the ddNFs behave very well on our benchmark sets.

Atomic predicates always correspond to a union of nodes in the ddNF built from routers. This is because each atomic predicate is an intersection of DOCs corresponding to rules and each such intersection corresponds to a union of nodes in a ddNF. Thus, the number of ddNF nodes is always at least the number of atomic predicates. Our experiments show that in practice this number is pretty small, even though the worst case is prohibitive. The ddNFs originating from rules from example 1 grow exponentially. The ddNF for that example contained 8 nodes, while there are only three atomic predicates: $1\star\star, 01\star, 001$, but the ddNF grows exponentially with the bit-width. More generally, rules for a single router create only one atomic predicate per output port, while the number of nodes in a ddNF is potentially exponential for a fixed router. The number of atomic predicates collected for a set of routers can of course be exponential for the same reasons that ddNFs can be of exponential size.

4.4   ddNFs and DOCs and Multi-dimensional Prefix Tries

The HSA [7] tool uses linear search over DOCs to process symbolic headers represented as TBVs and figure out the forwarding behavior for a set of packets. It does not use any specific indexing techniques to speed up matching. The Veriflow tool [8] integrates some indexing. It uses multi-dimensional prefix tries to represent rules. It is inspired by traditional packet classification data structures. Each dimension corresponds to a header field, and each trie branches on one bit at a time. The approach suggested with ddNF here would correspond to a single dimension of such a trie, or a collapsed multi-dimensional trie. One can of course create multi-dimensional structures from ddNFs, but we have not found a use for it yet. On the other hand, Veriflow uses the tries to compute the set of ports based on symbolic headers represented as TBVs. It does not pre-compute labels.

4.5   Handling Rules that Update Packets

Let us briefly describe one way to extend using ddNFs for analysis of networks where rules can update packet headers. We limit the discussion to header transformations that have match-action rules of the form $\langle p_{in}, tbv, upd, p_{out} \rangle$, where tbv is the matching condition and upd is a ternary bit-vector, and p_{in}, p_{out} are input and output ports. A packet header t matches the rule if $t \cap tbv = t$, and it is transformed to a header $t \downarrow upd$, such that $(t \downarrow upd)[i] = (upd[i] = \star)?t[i] : upd[i]$, for each bit-position i in t. The relevant question is how to efficiently compute updates for sets of headers given by a difference of cube. If we attempt to apply rewrites on difference of cubes we quickly realize that the operations require in general to eliminate existential variables: since symbolic execution of a set of states (regardless of their representation) corresponds to working with strongest post-conditions. On the other hand, pre-conditions of guarded assignments correspond to basic substitutions with the assignment and intersections with the guard. It is therefore more convenient to close ddNFs under pre-images. The procedure for closing ddNFs under pre-images over a set of configurations $\langle doc_1, p_1 \rangle, \ldots, \langle doc_n, p_n \rangle$ of DOCs and ports $p_1, \ldots, p_n$ is obtained by computing the fixedpoint under

$$wpc(\langle p_{in}, tbv, upd, p_{out} \rangle, \langle doc_{out}, p_{out} \rangle) := \langle doc_{in} \cup tbv \cap (doc_{out} \downarrow upd), p_{in} \rangle$$

Note that the operations on the resulting DOCs can be performed directly over ddNFs.

5   Experiments

We measured the efficiency of the ddNF data structure in comparison with [17] using benchmarks from the Stanford Campus Network [7] and IP forwarding tables provided from selected Azure data-centers. We used a modest laptop running Intel Core i5-3317U 1.70 GHz, 8 GB Ram, running 64 bit Windows 8.1. Our implementation of [17] uses the BuDDy BDD library [15] and otherwise follows almost verbatim the presentation of [17] with one minor change. The algorithm suggested in [17] for inserting a set P into an existing set of partitions $R_1, \ldots, R_n$ is to compute $\{P \cap R_i, \overline{P} \cap R_i \mid i = 1, \ldots, n\}$ and remove empty sets from the result. Our approach is, for each i, to first compute $P \cap R_i$. If the result is empty then we produce R_i, otherwise compute also $\overline{P} \cap R_i$ and set P to $P \cap \overline{R}_i$. We found this approach to be crucial to make the BDD based approach work.

Table 1 summarizes the comparison. We note that the ddNF-based implementation runs at least one order of magnitude faster, with the runtime being a fraction of a second even for the largest benchmark. This makes the ddNF-based approach well-suited for use with real-time updates of router rules. We also noticed that (perhaps unsurprisingly) the BDD based approach is sensitive to the initial variable order. For instance, for the Stanford benchmark set, the BDD approach is 10x faster if the initial variable order is reversed from least to most significant digit (this remains slower than ddNF, nonetheless).

Table 1. Measurements from five different network topologies. The Stanford benchmark is obtained from [7] and is used as a standard benchmark. We extracted only the forwarding rules from these benchmarks for our measurements. The networks DC 1–4 represent different snapshots from Azure data-centers of different size from around the globe. The numbers in the BDD and ddNF columns are time in seconds and number of generated labels. The ddNF for the Stanford network contains 5149 labels before compression and only 17 labels after line 11 of Algorithm 3. For the other networks, compression has no effect.

	# Rules	BDD		ddNF	
		sec.	#labels	sec.	#labels
Stanford	8137	3.4	178	0.19	5149/17
DC 1	9060	2.0	829	0.05	1005
DC 2	7446	2.3	979	0.04	1157
DC 3	89871	17.7	2627	0.49	3058
DC 4	113131	29.8	3272	0.66	4077

We also applied the ddNF data-structure in [14] as an integral part of a set of network surgeries aimed to speed up reachability queries on networks. Let us here recall main elements of our experiments there. Our experimental setup there used a Microsoft production data center located in Singapore, similar to DC 4. In more detail, the it is a fairly large switching network, with 52 core routers, each with about 800 forwarding rules (but no ACLs), and with 90 ToRs with about 800 rules and 100 ACLs each. In total, this network has about 820 K forwarding and ACL rules and is a reasonable example of a complex data center.

After reducing the network with respect to the header equivalences we split forwaring rules so that each rule operates on a single header equivalence class. Then, for each such class h we compute a forwarding equivalence relation as a congruence closure relation: it is computed bottom up from reachable nodes: two nodes are equivalent with respect to a header equivalence class h if they forward h the same way. In particular, two nodes that have no forwarding rules for h are equivalent. Then, inductively, two nodes become equivalent with respect to h, if the successors are pairwise equivalent. We could have opted for a stronger equivalence relation that considers two nodes forwarding equivalent with respect to h using a (co-inductive) bisimulation relation, but in the case of packet forwarding, we may expect most forwarding paths to be acyclic. Luckily, in the acyclic case, there is no difference between inductive congruence closure and co-inductive bisimulation relations. In this way, we transformed a network with nearly a million rules to a new network with just over 10,000 rules and obtained a corresponding two-orders of magnitude speedup over analyzing the original network.

6 Conclusions

This paper developed ddNFs to quickly and incrementally decompose the header space into a much smaller set of equivalence classes. We found ddNFs an order of magnitude faster than previous approaches [17] on our benchmarks, making ddNFs especially suitable for incremental verification when router rules change rapidly.

References

1. Al-Shaer, E., Al-Haj, S.: FlowChecker: configuration analysis and verification of federated OpenFlow infrastructures. In: SafeConfig (2010)
2. Bosshart, P., Daly, D., Gibb, G., Izzard, M., McKeown, N., Rexford, J., Schlesinger, C., Talayco, D., Vahdat, A., Varghese, G., Walker, D.: P4: programming protocol-independent packet processors. SIGCOMM Comput. Commun. Rev. **44**(3), 87–95 (2014)
3. Bosshart, P., Gibb, G., Kim, H.-S., Varghese, G., McKeown, N., Izzard, M., Mujica, F., Horowitz, M.: Forwarding metamorphosis: fast programmable match-action processing in hardware for SDN. In: SIGCOMM (2013)
4. Bryant, R.E.: Graph-based algorithms for Boolean function manipulation. IEEE Trans. Comput. **35**(8), 677–691 (1986)
5. Greenberg, A., Hamilton, J., Maltz, D.A., Patel, P.: The cost of a cloud: research problems in data center networks. SIGCOMM Comput. Commun. Rev. **39**(1), 68–73 (2008)
6. Kazemian, P., Chang, M., Zeng, H., Varghese, G., McKeown, N., Whyte, S.: Real time network policy checking using header space analysis. In: NSDI (2013)
7. Kazemian, P., Varghese, G., McKeown, N.: Header space analysis: static checking for networks. In: NSDI, pp. 113–126 (2012)
8. Khurshid, A., Zou, X., Zhou, W., Caesar, M., Godfrey, P.B.: Veriflow: verifying network-wide invariants in real time. In: NSDI (2013)
9. Lopes, N., Bjørner, N., Godefroid, P., Jayaraman, K., Varghese, G.: Checking beliefs in dynamic networks. In: NSDI (2015)
10. Mai, H., Khurshid, A., Agarwal, R., Caesar, M., Godfrey, P.B., King, S.T.: Debugging the data plane with anteater. In: SIGCOMM (2011)

11. McKeown, N.: Mind the gap. In: SIGCOMM (2012). http://youtu.be/Ho239zp KMwQ
12. Nelson, T., Barratt, C., Dougherty, D.J., Fisler, K., Krishnamurthi, S.: The margrave tool for firewall analysis. In: LISA (2010)
13. Pathak, A., Zhang, M., Hu, Y.C., Mahajan, R., Maltz, D.: Latency inflation in MPLS-based traffic engineering. In: Internet Measurement Conference (IMC) (2011)
14. Plotkin, G.D., Bjørner, N., Lopes, N.P., Rybalchenko, A., Varghese, G.: Scaling network verification using symmetry and surgery. In: Bodík, R., Majumdar R. (eds.) Proceedings of the 43rd Annual ACM SIGPLAN-SIGACT Symposium on Principles of Programming Languages, POPL 2016, St. Petersburg, FL, USA, January 20–22, 2016, pp. 69–83. ACM (2016)
15. The BuDDy BDD package. http://buddy.sourceforge.net/manual/main.html
16. Xie, G.G., Zhan, J., Maltz, D.A., Zhang, H., Greenberg, A.G., Hjálmtýsson, G., Rexford, J.: On static reachability analysis of IP networks. In: INFOCOM (2005)
17. Yang, H., Lam, S.S.: Real-time verification of network properties using atomic predicates. In: ICNP, pp. 1–11 (2013)

Probabilistic Fault Localisation

David Landsberg[1(✉)], Hana Chockler[2], and Daniel Kroening[1]

[1] Department of Computer Science, University of Oxford, Oxford, UK
david.landsberg@linacre.ox.ac.uk
[2] Department of Informatics, King's College London, London, UK

Abstract. Efficient fault localisation is becoming increasingly important as software grows in size and complexity. In this paper we present a new formal framework, denoted *probabilistic fault localisation* (PFL), and compare it to the established framework of spectrum based fault localisation (SBFL). We formally prove that PFL satisfies some desirable properties which SBFL does not, empirically demonstrate that PFL is significantly more effective at finding faults than all known SBFL measures in large scale experimentation, and show PFL has comparable efficiency. Results show that the user investigates 37 % more code (and finds a fault immediately in 27 % fewer cases) when using the best performing SBFL measures, compared to the PFL framework. Furthermore, we show that it is theoretically impossible to design strictly rational SBFL measures that outperform PFL techniques on a large set of benchmarks.

Keywords: Fault localisation · Spectrum based fault localisation · Triage and debug technologies

1 Introduction

Faulty software is estimated to cost 60 billion dollars to the US economy per year [1] and has been single-handedly responsible for major newsworthy catastrophes[1]. This problem is exacerbated by the fact that debugging (defined as the process of finding and fixing a fault) is complex and time consuming – estimated to consume 50–60 % of the time a programmer spends in the maintenance and development cycle [2]. Consequently, the development of effective and efficient methods for software fault localisation has the potential to greatly reduce costs, wasted programmer time and the possibility of catastrophe.

In this paper we advance the state of the art in lightweight fault localisation by building on research in spectrum-based fault localisation (SBFL). In SBFL, a *measure* is used to determine the degree of suspiciousness each line of code is with respect to being faulty, where this degree is defined as a function of the number of passing/failing traces that do/do not cover that code. SBFL is one of the most prominent areas of software fault localisation research, has recently

---

[1] https://www.newscientist.com/gallery/software-faults/.

© Springer International Publishing AG 2016
R. Bloem and E. Arbel (Eds.): HVC 2016, LNCS 10028, pp. 65–81, 2016.
DOI: 10.1007/978-3-319-49052-6_5

been estimated to make up 35 % of published work in the field [3] and has been consistently demonstrated to be effective and efficient at finding faults [4–21].

However, so far there have not been many formal properties about the general problem of fault localisation which SBFL measures have been shown to satisfy, representing a potential theoretical shortcoming of the approach. Although properties that measures should satisfy a priori (such as strict rationality [22]) have been discussed, and measures that solve fault localisation sub-problems have been presented (such as single bug optimal measures [15]), there is not yet a SBFL measure that solves the problem of fault localisation for all benchmarks. Indeed, recently Yoo et al. have established theoretical results which show that a "best" performing suspicious measure does not exist [23]. In light of this, the SBFL literature has favoured developing measures with good experimental performance as opposed to developing them according to a priori requirements. This has facilitated a culture of borrowing measures from other domains [11,15,16], manually tweaking measures [13,17], or using machine learning methods [19,20,24]. Thus, there remains the challenge of developing new, better performing and comparably efficient methods that can satisfy key properties of fault localisation. Our contributions in this paper are as follows:

- We introduce and motivate a new formal framework denoted *Probabilistic Fault Localisation* (PFL), which can leverage any SBFL measure.
- We formally prove that PFL satisfies desirable formal properties which SBFL does not.
- We demonstrate that PFL techniques are substantially and statistically significantly more effective (using $p = 0.01$) than all known (200) SBFL measures at finding faults on what, to our knowledge, is the largest scale experimental comparison in software fault localisation to date.
- We show that it is theoretically impossible to define strictly rational SBFL measures that can outperform given PFL techniques on many of our benchmarks.
- We demonstrate that PFL maintains efficiency comparable to SBFL.

The rest of the paper is organised as follows. In Sect. 2 we present the formal preliminaries common to the approaches discussed in this paper and in Sect. 3 introduce a small illustrative example of SBFL. In Sect. 4, we introduce and motivate the formal theory underlying the PFL approach and formally prove it satisfies desirable fault localisation properties which SBFL does not. Section 5 presents our experimental comparison of PFL techniques against SBFL measures. Finally, we present related work and general conclusions.

2 Preliminaries

In this section we summarise the formal apparatus common to the approaches in this paper.

We model each *program* as an ordered set $P = \langle C_1, \ldots, C_n \rangle$. Intuitively, each C_i can be thought of as a program entity, event, or proposition, which is executed, occurs, or is true if a corresponding program entity is covered in a given execution. A program entity (or component) can be thought of as a program statement, branch, path, or block of code [7,25]. A component is called *complex* if it is the union of other components, and *atomic* otherwise. In practice, P is modelled as a set of atomic components in order to reduce overhead [4–21].

We model each *test suite* as an ordered set of test cases $T = \langle t_1, \ldots, t_m \rangle$. Each test case t_i is a Boolean vector of length $|P|$ such that $t_k = \langle c_1^k, \ldots, c_{|P|}^k \rangle$, and where we have $c_i^k = \top$ if C_i is covered/occurs/is true in t_k and $\bot$ otherwise. We also use 1 and 0 for $\top$ and $\bot$ respectively. $C_{|P|}$ can be thought of as the event of the error (denoted by E), where $c_{|P|}^k = e^k = \top$ if the test case *fails* and $\bot$ if it *passes*. Intuitively, each test case records the coverage details of a given execution, and is failing/passing if that execution violates/satisfies a given specification, where a specification is a logically contingent proposition stated in some formal language.

Each test suite may be partitioned $T = F \cup P$, where F and P are the set of failing and passing test cases respectively. By convention each test suite is ordered such that the failing traces appear before the passing. In general, we assume that every failing test case covers at least one component, and that every component is covered by at least one failing test case. We may represent a test suite with an $m \times n$ *coverage matrix*, in which the k-th row of the i-th column represents whether C_i occurred in t_k. An example of a coverage matrix is given in Fig. 2.

For each $C_i \in P$ we can construct its *program spectrum* using a test suite. A program spectrum is defined as a vector of four elements $\langle a_{ef}^i, a_{nf}^i, a_{ep}^i, a_{np}^i \rangle$, where a_{ef}^i is the number of failing test cases in T that cover C_i, a_{nf}^i is the number of failing test cases in T that do not cover C_i, a_{ep}^i is the number of passing test cases in T that cover C_i and a_{np}^i is the number of passing test cases in T that do not cover C_i. Probabilistic expressions may be defined as a function of program spectra as follows. We identify $P(C_i \cap E)$, $P(\overline{C_i} \cap E)$, $P(C_i \cap \overline{E})$ and $P(\overline{C_i} \cap \overline{E})$ with $\frac{a_{ef}^i}{|T|}$, $\frac{a_{nf}^i}{|T|}$, $\frac{a_{ep}^i}{|T|}$ and $\frac{a_{np}^i}{|T|}$ respectively. Using definitions from probabilistic calculus [26], we may then identify many measures with a probabilistic expression.

A *suspiciousness measure* w maps a program entity to a real number as a function of its spectrum [15], where this number is called the program entity's degree of suspiciousness. The higher the degree the more suspicious the program entity C_i is assumed to be with respect to being a fault. In practical SBFL the components in the program are investigated in descending order of suspiciousness until a fault is found. Prominent measures include Zoltar $= \frac{a_{ef}^i}{a_{ef}^i + a_{nf}^i + a_{ep}^i + k}$ where $k = \frac{10000 a_{nf}^i a_{ep}^i}{a_{ef}^i}$ [15], Kulczynski2 $= \frac{1}{2}(P(E|C_i) + P(C_i|E))$ [15], Ochiai $= P(C_i \cap E)/\sqrt{P(C_i)P(E)}$ [4], and Positive predictive power (PPV) $= P(E|C_i)$ [6]. PPV is equivalent to the Tarantula measure [27].

Some suspiciousness measures are informally known as measures of *causal strength* [11]. Measures of causal strength are designed to measure the propensity of an event in causing a given effect. Any measure can be proposed as a measure of causal strength. Historically such measures have been developed around the premise that causes raise the probability of their effects. Prominent measures include Lewis $= P(E|C_i)/P(E|\neg C_i)$, Fitelson $= P(E|C_i)/P(E)$, Suppes $= P(E|C_i) - P(E|\neg C_i)$, and Eels $= P(E|C_i)/P(E)$ (see [11]).

Formally, a suspiciousness measure w is *rational* if and only if for all $c > 0$ (1) $w(a_{ef}, a_{nf}, a_{ep}, a_{np}) \leq w(a_{ef} + c, a_{nf} - c, a_{ep}, a_{np})$, and (2) $w(a_{ef}, a_{nf}, a_{ep} + c, a_{np} - c) \leq w(a_{ef}, a_{nf}, a_{ep}, a_{np})$. The property of *strict rationality* is defined by replacing $\leq$ with $<$ in the latter two conditions. Roughly speaking, a measure is rational/strictly-rational if more failing traces covering a component make it more suspicious, and more passing traces maek it less suspicious – conforming to our intuition of suspiciousness. Many suspiciousness measures have been shown to satisfy strict rationality, at least when $a_{ef}, a_{ep} > 1$ [15,22]. Naish et al. argue that it is reasonable to restrict the SBFL approach to rational measures [28].

We now discuss established methods for evaluating the performance of a suspiciousness measure. First, there are *wasted effort* scores (or W-scores). W-scores estimate the percentage of non-faulty components a user will look through until a fault is found. Best case, worst case, and average case W-scores have been defined [4,11,13,15]. Where w is a measure, b is a fault with the highest degree of suspiciousness, and f is the number of faults which are equally suspicious to the most suspicious fault, we use the following definitions: $best(w) = \frac{|\{x|w(x)>w(b)\}|}{|P|-1}100$, $worst(w) = \frac{|\{x|m(x)\geq w(b)\}-1|}{|P|-1}100$, $average(w) = best(w) + \frac{worst(w)-best(w)}{f+1}$. We use *avg* W-scores. Second, there are *absolute scores* (or A-scores) [29]. A-scores measure whether a given measure found a fault after inspecting n non-faulty components [29]. Thus, for a given n a suspiciousness measure receives 100 % if the user found a fault after investigating n non-faulty components, otherwise it received 0 %. We use $n = 0$. A suspiciousness measure performs well if it has have low mean W-scores and a high mean A-scores.

Finally, Naish et al. define the *unavoidable costs* of any strictly rational measure. These are the scores that the best performing strictly rational measure can possibly receive [28]. To determine this score, one constructs an ordered list with the property that for every component, C_i is ranked higher than a given fault C_j just in case every strictly rational measure would rank C_i higher than C_j. The W/A-scores of this list are the unavoidable cost W/A-scores. Unavoidable cost scores estimate the upper bound limit for the performance of the SBFL approach in general (see [28] for details).

3   Example

We present a small example to illustrate SBFL. Consider the C program **min-max.c** in Fig. 1 (from [30]). The program is formally modelled as the following set of program entities $\boldsymbol{P} = \langle C_1, C_2, C_3, C_4, E \rangle$, where E models the event in which the specification `assert(least <= most)` is violated. The program fails to always satisfy this specification. The explanation for the failure is the fault at C_3, which should be an assignment to `least` instead of `most`. We collected coverage data from ten test cases to form our test suite $\boldsymbol{T} = \langle t_1, \ldots, t_{10} \rangle$. The

```
int main() {
  int input1, input2, input3;
  int least = input1;
  int most = input1;

  if (most < input2)
    most = input2;   // C1
  if (most < input3)
    most = input3;  // C2
  if (least > input2)
    most = input2;  // C3 (fault)
  if (least > input3)
    least = input3;  // C4

  assert(least <= most);  // E
}
```

	C_1	C_2	C_3	C_4	E
t_1	0	1	1	0	1
t_2	0	0	1	1	1
t_3	0	0	1	0	1
t_4	1	0	0	0	0
t_5	0	1	0	0	0
t_6	0	0	0	1	0
t_7	0	0	1	1	0
t_8	0	0	0	0	0
t_9	1	0	0	1	0
t_{10}	1	1	0	0	0

Fig. 1. `minmax.c`   **Fig. 2.** Coverage matrix

coverage matrix for these test cases is given in Fig. 2. Three of the test cases fail and seven pass. We compute the program spectrum for each component using the coverage matrix. For example, the program spectrum for C_3 is $\langle 3, 0, 1, 6 \rangle$.

To illustrate an instance of SBFL we use the suspiciousness measure Wong-2 = $a^i_{ef} - a^i_{ep}$ [13]. The user inspects the program in decreasing order of suspiciousness until a fault is found. C_3 is inspected first with a suspiciousness of 2 and thereby a fault is found immediately. The example illustrates that SBFL measures can be successfully employed as heuristics for fault localisation, but that the formal connection to fault localisation could potentially be improved.

4   Estimating Fault Probability

In this section, we introduce assumptions to generate our estimation of fault probability and then prove this estimation satisfies important properties that are not satisfied by any SBFL measure.

We begin as follows. We introduce a probability function P the domain of which is a set of propositions. To define the set of propositions, we first define two sets of atomic propositions $\mathbf{H} = \{h_i | C_i \in \boldsymbol{P}\}$ and $\mathbf{C} = \{h_i^k | C_i \in \boldsymbol{P} \wedge t_k \in \mathbf{T}\}$. Intuitively, $\mathbf{H}$ is a set of fault hypotheses, where h_i expresses the hypothesis that C_i is faulty, and $\mathbf{C}$ is a set of causal hypotheses, where h_i^k expresses the hypothesis that C_i was the cause of the error E in execution t_k. The set of propositions is then defined inductively as follows. For each $p, q \in \mathbf{H} \cup \mathbf{C}$, p and q are propositions. If p and q are propositions, then $p \wedge q$, $p \vee q$, $\neg p$ are propositions. We also assume the following standard properties of probability [26]. For each proposition p and q: $P(p) = 1$ if $p = \top$. $P(p) = 0$ if $p = \bot$. $P(p \vee q) = P(p) + P(q) - P(p \wedge q)$. $P(\neg p) = 1 - P(p)$. $P(p|q) = P(p \wedge q)/P(q)$.

We now present assumptions **A1-7** which are designed to be plausible in any probability space induced by a test suite **T** for a faulty program **P**.

A1. For all $h_i \in \mathbf{H}$, $h_i = \bigvee_{k=1}^{|\mathbf{T}|} h_i^k$.

This states that C_i is faulty just in case C_i was the cause of the error E in some execution of the program.

A2. For all $t_k \in \mathbf{F}$, $\bigvee_{i=1}^{|P|} h_i^k = \top$.

This states that for every failing trace, there is some component $C_i \in \mathbf{P}$ which caused the error E in that trace. In other words, if an error occurred then something must have caused it. For all $h_i^k \in \mathbf{C}$ we also have the following

A3. if $h_i^k = \top$ then $C_i \neq E$.

A4. if $h_i^k = \top$ then $c_i^k = \top$ and $e^k = \top$.

These assumptions state that if C_i was the cause of E in t_k, then C_i must have been a different event to E (**A3**), and C_i and E must have actually occurred (**A4**). These two assumptions have been described as fundamental properties about causation [31]. For all $h_i^k, h_j^k \in \mathbf{C}$

A5. if $C_i \neq C_j$ then $h_i^k \wedge h_j^k = \bot$.

This states that no two events could have both been the cause of the error in a given trace. In other words, different causal hypotheses for the same trace are mutually exclusive. The rationale for this is that the intended meaning of h_i^k is C_i was *the* cause of E in t_k, and as *the* implies uniqueness, no two events could have been *the* cause. In general, any union of events may be said to be *the* cause so long as that union is in **P**. For all $h_i^k \in \mathbf{C}$ and every sample $\mathbf{S} \subseteq \mathbf{T} - \{t_k\}$

A6. $P(h_i^k | \bigvee_{t_n \in S} h_i^n) = P(h_i^k)$.

This states that the probability that C_i was the cause in one trace is not affected by whether it was in some others. In other words, whether it was the cause in one is statistically independent of whether it was in others. Here, we assume that our probabilities describe objective chance, and that the causal properties of each execution is determined by the properties of the events in that execution alone, and therefore cannot affect the causal properties of other executions. Independence principles are well established in probability theory [26].

In light of the above assumptions we may define $c(t_k) = \{C_i | C_i \in \mathbf{P} \wedge c_i^k = e^k = \top \wedge C_i \neq E\}$ as the set of candidate causes of E in t_k. Following this, for some measure w, and all $C_i, C_j \in c(t_k)$, we assume

A7. $P(h_i^k)/P(h_j^k) = w(C_i)/w(C_j)$.

Here, we assume w measures the propensity of a given event to cause the error (and is thus motivated as a measure of causal strength as described in the preliminaries). Accordingly, the assumption states that the relative likelihood that one event caused the error over another, is directly proportional to their propensities to do so. In general, any suspiciousness measure w from the SBFL literature may be proposed as a measure of causal strength, and thus there is great room for experimentation over the definition of w. One formal proviso is that measures be re-scaled so $w(C_i) > 0$ if $a_{ef}^i > 0$ (this avoids divisions by zero). We use the notation PFL-w when measure w is being used.

We now show that the assumptions **A1-7** (henceforth PFL assumptions) imply Eqs. (1), (2) and (3) (henceforth PFL equations). The PFL equations can be used to determine the probability that a given component C_i is faulty. For all $h_i^k \in \mathbf{C}$

$$P(h_i) = P(\bigvee_{n=1}^{|\mathbf{T}|} h_i^n) \tag{1}$$

$$P(\bigvee_{j=n}^{|\mathbf{T}|} h_i^j) = P(h_i^n) + P(\bigvee_{j=n+1}^{|\mathbf{T}|} h_i^j) - P(h_i^n)\, P(\bigvee_{j=n+1}^{|\mathbf{T}|} h_i^j) \tag{2}$$

$$P(h_i^k) = \begin{cases} \dfrac{w(C_i)}{\sum\limits_{C_j \in c(t_k)} w(C_j)} & \text{if } C_i \in c(t_k) \\ 0 & \text{otherwise} \end{cases} \tag{3}$$

Proposition 1. *The* PFL *assumptions imply the* PFL *equations.*

Proof. We first show Eq. (1). $h_i = \bigvee_{k=1}^{|\mathbf{T}|} h_i^k$ (by **A1**). Thus $P(h_i) = P(\bigvee_{k=1}^{|\mathbf{T}|} h_i^k)$ (by Leibniz's law). We now show Eq. (2). The definition of disjunction states $P(\bigvee_{j=n}^{|\mathbf{T}|} h_i^j) = P(h_i^n) + P(\bigvee_{j=n+1}^{|\mathbf{T}|} h_i^j) - P(h_i^n \wedge \bigvee_{j=n+1}^{|\mathbf{T}|} h_i^j)$. It remains to show $P(h_i^n \wedge \bigvee_{j=n+1}^{|\mathbf{T}|} h_i^j) = P(h_i^n)P(\bigvee_{j=n+1}^{|\mathbf{T}|} h_i^j)$. $P(h_i^n \wedge \bigvee_{j=n+1}^{|\mathbf{T}|} h_i^j)$ is equal to $P(h_i^n | \bigvee_{j=n+1}^{|\mathbf{T}|} h_i^j)P(\bigvee_{j=n+1}^{|\mathbf{T}|} h_i^j)$ (by probabilistic calculus). This is equal to $P(h_i^n)P(\bigvee_{j=n+1}^{|\mathbf{T}|} h_i^j)$ (by **A6**).

We now show Eq. (3). We have two cases to consider: $C_i \in c(t_k)$ and $C_i \notin c(t_k)$. Assume $C_i \in c(t_k)$. We may assume t_k is ordered such that $\bigwedge_{i=1}^{n} c_i^k = \top$, $\bigwedge_{i=n+1}^{|P|-1} c_i^k = \bot$ and $c_{|P|}^k = e^k = \top$ (such that $c(t_k) = \{C_1, \ldots, C_n\}$). Now, for all $C_i, C_j \in c(t_k)$ $P(h_i^k)/P(h_j^k) = w(C_i)/w(C_j)$ (by **A7**). Thus, for $C_i, C_j \in c(t_k)$ $w(C_i)/P(h_i^k) = w(C_j)/P(h_j^k)$ (as $x/y = w/z \equiv z/y = w/x$). So, $w(C_1)/P(h_1^k) = w(C_2)/P(h_2^k) = \ldots = w(C_n)/P(h_n^k)$. Thus, there is some c such that for all $C_i \in c(t_k)$, $c = w(C_i)/P(h_i^k)$ (by the last result). Equivalently, there is some c such that for all $C_i \in c(t_k)$, $P(h_i^k) = w(C_i)/c$. To complete the proof it remains to prove $c = \sum_{C_j \in c(t_k)} w(C_j)$. $\bigvee_{i=1}^{|P|} h_i^k = \top$ (by **A2**). But, $\bigvee_{i=n+1}^{|P|-1} h_i^k = \bot$ (by **A4**), and $h_{|P|}^k = \bot$ (by **A3**). Thus, $\bigvee_{i=1}^{n} h_i^k = \top$ (by $\vee$-elimination). So, $P(\bigvee_{i=1}^{n} h_i^k) = 1$ (by probabilistic calculus). Thus, $\sum_{i=1}^{n} P(h_i^k) = 1$ (by probabilistic calculus and **A5**). So, $\sum_{i=1}^{n}(w(C_i)/c) = 1$. Thus, $(\sum_{i=1}^{n} w(C_i))/c = 1$. Equivalently, $\sum_{i=1}^{n} w(C_i) = c$. So, $\sum_{C_i \in c(t_k)} w(C_i) = c$ (by def. of $c(t_k)$ above). We now do the second condition. Assume $C_i \notin c(t_k)$. Then $\neg(c_i^k = e^k = \top \wedge C_i \neq E)$ (by def. of $c(t_k)$). Thus $c_i^k = \bot$ or $e^k = \bot$ or $C_i = E$. If $C_i \neq E$, then $P(h_i^k) = 0$ (by **A3**). If $c_i^k = \bot$, then $P(h_i^k) = 0$ (by **A4**). If $e^k = \bot$, then $P(h_i^k) = 0$ (by **A4**). Thus, if $C_i \notin c(t_k)$, then $P(h_i^k) = 0$.

To use the PFL equations, it remains for the user to choose a measure w for **A7**. One proposal is $w(C_i) = P(E|C_i)$ (the PPV measure [11]) or $P(E|C_i)/P(E)$ (the Fitelson measure of causal strength [32]). For the purposes of defining $P(h_i^k)$ both proposals are equivalent (observe $P(h_i^k)/P(h_j^k) = P(E/C_i)/P(E/C_i) = (P(E/C_i)/P(E))/(P(E/C_j)/P(E))$ using **A7**).

The proposal captures three potentially plausible intuitions about causal likelihood. Firstly, it captures an intuition that the more something raises the probability of the error, the more likely it is to be the cause of it (to see this, observe we have $P(h_i^k)/P(h_j^k) = P(E|C_i)/P(E|C_j)$ using **A7**). Secondly, it captures an intuition that events which do not affect the error's likelihood are equally unlikely to have caused it (to see this, assume both C_i and C_j are independent of E i.e. $P(E) = P(E|C_i)$ and $P(E) = P(E|C_j)$, then it follows $P(h_i^k) = P(h_j^k)$ using **A7**). Thirdly, a plausible estimate of $w(C_i)$ as a measure of C_i's causal strength is the probability that C_i causes E given C_i, and $P(E|C_i)$ accordingly provides an upper bound for this estimate. In our running example PFL-PPV returns $P(h_2) = 0.00$, $P(h_2) = 0.31$, $P(h_3) = 1.00$, and $P(h_4) = 0.25$, which correctly identifies the correct hypothesis with the most probable one.

Finally, given a test suite $\mathbf{T}$ and measure w, an algorithm to find a single fault in a program $\mathbf{P}$ is as follows. Step one, find $\max_{h_i \in \mathbf{H}}(P(h_i))$ by computing the value of $P(h_i)$ for each $h_i \in \mathbf{H}$ using the PFL equations. If the most probable hypothesis represents a fault in the program, the procedure stops. Otherwise, h_j is removed from the set of candidates by setting $c_j^k = \bot$ for each t_k, and return to step one. We call this the PFL algorithm. A property of this algorithm is that yet to be investigated components can change in fault likelihood at each iteration.

We now identify desirable formal properties which we prove the PFL equations satisfies, but no SBFL suspiciousness measure can.

Definition 1. *Fault Likelihood Properties. For all $C_i, C_j \in \mathbf{P}$, where $C_i \neq C_j$, we define the following:*

1. *Base case. If there is some failing trace which only covers C_i, but this property does not hold of C_j, then C_i is more suspicious than C_j.*
2. *Extended case. Let $\mathbf{T}_1$ be a test suite in which all failing traces cover more than one component, and let $\mathbf{T}_2$ be identical to $\mathbf{T}_1$ except $c_i^k = 1$ and $c_j^k = 1$ in $\mathbf{T}_1$ and $c_i^k = 1$ and $c_j^k = 0$ in $\mathbf{T}_2$, then the suspiciousness of C_i in $\mathbf{T}_2$ is more than its suspiciousness in $\mathbf{T}_2$.*

These properties capture the intuition that the fewer covered entities there are in a failing trace, the fewer places there are for the fault to"hide", and so the a priori likelihood that a given covered entity is faulty must increase. Upper bounds for this increase is established by the base case – if a failing trace only covers a single component then that component must be faulty. We now formally establish that the PFL equations, but no SBFL measure, satisfies these properties.

Proposition 2. *The PFL equations satisfies the fault likelihood properties.*

Proof. We first prove the base property. We first show that if there is some failing trace t_k which only covers C_i, then nothing is more suspicious than it. Let t_1 be a failing trace which only covers C_i. Then $P(h_i^1) = \frac{w(C_i)}{w(C_i)} = 1$ (by Eq. (3)). Letting n abbreviate $P(\bigvee_{j=2}^{|\mathbf{T}|} h_i^j)$, we then have $P(\bigvee_{k=1}^{|\mathbf{T}|} h_i^k) = (1+n) - (1n) = 1$ (by Eq. (2)). So $P(h_i) = 1$ (by Eq. (1)). Thus, nothing can be more suspicious than C_i. We now show that if there is no failing trace which only covers C_j, then C_j must be less suspicious than C_i. Assume the antecedent, then for each t_k we have $P(h_i^k) = \frac{w(C_i)}{w(C_i) + \cdots + w(C_k)} < 1$ (by Eq. (3)). Thus $P(\bigvee_{k=1}^{|\mathbf{T}|} h_i^k) < 1$ (by Eqs. (2) and (3)). Thus $P(h_j) < 1$ (by Eq. (1)). Thus $P(h_j) < P(h_i)$, which means C_i is more suspicious than C_j.

We now prove the extended property. Let $\mathbf{T}_1$ be a test suite in which all failing traces cover more than one component, and let $\mathbf{T}_2$ be identical to $\mathbf{T}_1$ except $c_i^1 = 1$ and $c_j^1 = 1$ in $\mathbf{T}_1$ and $c_i^1 = 1$ and $c_j^1 = 0$ in $\mathbf{T}_2$. Let n abbreviate $P(\bigvee_{m=2}^{|\mathbf{T}|} h_i^m)$ $P(h_i) = P(h_i^1) + n - (P(h_i^1)n)$ (by Eqs. (1) and (2)). It remains to first show that $P(h_i^1)$ is greater in $\mathbf{T}_2$, and secondly show n has the same value for both test suites where $n < 1$. For the former, let $P(h_i^1) = \frac{w(C_i)}{w(C_1) + \cdots + x + \cdots + w(C_{|c(t_k)|})}$ for both test suites (using Eq. (3)), where we let $x = w(C_j)$ for $\mathbf{T}_1$ (where $w(C_j) > 0$), and $x = 0$ for $\mathbf{T}_2$ (as $c_j^k \notin c(t_k)$ for $\mathbf{T}_2$). So, the equation for $P(h_i^1)$ is greater in $\mathbf{T}_2$. To show the latter, we observe that for all $1 < m \leq |\mathbf{T}_1|$ we have $P(h_i^m) < 1$ (by assumption each $t_m \in \mathbf{F} \subseteq \mathbf{T}_1$ covers at least 2 components) and that $P(h_i^m)$ is the same in both $\mathbf{T}_1, \mathbf{T}_2$, thus $n < 1$ (by Eq. (2)) and n has the same value for both.

Proposition 3. *No SBFL measure satisfies either property.*

Proof. To show that no suspiciousness measure w satisfies the base property, we show that for any w we can construct a test suite in which (1) there is a failing trace which only covers C_i, (2) there is some C_j such that there is no failing trace which only covers it, and (3) $w(C_i) = w(C_j)$. A simple example is as follows. Let $\mathbf{P} = \langle C_1, C_2, C_3, E \rangle$ and $\mathbf{T} = \langle \langle 1, 1, 1, 1 \rangle, \langle 0, 1, 1, 1 \rangle, \langle 1, 0, 0, 1 \rangle \rangle$. Thus the spectrum for C_1 and C_2 is $\langle 2, 0, 0, 0 \rangle$, and so $w(C_i) = w(C_j)$.

To show that no suspiciousness measure w satisfies the extended property, we show that for any w we can construct a pair of test suites $\mathbf{T}_1$ and $\mathbf{T}_2$ which are otherwise identical except (1) $c_i^k = 1$ and $c_j^k = 1$ in $\mathbf{T}_1$ (2) $c_i^k = 1$ and $c_j^k = 0$ in $\mathbf{T}_2$, and (3) $w(C_i) = w(C_j)$. The simplest example is as follows. Let $\mathbf{P} = \langle C_1, C_2, E \rangle$ and $\mathbf{T}_1 = \langle \langle 1, 1, 1 \rangle \rangle$ and $\mathbf{T}_2 = \langle \langle 1, 0, 1 \rangle \rangle$. Thus the spectrum for C_1 is $\langle 1, 0, 0, 0 \rangle$ in both cases, and so $w(C_i) = w(C_j)$.

The proof of the last proposition suggests that there are large classes of test suites in which SBFL measures violate the properties. SBFL measures do not have the resources to satisfy the properties because each C_i's suspiciousness is only a function of its program spectrum, which itself is only a function of the i-th column of a coverage matrix.

5   Experimentation

In this section we discuss our experimental setup and our results. The aim of the experiment is to compare the performance of the PFL algorithm against SBFL measures at the practical task of finding a fault in large faulty programs.

5.1   Setup

We use the Steimann test suite in our experiments, described in Table 1 [33]. M is the number of methods, UUT the number of units under test, b the number of blocks of code, UUT/b the mean number of UUTs per block, t the number of test cases. The last column gives the number of program versions with 1/2/4/8/16/32 faults respectively. The average number of covered components that were faulty for all 1/2/4/8/16/32 fault benchmarks was found to be 1.00/1.92/3.63/6.71/11.81/20.02 respectively (7.52 on average). Steimann's test suite is the only test suite found to represent large programs with a large range of faults and a large number of program versions. For more about the suite see [33]. The suite came with a program that generated the coverage matrices (see [33]).

We used blocks as our atomic program entity, and only considered atomic blocks for all methods compared. A block corresponds to a maximal set of executable statements with the same traces covering them. This correspondence provides a natural grouping, as the degree of suspiciousness of lines of code is the same as the block to which they belong, and does not effect the fault localisation process from the user's point of view. In the majority of cases blocks represented a continuous chunk of the program and were similar in size – the average size of these blocks are reported in the UUT/b column of Table 1, and can often be quite large.

Table 1. Benchmarks

Benchmark	M	UUT	b	UUT/b	t	1/2/4/8/16/32v
Daikon 4.6.4	14387	1936	48	40	157	353/1000/1000/...
Eventbus 1.4	859	338	68	5	91	577/1000/1000/...
Jaxen 1.1.5	1689	961	228	4	695	600/1000/1000/...
Jester 1.37b	378	152	25	6	64	411/1000/1000/...
Jexel 1.0.0b13	242	150	48	3	335	537/1000/1000/...
JParsec 2.0	1011	893	240	4	510	598/1000/1000/...
AC Codec 1.3	265	229	57	4	188	543/1000/1000/...
AC Lang 3.0	5373	2075	78	27	1666	599/1000/1000/...
Eclipse.Draw2d 3.4.2	3231	878	74	12	89	570/1000/1000/...
HTML Parser 1.6	1925	785	148	5	600	599/1000/1000/

We now discuss techniques compared. We include all known SBFL techniques; which includes the 157 measures in [11], which itself includes 30 measures from the studies of Naish [15] and the 40 measures Lo [16]. We include the 30 genetic measures of Yoo [20], the Dstar measures [17] and the 6 "combination" measures of Kim et al. [21]. This brings the number of SBFL measures to almost 200, which to our knowledge is the largest comparison of SBFL measures to date. We now discuss the PFL techniques. We used the weighted model PFL-w, and used the PPV, Ochiai, Kulczynski2, and Suppes measures (see preliminaries) as values for w. Not all measures could be tested because PFL techniques take slightly longer to run. To our knowledge SBFL and PFL techniques are the only ones which can feasibly scale to our experiments. Techniques which take 10 min on average to localise a fault in one program version would take almost a year to complete the experiment.

We evaluated the effectiveness of a technique using *avg* W-scores and A-scores (see preliminaries). We define higher level W/A-scores as follows. For each $n \in \{1, 2, 4, 8, 16, 32\}$ a basic score for the n-fault versions of a given benchmark is the mean of the scores for all versions of that benchmark with n-faults. The score for the n-fault versions is the mean of the ten basic scores for the n-fault versions. The AVG score is the mean of the 60 basic scores. We used *Wilcoxon rank-sum tests* to determine to whether a technique's 60 W/A basic scores were statistically significantly better than another (using $p = 0.01$). To provide a *lower bound* for SBFL performance, we included scores for the Random measure (defined as a measure which outputs a random number). To provide an *upper bound*, we computed the unavoidable costs for W/A-scores (discussed in Sect. 2).

5.2   Results

We begin with overall results. Zoltar was the SBFL measure with the highest AVG W-score of 2.59. PFL-PPV improved on this score with a AVG W-score of 1.88. Thus, the user has to investigate 37.77 % more code when using the best SBFL measure. Klosgen was the SBFL measure with the highest AVG A-score of 55.2. (PFL-PPV) improved on this score with a AVG A-score of 76.2. Thus, the user finds a fault immediately 27.56 % less frequently using the next best SBFL measure. Both PFL-PPV's W/A 60 scores were a statistically significant improvement over the next best performing SBFL measures using $p = 0.01$. Thus, the PFL approach was a substantial and significant improvement at localising faults.

We now discuss unavoidable cost (UC) scores. UC's AVG W/A-scores were 76.45 and 1.38 respectively. PFL-PPV outperformed UC's W-scores at 30/60 benchmarks, and UC's A-scores at 24/60 benchmarks. It is thus theoretically impossible to design a strictly rational SBFL measure that can outperform PFL-PPV on many benchmarks.

To get an impression for the overall range of performance, we present the following additional AVG scores. Kulkzynski2, Ochiai, Suppes, PPV (Tarantula), Random had AVG W-scores of 2.69, 2.97, 3.60, 3.88, 19.77, and AVG A-scores of 52.65, 52,47, 52.47, 49.73, 12.97 respectively. When PFL-w was used in conjunction with the first three measures (scaled [0,1]), the techniques had AVG

W-scores of 2.31, 2.05, 2.09 and AvG A-scores of 70.57, 72.55, 72.30. Thus, all our PFL-w approaches outperformed all SBFL measures regardless of choice of w. This suggests that the PFL-w framework is more responsible for the improvement of fault localisation effectiveness than the choice of weight w.

We now discuss how measures behave as more faults are introduced into a program. In Figs. 3 and 4 we graphically compare a range of techniques. Firstly, we represented the unavoidable cost scores to show how PFL-PPV approximates (and in some cases exceeds) the idealised upper bounds for performance of strictly rational SBFL measures. Secondly, we represented Zoltar as it was the SBFL measure which the best W-scores. Thirdly, we represented Tarantula (equivalent to PPV) to show how using PFL-PPV improves performance. Each column represents a technique's score for the n-fault versions of that suite, with the key shade representing the value of n (for example, the W-score for PFL-PPV at the 2-fault benchmarks is 1.94).

We observed the following trends: In general, the more faults there were in a program the better an SBFL measure's W-scores, but the worse that measure's A-scores. A proposed explanation for this is that the more faults there were in

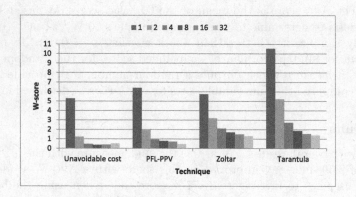

Fig. 3. W-scores for selected techniques

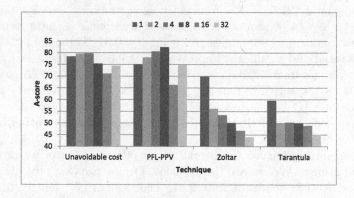

Fig. 4. A-scores for selected techniques

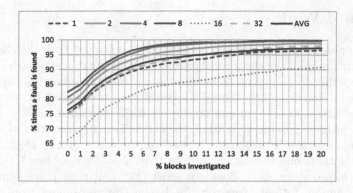

Fig. 5. PFL-PPV performance

a program, the more likely it was to find a fault early (due to increased luck –
thus improving W-scores), but the less likely to find a fault immediately (due to
increased noise – thus worsening A-scores). These trends were noticed in all of
our SBFL measures, of which Zoltar and Tarantula are examples. By contrast, a
negative trend for the A-scores was not noticed for our variants of PFL-w, which
demonstrated a superior ability to deal with noise introduced by multiple faults.

We now discuss Fig. 5. For each set of n-fault benchmarks, if $y\%$ of the
program versions received a W-score of $\leq x\%$, a point was plotted on that
graph at (x, y). The mean (AVG) of the 6 graphs is also plotted. The figure
demonstrates that if we limit fault localisation to only 10 % of the blocks, on
AVG we would expect to find a fault 95 % of the time using PFL-PPV. An outlier
is that PFL-PPV does slightly worse on the 16-fault benchmarks. In general, the
graph confirms the conclusion that PFL-PPV's performance is not substantially
worsened by the number of faults in the program.

We now discuss time efficiency. In our implementation it took under a second
to find the most suspicious component in SBFL/PFL procedures. The complete
PFL procedure (as per the algorithm in Sect. 4), took an average of 6.16 s (with
potential for optimisation) – thus establishing PFL's negligible overhead.

In summary, PFL approaches substantially, and statistically significantly
improve over the best performing SBFL approaches in our large multiple fault
programs, and are comparably efficient. Furthermore, they outperform theoretically optimum performance of SBFL measures on a large class of benchmarks.

We briefly report results (AVG scores) in additional experiments which were
of much lower quality and size. We generated 500+ 1/2/3/4 fault versions using
the methodology and 10 SIR benchmarks of [34]. 80 % of the faults were covered
by all failing traces which made it less challenging for our techniques in terms of
noise. The highest scoring SBFL measure was Kulczynski2 (K2) (W-score 8.76,
A-score 33.75). PFL-Suppes, PFL-K2, PFL-Ochiai came second (W-scores 9.66,
10.27, 10.40, and A-scores 25.73, 24.43, 28.43 respectively). K2's scores were not
statistically significantly better. The BARINEL tool (see [34]) came 43rd overall
and was not competitive. PFL-PPV came 6th after SBFL measures (W-score 11.39,
A-score 29.15). The experiments confirm PFL as high performing.

6   Related Work

The most prominent lightweight approach to software fault localisation is
SBFL [3], and provides the theoretical groundwork for the PFL approach. Research
is driven by the development of new measures and experimentally comparing
them on benchmarks [4–21]. Causal measures were introduced to SBFL in [11].
Threats to the value of empirical studies of SBFL is studied in [33]. Theoretical results include proving potentially desirable formal properties of measures
and finding equivalence proofs for classes of measures [10,11,15,22,35]. Yoo
et al. have established theoretical results that show that a "best" performing
suspicious measure for SBFL does not exist [23], and thus there remains the
problem of finding formal properties for lightweight techniques to exploit. We
have tried to address this problem in this paper.

A prominent probabilistic approach is BARINEL, which differs to PFL insofar
as it uses Bayesian methods to generate likelihoods of given hypotheses [34],
and a minimal hitting set algorithm STACCATO to generate hypotheses. Their
approach is designed for the simultaneous fault localisation of sets of multiple
faults, and were only scalable to our additional experiments. Other heavyweight
techniques are similarly unscalable [30,36–41], which emphasises the importance
of developing lightweight techniques such as PFL/SBFL.

In general, SBFL methods have been successfully used in the following applications. Firstly, in semi-automated fault localisation in which users inspect code
in descending order of suspiciousness [29]. Secondly, in fully-automated fault
localisation subroutines within algorithms which inductively synthesise (such as
CEGIS [42]) or repair programs (such as GENPROG [43]). Thirdly, as a substitute for heavyweight methods which cannot scale to large programs [30,36,37].
Fourthly, as a technique combined with other methods [21,24,44–50]. In general,
PFL may be used as a substitute for SBFL measures in all these applications. For
a major recent survey we defer to Wong et al. [3].

7   Conclusions

In this paper we have presented a new formal framework which we call PFL,
and compared it to SBFL in terms of (1) desirable theoretical properties, (2) its
effectiveness at fault localisation and (3) its efficiency. Regarding (1), the PFL
equations were formally proven to satisfy desirable fault likelihood properties
which SBFL measures could not. Regarding (2), PFL-PPV was shown to substantially and statistically significantly (using $p = 0.01$) outperform all known
SBFL measures at W and A-scores in what is to our knowledge the largest scale
experimental comparison in software fault localisation to date. We found that
the user has to investigate over 37.77 % more blocks of code (and finds a fault
immediately 27.56 % less frequently) than PFL-PPV when using the best SBFL
measures. Furthermore, we show that for a third/quarter of our benchmarks it
is theoretically impossible to design strictly rational SBFL measures which outperforms PFL-PPV's W/A-scores respectively. Regarding (3), we found that the

PFL approach maintains a comparably negligible overhead to SBFL. Thus, our results suggest the PFL framework has theoretical and practical advantages over SBFL.

For future work, we would like to find additional suspiciousness measures for use with PFL-w. Secondly, we would like find a method to determine upper bound scores for PFL performance (similar to Naish's unavoidable costs). Thirdly, we would like to implement PFL in an easy to use tool for engineers.

References

1. Zhivich, M., Cunningham, R.K.: The real cost of software errors. IEEE Secur. Priv. **7**(2), 87–90 (2009)
2. Collofello, J.S., Woodfield, S.N.: Evaluating the effectiveness of reliability-assurance techniques. J. Syst. Softw. **9**(3), 745–770 (1989)
3. Wong, W.E., Gao, R., Li, Y., Abreu, R., Wotawa, F.: A survey on software fault localization. IEEE Trans. Softw. Eng. (99) (2016)
4. Abreu, R., Zoeteweij, P., van Gemund, A.J.C.: On the accuracy of spectrum-based fault localization. In: TAICPART-MUTATION, pp. 89–98. IEEE (2007)
5. Briand, L.C., Labiche, Y., Liu, X.: Using machine learning to support debugging with Tarantula. In: ISSRE, pp. 137–146 (2007)
6. Jones, J.A., Harrold, M.J.: Empirical evaluation of the Tarantula automatic fault-localization technique. In: ASE, pp. 273–282. ACM (2005)
7. Liblit, B., Naik, M., Zheng, A.X., Aiken, A., Jordan, M.I.: Scalable statistical bug isolation. SIGPLAN Not. **40**(6), 15–26 (2005)
8. Liu, C., Fei, L., Yan, X., Han, J., Midkiff, S.P.: Statistical debugging: a hypothesis testing-based approach. IEEE Trans. Softw. Eng. **32**(10), 831–848 (2006)
9. Zhang, Z., Chan, W.K., Tse, T.H., Jiang, B., Wang, X.: Capturing propagation of infected program states. In: ESEC/FSE, pp. 43–52. ACM (2009)
10. Xie, X., Chen, T.Y., Kuo, F.C., Xu, B.: A theoretical analysis of the risk evaluation formulas for spectrum-based fault localization. ACM TSEM **22**(4), 31:1–31:40 (2013)
11. Landsberg, D., Chockler, H., Kroening, D., Lewis, M.: Evaluation of measures for statistical fault localisation and an optimising scheme. In: Egyed, A., Schaefer, I. (eds.) FASE 2015. LNCS, vol. 9033, pp. 115–129. Springer, Heidelberg (2015). doi:10.1007/978-3-662-46675-9_8
12. Renieris, M., Reiss, S.P.: Fault localization with nearest neighbor queries. In: ASE, pp. 30–39 (2003)
13. Wong, W.E., Qi, Y., Zhao, L., Cai, K.Y.: Effective fault localization using code coverage. In: COMPSAC, pp. 449–456 (2007)
14. Pytlik, B., Renieris, M., Krishnamurthi, S., Reiss, S.: Automated fault localization using potential invariants. Arxiv preprint cs.SE/0310040 (2003)
15. Naish, L., Lee, H.J., Ramamohanarao, K.: A model for spectra-based software diagnosis. ACM Trans. Softw. Eng. Methodol. **20**(3), 1–11 (2011)
16. Lucia, L., Lo, D., Jiang, L., Thung, F., Budi, A.: Extended comprehensive study of association measures for fault localization. J. Softw. Evol. Process **26**(2), 172–219 (2014)
17. Wong, W., Debroy, V., Gao, R., Li, Y.: The DStar method for effective software fault localization. IEEE Trans. Reliab. **63**(1), 290–308 (2014)

18. Wong, W.E., Debroy, V., Choi, B.: A family of code coverage-based heuristics for effective fault localization. J. Syst. Softw. **83**(2), 188–208 (2010)
19. Wong, W.E., Debroy, V., Golden, R., Xu, X., Thuraisingham, B.M.: Effective software fault localization using an RBF neural network. IEEE Trans. Reliab. **61**(1), 149–169 (2012)
20. Yoo, S.: Evolving human competitive spectra-based fault localisation techniques. In: Fraser, G., Teixeira de Souza, J. (eds.) SSBSE 2012. LNCS, vol. 7515, pp. 244–258. Springer, Heidelberg (2012). doi:10.1007/978-3-642-33119-0_18
21. Kim, J., Park, J., Lee, E.: A new hybrid algorithm for software fault localization. In: IMCOM, pp. 50:1–50:8. ACM (2015)
22. Naish, L., Lee, H.J.: Duals in spectral fault localization. In: Australian Conference on Software Engineering (ASWEC), pp. 51–59. IEEE (2013)
23. Yoo, S., Xie, X., Kuo, F., Chen, T., Harman, M.: No pot of gold at the end of program spectrum rainbow: greatest risk evaluation formula does not exist. Department of Computer Science, UCL (2014)
24. Xuan, J., Monperrus, M.: Learning to combine multiple ranking metrics for fault localization. In: ICSME (2014)
25. Wong, W.E., Qi, Y.: Effective program debugging based on execution slices and inter-block data dependency. JSS **79**(7), 891–903 (2006)
26. Keynes, J.M.: A Treatise on Probability. Dover Publications, New York (1921)
27. Baah, G.K., Podgurski, A., Harrold, M.J.: Causal inference for statistical fault localization. In: International Symposium on Software Testing and Analysis (ISSTA), pp. 73–84. ACM (2010)
28. Naish, L., Lee, H.J., Ramamohanarao, K.: Spectral debugging: how much better can we do? In: Australasian Computer Science Conference (ACSC), pp. 99–106 (2012)
29. Parnin, C., Orso, A.: Are automated debugging techniques actually helping programmers? In: ISSTA, pp. 199–209 (2011)
30. Groce, A.: Error explanation with distance metrics. In: Jensen, K., Podelski, A. (eds.) TACAS 2004. LNCS, vol. 2988, pp. 108–122. Springer, Heidelberg (2004). doi:10.1007/978-3-540-24730-2_8
31. Lewis, D.: Causation. J. Philos. **70**(17), 556–567 (1974)
32. Fitelson, B., Hitchcock, C.: Probabilistic measures of causal strength. In: Illari, P.M., Russo, F., Williamson, J. (eds.) Causality in the Sciences. Oxford University Press, Oxford (2011)
33. Steimann, F., Frenkel, M., Abreu, R.: Threats to the validity and value of empirical assessments of the accuracy of coverage-based fault locators. In: ISSTA, pp. 314–324 (2013)
34. Abreu, R., Zoeteweij, P., van Gemund, A.J.C.: Spectrum-based multiple fault localization. In: ASE, pp. 88–99 (2009)
35. Debroy, V., Wong, W.E.: On the equivalence of certain fault localization techniques. In: SAC, pp. 1457–1463 (2011)
36. Mayer, W., Stumptner, M.: Evaluating models for model-based debugging. In: ASE, pp. 128–137 (2008)
37. Yilmaz, C., Williams, C.: An automated model-based debugging approach. In: ASE, pp. 174–183. ACM (2007)
38. Zeller, A.: Isolating cause-effect chains from computer programs. In: SIGSOFT-/FSE, pp. 1–10. ACM (2002)
39. Jeffrey, D., Gupta, N., Gupta, R.: Effective and efficient localization of multiple faults using value replacement. In: ICSM, pp. 221–230. IEEE (2009)

40. Zhang, X., Gupta, N., Gupta, R.: Locating faults through automated predicate switching. In: ICSE, pp. 272–281. ACM (2006)
41. Jobstmann, B., Griesmayer, A., Bloem, R.: Program repair as a game. In: Etessami, K., Rajamani, S.K. (eds.) CAV 2005. LNCS, vol. 3576, pp. 226–238. Springer, Heidelberg (2005). doi:10.1007/11513988_23
42. Jha, S., Seshia, S.A.: Are there good mistakes? A theoretical analysis of CEGIS. In: 3rd Workshop on Synthesis (SYNT), pp. 84–99, July 2014
43. Goues, C.L., Nguyen, T., Forrest, S., Weimer, W.: GenProg: a generic method for automatic software repair. IEEE Trans. Softw. Eng. 1, 54–72 (2012)
44. Baudry, B., Fleurey, F., Le Traon, Y.: Improving test suites for efficient fault localization. In: ICSE, pp. 82–91. ACM (2006)
45. Gopinath, D., Zaeem, R.N., Khurshid, S.: Improving the effectiveness of spectra-based fault localization using specifications. In: ASE, pp. 40–49 (2012)
46. Abreu, R., Mayer, W., Stumptner, M., van Gemund, A.J.C.: Refining spectrum-based fault localization rankings. In: SAC 2009, pp. 409–414 (2009)
47. Debroy, V., Wong, W.E.: A consensus-based strategy to improve the quality of fault localization. Softw. Pract. Exp. 43(8), 989–1011 (2013)
48. Lucia, L., D., Xia, X.: Fusion fault localizers. In: Automated Software Engineering (ASE), pp. 127–138. ACM (2014)
49. Debroy, V., Wong, W.E.: On the consensus-based application of fault localization techniques. In: 2011 IEEE 35th Annual COMPSACW, pp. 506–511, July 2011
50. Ju, X., Jiang, S., Chen, X., Wang, X., Zhang, Y., Cao, H.: HSFal: effective fault localization using hybrid spectrum of full and execution slices. JSS 90, 3–17 (2014)

Iterative User-Driven Fault Localization

Xiangyu Li[1]([⊠]), Marcelo d'Amorim[2], and Alessandro Orso[1]

[1] Georgia Institute of Technology, Atlanta, USA
{xiangyu.li,orso}@cc.gatech.edu
[2] Federal University of Pernambuco, Recife, Brazil
damorim@cin.ufpe.br

Abstract. Because debugging is a notoriously expensive activity, numerous automated debugging techniques have been proposed in the literature. In the last ten years, statistical fault localization emerged as the most popular approach to automated debugging. One problem with statistical fault localization techniques is that they tend to make strong assumptions on how developers behave during debugging. These assumptions are often unrealistic, which considerably limits the practical applicability and effectiveness of these techniques. To mitigate this issue, we propose Swift, an iterative user-driven technique designed to support developers during debugging. Swift (1) leverages statistical fault localization to identify suspicious methods, (2) generates *high-level* queries to the developer about the correctness of specific executions of the most suspicious methods, (3) uses the feedback from the developer to improve the localization results, and (4) repeats this cycle until the fault has been localized. Our empirical evaluation of Swift, performed on 26 faults in 5 programs, produced promising results; on average, Swift required less than 10 user queries to identify the fault. Most importantly, these queries were only about input/output relationships for specific executions of the methods, which developers should be able to answer quickly and without having to look at the code. We believe that Swift is a first important step towards defining fault localization techniques that account for the presence of humans in the loop and are practically applicable.

1 Introduction

Debugging contributes greatly to software development costs [25]. It is therefore not surprising that researchers and practitioners alike invested much effort in defining techniques that can help developers in this task. Statistical fault localization (SFL) techniques, in particular, became extremely popular in recent years (*e.g.,* [4,6–8,14,15,18,22,27,28]). These techniques compute suspiciousness values for various program entities using coverage information of passing and failing test cases and use theses values to produce a ranked list of program entities in decreasing order of suspiciousness. While significant progress has been made in this field, there is evidence that (1) asking developers to examine a possibly long list of suspicious program entities in order and (2) expecting developers to recognize faulty lines by simply looking at them are both unrealistic expectations. In

© Springer International Publishing AG 2016
R. Bloem and E. Arbel (Eds.): HVC 2016, LNCS 10028, pp. 82–98, 2016.
DOI: 10.1007/978-3-319-49052-6_6

fact, even when provided with SFL tools, developers tend not to use them and rely on traditional manual debugging approaches instead [21].

There is thus a disconnect between research and practice in the area of software debugging and, in particular, fault localization. In standard practice, a debugging task typically proceeds as follows. Developers observe that a program execution exhibits some unintended behavior, make hypotheses on what program entities caused that behavior, and confirm or reject these hypotheses by examining the execution at specific points. They then incorporate the additional knowledge acquired in the process to refine their hypotheses, possibly observing the faulty execution at different points and continuing this feedback loop until they identify the fault responsible for the observed unintended behavior. In this setting, debugging is an art that mainly relies on developers' knowledge and their familiarity with the software system being debugged.

To support the above process, while trying to automate it as much as possible, we present Swift, an iterative user-driven technique designed to help developers during debugging in a natural way. Figure 1 provides a high-level view of Swift, which performs *SFL with humans in the loop* as follows. First, it leverages traditional SFL techniques to identify and rank suspicious methods. Second, it generates queries to the developer about the correctness of specific executions of the most suspicious method. A query consists of

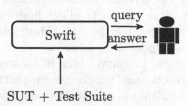

Fig. 1. Swift's interaction with the user (SUT stands for System Under Test).

the inputs to that method and the corresponding outputs, possibly including relevant program states. The developer answers a query by asserting whether the outputs are correct for those inputs. Third, Swift uses the response provided by the developer by incorporating it in the form of a "virtual" test case and using this additional information to improve localization results. Swift reiterates these steps until the SFL results become precise enough that the fault can be localized by the developer.

A key aspect of Swift is the use of high-level abstractions to gather input from the developer. Unlike traditional SFL, in which developers are simply provided with a list of statements and must follow the list with no guidance and no additional context, Swift guides the developers towards the fault through an iterative process that only requires them to check high-level input-output relationships at the method level.

To assess the effectiveness of Swift, we implemented it in a prototype tool and performed an empirical study on 5 programs and 26 faults for these programs, while simulating the developers' answers using an automated oracle. The results of our study, albeit preliminary, are promising and provide support for further research in this direction. On average, for the faults considered, Swift required less than 10 user queries to identify the fault, which is an initial indication of the practical applicability and potential usefulness of our approach.

The main contributions of this paper are: (1) a novel technique that overcomes some of the limitations of existing SFL approaches by leveraging user feedback in a natural way; (2) an implementation of our approach for Java programs that is publicly available at http://www.cc.gatech.edu/~orso/software/swift/, together with our experimental infrastructure; and (3) an empirical evaluation that provides initial evidence of the potential usefulness of our approach and identifies several directions for future work.

2   Running Example

Figure 2 shows class `BoundedStack` and its test suite with two test cases, `t1` and `t2`. In this example, test `t2` fails with an `ArrayIndexOutOfBoundsException` when calling `bs.peek()`. That happens because of a fault at line 11. The method `pop()` is expected to have no effect when the stack is empty, but it incorrectly subtracts `numElems` even when `numElems == 0`, resulting in a negative stack size. A check on the size of the stack would fix the problem in this case.

For this example, SFL would rank line 18 as the most suspicious because the line is executed in the failing test case, but not in the passing test case. All other statements, except the one at line 15 have the same suspiciousness values. Thus, in this case, fault localization alone does not help the developer to diagnose the fault.

3   Approach

Figure 3 shows the workflow of Swift, which takes as input the system under test (SUT) and a test suite for the SUT with at least one failing test case.

```
1    public class BoundedStack {
2      Integer[] elems; int numElems;
3
4      BoundedStack(int max) {
5        elems = new Integer[max]; }
6
7      void push(Integer k) {
8        /* check size */
9        elems[numElems++] = k; }
10
11     void pop() { --numElems; }
12
13     Integer peek() {
14       if (size() == 0)
15         return null;
16       else return elems[size()-1];}
17
18     void clear() { numElems = 0; }
19
20     int size() { return numElems; }
21     ...
22   }
23
24   // tests
25   @Test t1() {
26     BoundedStack bs =
27       new BoundedStack(3);
28     bs.push(5); bs.push(6);
29     bs.pop();
30     assertEquals(5, bs.peek());}
31
32   @Test t2() {
33     BoundedStack bs =
34       new BoundedStack(3);
35     bs.push(7); bs.push(8);
36     bs.clear();
37     bs.pop();
38     assertEquals(null, bs.peek());
```

Fig. 2. Faulty BoundedStack [24].

In Step 1, Swift executes the provided test suite and collects runtime data about each test, including (1) coverage and pass/fail information, for performing fault localization, and (2) dynamic call information, for suitably incorporating developers' feedback. In Step 2, Swift leverages existing fault localization techniques to compute the suspiciousness of program entities based on the collected runtime information. Initially, only the executions of the existing test cases are considered. As developers interact with Swift while debugging, their knowledge regarding the examined parts of the executions is incorporated as additional runtime data, providing extra information for fault localization.

In Step 3, Swift guides the developer to examine the parts of a failing test execution where highly suspicious program entities are being executed, by means of debugging queries. In this setup, the developer is expected to check correctness of the method execution based on the provided input and output, with possibly partial state information, and give the answer back to Swift. Step 4 incorporates the developer's answer to the debugging query by modifying and augmenting the runtime data. The interactive debugging process then loops back to Step 2. Swift refines fault localization results with the additional knowledge from the developer and generates another debugging query using the refined suspiciousness values. This process continues until either the fault is found or the developer gives up and stops Swift.

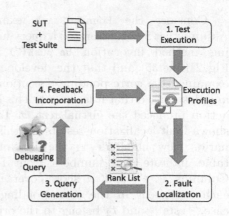

Fig. 3. Workflow overview

3.1   Technical Details

We now discuss the steps of Swift in detail. For each step, we first describe the step and then illustrate it on the example faulty program from Sect. 2.

Test Execution. In this initial step, Swift executes the test suite for the SUT and collects an execution tree for each test. Figure 4 shows the execution tree that corresponds to test case t2 in the BoundedStack example of Fig. 2. In the figure, each box represents a method invocation node. The labels of the nodes show the method name on the first line and the direct statement coverage information on the second line. The set of numbers inside the brackets indicates the covered statements, corresponding to the line numbers in Fig. 2.

Fault Localization. Any fault localization technique that uses coverage information to rank program entities according to their fault suspiciousness can be used in our approach. Swift currently uses Ochiai, as it has been shown to perform well in practice [3,20]. In its first iteration, Swift uses the input test suite to perform traditional fault localization. In later

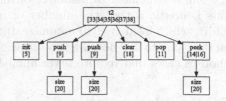

Fig. 4. Execution tree corresponding to test t2 (see Fig. 2).

iterations, it also includes *virtual tests*. These additional tests model developer answers to queries in the form of synthetic execution trees and have the effect of fine tuning the fault suspiciousness values based on developer's input.

Consider the `BoundedStack` example. Assume that Swift generated a query involving method invocation `bs.push(7)` from Fig. 2 (line 35) and that the developer has examined the corresponding execution tree and determined that it is correct. This interaction produced the virtual test vt. Table 1 shows fault localization results for this scenario. Row numbers to the left of the table indicate line numbers from Fig. 2. Columns t_1, t_2, and vt show coverage for each statement in the corresponding test case. Tests t_1 and t_2 belong to the original

Table 1. Example of coverage and suspiciousness information for the `BoundedStack` example.

	✓	✗	✓	
	t_1	t_2	vt	$susp.$
5	1	1	0	0.7
9	1	1	1	0.6
11	1	1	0	0.7
14	1	1	0	0.7
15	0	0	0	0.0
16	1	1	0	0.7
18	0	1	0	1.0
20	1	1	1	0.6

test suite whereas test vt is the virtual test corresponding to the execution tree rooted at the `bs.push(7)` invocation. It reflects the developer's feedback that this method invocation produces a correct result. The symbol "✓" above the name of the test indicates that the test is passing whereas "✗" indicates a failure. Column $susp.$ shows the suspiciousness of a statement as computed by the Ochiai formula. Lines 9 and 20 have lower suspiciousness because of the additional test vt.

Query Generation. Swift asks developers for feedback through debugging queries, which basically consist of the input and output of a method invocation. Developers are expected to assess the correctness of the computation for that invocation. The rationale for this choice is that we expect the semantics of methods to be relatively well understood by developers who are familiar with the program being debugged.

Swift determines which method invocation to select for generating a debugging query from the fault localization results computed in Step 2. Swift picks, from the failing executions, a method invocation that directly covers the most suspicious statement. In case multiple statements are ranked at the top, one is chosen randomly. And if there are multiple failing executions that cover the most suspicious statement, Swift picks the invocation from the test that executes the smallest number of instances of the suspicious statement. The rationale for this heuristic is that the number of queries is a reasonable proxy for human effort, which Swift tries to minimize. Intuitively, the heuristic we presented above enables one to diagnose highly-suspicious statements more quickly, as it eagerly chooses cases that require fewer number of queries for the user to answer.

Feedback Incorporation. Developers' answers to debugging queries provide Swift with additional knowledge about the correctness of *partial program executions*. This section discusses how Swift uses this information to update the execution trees and thus incorporate developers' feedback. Figure 5 shows the pseudo-code of the algorithm for this part of our technique.

The algorithm takes as input the user feedback, represented by class `Feedback` (lines 1–5). Type `Invocation` represents a method invocation node in the

```
1    class Feedback {
2      Invocation invocation;
3      Invocation fromProfile;
4      bool isCorrect;
5    }
6
7    List<Invocation> correctProfiles = ...
8    List<Invocation> incorrectProfiles = ...
9
10   incorporateUserFeedback(Feedback feedback) {
11     if (feedback.isCorrect) {
12       feedback.invocation.removeFromParent();
13       correctProfiles.add(feedback.invocation);
14       for (Statement s
15         : feedback.invocation.getCoverage()) {
16       if (!feedback.fromProfile.covers(s)) {
17         for (Invocation incorrectProfile
18           : incorrectProfiles) {
19         incorrectProfile.removeCoverage(s); }}}
20     } else {
21       for (Invocation incorrectProfile
22         : incorrectProfiles) {
23       for (Statement s
24         : incorrectProfile.getCoverage()) {
25       if (!feedback.invocation.covers(s)) {
26         incorrectProfile.removeCoverage(s); }}}}}
```

Fig. 5. Algorithm for incorporating user feedback into execution profiles.

execution tree. Field `invocation` references the method invocation selected for this debugging query. Field `fromProfile` refers to the root of the incorrect execution profile from which `invocation` is selected. Finally, field `isCorrect` indicates developer's answer to the correctness of the invocation. Lines 7 to 8 correspond to the two sets of execution trees whose correctness is known. They are maintained by Swift throughout the debugging process and used by the fault localization component for suspiciousness computation.

For a particular debugging query, if the developer determines that the corresponding method execution is correct, Swift can conclude that this method invocation instance is not responsible for the failure (under the simplifying assumption that the developer is correct). In these situations, Swift removes the execution tree rooted at this method invocation node from its parent and marks this execution tree as a correct execution. Swift then checks whether the modified `fromProfile` no longer covers some statements it originally covered. Because these statements cannot be the cause of the failure at hand, they are excluded from consideration. Lines 12 to 19 show the pseudo-code for this case. Note that it is not necessarily true that the method invocation that is determined as correct does not exercise the faulty statement. The issue of coincidental correctness, which is considered to negatively affect the precision of fault localization techniques [4,26], could also happen for method invocations. However, we conjecture that this issue is less likely to occur for these shorter executions.

We show an example of how positive feedback is incorporated using the `BoundedStack` program. For illustration purpose, we assume that, at the initial state, the first debugging query generated is about the method invocation `bs.push(7)` on line 35 in failing test `t2`. The developer determines that this method invocation is correct. Figure 6a shows the execution profiles before and after this feedback is incorporated. The structure and the coverage information of the execution tree for test t1 is irrelevant and thus omitted.

A negative answer to a query corresponds to the case of a developer indicating that the method invocation in the query should have produced a different result. Swift incorporates a negative answer by reducing the set of statements potentially faulty. Specifically, Swift limits the suspicious set of statements to those that are executed by the method invocation in this debugging query by removing the coverage of all the other statements from the execution profiles (lines 21 to 26 in the pseudo-code).

Continuing the previous example on the BoundedStack program, we assume that the second debugging query generated is about the method invocation bs.pop() on line 35. This is the actual faulty method invocation, and the developer would determine that it is incorrect. Figure 6b shows the execution profiles after this negative feedback is incorporated.

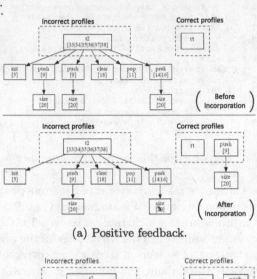

(a) Positive feedback.

(b) Negative feedback.

Fig. 6. Incorporating feedback.

3.2 Complete Debugging Session

This section applies Swift to our faulty program BoundedStack to illustrate a complete debugging session, including how Swift generates each debug query and incorporates developer feedback to update the fault localization results.

The tables in Fig. 8 show, for each iteration of Swift's debugging-query loop, the coverage matrix used for fault localization computation and the suspiciousness of each statement. Row numbers to the left of the tables correspond to the lines of code in Fig. 2. Columns t_x show the coverage of each statement in the corresponding test case. As before, tests t_1 and t_2 are in the original test suite in the code, whereas t_3 and t_4 are additional "virtual tests" created from the answers to debugging queries. Column s in each table shows the suspiciousness of the statements as computed by the Ochiai formula. Table cells with a blue background contain values that are changed with respect to the previous iteration. Due to space limit, the execution trees from which the coverage matrices are derived are not shown.

The initial fault localization computation ranks line 18 at the top because it is executed only in the failing test case t_2, while the actual fault (*i.e.*, line 11) is ranked lower since it is executed in both passing and failing tests. Swift generates the first debugging query Q_1, asking the developer to examine the method invocation `bs.clear()` called on line 36.

Q_1: `BoundedStack.clear()`#0 in t_2	
Input:	Output:

this: {
  elems: {7, 8, null}
  numElems: 2
}
	this: {
	  elems: {7, 8, null}
	  numElems: 0
	}

Fig. 7. Debugging query Q_1.

Figure 7 shows the details of the debugging query. Based on the information provided, the developer determines that this method invocation actually executed correctly. Swift removes the sub-tree that represents this method invocation from the execution tree of the failing test case t_2 and marks the sub-tree as a correct execution. The effect of this operation on the fault localization computation is shown in the second table from the left in Fig. 8. Since line 18 is executed only once in the invocation of `clear()`, its coverage flag in t_2 is removed. A "virtual test" t_3, which corresponds to the new correct execution of the `clear()` invocation, is also added to the coverage matrix. The suspiciousness of line 18 is changed to 0, as it is no longer covered by failing executions.

	t_1	t_2	s
5	1	1	0.7
9	1	1	0.7
11	1	1	0.7
14	1	1	0.7
15	0	0	0.0
16	1	1	0.7
18	0	1	1.0
20	1	1	0.7

$\xrightarrow{Q_1}$

	t_1	t_2	t_3	s
5	1	1	0	0.7
9	1	1	0	0.7
11	1	1	0	0.7
14	1	1	0	0.7
15	0	0	0	0.0
16	1	1	0	0.7
18	0	0	1	0.0
20	1	1	0	0.7

$\xrightarrow{Q_2}$

	t_1	t_2	t_3	t_4	s
5	1	1	0	0	0.7
9	1	1	0	1	0.6
11	1	1	0	0	0.7
14	1	1	0	0	0.7
15	0	0	0	0	0.0
16	1	1	0	0	0.7
18	0	0	1	0	0.0
20	1	1	0	1	0.6

$\xrightarrow{Q_3}$

	t_1	t_2	t_3	t_4	s
5	1	0	0	0	0.0
9	1	0	0	1	0.0
11	1	1	0	0	0.7
14	1	0	0	0	0.0
15	0	0	0	0	0.0
16	1	0	0	0	0.0
18	0	0	1	0	0.0
20	1	0	0	1	0.0

Fig. 8. Complete debugging session.

After the answer to the debugging query Q_1 is incorporated, lines 5, 9, 11, 14, 16 and 20 are ranked at the top and have the same suspiciousness value. Swift randomly picks one of them to generate the next debugging query. Assume that Swift picks line 9 and selects the method invocation `bs.push(8)` called on line 35 to generate debugging query Q_2. The developer determines that the execution of this method invocation is also correct. Swift modifies the execution profiles in the same way as before. Another passing "virtual test" t_4 that covers lines 9 and 20 is added to the coverage matrix and, as a result, the suspiciousness values of these 2 lines are reduced.

For the third debugging query, Q_3, assume that Swift picks line 11, which is the actual fault. Method invocation `bs.pop()` on line 37 is selected. Figure 9 shows the details of the query. The developer determines that this method invocation is incorrect by spotting `numElems == -1` in its output data.

Q_3: `BoundedStack.pop()`#0 in t_2	
Input:	Output:

this: {
  elems: {7, 8, null}
  numElems: 0
}
	this: {
	  elems: {7, 8, null}
	  numElems: -1
	}

Fig. 9. Debugging query Q_3.

In a realistic debugging session, the

developer would have found the fault at this point and concluded the debugging activity, as the faulty program state is infected in the current method invocation by a statement in its method body. For the purpose of illustration, we assume that the developer answers this debugging query instead and continues. Swift incorporates the feedback by removing the coverage flag of all the statements, except for the ones covered by the incorrect `pop()` invocation, from the failing executions. Consequently, after this debugging query is considered, the coverage of t_2 contains only line 11, which is also ranked at the top by Swift's fault localization component.

4   Empirical Evaluation

In our evaluation, we investigate the following two main research questions:

R1 – Can Swift locate the fault with a small number of debugging queries?
R2 – How does user feedback affect fault ranking?

The rest of this section describes the subject programs and faults we used (Sect. 4.1), explains the experimental setup we used (Sect. 4.2), and discusses experimental results to answer these questions (Sect. 4.3).

4.1   Subjects and Faults

To empirically assess the effectiveness of Swift, we implemented the technique in a prototype tool that works on Java programs. We evaluated the effectiveness of Swift on a benchmark with 26 faults distributed across 5 open-source applications from three repositories: SIR [2], Defects4J [16], and SAEG [1]. Each subject program contains multiple faulty versions. We selected versions that contain single non-concurrent faults that can be revealed by at least one failing test case in the original test suite. Furthermore, to better identify the benefits of Swift in the debugging process, we

Table 2. Characterization of subjects and faults.

Subject	Repo.	Fault ID	P-F	#Cls.	#Meths.	kLOC
jtopas	[2]	FAULT_2	123-3	25	251	7
		FAULT_6	125-1	25	251	7
commons-math	[2]	C_AK_1	1162-1	236	1723	43
		EDI_AK_1	1162-1	236	1723	43
		F_AK_1	1162-1	236	1723	43
		M_AK_1	1162-1	236	1723	43
		VS_AK_1	1162-1	236	1723	43
		CDI_AK_1	2048-2	477	3899	83
		MU_AK_1	2048-2	477	3899	83
		MU_AK_4	2049-1	477	3899	83
		URSU_AK_1	2048-2	477	3899	83
xml-security	[2]	CN2_AK_2	89-2	198	1278	40
		C2E_AK_1	92-2	198	1275	41
jsoup	[1]	1_3_4_b3	225-1	75	611	8
		1_4_2_b2	295-1	89	698	9
		1_5_2_b2	236-4	86	682	9
		1_5_2_b5	243-1	86	682	9
		1_6_1_b1	290-2	198	979	13
		1_6_3_b3	323-1	206	1032	14
commons-lang	[16]	b6	2125-3	169	2281	57
		b9	2057-8	170	2224	54
		b10	2055-8	170	2224	54
		b16	1913-1	160	2142	53
		b24	1698-1	143	2022	50
		b26	1677-1	139	2000	50
		b39	1566-1	123	1835	45

excluded cases where the initial fault localization results ranked the faulty statement alone at the top. The cases where the fault is initially ranked at the top together with a large number of other statements are included in the experiment because in this situation the fault is still difficult to identify and Swift can reduce the suspiciousness of non-faulty statements. Table 2 characterizes the faults we considered. Column "*Repo.*" shows the repository from which we obtained the subject. Column "*Fault ID*" shows the identifier of a given fault, as documented in their source repository. Column "*P-F*" shows the number of passing (P) and failing (F) tests for that fault. The last three columns show the number of classes, methods, and lines of code in the faulty version.

4.2   Experimental Setup

For each of the faults that we considered in the experiment, we applied Swift and recorded the number of debugging queries needed to locate the fault. We consider the fault to be located if the currently selected method invocation is the one that directly infected the state. To track how fault localization results change during the debugging process, we record the debugging query, its answer, and the updated ranking at each iteration step of Swift's main loop.

In this study, we used an automated oracle, instead of a human developer, to answer queries. For each of the faults in our experiment, we obtained the fixed version of the program and confirmed that all the tests pass. We also made sure that all code changes between the two versions involved faulty statements. Therefore, any difference in their execution must be caused by the fault. The automated oracle answers debugging queries by executing the fixed program to get the expected output of the invocation in the query, and compare it with the observed output.

One limitation of our current implementation of the automated oracle is that it does not handle infected program states in external resources (*e.g.*, files, and network communications). The subject programs we used do not have cases where the faulty state is manifested only in external resources.

There are cases in which the oracle is unable to find the corresponding method invocation that has the same input in the execution of the fixed program. This happens when the input of the method invocation in the debugging query has already been infected by the fault, and thus does not exist in the execution of the fixed version. In these cases, the oracle reports to Swift that it cannot answer the query, which is considered inconclusive and does not result in the generation of a virtual test. However, to be conservative in assessing the effectiveness of Swift, we still count these queries (*i.e.*, we add the query to the set of queries needed to locate the fault). It is important to note that, in our benchmark, these cases happen infrequently.

4.3   Results

Table 3 summarizes our results. Column "*#Queries*" shows the number of queries that Swift requires to locate the fault. Columns "*Stmt Initial Rank*"

Table 3. Summary of results.

Subject	Fault ID	#Queries	Stmt. Initial Rank	Stmt. Final Rank	Methods Initial Rank	Invocations Initial Rank
jtopas	FAULT_2	1	1/11	1/10	1/2	1/4
	FAULT_6	52	69/71	1/2	20/21	1231/1238
commons-math	C_AK_1	1	3/5	1/1	2/3	2/3
	EDI_AK_1	7	7/37	4/15	3/7	5/15
	F_AK_1	2	11/38	4/8	4/4	5/5
	M_AK_1	14	94/105	1/3	23/24	15,541/15,542
	VS_AK_1	4	2/16	2/9	1/4	1/8
	CDI_AK_1	1	12/26	11/25	2/2	2/2
	MU_AK_1	11	27/29	3/5	2/2	11/11
	MU_AK_4	11	12/36	1/6	3/6	6,065/16,971
	URSU_AK_1	1	28/37	4/13	10/10	16/16
xml-security	CN2_AK_2	1	2/9	1/2	1/1	3/5
	C2E_AK_1	26	300/456	36/67	35/49	211/348
jsoup	1_3__4_b3	5	232/248	1/1	46/52	789/795
	1_4_2_b2	8	45/49	3/7	10/10	20/20
	1_5_2_b2	10	51/60	2/8	16/18	27/29
	1_5_2_b5	1	4/20	2/4	3/6	15/25
	1_6_1_b1	19	54/59	1/6	14/14	33/33
	1_6_3_b3	4	167/176	7/14	111/112	353/359
commons-lang	b6	3	120/121	1/2	34/34	126/126
	b9	15	46/73	2/24	14/17	26/34
	b10	7	61/63	1/3	15/15	73/73
	b16	3	24/53	4/15	1/5	1/20
	b24	39	1/65	1/1	1/3	1/71
	b26	4	112/114	1/3	17/17	20/20
	b39	5	4/53	2/11	2/2	15/15

and "*Stmt Final Rank*" show the statement-level ranking of the fault before and after running Swift. Column "*Methods Initial Rank*" shows the method-level ranking of the fault in the initial state. We report rankings in the format "best-case rank/worst-case rank", as the faulty program entities can share the same suspiciousness values as other program entities. Note that we omitted the final method-level ranking. This is because the faulty methods are always ranked at the top after running Swift. It is also important to note that, in the final state of the debugging process, the statements ranked as high as (or higher than) the actual faulty statement are all in the same method that contains the fault. Column "*Invocations Initial Rank*" shows the number of method invocations to be examined before reaching the first faulty method invocation when the answers to debugging queries are not incorporated. We also refer to these numbers as the initial method-invocation ranking. These numbers are also shown in "best case/worst case" format, depending on the position of the fault in the ranking among the statements that have the same suspiciousness value.

Overall Effectiveness. For 23 out of the 26 faulty program versions that we considered, the fault is found with less than 20 debugging queries (column "#Queries"). The average number of queries across all versions is about 10. Overall, these results indicate that a relatively small number of queries suffice to guide developers to the places where the fault infects the program state.

Note that, for this study, there are no obvious baselines to directly compare Swift against, beside a vanilla statistical fault localization approach. As the results show, inspecting code according to the output of statistical fault localization alone would be challenging (see column "Stmt. Initial Rank"). For xml-security's fault C2E_AK_1, for example, a statistical fault localization approach would require the developer to inspect 300 statements in the best case and 456 statements in the worst case. In contrast, Swift only needs 26 queries to isolate the faulty method invocation (see column "#Queries").

We note that the faulty statement is not always ranked among the most suspicious statements, even after the faulty method invocation has been isolated. This could happen if (1) executing the faulty code does not always infect the state and (2) other statements in the same method are executed more often than the number of times the state is infected. In this case, the faulty statement is covered by a relatively higher number of correct execution profiles, which reduces its suspiciousness score. Note, however, that this is not central to Swift as the technique focuses on isolating the faulty method invocation, not on optimizing the ranking of statements.

Progress of Fault Rankings. We elaborate on the effects of incorporating answers of debugging queries in Swift.

Figure 10 shows the progress of fault localization ranking as Swift incorporates answers on 2 representative faulty subject versions. We considered worst-case statement-level ranking in the plots. The x-axis denotes the number of queries answered over time and the y-axis denotes the ranking of the fault.

The plot of joup_1_4_2_b2 represents the case of the majority of the faults from the experiment (22 out of 26 cases). In this case, the ranking of the faulty statement monotonically decreases (*i.e.*, the faulty statement becomes more suspicious) from 49 down to 7

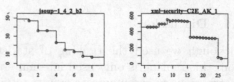

Fig. 10. Progress of stmt.-level suspiciousness.

as 8 debugging queries are answered. In contrast, the fault ranking of xml-security_C2E_AK_1 first increases, when incorporating the first 12 answers, and decreases afterwards. The reason for this type of progress pattern is that the execution of the faulty statement does not always infect the state. The first 12 queries are all classified as correct, for instance; although some of these queries indeed cover the faulty statement, they do not infect the state. For this reason, in the beginning of the debugging process, the faulty statement appears relatively more often associated with correct execution profiles, leading to an initial increase in the ranking.

Considering all the faults we analyzed in this experiment, xml-security_C2E_AK_1 and commons-lang_b24 are the only ones where the fault ranking increases by a significant amount at some stage during the debugging process. We found that, for these cases, the number of queries needed to locate the fault was also larger compared to the other versions. Intuitively, these scenarios can be further explained by considering that the basic assumption of statistical fault localization is that the execution of faulty code is more correlated with failing than passing runs. However, if faulty statements infect the state infrequently when executed, this assumption becomes invalid. Swift handles these situations by calibrating suspiciousness scores of highly suspicious but non-faulty program entities.

Effect of Feedback Incorporation. In addition to looking at how Swift improves fault localization rankings, we also assessed how effective the updates to the ranking list are for guiding the search of the faulty method invocation (column "*Invocations Initial Rank*"). To that end, for each faulty version, we measured the number of queries that would be generated if Swift did not update the fault localization results using the answers to debugging queries. In this setup, Swift would start from the beginning of the initial ranking list of statements and would present all method invocations that covered the most suspicious statement to the developer. It would then go to the next statement of the ranking list when all method invocations of the current statement are answered.

By comparing this number with the number of queries needed to locate the faulty method invocation (column "*#Queries*"), we can observe a significant reduction in the number of methods to examine when query answers are considered. Furthermore, in 4 of the 26 faults, the number of method invocations to examine without feedback incorporation is larger than 500, making the task of examining all of them prohibitive. This result highlights the important role that feedback incorporation can play in the iterative debugging process.

4.4   Discussion

Although we used the ranking of statistical fault localization in our evaluation, this ranking is only used internally in Swift. The technique uses high-level abstractions to communicate results to users, who do not have to deal with the low-level abstractions used within the tool.

It is important to recall that to facilitate automation of our experiments we stop the debugging session when Swift is able to generate a query associated to a method invocation that injects the fault (see Sect. 4.2). In practice, however, users can stop (and later continue) using Swift at any point in time. This could be triggered, for instance, by the desire to check a debugging hypothesis from a suspicious fault manifestation.

The important problem of deciding how to present queries to users is outside the scope of this paper, which mainly focuses on the feasibility of the general approach. In future work, we will explore this aspect in depth and investigate different approaches, such as highlighting/obfuscating (ir)relevant fields, using program slicing, and using suitable visualization techniques. In a continuous software development environment, the users' effort of answering debugging queries can be further reduced by caching previous answers.

Our preliminary empirical evaluation shows that Swift is promising, as it provides initial evidence that Swift can locate faults by generating a relatively small number of user queries (Sect. 4.3). The evaluation also shows that our results do not seem to be coincidental, as the systematic incorporation of answers to queries improves the overall diagnosis (Sects. 4.3 and 4.3).

4.5   Threats to Validity

The main threats to validity are as follows. **External Validity**: The selection of subjects and faults we used may not generalize to other cases. To mitigate this threat, we used subjects from a variety of sources and selected according to a documented criteria, described in detail in Sect. 4.1. Another threat is that using automated oracles to simulate real users might have produced results that are not representative of a typical developer's performance. However, for an initial study that is meant to assess the feasibility of our new approach, we believe that this approximation is justified. **Internal Validity**: Errors in our implementation could affect the validity of our results. To mitigate this threat, we thoroughly checked our implementation and our experimental results, looking for discrepancies that would signal potential errors.

5   Related Work

There is an enormous body of related work on statistical fault localization and debugging in general (*e.g.,* [3,7,13,14,18,28]). In the interest of space, and because our work builds on and extends traditional fault localization, we do not discuss this work here and focus instead on techniques that share our specific goals and general approach.

Ko and Myers proposed Whyline [17], an interactive debugger that allows developers to ask high-level questions about how values in the state came to be. Similar in spirit to dynamic backward slicing, developers can use Whyline to localize faults by iteratively asking "why" questions involving parts of the state that seem suspicious. In our approach, the tool asks questions to the developer instead, and does so by focusing on suspicious parts of the computation.

Several existing techniques use developer feedback to improve fault localization. Algorithmic Debugging (AD) [23] is a debugging technique that is popular in the functional programming community. It asks questions to testers based on the structure of the execution tree induced from one failing test and systematically prunes the tree based on the answers to get to a point where the fault can be isolated. In contrast to Swift, AD does not take coverage profiles of multiple test runs into account to guide the debugging process. The work presented in [5,10] incorporates developer answers about the correctness of statements to refine a ranked list of suspicious statements. Swift differs from these techniques in that it asks questions about concrete input-output pairs during execution and does not rely on developers' ability to assess the correctness of individual program statements. The techniques in [11,12] suggest breakpoints using fault localization techniques and refine the suggestions based on developers' feedback on the correctness of program states. At each breakpoint, they ask the developers to examine the program states using a debugger and determine whether the state has been infected, and then increase or decrease the suspiciousness of related statements by a fixed ratio based on the feedback. In contrast, Swift generates user queries at the level of abstraction of methods in the program, whose semantics is more likely to be understood by developers than that of program states considered in isolation.

At a high-level, Swift employs a form of supervised learning to solve a program analysis problem. Recently, user supervision has been explored to solve undecidable problems in program analysis. Dillig *et al.* [9] and Mangal *et al.* [19] independently explored the feedback given by domain specialists to improve precision and recall in static analyses. In their context, user feedback indicates whether or not a warning is correct, and feedback is restricted to the output of the analysis. Swift, conversely requests user feedback on partial executions and is a dynamic (rather than static) analysis that supports debugging (rather than bug finding).

6   Conclusions

We presented Swift, a technique that aims to mitigate the existing disconnect between research and practice in the area of software debugging, and in particular in fault localization. Swift operates in an iterative and user-driven fashion. At each iteration, developers are provided with queries about the correctness of a specific method execution; Swift then processes the answers to these question and suitably increases or decreases the suspiciousness of the program entities involved in the computation. This process allows Swift to improve the localization results and guide the developer increasingly closer to the fault at hand.

We implemented Swift in a prototype that is publicly available, together with our experimental infrastructure. We used our implementation to perform an empirical evaluation of Swift on 5 programs and 26 faults for these programs. Our results show that Swift can, in most of the cases we considered, converge to the fault using only a small number of queries (less than 10, on average).

Our first goal for future work is to investigate ways to encode and visualize the queries so that they are as easy to consume and answer as possible for the developers. We will then perform a user study to assess how our approach performs in a real-world scenario, in which actual developers are answering the queries produced by Swift and performing debugging tasks.

Acknowledgments. Mayur Naik was engaged in early discussions about this work. Higor Amario de Souza shared the jsoup code. This work was partially supported by CNPq grants 457756/2014-4 and 203981/2014-6, by NSF grants CCF1320783 and CCF1161821, and by funding from Google, IBM Research, and Microsoft Research.

References

1. SAEG - Software Analysis and Experimentation Group (at Universidade de São Paulo (USP), Brazil). https://github.com/saeg/experiments/tree/master/jaguar-2015
2. SIR Repository. http://sir.unl.edu/portal/index.php
3. Abreu, R., Zoeteweij, P., van Gemund, A.J.C.: An evaluation of similarity coefficients for software fault localization. In: Proceedings of the 12th Pacific Rim International Symposium on Dependable Computing, PRDC 2006, pp. 39–46. IEEE Computer Society, Washington (2006)
4. Ball, T., Naik, M., Rajamani, S.K.: From symptom to cause: localizing errors in counterexample traces. In: POPL, pp. 97–105 (2003)
5. Bandyopadhyay, A., Ghosh, S.: Tester feedback driven fault localization. In: Proceedings of the 2012 IEEE Fifth International Conference on Software Testing, Verification and Validation, ICST 2012, pp. 41–50. IEEE Computer Society, Washington (2012)
6. Chandra, S., Torlak, E., Barman, S., Bodik, R.: Angelic debugging. In: ICSE, pp. 121–130 (2011)
7. Cleve, H., Zeller, A.: Locating causes of program failures. In: ICSE, pp. 342–351 (2005)
8. Demsky, B., Ernst, M.D., Guo, P.J., McCamant, S., Perkins, J.H., Rinard, M.: Inference and enforcement of data structure consistency specifications. In: ISSTA, pp. 233–244 (2006)
9. Dillig, I., Dillig, T., Aiken, A.: Automated error diagnosis using abductive inference. In: PLDI, pp. 181–192 (2012)
10. Gong, L., Lo, D., Jiang, L., Zhang, H.: Interactive fault localization leveraging simple user feedback. In: 2012 28th IEEE International Conference on Software Maintenance (ICSM), pp. 67–76, September 2012
11. Hao, D., Zhang, L., Xie, T., Mei, H., Sun, J.-S.: Interactive fault localization using test information. J. Comput. Sci. Technol. **24**(5), 962–974 (2009)
12. Hao, D., Zhang, L., Zhang, L., Sun, J., Mei, H.: Vida: Visual interactive debugging. In: 2009 IEEE 31st International Conference on Software Engineering, pp. 583–586, May 2009
13. Jones, J.A., Bowring, J.F., Harrold, M.J.: Debugging in parallel. In: Proceedings of the 2007 International Symposium on Software Testing and Analysis, ISSTA 2007, pp. 16–26. ACM, New York (2007)
14. Jones, J.A., Harrold, M.J., Stasko, J.: Visualization of test information to assist fault localization. In: ICSE, pp. 467–477 (2002)
15. Jose, M., Majumdar, R.: Cause clue clauses: error localization using maximum satisfiability. In: PLDI, pp. 437–446 (2011)
16. Just, R., Jalali, D., Ernst, M.D.: Defects4J: a database of existing faults to enable controlled testing studies for Java programs. In: Proceedings of the International Symposium on Software Testing and Analysis (ISSTA), San Jose, CA, USA, pp. 437–440, July 23–25 (2014)

17. Ko, A.J., Myers, B.A.: Designing the whyline: a debugging interface for asking questions about program behavior. In: Proceedings of the SIGCHI Conference on Human Factors in Computing Systems, CHI 2004, pp. 151–158. ACM, New York (2004)

18. Liblit, B., Naik, M., Zheng, A.X., Aiken, A., Jordan, M.I.: Scalable statistical bug isolation. In: PLDI, pp. 15–26 (2005)

19. Mangal, R., Zhang, X., Nori, A.V., Naik, M.: A user-guided approach to program analysis. In: ESEC/FSE, pp. 462–473 (2015)

20. Naish, L., Lee, H.J., Ramamohanarao, K.: A model for spectra-based software diagnosis. ACM Trans. Softw. Eng. Methodol. **11:20**(3), 1–11:32 (2011)

21. Parnin, C., Orso, A.: Are automated debugging techniques actually helping programmers? In: ISSTA, pp. 199–209 (2011)

22. Renieris, M., Reiss, S.P.: Fault localization with nearest neighbor queries. In: ASE, pp. 30–39 (2003)

23. Shapiro, E.Y.: Algorithmic Program DeBugging. MIT Press, Cambridge (1983)

24. Stotts, P.D., Lindsey, M., Antley, A.: An informal formal method for systematic junit test case generation. In: Proceedings of the Second XP Universe and First Agile Universe Conference on Extreme Programming and Agile Methods - XP/Agile Universe 2002, pp. 131–143 (2002)

25. Vessey, I.: Expertise in debugging computer programs: An analysis of the content of verbal protocols. IEEE Trans. Syst. Man Cybern. B Cybern. **16**(5), 621–637 (1986)

26. Wang, X., Cheung, S.C., Chan, W.K., Zhang, Z.: Taming coincidental correctness: coverage refinement with context patterns to improve fault localization. In: Proceedings of the 31st International Conference on Software Engineering, ICSE 2009, pp. 45–55. IEEE Computer Society , Washington (2009)

27. Zhang, X., Gupta, N., Gupta, R.: Locating faults through automated predicate switching. In: ICSE, pp. 272–281 (2006)

28. Zheng, A.X., Jordan, M.I., Liblit, B., Naik, M., Aiken, A.: Statistical debugging: simultaneous identification of multiple bugs. In: ICML, pp. 1105–1112 (2006)

Improving Efficiency and Accuracy
of Formula-Based Debugging

Wei Jin[1] and Alessandro Orso[2]([⊠])

[1] Georgia Institute of Technology and Google Inc., Mountain View, California, USA
weijin@gatech.edu
[2] Georgia Institute of Technology, Atlanta, Georgia, USA
orso@gatech.edu

Abstract. Formula-based debugging techniques are extremely appealing, as they provide a principled way to identify potentially faulty statements together with information that can help fix such statements. These approaches are however computationally expensive, which limits their practical applicability. Moreover, they tend to focus on failing test cases and ignore the information provided by passing tests. To mitigate these issues, we propose on-demand formula computation (OFC) and clause weighting (CW). OFC improves the overall efficiency of formula-based debugging by exploring all and only the parts of a program that are relevant to a failure. CW improves the accuracy of formula-based debugging by leveraging statistical fault-localization information that accounts for passing tests. Although OFC and CW are only a first step towards making formula-based debugging more applicable, our empirical results show that they are effective and improve the state of the art.

1 Introduction

Because debugging is expensive and time consuming, there has been a great deal of research on automated techniques for supporting various debugging tasks (*e.g.,* [3,5,14,17,24,25]). Recently, in particular, we have witnessed a considerable interest in techniques that can perform fault localization in a more principled way (*e.g.,* [7,11,15,21]). These techniques, collectively called *formula-based debugging* [20], model faulty programs and failing executions as formulas and perform fault localization by manipulating and solving these formulas. As a result, they can provide developers with the possible location of the fault, together with a mathematical explanation of the failure (*e.g.,* the fact that an expression should have produced a different value or that a different branch should have been taken at a conditional statement).

BugAssist [15] is a technique of particular interest in this arena. Given a faulty program, a failing input, and a corresponding (violated) assertion, BugAssist performs fault localization by constructing an unsatisfiable Boolean formula that encodes (1) the input values, (2) the semantics of (a bounded version of) the faulty program, and (3) the assertion. It then uses a pMAX-SAT solver to find maximal sets of clauses in this formula that can be satisfied together

© Springer International Publishing AG 2016
R. Bloem and E. Arbel (Eds.): HVC 2016, LNCS 10028, pp. 99–116, 2016.
DOI: 10.1007/978-3-319-49052-6_7

and outputs the complement sets of clauses (CoMSS) as potential causes of the error. Intuitively, each set of clauses in CoMSS indicates a corresponding set of statements that, if suitably modified (*e.g.,* replacing the statements with angelic values [6]), would make the program behave correctly for the considered input.

Although effective, BugAssist is computationally expensive, as it builds a formula for (a bounded unrolling of) *all possible paths* in a program. Moreover, like most formula-based debugging approaches, BugAssist does not take into account passing test cases, thus missing two important opportunities. First, passing executions can help identify statements, and thus parts of the formulas, that are less likely to be related to the fault, which can help optimize the search for a solution. Second, passing executions can help filter out locations that may be potential fixes for the failing executions considered but could break previously passing test cases if modified [6].

We propose two possible ways of addressing these issues: *on-demand formula computation (OFC)* and *clause weighting (CW)*. OFC is an on-demand algorithm that can dramatically reduce the number of paths encoded in a formula, and thus the overall complexity of such formula and the cost of computing a pMAX-SAT solution for it. Intuitively, our algorithm (1) builds a formula for the path in the original failing trace, (2) analyzes the formula to identify additional relevant paths to consider, (3) expands the formula by encoding these additional paths, (4) repeats (2) and (3) until no more relevant paths can be identified, at which point it (5) reports the computed solution. CW accounts for the information provided by passing test cases by assigning weights to the different clauses in an encoded formula based on the suspiciousness values computed by a statistical fault localization technique. Doing so has the potential to improve the accuracy of the results by helping the solver compute CoMSSs that are more likely to correspond to faulty statements.

To evaluate our approach, we performed an empirical study in which we compared the performance of BugAssist, used as a baseline, with that of a technique that also uses CW, OFC, or both. In the study, we first applied the techniques considered to 52 versions of two small programs, to assess several tradeoffs involved in the use of CW and OFC and compare with related work, and then performed a case study on a real-world bug in a popular open source project. Our results show that CW and OFC can improve the performance of BugAssist in several respects. First, the use of CW resulted in more accurate results—in terms of position of the actual fault in the ranked list of statements reported to developers—in the majority of the cases considered. Second, CW and OFC were able to reduce the computational cost of BugAssist by 27% and 75% on average, respectively, with maximum speedups of over 70X for OFC. Overall, our results show that CW and OFC are promising, albeit initial, steps towards more practically applicable formula-based debugging techniques.
The main contributions of this paper are:

- The definition of CW and OFC, two approaches for improving the accuracy and efficiency of formula-based debugging.

– A prototype implementation of our technique that is available for download, together with our experimental infrastructure and benchmark programs (see http://www.cc.gatech.edu/~orso/software/odin/).
– Initial empirical evidence that CW and OFC are as effective and more efficient than existing approaches.

2   Improving Formula-Based Debugging

2.1   Clause Weighting (CW)

CW consists of using the information from passing executions to inform a wpMAX-SAT solver. More precisely, CW leverages the suspiciousness values computed by a statistical fault localization technique and assigns to each program entity en, and thus to the corresponding clause in the program formula, a weight inversely proportional to its suspiciousness $susp(en)$: $weight(en) = 1/susp(en)$. If the suspiciousness value of an entity is zero, which means that the entity is only executed by passing tests, CW assigns to it the largest possible weight. By assigning different weights to different clauses, CW transforms the original pMAX-SAT problem in BugAssit into a wpMAX-SAT problem. The rationale for CW is that, by the definition of wpMAX-SAT, clauses with higher weights are more likely to be included in an MSS (*i.e.*, less likely to be identified as causes of the faulty behavior), while clauses with lower weights are less likely to be included in an MSS (*i.e.*, more likely to be included in a CoMSS and thus be identified as causes of the faulty behavior).

Formula-based debugging techniques such as BugAssist consider all possible pMAX-SAT solutions equally and simply report them. Conversely, by leveraging the heuristics in statistical fault localization, CW is more likely to rank the set of clauses corresponding to the fault at the top of the list of solutions, thus reducing developers' debugging effort. This potential advantage, however, comes at a cost. Solving wpMAX-SAT problems can be computationally more expensive than solving a pMAX-SAT problem, which can outweigh CW's benefits. To understand this tradeoff, in our empirical evaluation we assess how CW affects the accuracy and efficiency of formula-based debugging (see Sect. 3.2).

2.2   On-Demand Formula Computation (OFC)

OFC is our second, and more substantial, improvement over traditional formula-based debugging. Figure 1 shows an overall view of OFC and its workflow. The inputs to the algorithm are a faulty program, represented as an Interprocedural Control Flow Graph (ICFG), and a test suite that contains a set of passing tests and one

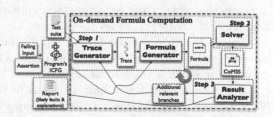

Fig. 1. Overview of OFC.

failing test. As it is common practice for debugging techniques, we assume that a failure can be expressed as the violation of an assertion in the program. Given these inputs, OFC produces as output a set of clauses and their corresponding program entities (*i.e.,* branches and statements). These are entities that, if suitably modified, would make the failing execution pass. The expressions in the reported clauses provide developers with additional information on the failure, and can be considered a "mathematical explanation" of the failure. Similar to other formula-based debugging techniques, OFC is capable of handling failures that are triggered by multiple faults. In these cases, all faults that affect the failure would appear in the set of program entities identified by the approach.

As Fig. 1 shows, OFC consists of three main steps. The key idea behind OFC is to reason about the failure incrementally, by starting with the entities traversed in a single failing trace, computing CoMSS solutions for the partial program exercised by the trace, and then expanding the portion of the program considered in the analysis when such solutions indicate that additional control-flow paths should be taken into consideration to "explain" the failure. Specifically, in its first step (*Trace Generator and Formula Generator*), OFC generates a new trace (the original failing trace, in the first iteration) and suitably updates the trace formula, which encodes the semantics of the traces generated so far. OFC's second step (*Solver*) computes the CoMSSs of the (unsatisfiable) formula built in the previous step. Finally, in OFC's third step (*Result Analyzer*), the algorithm checks whether there is any additional relevant branch to consider in the program. If so, OFC returns to Step 1. Otherwise, it computes all possible CoMSSs of the final formula to report to developers the set of relevant clauses and their corresponding program entities.

Algorithm 1 shows the main algorithm, which takes as inputs the ICFG of the faulty program and the program's test suite and performs the three steps we just described. We discuss each step in detail in the rest of this section.

Trace Generator and Formula Generator. After an initialization phase, OFC iterates Steps 1, 2, and 3. Step 1 performs two tasks: trace generation and formula generation.

Trace Generator. In its first part, Step 1 invokes the *Trace Generator* (Algorithm 2). In the first iteration of the algorithm, *Trace Generator* generates the trace corresponding to the failing input. In subsequent iterations, it generates a trace that covers the new program entities identified as relevant by Step 3 (see *Result Analyzer*), so as to augment the scope of the analysis. The inputs to *TraceGenerator* are the failing input, the map that associates each branch covered so far with the trace in which it was first covered, and the new relevant branch for which a trace must be generated (by flipping it).

If *flip_br* is null, which only happens in the first iteration of the algorithm, *TraceGenerator* generates a trace by simply providing the failing input to the program and collecting its execution trace (line 3). Otherwise, for subsequent iterations, *TraceGenerator* retrieves *old_trace* (line 5), the trace that first reached

---

Algorithm 1. OFC

```
Input  :  ICFG: ICFG of the faulty program
          TestSuite: test suite for the program
Output:  faulty statements and their corresponding clauses
1  begin
2  |    FIN ← GetFailingInput(TestSuite)
3  |    ASSERT ← GetFailingAssertion(TestSuite)
4  |    TF ← {}, SP ← {}, clause_origin ← {}, visited_branches ← {}, flip_br ← null
   |    // Step 1
5  |    new_trace ← TraceGenerator(FIN, visited_branches, flip_br)
6  |    flip_br ← null
7  |    TF ← FormulaGenerator(new_trace, TF, ICFG, SP, clause_origin)
   |    // Step 2
8  |    CoMSSs ← Solver(FIN, ASSERT, TF)
   |    // Step 3
9  |    foreach CoMSS in CoMSSs do
10 |    |    foreach clause in CoMSS do
11 |    |    |    st ← clause_origin(clause)
12 |    |    |    if st is a conditional statement then
13 |    |    |    |    <true_br, false_br> ← getBranches(st)
14 |    |    |    |    if visited_branches(true_br)==null then
15 |    |    |    |    |    flip_br ← false_br
16 |    |    |    |    |    go back to Step 1
17 |    |    |    |    end
18 |    |    |    |    if visited_branches(false_br)==null then
19 |    |    |    |    |    flip_br ← true_br
20 |    |    |    |    |    go back to Step 1
21 |    |    |    |    end
22 |    |    |    end
23 |    |    end
24 |    end
25 |    foreach CoMSS in CoMSSs do
26 |    |    foreach clause in CoMSS do
27 |    |    |    report clause and clause_origin(clause)
28 |    |    end
29 |    end
30 end
```

---

branch *flip_br* and generates a new trace, *new_trace* (line 5). To generate the trace, the algorithm provides the failing input to the program, forces the program to follow *old_trace* up to *flip_br*, and flips *flip_br* so that the program follows its alternative branch (using execution hijacking [22]). The algorithm also updates map *visited_branches* by adding to it an entry for every branch newly covered by *new_trace*, including *flip_br*'s alternative branch (lines 8–12).

Formula Generator. After generating a trace, OFC invokes *FormulaGenerator* (Algorithm 3), which constructs a new formula *TF*, either from scratch (in the first iteration) or by expanding the current formula based on the program entities in *new_trace* (in subsequent iterations).

The inputs to *FormulaGenerator* are the ICFG of the faulty program, the current trace formula, the portion of the program currently considered (and encoded in the current trace formula), the trace newly generated by *TraceGenerator*, and a map from clauses to statements that originated them.

In its main loop, *FormulaGenerator* processes each statement *st* in the new trace, *new_trace*, one at a time. If *st* is not yet part of *SP*, the portion of the program currently considered, the algorithm (1) adds *st* to *SP*, (2) encodes its semantics in a new Boolean clause $clause_{st}$, (3) conjoins $clause_{st}$ and *TF*, and (4) updates map *clause_origin* by mapping $clause_{st}$ to *st*.

Similar to other symbolic analyses (*e.g.,* [8,15,21]), OFC operates on an static single assignment (SSA) form of the faulty program [9,13]. The formula generator models three types of statements in the program (and its trace):

Algorithm 2. TraceGenerator

```
Input  : FIN: failing input
         visited_branches: map from branches to traces that covered them
         flip_br: branch for which a new trace must be generated
Output : new_trace: newly generated trace
1  begin
2      if flip_br==null then
3      |   new_trace ← Execute(Input, null, null)
4      else
5      |   old_trace ← visited_branches(flip_br)
6      |   new_trace ← Execute(Input, old_trace, flip_br)
7      end
8      foreach br in new_trace do
9      |   if visited_branches(br)==null then
10     |   |   visited_branches(br) ← new_trace
11     |   end
12     end
13     return new_trace
14 end
```

Algorithm 3. FormulaGenerator

```
Input  : ICFG: ICFG of the faulty program
         TF: current trace formula
         SP: portion of the program currently considered
         new_trace: newly generated trace
Output : TF: updated trace formula
         SP: updated portion of the program currently considered
1  clause_origin: map from clauses to statements that originated them
2  begin
3      foreach st ∈ new_trace do
4          if st ∉ SP then
5              SP ← SP + st
6              if st is a conditional statement then
7                  predicate_st ← GetPredicate(st)
8                  clause_st ← (guard_st = predicate_st)
9              else
10                 if st is a φ function then
11                     phi ← φ function in st
12                     cs ← φ's conditional statement
13                     guard_cs ← cs's condition
14                     clause_st ← ((guard_cs ∧ (st_LHS = st_RHS,t)) ∨ (¬guard_cs ∧ (st_LHS =
                           st_RHS,f)))
15                 else
16                 |   clause_st ← (st_LHS = st_RHS)
17                 end
18             end
19             clause_origin(clause_st) = st
20             TF ← TF ∧ clause_st
21         end
22     end
23     return TF
24 end
```

---

conditional statements, definitions that involve a ϕ function and definitions that do not involve a ϕ function. To perform a correct semantic encoding, when deriving $clause_{st}$ from st, *FormulaGenerator* must treat these three types of statements differently.

If st is a conditional statement with predicate $predicate_{st}$, the algorithm retrieves such predicate from st (GetPredicate at line 7) and encodes st as $(guard_{st}=predicate_{st})$, where $guard_{st}$ is a Boolean variable that represents st's condition (line 8).

If st involves a ϕ function phi, the algorithm generates a clause $(guard_{cs} \wedge (st_{LHS} = st_{RHS,t})) \vee (\neg guard_{cs} \wedge (st_{LHS} = st_{RHS,f}))$, where (1) cs is phi's conditional and, similar to above, $guard_{cs}$ represents cs's condition, (2) st_{LHS} is the variable being defined at st, and (3) $st_{RHS,t}$ and $st_{RHS,f}$ are the definitions selected by phi along cs's *true* and *false* branches. Basically, this clause explicitly represents the semantics of *phi* and encodes both the data- and the control-flow aspects of the execution, which allows OFC to handle faults in both. Algorithm 3 performs this encoding at lines 10–14.

Finally, if *st* is a traditional assignment statement, the algorithm encodes *st* as $st_{LHS} = st_{RHS}$, the equivalence relation between the variable on *st*'s lefthand side and the expression on its righthand side (line 16). Because each assignment in SSA form defines a new variable, $clause_{st}$ can be simply conjoined with the current formula *TF* (line 20).

After processing a statement *st* and generating the corresponding clause $clause_{st}$, the algorithm records that $clause_{st}$ was generated from *st* and suitably updates the trace formula *TF* (lines 19 and 20). Finally, after processing all statements in *new_trace*, *FormulaGenerator* returns *TF*.

Solver. In its second step, OFC leverages a pMAX-SAT solver to find all possible causes of the failure being considered. To do so, it invokes function *Solver* and passes to it the failing input, the failing assertion, and the trace formula constructed in Step 1 (line 8 of Algorithm 1). Function *Solver* will first generate a formula by conjoining the input clauses (*i.e.,* clauses that assert that the input is the failing input *FIN*), the current trace formula *TF*, and the failing assertion *ASSERT*. Because *FIN* causes the program to fail, that is, to violate *ASSERT*, the resulting formula is unsatisfiable.

To suitably define the pMAX-SAT problem, *Solver* encodes (1) the input clauses and the failing assertion as hard clauses, (2) the clauses in *TF* generated from ϕ functions as hard clauses, and (3) the other clauses in *TF* as soft clauses. The input clauses and the assertion are encoded as hard clauses because the failure could be trivially eliminated by changing the input or the assertion, which would not provide any information on where the problem is in the program. Encoding clauses generated by ϕ functions as hard clauses, conversely, ensures that control-flow related information is kept in the results, which is necessary to handle control-flow related faults. At this point, function *Solver* passes the so defined pMAX-SAT problem to an external solver and retrieves from it all possible CoMSSs for the problem. If CW were also used, OFC would generate a wpMAX-SAT problem instead by assigning a weight to each soft clause based on the suspiciousness of the corresponding program entity (*i.e.,* *clause_origin(clause)*), as described in Sect. 2.1.

Result Analyzer. OFC's third step takes the set of CoMSSs for the failure being investigated, produced by Step 2, and generates a report with a set of program entities (or an ordered list of entities, if we use CW and a wpMAX-SAT solver) and corresponding clauses. The entities are statements that, if suitably modified, would make the failing execution pass (*i.e.,* the potential causes of the failure being investigated). The expressions in the clauses associated with the statements provide developers with additional information on how the statements contribute to the failure, and as stated above, can thus be seen as a mathematical explanation of the failure.

This part of OFC, corresponding to lines 9–23 of Algorithm 1, iterates through each clause of each CoMSS computed in Step 2. For each clause, it first retrieves the corresponding statement *st*. If *st* is a conditional statement, the predicate in the conditional statement is potentially faulty, and taking a different branch may fix the program. To account for this possibility, the algorithm checks whether the conditional has one branch that has not been executed in any previously computed trace and, if so, expands the scope of the analysis by selecting that branch as a new branch to analyze and going back to Step 1 (lines 12–20). Step 1 would then add such branch to the list of relevant branches, generate a new trace, constructs a new formula, and perform an additional iteration of the analysis. Conversely, if both branches have already been covered, or *st* is not a conditional statement, the algorithm processes the next clause.

If no clause in any CoMSS contains a conditional statement for which one of the branches has not been covered, it means that the analysis already considered the portion of the program relevant to the failure, so the algorithm can terminate and produce a report (lines 25–28). To do so, OFC iterates once more through the set of CoMSSs computed during its last iteration. For each clause in each CoMSS, OFC reports it to developers, together with its corresponding statement, as a possible cause (and partial explanation) of the failure.

3   Empirical Evaluation

To evaluate CW and OFC, we have developed a prototype tool for C programs that implements four different formula-based debugging techniques: BugAssist (BA), BugAssist with clause weighting (BA+CW), on-demand formula computation (OFC), and on-demand formula computation with clause weighting (OFC+CW). We have empirically investigated the following research questions:

RQ1: Does BA+CW produce more accurate results than BA? If so, what is CW's effect on efficiency?

RQ2: Does OFC improve the efficiency of all-paths formula-based debugging?

RQ3: Does OFC+CW combine the benefits of OFC and CW? If so, can it handle programs that an all-paths technique could not handle?

3.1   Evaluation Setup

Implementation. Our implementation leverages the LLVM compiler infrastructure (http://llvm.org/), the Yices SMT solver (http://yices.csl.sri.com/) and the Z3 theorem prover (http://z3.codeplex.com/).

Benchmarks. For our evaluation, we selected multiple faulty versions of two programs (tcas and tot_info) from the SIR repository (http://sir.unl.edu/) and a real faulty version of the Redis open-source project [1]. tcas has 41 versions and ˜200 LOC, and tot_info has 11 versions and ˜500 LOC. Both programs come with test cases and a golden version that can be used as an oracle and were also used to evaluate BugAssist [15], which lets us directly compare our results with an all-paths formula-based technique in terms of accuracy and efficiency. The third benchmark is a (faulty) module of Redis that processes Lua scripts (www. lua.org/) and consists of ˜1KLOC. We selected this module because it is a more realistic piece of software that also comes with a set of test cases. The bug in the module is a potential buffer overflow.

Study Protocol. For each faulty program version considered, we proceeded as follows. *First*, we identified passing and failing test cases for that version. For tcas and tot_info, we did so by defining the assertion for a test using the output generated by the same test when run against their golden implementation. For the bug in Redis, we used the bug description [1] and the corresponding test [2]. We then ran all programs instrumented to collect coverage information for all passing and failing tests at the same time. We used this coverage information to compute the suspiciousness values for the branches and statements in each program version using the Ochiai metric [3]. These are the values that BA+CW and OFC+CW use to assign weights to the clauses in the program formula. *Second*, for each failing input, we ran all four techniques on the faulty version. Because the all-paths techniques timed out or could not build a formula for the bugs in tot_info and Redis (see Sect. 3.2 for details), we could only investigate RQ1 and RQ2 on tcas, whereas we used tcas, tot_info, and Redis for RQ3. (For fairness, we note that Reference [15] reports results for 2 versions of tot_info. However, the authors mention that those results were obtained working on a program slice, and there are no details on how the slice was computed and on which version, so we could not replicate them using either our or their implementation of BA.) For each faulty version and each technique that successfully ran on that version, the technique generated a report for the developers. To do a complete assessment of the performance of the techniques, we also recorded the average CPU time of each technique for each failing input, the number of iterations of the OFC algorithm, whether the generated report contained the fault, and, if so, the rank of the fault in the report.

3.2   Results and Discussion

RQ1—BA+CW Versus BA. To answer this research question, we compared the accuracy and the computational cost of BA+CW and BA. To do so, we ran both techniques on the 41 faulty versions of tcas and computed the results as described in Sect. 3.1. Table 1 presents these results. The columns in the table show the version ID, the number of lines of code a developer would have to examine before getting to the fault, and the average CPU time consumed by BA and BA+CW to compute their results. For comparison purposes, in the last column we also report the results of a traditional fault-localization technique (Ochiai). Note that, for BA+CW, the number of lines of code to examine corresponds to the actual rank of the faulty line of code in the report produced by the technique. BA, however, does not rank the potentially faulty lines of code, but simply reports them as an unordered set to developers. Therefore, the number in the table corresponds to the number of lines of code developers would have to investigate if we assume they examine the entities in the set in a random order (*i.e.*, half of the size of the set).

As Table 1 shows, both techniques were able to identify the faulty statements for all versions considered. We can also observe that both BA and BA+CW produced overall more accurate results than Ochiai (significance level of 0.05 for both BA and BA+CW for *a paired t-test*). Although this was not a goal of the study, it provides evidence that formula-based techniques, by reasoning on the semantics of a failing execution, can provide more accurate results than a purely statistical approach. As for the comparison of BA and BA+CW, BA+CW produced better results than BA, with a significance level of 0.05 for *a paired t-test*. On average, a developer would have to examine 4.7 statements per fault for BA+CW versus 6.5 for BA. By leveraging the suspiciousness values computed by statistical fault localization, BA+CW can thus outperform BA in most cases (33 out of 41). For the 8 cases in which BA+CW was slightly outperformed by BA, manual analysis of the results showed that the weights computed by

Table 1. Results for BA and BA+CW when run on tcas.

Version	BA		BA+CW		Ochiai	Version	BA		BA+CW		Ochiai
	Rank	Time	Rank	Time	Rank		Rank	Time	Rank	Time	Rank
v1	7.5	26 s	2	27 s	4	v22	4	7 s	5	7 s	22
v2	4	15 s	4	16 s	3	v23	5.5	15 s	10	12 s	23
v3	8.5	292 s	1	183 s	3	v24	7.5	30 s	8	23 s	23
v4	8	11 s	3	11 s	1	v25	5.5	297 s	4	216 s	2
v5	7.5	352 s	3	323 s	18	v26	8	160 s	5	123 s	21
v6	7.5	569 s	5	316 s	4	v27	9.5	443 s	4	393 s	21
v7	8	484 s	8	238 s	8	v28	5	41 s	3	40 s	2
v8	7.5	21 s	13	18 s	48	v29	5	25 s	1	27 s	20
v9	4.5	18 s	10	15 s	23	v30	5	11 s	6	14 s	20
v10	8	125 s	3	96 s	4	v31	8.5	958 s	2	909 s	4
v11	5.5	130 s	1	91 s	21	v32	8.5	171 s	1	145 s	3
v12	8	22 s	11	20 s	49	v33	6	79 s	1	70 s	3
v13	8	24 s	7	21 s	1	v34	7.5	164 s	5	144 s	23
v14	7	28 s	1	28 s	1	v35	5	38 s	3	40 s	2
v15	6.5	14 s	5	14 s	21	v36	2.5	19 s	1	17 s	1
v16	8	331 s	12	228 s	49	v37	7.5	127 s	1	136 s	3
v17	8	626 s	8	285 s	49	v38	6.5	8 s	1	8 s	2
v18	6	378 s	6	245 s	49	v39	6	244 s	4	272 s	2
v19	8	399 s	5	167 s	49	v40	5.5	219 s	3	219 s	4
v20	8	504 s	8	247 s	21	v41	7.5	6 s	2	5 s	6
v21	7.5	252 s	8	194 s	21	Average	6.5	187 s	4.7	137 s	17

fault localization were too inaccurate and caused the solver to first produce CoMSSs that did not include the faulty statements. Despite these negative cases, the results justify the use of statistical fault-localization information: BA+CW ranked the faulty statement first for 9 out of 41 versions, among the top 3 statements in another 8 cases, and at a position less than 10 in all but 3 cases.

The data in Table 1 also allow us to investigate the second part of RQ1, that is, the effect of CW on efficiency. As we discussed in Sect. 2.1, solving wpMAX-SAT problems may be computationally more expensive than solving a pMAX-SAT problem, so the use of CW may negatively affect the efficiency of formula-based debugging. As the table shows, on average BA+CW performs significantly better than BA (137 s versus 187 s, significance level of 0.05). Although these results may seem counterintuitive, we discovered that the extra information provided by the weights can in many cases unintentionally help the solver find CoMSSs more efficiently.

In summary, our results provide initial evidence that CW can improve formula-based debugging, both in terms of accuracy and in terms of efficiency.

RQ2—OFC Versus BA. To investigate RQ2, we compared OFC and BA in terms of efficiency. As we did for RQ1, we ran the two techniques on the 41 faulty versions of tcas and measured their performance. The results are shown in Table 2. The table shows the version ID, the average CPU time spent by BA and OFC, respectively, on each failing input, the average number of iterations (*i.e.*, path expansions) of the OFC algorithm, and the average CPU time spent by OFC in each iteration. For example, for a failing input in tcas.v1, it took, on average, 26 s (BA) and 7 s (OFC) to generate the results, OFC iterated 9 times, and, for each expansion, it took OFC 0.8 s to find all CoMSS solutions.

Overall, OFC was more efficient than BA in 33 out of 41 cases by looking at the second and third columns and could achieve almost 4X speed-ups on average (48 versus 187 s, significance level of 0.05) and over 70X speed-ups in the best case (7 versus 504 s).

To understand the reason of OFC outperforming BA in terms of efficiency, we also present the average number of iterations and time spent in each iteration in OFC. The second and fifth columns in the table clearly show that it took considerably less time for the pMAX-SAT solver to find solutions for formulas generated in one iteration of OFC (4 s) than for formulas generated by BA (187 s). The statistically significant gain of efficiency (significance level of 0.05) is caused, as expected, by the difference in the complexity of the encoded formulas—OFC only encodes the subset of the program relevant to the failure into the formulas passed to the solver, while BA generates a much more complex formula that encodes the semantics of the entire program.

The results in the fourth column of Table 2 indicate that OFC performed 12 iterations per fault, on average. Therefore, the benefits of generating a simpler formula were in some cases (*e.g.*, tcas.v2) outweighed by the cost of solving multiple pMAX-SAT problems during on-demand expansion, thus making OFC less efficient than BA. In fact, comparing the results in the second and third

Table 2. Performance results for BA and OFC on tcas.

Version	BA	OFC	#Iteration	Time per iteration	Version	BA	OFC	#Iteration	Time per iteration
v1	26 s	7 s	9	0.8 s	v22	7 s	6 s	13.2	0.4 s
v2	15 s	38 s	12	3.2 s	v23	15 s	24 s	11	2.1 s
v3	292 s	19 s	14	1.4 s	v24	30 s	7 s	10	0.7 s
v4	11 s	6 s	9.2	0.6 s	v25	297 s	244 s	12	20.3 s
v5	352 s	15 s	13.4	1.1 s	v26	160 s	17 s	13	1.3 s
v6	569 s	17 s	13	1.3 s	v27	443 s	15 s	13.4	1.1 s
v7	484 s	104 s	14.8	7.1 s	v28	41 s	24 s	11.2	2.2 s
v8	21 s	5 s	10	0.5 s	v29	25 s	6 s	9.8	0.6 s
v9	18 s	28 s	12	2.4 s	v30	11 s	24 s	11	2.2 s
v10	125 s	22 s	14	1.6 s	v31	958 s	33 s	10.8	3 s
v11	130 s	11 s	8.4	1.3 s	v32	171 s	14 s	13	1.1 s
v12	22 s	17 s	14.2	1.2 s	v33	79 s	178 s	13	13.7 s
v13	24 s	15 s	13.3	1.2 s	v34	164 s	21 s	13	1.6 s
v14	28 s	20 s	13.8	1.4 s	v35	38 s	22 s	14	1.5 s
v15	14 s	20 s	13.2	1.5 s	v36	19 s	11 s	11.2	1 s
v16	331 s	16 s	13	1.2 s	v37	127 s	251 s	14	18 s
v17	626 s	73 s	14.2	5.1 s	v38	8 s	95 s	16	5.9 s
v18	378 s	96 s	13.4	7.2 s	v39	244 s	213 s	12	17.8 s
v19	399 s	17 s	13.2	1.3 s	v40	219 s	180 s	10.4	17.3 s
v20	504 s	7 s	9.4	0.8 s	v41	6 s	5 s	8.2	0.6 s
v21	252 s	6 s	8.8	0.7 s	Average	187 s	48 s	12	4 s

columns of the table, we can observe that there were 8 cases in which OFC performed worse than BA.

It is also worth noting that our results on the number of iterations performed by OFC provide some evidence that techniques that operate on a single-trace formula (*e.g.,* [7,11]) may compute inaccurate results, even when they encode both data- and control-flow information. Because each expansion adds new constraints that must be taken into account in the analysis, limiting the analysis to a single trace is likely to negatively affect the quality of the results.

Finally, as a sanity check, we examined the sets of suspicious entities reported by the two techniques. This examination confirmed that OFC reports the same sets as BA (*i.e.,* the fault-ranking results for OFC were the same as those for BA, shown in Table 1). That is, it confirmed that OFC is able to build smaller yet conservative formulas and can thus produce the same result as an approach that encodes the whole program.

In summary, our results for RQ2 provide initial, but clear evidence that OFC can considerably improve the efficiency of formula-based debugging without losing effectiveness with respect to an all-paths technique.

RQ3—OFC+CW Versus BA, BA+CW, and OFC. To answer the first part of RQ3, we compared the performance of OFC+CW with that of the other three techniques considered, in terms of both accuracy and efficiency, when run on the 41 tcas versions. For accuracy, we found that the results for OFC+CW, not reported here for brevity, were the same as those listed in the "BA+CW" column of Table 1. This is not surprising, as OFC reports the same sets as BA, as we just discussed, and we expect CW to benefit both techniques in the same way. Therefore, the results show that OFC+CW is as accurate as BA+CW and more accurate than BA and OFC.

To compare the efficiency of the four techniques considered, we measured the average CPU time required by the techniques to process one fault in tcas: BA is 187 s, BA+CW is 137 s, OFC is 48 s, and BA+CW is 36 s. As the result shows, for the cases considered, combining OFC and CW can further reduce the cost of formula-based debugging by 25 % with respect to OFC and by over 80 % with respect to our baseline, BA. (Note that, to assess whether our results depended on the use of a specific solver, we replaced Yices with Z3 and recomputed the average CPU time. As we further discuss in our companion technical report [13], we obtained comparable results also with this alternative solver.) Although these are considerable improvements, it is unclear whether they can actually result in more practically applicable debugging techniques. This is the focus of the second part of RQ3, which aims to assess the potential increase in applicability that our two improvements can provide. To answer this part of RQ3, we ran the techniques considered on our two additional benchmarks: tot_info and Redis.

tot_info Results for RQ3. Unlike tcas, tot_info contains loops, calls to external libraries, and complex floating point computations. (We considered all faults except those directly related to calls to external *system* libraries, which our current implementation does not handle.) Because of the presence of loops, we set an upper bound of 5 to the size of clauses in a CoMSS [13]. (We believe 5 is a reasonable value, as it means that the technique would be able to handle all faults that involve up to 5 statements.) As we discussed in Sect. 3.1, for BA and BA+CW the program formula generated was too large, and the solver was not able to compute the set of CoMSSs within two hours (the time limit we used for the study) for the faults considered. Conversely, OFC and OFC+CW were able to compute a result within the time limit for all faults, which provides initial evidence that our improvements can indeed result in more scalable formula-based techniques. By focusing only on the relevant parts of a failing program and leveraging statistical fault localization, OFC+CW can reduce the complexity of the analysis and successfully diagnose faults that an all-paths technique may not be able to handle. To also assess the accuracy of the produced results, in Table 3 we show the results computed by OFC+CW. The columns in the table show the program version and the number of lines of code a developer would have to examine before getting to the fault in that version. As the table shows, OFC+CW was able to rank all 11 faults within the top 10 statements in the list reported to the developer, and 4 of them at the top of the list.

Table 3. Ranking results of OFC+CW on tot_info.

Version	OFC+CW	Version	OFC+CW	Version	OFC+CW	Version	OFC+CW
tot_info.v1	2	tot_info.v11	3	tot_info.v16	2	tot_info.v22	6
tot_info.v3	1	tot_info.v14	1	tot_info.v18	3	tot_info.v23	8
tot_info.v4	1	tot_info.v15	1	tot_info.v20	3		

Redis Results for RQ3. To further assess the practical applicability of OFC+CW, we ran the techniques considered on our third benchmark, a real-world bug [1] in Redis, which is considerably larger and more complex than tcas and tot_info.

Figure 2 shows an excerpt of the code that contains the bug. The original version of the code fails to check whether the size of the script from the command line is greater than the size of the memory in which it is stored. If the script is too large, the program generates an out-of-boundary memory access and fails.

We inserted assertions that are triggered when a buffer overflow occurs, and applied OFC+CW to the faulty code. Our tool generated the report shown in Fig. 3, which contains five suspicious statements and program locations. The first entry in our report suggests that a control statement should be changed after line 237 of scripting.c to avoid the out-of-boundary access in the next statement. This is also the location where the developers of Redis fixed the bug [1]. Also in this case, we tried to run the all-paths techniques on the module,

```
203 #define LUA_CMD_OBJCACHE_SIZE 32
...
206 int j, argc = lua_gettop(lua);
...
214 static robj *cached_objects[LUA_CMD_OBJCACHE_SIZE];
...
218 if (argc == 0)
...
221   return 1;
222
...
232 for (j = 0; j < argc; j++) {
233   char *obj_s;
234   size_t obj_len;
236   obj_s = (char*)lua_tolstring(lua,j+1,&obj_len);
237   if (obj_s == NULL) break; /* Not a string. */
      /* Try to use a cached object. */
      /* bug fixes */
240-  if (cached_objects[j] &&
          cached_objects_len[j] >= obj_len) {
240+  if (j < LUA_CMD_OBJCACHE_SIZE &&
          cached_objects[j] &&
241+      cached_objects_len[j] >= obj_len) {
...
```

Fig. 2. Excerpt of the bug in Redis.

but they were not successful. Because BA relies on a static model checker that unrolls loops based on a predetermined (low) bound, whereas the loop in the code needs to be executed a large number of times for the bug to be triggered, BA is unable to build a formula for the failure at hand. Unfortunately, increasing the number of times loops are unrolled is not a viable solution, as it causes the number of encoded paths to explode and results in the solver timing out.

Although this is just one bug in one program, we find the results very encouraging. They provide evidence that our approach can improve the applicability of formula-based debugging.

Rank	Source Location	Statement
1	scripting.c:237	if (obj_s == NULL) break;
2	scripting.c:236	obj_s = (char*)lua_tolstring(lua,j+1,&obj_len);
3	scripting.c:232	j++
4	scripting.c:206	int j, argc = lua_gettop(lua);
5	scripting.c:218	if (argc == 0)

Fig. 3. OFC+CW results on Redis.

4   Related Work

Our work is closely related to other formula-based debugging techniques [20]. In particular, OFC builds on BugAssist [15], which encodes a faulty program as an unsatisfiable Boolean formula, uses a MAX-SAT solver to find maximal sets of satisfiable clauses in this formula, and reports the complement sets of clauses as potential causes of the error. The dual of MAX-SAT, that is the problem of computing minimal unsatisfiable subsets (or unsatisfiable cores), can also be leveraged in a similar way to identify potentially faulty statements, as done by Torlak, Vaziri, and Dolby [21]. This kind of techniques have the advantage of performing debugging in a principled way, but tend to rely on exhaustive exploration of (a bounded version of) the program state, which can dramatically limit their scalability. OFC, by operating on demand, can produce results that are at least as good as those produced by these techniques at a fraction of the cost. Moreover, by working on a single path at a time, OFC can directly benefit from various dynamic optimizations. Finally, CW leverages the additional information provided by passing test cases, which are not considered by most existing techniques in this arena.

Another related approach, called Error Invariants, transforms program entities on a single failing execution into a path formula [11]. This technique leverages Craig interpolants to find the points in the failing trace where the state is modified in a way that affects the final outcome of the execution. The statements in these points are then reported as potential causes of the failure. This technique cannot handle control-flow related faults because, as also recognized by the authors, it does not encode control-flow information in its formula. To address this limitation, in followup work the authors developed a version of their approach that encodes partial control-flow information into the path formula [7]; with this extension, their approach can identify conditional statements that may be the cause of a failure. Their approach, however, computes preconditions as the conjunction of all predicates on which a statement is control dependent, which in most cases results in much more complex preconditions than those computed by our OFC technique. In fact, our algorithm only needs to encode the predicate on which the ϕ function is directly dependent. In addition, the two approaches handle potentially faulty conditional statements very differently. OFC considers additional paths induced by a possible modification of the faulty conditionals, and can therefore safely identify additional faulty statements along these paths. Their technique simply reports the identified conditionals to developers, who may thus miss important information and produce a partial, or even incorrect, fix. Because of these substantial (both conceptual and practical) differences between the two techniques, which would make it difficult to perform an apple-to-apple comparison, we did not perform a direct comparison between OFC and their approach in our empirical study.

Our work is also related to statistical fault localization techniques (*e.g.,* [3,5,14,17,18]). Although efficient, these techniques often produce long lists of program entities with no context information, which can limit their usefulness [19]. In CW, we use the results of statistical fault localization as a starting point to inform formula-based debugging and guide the analysis. As our results show, these can result in considerably more accurate (and more informative) fault-localization results.

Other approaches for identifying potentially faulty statements are static and dynamic slicing [4,23] and delta debugging [24]. These approaches are orthogonal to ours and to formula-based debugging techniques in general, and can be leveraged to achieve further improvements.

Finally, automated repair techniques (*e.g.,* [10,12,16]) are related to our work. However, these techniques are mostly orthogonal to fault-localization approaches, as they require some form of fault localization as a starting point.

(One exception is Angelic Debugging, by Chandra and colleagues [6], which combines fault localization and a limited form of repair.) In this sense, we believe that the information produced by our approach could be used to guide the automated repair generation performed by these techniques, which is something that we plan to investigate in future work.

5   Conclusion and Future Work

We presented clause weighting (CW) and on-demand formula computation (OFC), two ways to improve existing formula-based debugging techniques and mitigate some of their limitations. CW incorporates the (previously ignored) information provided by passing test cases into formula-based debugging techniques to improve their accuracy. OFC is a novel formula-based debugging algorithm that, by operating on demand, can analyze a small fraction of a faulty program and yet compute the same results that would be computed analyzing all paths of the program, at a much higher cost.

To evaluate CW and OFC, we empirically assessed the improvements that they can achieve over a formula-based debugging approach. Our results show that formula-based debugging remains an expensive approach with limited scalability (mostly because of the cost of solving MAX-SAT problems). Nevertheless, the fact that CW and OFC can considerably improve the accuracy and efficiency of this approach motivate further research in this area.

In future work, we will perform additional studies, including user studies, to further show the usefulness of our approach. We will also apply our on-demand algorithm to other types of formula-based techniques, such as those based on single-trace analysis (e.g., [7,11]), to assess whether we can achieve similar, or even better improvements for these techniques. We will investigate approaches that can further address the inherently limited scalability of formula-based debugging. In particular, we will consider two research directions: (1) further simplifying the constructed MAX-SAT problems to decrease the cost of solving them and (2) trying to decompose the debugging problem into several subproblems (e.g., at the procedure level) that can be solved modularly. Finally, we will investigate whether formula-based debugging techniques can help automated program repair. Intuitively, the clauses in the CoMSSs produced by the former should be able to inform and guide the latter in finding or synthesizing suitable repairs.

Acknowledgments. This work was partially supported by NSF grants CCF1320783 and CCF1161821, and by funding from Google, IBM Research, and Microsoft Research.

References

1. LUA_OBJCACHE segfault bug in Redis, July 2016. https://github.com/antirez/redis/commit/ea0e2524aae1bbd0fa6bd29e1867dc1ca133bfa5
2. Test cases for scripting.c in Redis, July 2016. https://github.com/antirez/redis/blob/7f772355f403a1be9592e60f606d457d117fccc5/tests/unit/scripting.tcl
3. Abreu, R., Zoeteweij, P., Gemund, A.J.C.V.: An evaluation of similarity coefficients for software fault localization. In: Proceedings of the 12th Pacific Rim International Symposium on Dependable Computing, pp. 39–46 (2006)
4. Agrawal, H., Horgan, J.R.: Dynamic program slicing. In: Proceedings of the 1990 ACM SIGPLAN Conference on Programming Language Design and Implementation, pp. 246–256 (1990)
5. Artzi, S., Dolby, J., Tip, F., Pistoia, M.: Directed test generation for effective fault localization. In: Proceedings of the 19th International Symposium on Software Testing and Analysis, pp. 49–60 (2010)
6. Chandra, S., Torlak, E., Barman, S., Bodik, R.: Angelic debugging. In: Proceedings of the 33rd International Conference on Software Engineering, pp. 121–130 (2011)
7. Christ, J., Ermis, E., Schäf, M., Wies, T.: Flow-sensitive fault localization. In: Giacobazzi, R., Berdine, J., Mastroeni, I. (eds.) VMCAI 2013. LNCS, vol. 7737, pp. 189–208. Springer, Heidelberg (2013). doi:10.1007/978-3-642-35873-9_13
8. Clarke, E., Kroening, D., Lerda, F.: A tool for checking ANSI-C programs. In: Jensen, K., Podelski, A. (eds.) TACAS 2004. LNCS, vol. 2988, pp. 168–176. Springer, Heidelberg (2004). doi:10.1007/978-3-540-24730-2_15
9. Cytron, R., Ferrante, J., Rosen, B.K., Wegman, M.N., Zadeck, F.K.: Efficiently computing static single assignment form and the control dependence graph. ACM Trans. Program. Lang. Syst. **13**(4), 451–490 (1991)
10. Dallmeier, V., Zeller, A., Meyer, B.: Generating fixes from object behavior anomalies. In: Proceedings of the 24th IEEE International Conference on Automated Software Engineering, pp. 550–554. IEEE Computer Society (2009)
11. Ermis, E., Schäf, M., Wies, T.: Error invariants. In: Giannakopoulou, D., Méry, D. (eds.) FM 2012. LNCS, vol. 7436, pp. 187–201. Springer, Heidelberg (2012). doi:10.1007/978-3-642-32759-9_17
12. Jeffrey, D., Feng, M., Gupta, N., Gupta, R.: BugFix: a learning-based tool to assist developers in fixing bugs. In: Proceedings of the 17th International Conference on Program Comprehension, pp. 70–79 (2009)
13. Jin, W., Orso, A.: Improving efficiency and scalability of formula-based debugging. Technical report, Georgia Institute of Technology, College of Computing, September 2014. https://arxiv.org/abs/1409.1989
14. Jones, J.A., Harrold, M.J., Stasko, J.: Visualization of test information to assist fault localization. In: Proceedings of the 24th International Conference on Software Engineering, pp. 467–477 (2002)
15. Jose, M., Majumdar, R.: Cause clue clauses: error localization using maximum satisfiability. In: Proceedings of the 2011 ACM SIGPLAN Conference on Programming Language Design and Implementation, pp. 437–446 (2011)
16. Le Goues, C., Nguyen, T., Forrest, S., Weimer, W.: GenProg: a generic method for automatic software repair. IEEE Trans. Softw. Eng. **38**(1), 54–72 (2012)
17. Liblit, B., Aiken, A., Zheng, A.X., Jordan, M.I.: Bug isolation via remote program sampling. In: Proceedings of the 2003 ACM SIGPLAN Conference on Programming Language Design and Implementation, pp. 141–154 (2003)

18. Naish, L., Lee, H.J., Ramamohanarao, K.: A model for spectra-based software diagnosis. ACM Trans. Softw. Eng. Methodol. **20**(3), 11:1–11:32 (2011)
19. Parnin, C., Orso, A.: Are automated debugging techniques actually helping programmers? In: Proceedings of the 2011 International Symposium on Software Testing and Analysis, Toronto, Canada, pp. 199–209, July 2011
20. Roychoudhury, A., Chandra, S.: Formula-based software debugging. Commun. ACM **59**(7), 68–77 (2016)
21. Torlak, E., Vaziri, M., Dolby, J.: MemSAT: checking axiomatic specifications of memory models. In: Proceedings of the 2010 ACM SIGPLAN Conference on Programming Language Design and Implementation, pp. 341–350 (2010)
22. Tsankov, P., Jin, W., Orso, A., Sinha, S.: Execution hijacking: improving dynamic analysis by flying off course. In: Proceedings of the 4th International Conference on Software Testing, pp. 200–209. IEEE (2011)
23. Weiser, M.: Program slicing. In: Proceedings of the 5th International Conference on Software Engineering, pp. 439–449 (1981)
24. Zeller, A., Hildebrandt, R.: Simplifying and isolating failure-inducing input. IEEE Trans. Softw. Eng. **28**(2), 183–200 (2002)
25. Zhang, Z., Chan, W.K., Tse, T.H., Jiang, B., Wang, X.: Capturing propagation of infected program states. In: The 7th Joint Meeting of the European Software Engineering Conference and the ACM SIGSOFT Symposium on the Foundations of Software Engineering, pp. 43–52 (2009)

Improving Priority Promotion for Parity Games

Massimo Benerecetti[1], Daniele Dell'Erba[1], and Fabio Mogavero[2]([⊠])

[1] Università degli Studi di Napoli Federico II, Naples, Italy
[2] Oxford University, Oxford, UK
fabio.mogavero@cs.ox.ac.uk

Abstract. *Parity games* are two-player infinite-duration games on graphs that play a crucial role in various fields of theoretical computer science. Finding efficient algorithms to solve these games in practice is widely acknowledged as a core problem in formal verification, as it leads to efficient solutions of the model-checking and satisfiability problems of expressive temporal logics, *e.g.*, the modal μCALCULUS. Their solution can be reduced to the problem of identifying sets of positions of the game, called dominions, in each of which a player can force a win by remaining in the set forever. Recently, a novel technique to compute dominions, called *priority promotion*, has been proposed, which is based on the notions of quasi dominion, a relaxed form of dominion, and dominion space. The underlying framework is general enough to accommodate different instantiations of the solution procedure, whose correctness is ensured by the nature of the space itself. In this paper we propose a new such instantiation, called *region recovery*, that tries to reduce the possible exponential behaviours exhibited by the original method in the worst case. The resulting procedure not only often outperforms the original priority promotion approach, but so far no exponential worst case is known.

1 Introduction

The abstract concept of *game* has proved to be a fruitful metaphor in theoretical computer science [1]. Several *decision problems* can, indeed, be encoded as *path-forming games on graph*, where a player willing to achieve a certain goal, usually the verification of some property on the plays derived from the original problem, has to face an opponent whose aim is to pursue the exact opposite task. One of the most prominent instances of this connection is represented by the notion of *parity game* [18], a simple two-player turn-based perfect-information game played on directed graphs, whose nodes are labelled with natural numbers called *priorities*. The goal of the first (*resp.*, second) player, *a.k.a.*, even (*resp.*, odd) player, is to force a play π, whose maximal priority occurring infinitely often along π is of even (*resp.*, odd) parity. The importance of these games is due to the numerous applications in the area of system specification, verification, and synthesis, where it is used as algorithmic back-end of satisfiability and model-checking procedures for temporal logics [6,8,16], and as a core for several techniques employed in automata theory [7,10,15,17]. In particular, it has been proved to be linear-time interreducible with the model-checking problem for the

© Springer International Publishing AG 2016
R. Bloem and E. Arbel (Eds.): HVC 2016, LNCS 10028, pp. 117–133, 2016.
DOI: 10.1007/978-3-319-49052-6_8

modal μCALCULUS [8] and it is closely related to other games of infinite duration, such as *mean payoff* [5,11], *discounted payoff* [24], *simple stochastic* [4], and *energy* [3] games. Besides the practical importance, parity games are also interesting from a computational complexity point of view, since their solution problem is one of the few inhabitants of the UPTIME ∩ COUPTIME class [12]. That result improves the NPTIME ∩ CONPTIME membership [8], which easily follows from the property of *memoryless determinacy* [7,18]. Still open is the question about the membership in PTIME. The literature on the topic is reach of algorithms for solving parity games, which can be mainly classified into two families. The first one contains the algorithms that, by employing a *divide et impera* approach, recursively decompose the problem into subproblems, whose solutions are then suitably assembled to obtain the desired result. In this category fall, for example, *Zielonka's recursive algorithm* [23] and its *dominion decomposition* [14] and *big step* [19] improvements. The second family, instead, groups together those algorithms that try to compute a winning strategy for the two players on the entire game. The principal members of this category are represented by *Jurdziński's progress measure* algorithm [13] and the *strategy improvement* approaches [20–22].

Recently, a new *divide et impera* solution algorithm, called *priority promotion* (PP, for short), has been proposed in [2], which is fully based on the decomposition of the winning regions into *dominions*. The idea is to find a dominion for some of the two players and then remove it from the game, thereby allowing for a recursive solution. The important difference *w.r.t.* the other two approaches [14,19] based on the same notion is that these procedures only look for dominions of a certain size in order to speed up classic Zielonka's algorithm in the worst case. Consequently, they strongly rely on this algorithm for their completeness. On the contrary, the PP procedure autonomously computes dominions of any size, by suitably composing quasi dominions, a weaker notion of dominion. Intuitively, a *quasi dominion* Q for player $\alpha \in \{0, 1\}$ is a set of vertices from each of which player α can enforce a winning play that never leaves the region, unless one of the following two conditions holds: *(i)* the opponent $\overline{\alpha}$ can escape from Q (*i.e.*, there is an edge from a vertex of $\overline{\alpha}$ exiting from Q) or *(ii)* the only choice for player α itself is to exit from Q (*i.e.*, no edge from a vertex of α remains in Q). A crucial feature of quasi dominion is that they can be ordered by assigning to each of them a priority corresponding to an underapproximation of the best value for α the opponent $\overline{\alpha}$ can be forced to visit along any play exiting from it. Indeed, under suitable and easy to check assumptions, a higher priority quasi α-dominion Q_1 and a lower priority one Q_2, can be merged into a single quasi α-dominion of the higher priority, thus improving the approximation for Q_2. This merging operation is called a priority promotion of Q_2 to Q_1. The PP solution procedure has been shown to be very effective in practice and to often significantly outperform all other solvers. Moreover, it also improves the space complexity of the best know algorithm by an exponential factor, since it only needs $O(n \cdot \log k)$ space against the $O(k \cdot n \cdot \log n)$ required by Jurdziński's approach [13], where n and k are, respectively, the numbers of vertexes and priorities of the game. Unfortunately, the PP algorithm also exhibits exponential behaviours on a simple family of games. This is due to the fact that, in general, promotions to higher priorities requires resetting previously computed quasi dominions at lower ones.

In order to mitigate the problem, we propose in this paper a new algorithm, called RR for *region recovery*, which is built on top of PP and is based on a form of conservation property of quasi dominions. This property provides sufficient conditions for a subset a quasi α-dominion to be still a quasi α-dominion. By exploiting this property, the RR algorithm can significantly reduce the execution of the resetting phase, which is now limited to the cases when the conservation property is not guaranteed to hold. For the resulting procedure no exponential worst case has been found yet. Experiments on randomly generated games also show that the new approach performs significantly better than PP in practice, while still preserving the same space complexity.

2   Preliminaries

Let us first briefly recall the notation and basic definitions concerning parity games that expert readers can simply skip. We refer to [1, 23] for a comprehensive presentation of the subject.

Given a partial function $f : A \rightharpoonup B$, by $\mathsf{dom}(f) \subseteq A$ and $\mathsf{rng}(f) \subseteq B$ we denote the domain and range of f, respectively. In addition, $\uplus$ denotes the *completion operator* that, taken f and another partial function $g : A \rightharpoonup B$, returns the partial function $f \uplus g \triangleq (f \setminus \mathsf{dom}(g)) \cup g : A \rightharpoonup B$, which is equal to g on its domain and assumes the same values of f on the remaining part of A.

A two-player turn-based *arena* is a tuple $\mathcal{A} = \langle \mathrm{Ps}^\circ, \mathrm{Ps}^1, Mv \rangle$, with $\mathrm{Ps}^\circ \cap \mathrm{Ps}^1 = \emptyset$ and $\mathrm{Ps} \triangleq \mathrm{Ps}^\circ \cup \mathrm{Ps}^1$, such that $\langle \mathrm{Ps}, Mv \rangle$ is a finite directed graph. Ps° (*resp.*, Ps^1) is the set of positions of player 0 (*resp.*, 1) and $Mv \subseteq \mathrm{Ps} \times \mathrm{Ps}$ is a left-total relation describing all possible moves. A *path* in $V \subset \mathrm{Ps}$ is a finite or infinite sequence $\pi \in \mathrm{Pth}(V)$ of positions in V compatible with the move relation, *i.e.*, $(\pi_i, \pi_{i+1}) \in Mv$, for all $i \in [0, |\pi| - 1[$. For a finite path π, with $\mathsf{lst}(\pi)$ we denote the last position of π. A positional *strategy* for player $\alpha \in \{0, 1\}$ on $V \subseteq \mathrm{Ps}$ is a partial function $\sigma_\alpha \in \mathrm{Str}^\alpha(V) \subseteq (V \cap \mathrm{Ps}^\alpha) \rightharpoonup V$, mapping each α-position $v \in \mathsf{dom}(\sigma_\alpha)$ to position $\sigma_\alpha(v)$ compatible with the move relation, *i.e.*, $(v, \sigma_\alpha(v)) \in Mv$. With $\mathrm{Str}^\alpha(V)$ we denote the set of all α-strategies on V. A *play* in $V \subseteq \mathrm{Ps}$ from a position $v \in V$ *w.r.t.* a pair of strategies $(\sigma_0, \sigma_1) \in \mathrm{Str}^\circ(V) \times \mathrm{Str}^1(V)$, called $((\sigma_0, \sigma_1), v)$-*play*, is a path $\pi \in \mathrm{Pth}(V)$ such that $\pi_0 = v$ and, for all $i \in [0, |\pi| - 1[$, if $\pi_i \in \mathrm{Ps}^\circ$ then $\pi_{i+1} = \sigma^\circ(\pi_i)$ else $\pi_{i+1} = \sigma^1(\pi_i)$. The *play function* $\mathsf{play} : (\mathrm{Str}^\circ(V) \times \mathrm{Str}^1(V)) \times V \to \mathrm{Pth}(V)$ returns, for each position $v \in V$ and pair of strategies $(\sigma_0, \sigma_1) \in \mathrm{Str}^\circ(V) \times \mathrm{Str}^1(V)$, the maximal $((\sigma_0, \sigma_1), v)$-play $\mathsf{play}((\sigma^\circ, \sigma^1), v)$.

A *parity game* is a tuple $\eth = \langle \mathcal{A}, \mathrm{Pr}, \mathsf{pr} \rangle$, where $\mathcal{A}$ is an arena, $\mathrm{Pr} \subset \mathbb{N}$ is a finite set of priorities, and $\mathsf{pr} : \mathrm{Ps} \to \mathrm{Pr}$ is a *priority function* assigning a priority to each position. We denote with PG the class of parity games. The priority function can be naturally extended to games, sets of positions, and paths as follows: $\mathsf{pr}(\eth) \triangleq \max_{v \in \mathrm{Ps}} \mathsf{pr}(v)$; for a set of positions $V \subseteq \mathrm{Ps}$, we set

$\mathsf{pr}(V) \triangleq \max_{v \in V} \mathsf{pr}(v)$; for a path $\pi \in \mathrm{Pth}$, we set $\mathsf{pr}(\pi) \triangleq \max_{i \in [0,|\pi|[} \mathsf{pr}(\pi_i)$, if π is finite, and $\mathsf{pr}(\pi) \triangleq \limsup_{i \in \mathbb{N}} \mathsf{pr}(\pi_i)$, otherwise. A set of positions $V \subseteq \mathrm{Ps}$ is an α-*dominion*, with $\alpha \in \{0, 1\}$, if there exists an α-strategy $\sigma_\alpha \in \mathrm{Str}^\alpha(V)$ such that, for all $\overline{\alpha}$-strategies $\sigma_{\overline{\alpha}} \in \mathrm{Str}^{\overline{\alpha}}(V)$ and positions $v \in V$, the induced play $\pi = \mathsf{play}((\sigma_0, \sigma_1), v)$ is infinite and $\mathsf{pr}(\pi) \equiv_2 \alpha$. In other words, σ_α only induces on V infinite plays whose maximal priority visited infinitely often has parity α. The maximal α-dominion in a game, denoted Wn_α, is called winning region of player α. By $\eth \backslash V$ we denote the maximal subgame of $\eth$ with set of positions Ps' contained in $\mathrm{Ps} \backslash V$ and move relation Mv' equal to the restriction of Mv to Ps'.

The α-predecessor of V, in symbols $\mathsf{pre}^\alpha(V) \triangleq \{v \in \mathrm{Ps}^\alpha : Mv(v) \cap V \neq \emptyset\} \cup \{v \in \mathrm{Ps}^{\overline{\alpha}} : Mv(v) \subseteq V\}$, collects the positions from which player α can force the game to reach some position in V with a single move. The α-attractor $\mathsf{atr}^\alpha(V)$ generalises the notion of α-predecessor $\mathsf{pre}^\alpha(V)$ to an arbitrary number of moves. Thus, it corresponds to the least fix-point of that operator. When $V = \mathsf{atr}^\alpha(V)$, we say that V is α-maximal. Intuitively, V is α-maximal if player α cannot force any position outside V to enter this set. For such a V, the set of positions of the subgame $\eth \backslash V$ is precisely $\mathrm{Ps} \backslash V$. Finally, the α-*escape* of V, formally $\mathsf{esc}^\alpha(V) \triangleq \mathsf{pre}^\alpha(\mathrm{Ps} \backslash V) \cap V$, contains the positions in V from which α can leave V in one move. The dual notion of α-*interior*, defined as $\mathsf{int}^\alpha(V) \triangleq (V \cap \mathrm{Ps}^\alpha) \backslash \mathsf{esc}^\alpha(V)$, contains the α-positions from which α cannot escape with a single move, while the notion of α-*stay*, defined as $\mathsf{stay}^\alpha(V) \triangleq (V \cap \mathrm{Ps}^\alpha) \backslash \mathsf{esc}^{\overline{\alpha}}(V)$, denotes the α-positions from which α has a move to remain in V.

3   Quasi Dominion Approach

The priority promotion algorithm proposed in [2] attacks the problem of solving a parity game $\eth$ by computing one of its dominions D, for some player $\alpha \in \{0, 1\}$, at a time. Indeed, once the α-attractor $\mathrm{D}^\star$ of D is removed from $\eth$, the smaller game $\eth \backslash \mathrm{D}^\star$ is obtained, whose positions are winning for one player iff they are winning for the same player in the original game. This allows for decomposing the problem of solving a parity game to that of iteratively finding its dominions [14].

In order to solve the dominion problem, the idea described in [2] is to introduce a much weaker notion than that of dominion, called *quasi dominion*, which satisfies, under suitable conditions, a composition property that eventually brings to the construction of a dominion. Intuitively, a quasi α-dominion Q is a set of positions on which player α has a *witness strategy* σ_α, whose induced plays either remain inside Q forever and are winning for α or can exit from Q passing through a specific set of escape positions.

Definition 1 (Quasi Dominion [2]). *Let $\eth \in \mathrm{PG}$ be a game and $\alpha \in \{0, 1\}$ a player. A non-empty set of positions $Q \subseteq \mathrm{Ps}$ is a* quasi α-dominion *in $\eth$ if there exists an α-strategy $\sigma_\alpha \in \mathrm{Str}^\alpha(Q)$, called α-witness for Q, such that, for all $\overline{\alpha}$-strategies $\sigma_{\overline{\alpha}} \in \mathrm{Str}^{\overline{\alpha}}(Q)$, with $\mathsf{int}^{\overline{\alpha}}(Q) \subseteq \mathsf{dom}(\sigma_{\overline{\alpha}})$, and positions $v \in Q$, the induced play $\pi = \mathsf{play}((\sigma_0, \sigma_1), v)$ satisfies $\mathsf{pr}(\pi) \equiv_2 \alpha$, if π is infinite, and $\mathsf{lst}(\pi) \in \mathsf{esc}^{\overline{\alpha}}(Q)$, otherwise.*

Observe that, if all the plays induced by the witness σ_α remain in the set Q forever, this is actually an α-dominion and, therefore, a subset of the winning region Wn_α of α, with σ_α the projection over Q of some α-winning strategy on the entire game. In this case, the escape set of Q is empty, *i.e.*, $\mathrm{esc}^{\overline{\alpha}}(Q) = \emptyset$, and Q is said to be α-*closed*. In general, however, a quasi α-dominion Q that is not an α-dominion, *i.e.*, such that $\mathrm{esc}^{\overline{\alpha}}(Q) \neq \emptyset$, need not be a subset of Wn_α and it is called α-*open*. Indeed, in this case, some induced play may not satisfy the winning condition for that player once exited from Q, *e.g.*, by visiting a cycle containing a position with maximal priority of parity $\overline{\alpha}$. The set of triples $(Q, \sigma, \alpha) \in 2^{\mathrm{Ps}} \times \mathrm{Str} \times \{0,1\}$, where Q is a quasi α-dominion having σ as one of its α-witnesses, is denoted by QD, and is partitioned into the sets QD^- and QD^+ of open and closed quasi α-dominion triples, respectively.

Similarly to the other *divide et impera* techniques proposed in the literature, the one reported in [2], called PP, does not make any algorithmic use of the witness strategy σ_α associated with a quasi dominion Q, as this notion is only employed in the correctness proof. In this work, instead, we strongly exploit the effective computability of such a witness in order to considerably alleviate the collateral effects of a *reset operation* required by PP to ensure the soundness of the approach, which is also responsible for the exponential worst cases. Indeed, this algorithm needs to forget previously computed partial results after each compositions of two quasi-dominions, since the information computed during the entire process cannot ensure that these results can be still correctly used in the search for a dominion. In this work, instead, we exploit the following simple observation on the witness strategies, formally reported in Lemma 1, to determine which partial results can be safely preserved.

In general, quasi α-dominions are not closed under restriction. For example, consider the quasi 1-dominion $Q^\star = \{\mathsf{a}, \mathsf{c}, \mathsf{d}\}$ of Fig. 1 with unique 1-witness strategy $\sigma^\star = \{\mathsf{c} \mapsto \mathsf{a}, \mathsf{d} \mapsto \mathsf{c}\}$ and its subset $Q = \{\mathsf{d}\}$. It is quite immediate to see that Q is not a quasi 1-dominion, since $\mathrm{esc}^o(Q) = \emptyset$, but player 1 does not have a strategy that induces infinite 1-winning plays that remain in Q. Indeed, $\sigma^\star$ requires player 1 to exit from Q by going from d to c. On the contrary, the subset $Q = \{\mathsf{c}, \mathsf{d}\}$ is still a 1-dominion with 1-witness strategy $\sigma = \{\mathsf{d} \mapsto \mathsf{c}\} = \sigma^\star \!\upharpoonright\! \mathrm{stay}^1(Q)$, since $\mathrm{esc}^o(Q) = \{\mathsf{c}\}$. Hence, the restriction σ of $\sigma^\star$ to $\mathrm{stay}^1(Q) = \{\mathsf{d}\}$ is still a well-defined strategy on Q. Inspired by this observation, we provide the following sufficient criterion for a subset Q of a quasi α-dominion $Q^\star$ to be still a quasi α-dominion.

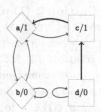

Fig. 1. Witness strategy

Lemma 1 (Witness Strategy). *Given a quasi α-dominion $Q^\star$ having $\sigma^\star \in \mathrm{Str}^\alpha(Q^\star)$ as α-witness and a subset of positions $Q \subseteq Q^\star$, the restriction $\sigma \triangleq \sigma^\star \!\upharpoonright\! \mathrm{stay}^\alpha(Q)$ is an α-witness for Q iff $\sigma \in \mathrm{Str}^\alpha(Q)$.*

The proof-idea behind this lemma is very simple. Any infinite play induced by the restriction of σ on Q is necessarily winning for player α, since it is coherent with the original α-witness $\sigma^\star$ of $Q^\star$ as well. Now, if $\sigma \in \text{Str}^\alpha(Q)$, we are also sure that any finite play ends in $\text{esc}^{\overline{\alpha}}(Q)$, as required by the definition of quasi dominion. Therefore, σ is an α-witness for Q, which is, then, a quasi α-dominion. On the other hand, if $\sigma \notin \text{Str}^\alpha(Q)$, there exists a finite play induced by σ that does not terminate in $\text{esc}^{\overline{\alpha}}(Q)$. Hence, σ is not an α-witness. In this case, we cannot ensure that Q is a quasi α-dominion.

The priority promotion algorithm explores a partial order, whose elements, called *states*, record information about the open quasi dominions computed along the way. The initial state of the search is the top element of the order, where the quasi dominions are initialised to the sets of positions with the same priority. At each step, a new quasi α-dominion Q together with

---

Algorithm 1: The Searcher.

signature $\text{src}_{\mathcal{D}} : S_{\mathcal{D}} \to \text{QD}^+_{\partial_{\mathcal{D}}}$
function $\text{src}_{\mathcal{D}}(s)$

1    $(Q, \sigma, \alpha) \leftarrow \Re_{\mathcal{D}}(s)$
2   **if** $(Q, \sigma, \alpha) \in \text{QD}^+_{\partial_{\mathcal{D}}}$ **then**
3 | **return** (Q, σ, α)
   else
4 | **return** $\text{src}_{\mathcal{D}}(s \downarrow_{\mathcal{D}} (Q, \sigma, \alpha))$

---

one of its possible α-witnesses σ is extracted from the current state, by means of a *query* operator $\Re$, and used to compute a successor state, by means of a *successor* operator $\downarrow$, if Q is open. If, on the other hand, it is closed, the search is over. Algorithm 1 implements the dominion search procedure $\text{src}_{\mathcal{D}}$. A *compatibility relation* $\succ$ connects the query and the successor operators. The relation holds between states of the partial order and the qua si dominions triples that can be extracted by the query operator. Such a relation defines the domain of the successor operator. The partial order, together with the query and successor operator and the compatibility relation, forms what is called a *dominion space*.

Definition 2 (Dominion Space). *A dominion space for a game $\partial \in \text{PG}$ is a tuple $\mathcal{D} \triangleq \langle \partial, \mathcal{S}, \succ, \Re, \downarrow \rangle$, where (1) $\mathcal{S} \triangleq \langle \text{S}, \top, \prec \rangle$ is a well-founded partial order w.r.t. $\prec \subset \text{S} \times \text{S}$ with distinguished element $\top \in \text{S}$, (2) $\succ \subseteq \mathcal{S} \times \text{QD}^-_\partial$ is the compatibility relation, (3) $\Re : \text{S} \to \text{QD}_\partial$ is the query operator mapping each element $s \in \text{S}$ to a quasi dominion triple $(Q, \sigma, \alpha) \triangleq \Re(s) \in \text{QD}_\partial$ such that, if $(Q, \sigma, \alpha) \in \text{QD}^-_\partial$ then $s \succ (Q, \alpha, \sigma)$, and (4) $\downarrow : \succ \to \text{S}$ is the successor operator mapping each pair $(s, (Q, \sigma, \alpha)) \in \succ$ to the element $s^\star \triangleq s \downarrow (Q, \sigma, \alpha) \in \text{S}$ with $s^\star \prec s$.*

The notion of dominion space is quite general and can be instantiated in different ways, by providing specific query and successor operators. In [2], indeed, it is shown that the search procedure $\text{src}_{\mathcal{D}}$ is sound and complete on any dominion space $\mathcal{D}$. In addition, its time complexity is linear in the *execution depth* of the dominion space, namely the length of the longest chain in the underlying partial order compatible with the successor operator, while its space complexity is only logarithmic in the space *size*, since only one state at the time needs to be maintained. A specific instantiation of dominion space, called PP *dominion space*, is the one proposed and studied in [2]. In the next section, we propose a different one, called RR *dominion space*, which crucially exploits Lemma 1 in order to prevent a considerable amount of useless reset operations after each quasi dominion composition, to the point that it does not seem obvious whether an exponential lower bound even exists for this new approach.

4   Priority Promotion with Region Recovery

In order to instantiate a dominion space, we need to define a suitable query function to compute quasi dominions and a successor operator to ensure progress in the search for a closed dominion. The priority promotion algorithm proceeds as follows. The input game is processed in descending order of priority. At each step, a subgame of the entire game, obtained by removing the quasi domains previously computed at higher priorities, is considered. At each priority of parity α, a quasi α-domain Q is extracted by the query operator from the current subgame. If Q is closed in the entire game, the search stops and returns Q as result. Otherwise, a successor state in the underlying partial order is computed by the successor operator, depending on whether Q is open in the current subgame or not. In the first case, the quasi α-dominion is removed from the current subgame and the search restarts on the new subgame that can only contain positions with lower priorities. In the second case, Q is merged together with some previously computed quasi α-dominion with higher priority. Being a dominion space well-ordered, the search is guaranteed to eventually terminate and return a closed quasi dominion. The procedure requires the solution of two crucial problems: *(a) extracting a quasi dominion* from a subgame and *(b) merging together two quasi α-dominions* to obtain a bigger, possibly closed, quasi α-dominion.

Solving problem *(b)* is not trivial, since quasi α-dominions are not, in general, closed under union. Consider the example in Fig. 2. Both $Q_1 = \{a, c\}$ and $Q_2 = \{b, d\}$ are quasi 0-dominions. Indeed, $\sigma_1 = \{c \mapsto c\}$ and $\sigma_2 = \{d \mapsto d\}$ are the corresponding 0-witnesses. However, their union $Q \triangleq Q_1 \cup Q_2$ is not a quasi 0-dominion, since the 1-strategy $\sigma = \{a \mapsto b, b \mapsto a\}$ forces player 0 to lose along any infinite play starting from either a or b.

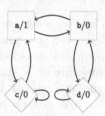

Fig. 2. Quasi dominions.

A solution to both problems relies on the definition of a specific class of quasi dominions, called *regions*. An α-region R of a game $\eth$ is a special form of quasi α-dominion of $\eth$ with the additional requirement that all the positions in $\mathsf{esc}^{\overline{\alpha}}(R)$ have the maximal priority $p \triangleq \mathsf{pr}(\eth) \equiv_2 \alpha$ in $\eth$. In this case, we say that α-region R has priority p. As a consequence, if the opponent $\overline{\alpha}$ can escape from the α-region R, it must visit a position with the highest priority in it, which is of parity α.

Definition 3 (Region [2]). *A quasi α-dominion R is an α-region in $\eth$ if $\mathsf{pr}(\eth) \equiv_2 \alpha$ and all the positions in $\mathsf{esc}^{\overline{\alpha}}(R)$ have priority $\mathsf{pr}(\eth)$, i.e., $\mathsf{esc}^{\overline{\alpha}}(R) \subseteq \mathsf{pr}^{-1}(\mathsf{pr}(\eth))$.*

Observe that, in any parity game, an α-region always exists, for some $\alpha \in \{0, 1\}$. In particular, the set of positions of maximal priority in the game always forms an α-region, with α equal to the parity of that maximal priority. In addition, the α-attractor of an α-region is always an (α-maximal) α-region. A closed α-region in a game is clearly an α-dominion in that game. These observations give us an easy and efficient way to extract a quasi dominion from every subgame: collect the α-attractor of the positions with maximal priority p in the subgame, where $p \equiv_2 \alpha$, and assign p as priority of the resulting region R. This priority, called *measure* of R, intuitively corresponds to an under-approximation of the best priority player α can force the opponent $\overline{\alpha}$ to visit along any play exiting from R.

Proposition 1 (Region Extension [2]**).** *Let $\partial \in$ PG be a game and $R \subseteq$ Ps an α-region in ∂. Then, $R^{\star} \triangleq \mathrm{atr}^{\alpha}(R)$ is an α-maximal α-region in ∂.*

A solution to the second problem, the merging operation, is obtained as follows. Given an α-region R in some game ∂ and an α-dominion D in a subgame of ∂ that does not contain R itself, the two sets are merged together, if the only moves exiting from $\overline{\alpha}$-positions of D in the entire game lead to higher priority α-regions and R has the lowest priority among them. The priority of R is called the *best escape priority* of D for $\overline{\alpha}$. The correctness of this merging operation is established by the following proposition.

Proposition 2 (Region Merging [2]**).** *Let $\partial \in$ PG be a game, $R \subseteq$ Ps an α-region, and $D \subseteq \mathrm{Ps}_{\partial \setminus R}$ an α-dominion in the subgame $\partial \setminus R$. Then, $R^{\star} \triangleq R \cup D$ is an α-region in ∂. Moreover, if both R and D are α-maximal in ∂ and $\partial \setminus R$, respectively, then $R^{\star}$ is α-maximal in ∂ as well.*

The merging operation is implemented by promoting all the positions of α-dominion D to the measure of R, thus improving the measure of D. For this reason, it is called a *priority promotion*. In [2] it is shown that, after a promotion to some measure p, the regions with measure lower than p might need to be destroyed, by resetting all the contained positions to their original priority. This necessity derives from the fact that the new promoted region may attract positions from lower ones, thereby potentially invalidating their status as regions. Indeed, in some cases, the player that wins by remaining in the region may even change from α to $\overline{\alpha}$. As a consequence, the reset operation

	1	2	3	4	5
8	a↓	=	=	a,b,c,d,h,i,j↓	=
7	j,k↓	=	=		
5	b↓	=	b,c,e,f,g,h↓		
4	c,d↓	=		k↓	=
3	e,f↓	e,f,g,h↑₅	d↓	e,f↓	e,f,g
1	g,h↑₃			g↑₃	
0			i↑₈		

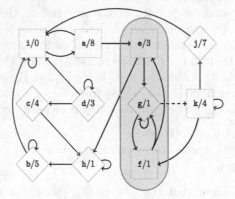

Fig. 3. Running example.

is, in general, unavoidable. The original priority promotion algorithm applies the reset operation to all the lower priority regions. As shown in [2], the reset operation is the main source of the exponential behaviours of the approach. We shall propose here a different approach that, based on the result of Lemma 1, can drastically reduce the number of resets needed.

Figure 3 illustrates the dominion search procedure on an example game. Diamond shaped positions belong to player 0 and square shaped ones to opponent 1. Each cell of the table contains a computed region. The downward arrow denotes that the region is open in the subgame where is computed, while the upward arrow means that the region gets to be promoted to the priority in the subscript. The measure of the region correspond to the index of the row in which the region is contained. Empty slots in the table represent empty regions, while a slot with symbol = in it means that the it contains the same region as the corresponding slot in the previous column.

Assume the dashed move (g,k) is not present in the game. Then, following the idea sketched above, the first region obtained is the single-position 0-region {a} at priority 8, which is open because of the two moves leading to e and i. At priority 7, the open 1-region {j,k} is formed, by attracting k to j according to Proposition 1, which is open in the subgame where {a} is removed. The procedures proceeds similarly, processing all the priorities down to 1 and extracting the regions reported in the first column of the table of Fig. 3. Those are all open regions in their corresponding subgames, except for the 1-region {g,h} at priority 1, which is closed in its subgames but not in the entire game. This region has a move (g,f) leading to region 3 and Proposition 2 is then applied, which promotes this region to 3, obtaining a new 1-region {e,f,g,h} with measure 3. This one is again closed in its subgames and, due to move (h,b), triggers another application of Proposition 2, which promotes all of its positions to region 5 and resets the positions in region 4 to their original priority. The search resumes at priority 5 and the maximization of that region attracts position c as well, forming region {b,c,e,f,g,h} with measure 5. In the resulting subgame, the procedure now extracts the open 1-region {d} at priority 3. The residual game only contains position i, that forms a closed 0-region with a move leading to region 8. This triggers a new promotion that resets the position of all the regions with measure lower than 8, namely the regions with measures 7 and 5. After maximization of the target region, positions b, c, d, h, and j are all attracted to form the 0-region in the first row of column 4. The reset of previous region 7 releases position k which now forms an open 0-region of priority 4. Similarly, positions e and f, reset by the last promotion, form an open 1-region at priority 3. Finally, at priority 1 the closed 1-region {g} is extracted and promoted, by move (g,f), to region 3, forming the set {e,f,g}. Since no move from 0-positions lead outside the set, this region is closed in the entire game and a 1-dominion has been found.

During the simulation above, three resets have been performed. The first one resets 0-region {c,d} with measure 4 in column 2, after promotion of region {e,f,g,h} to priority 5. Indeed, the maximization of the resulting region {b,e,f,g,h} attracts position c, leaving the set {d} with measure 4. However, according to Definition 1, this is not a quasi 0-dominion, since its 1-escape is empty and player 1 can win by remaining in the set forever. After the promotion of region {i} to 8 in column 3, both the regions in rows 7 and 5 get reset. The maximization of the target region of the promotion, *i.e.*, $\{a, i\}$, attracts positions b, c, d, h, and j. As a consequence, for similar reasons described above for position d, the residual position k at priority 7 must be reset to its original priority. Notice that, in both the considered cases, Lemma 1 does not apply. Indeed, the 0-witness strategy for region $\{c, d\}$ is $\sigma = \{d \mapsto c\}$, the 0-stay set of the residual region $\{d\}$ is the set itself, and the restriction of σ to $\{d\}$ leads outside $\{d\}$, hence, it does not belong to $\text{Str}^o(\{d\})$. A similar argument applies to set $\{k\}$ as well.

As opposed to this case, however, the reset of region 5 can be avoided, thanks to Lemma 1. Indeed, a 1-witness for that region is $\sigma = \{e \mapsto g, f \mapsto e\}$ and, in this case, the residual set after the promotion and the maximization of the target region 8 is $\{e, f, g\}$, whose 1-stay set is $\{e, f\}$. The restriction of σ to that set is, however, contained in $\text{Str}^1(\{e, f\})$ and the lemma applies. Note that, avoiding the reset of region with measure 5, containing $\{e, f, g\}$ in column 4, would also avoid the computation of regions 4, 3, and 1, and the promotion of region 1 to 3 that leads to column 5. Indeed, the residual region 5 is a 1-region, according to the lemma, and is also closed in the entire game.

If, however, the dashed move (g, k) was added to the game, the reset of region 5 would be necessary. The reason is that, in this case, the 0-escape set $\{e, f, g\}$ would contain position g, which can escape to position k. As a consequence, $\{e, f, g\}$ would not be a 1-region as the escape set contains a position with priority non-maximal in the subgame, contrary to what is required by Definition 3.

In summary, we can exploit Lemma 1 and Definition 3 to avoid resetting regions after a promotion whenever *(i)* the witness strategy of the residual region satisfies the condition of the lemma, and *(ii)* its escape set only contains positions of maximal priorities in the subgame. This is the core observation that allows the definition of the RR approach, which is formally defined in the following.

The RR *Dominion Space*. We can now provide the formal account of the RR dominion space. We shall denote with Rg the set of region triples in $\eth$ and with Rg^- and Rg^+ the sets of open and closed region triples, respectively.

Similarly to the PP algorithm, during the search for a dominion, the computed regions, together with their current measure, are kept track of by means of an auxiliary priority function $r \in \Delta \triangleq \text{Ps} \to \text{Pr}$, called *region function*. Given a priority $p \in \text{Pr}$, we denote by $r^{(\geq p)}$ (*resp.*, $r^{(>p)}$, $r^{(<p)}$, and $r^{(\neq p)}$) the function obtained by restricting the domain of r to the positions with measure greater than or equal to p (*resp.*, greater than, lower than, and different from p). Formally, $r^{(\sim p)} \triangleq r \upharpoonright \{v \in \text{Ps} : r(v) \sim p\}$, for $\sim \in \{\geq, >, <, \neq\}$. By $\eth_r^{\leq p} \triangleq \eth \setminus \text{dom}(r^{(>p)})$, we denote the largest subgame obtained by removing from $\eth$ all the positions in the domain of $r^{(>p)}$. In order for the RR procedure to exploit Lemma 1, it also needs to keep track of witness strategies of the computed region. To this end, we introduce the notion of witness core. A strategy $\sigma \in \text{Str}^\alpha(Q)$ is an α-*witness core* for an α-region R if *(i)* it is defined on all positions having priority lower than $\text{pr}(R)$, *i.e.*, $\{v \in R : \text{pr}(v) < \text{pr}(R)\} \subseteq \text{dom}(\sigma)$, and *(ii)* it is a restriction of some α-witness $\varsigma \in \text{Str}^\alpha$ for R, *i.e.*, $\sigma \subseteq \varsigma$. Intuitively, a witness core only maintains the essential part of a witness and can be easily transformed into a complete witness by associating every position $v \in \mathsf{stay}^{\alpha}(R) \setminus \mathsf{dom}(\sigma)$ with an arbitrary successor in R. The result of any such completion is an actual witness, since any infinite path passing through v is forced to visit a maximal priority of parity α.

Definition 4 (Region-Witness Pair). *Let* $r \in \Delta$ *be a priority function,* $\tau \in \mathrm{Str}$ *a strategy, and* $p \in \mathrm{Pr}$ *a priority. The pair* (r, τ) *is a* region-witness pair *w.r.t.* p *if, for all* $q \in \mathsf{rng}(r)$ *with* $\alpha \triangleq q \bmod 2$, $R \triangleq r^{-1}(q) \cap \mathrm{Ps}_{\supset_r^{\leq q}} \neq \emptyset$, *and* $\sigma \triangleq \tau {\restriction} R$, *the following two conditions hold:*

1. *if* $q \geq p$, *then* R *is an* α-region *in the subgame* $\supset_r^{\leq q}$ *with* α-witness core σ;
2. *if* $q < p$, *there exists a quasi* α-dominion $Q^{\star} \supseteq R$ *with* α-witness $\sigma^{\star}$ *such that* (i) $\mathsf{pr}(Q^{\star}) = q$, (ii) $\sigma \subseteq \sigma^{\star}$, *and* (iii) $(R \cap \mathrm{Ps}^{\alpha}) \setminus \mathsf{dom}(\sigma) \subseteq \mathsf{pr}^{-1}(q)$.

In addition, r *is* maximal above $p \in \mathrm{Pr}$ *iff, whenever* $q > p$, *it holds that* R *is* α-maximal in $\supset_r^{\leq q}$ *as well.*

As opposed to the PP approach, where a promotion to a priority p resets all the regions of measure lower than p, the RR algorithm resets lower regions only when it cannot ensure their validity. This is done one region at a time, during the descend phase. If, while reading a set $r^{-1}(q)$ at a certain priority $q < p$, the conditions of Lemma 1 are not met by $r^{-1}(q)$ or the escape of that region contains positions of priority lower than q, then $r^{-1}(q)$ is reset.

Contrary to PP, for which the set contained in r at each measure q must be an α-region, RR requires such a property only for those regions with measure $q \geq p$, as expressed by Item 1 of the previous definition. For each $q < p$, instead, we simply require the set of positions contained in r at that measure to be a subset of some previously computed quasi dominions of the same player. This is done by requiring that the strategies recorded in τ be subsets of witnesses of these dominions, as described in Item 2. In this way, to verify that $r^{-1}(q)$ is still a quasi α-dominion, RR can apply the property stated in Lemma 1.

The status of the search of a dominion is encoded by the notion of *state* s of the dominion space, which contains the current region-witness pair (r, τ) and the current priority p reached by the search in $\supset$. Initially, r coincides with the priority function pr of the entire game $\supset$, τ is the empty strategy, and p is set to the maximal priority $\mathsf{pr}(\supset)$ available in the game. To each of such states $s \triangleq (r, \_, p)$, we then associate the *subgame at s* defined as $\supset_s \triangleq \supset_r^{\leq p}$, representing the portion of the original game that still has to be processed.

The following state space specifies the configurations in which the RR procedure can reside and the relative order that the successor function must satisfy.

Definition 5 (State Space). *A* state space *is a tuple* $\mathcal{S} \triangleq \langle \mathrm{S}, \top, \prec \rangle$, *where:*

1. $\mathrm{S} \subseteq \Delta \times \mathrm{Str} \times \mathrm{Pr}$ *is the set of triples* $s \triangleq (r, \tau, p)$, *called* states, *where* (a) (r, τ) *is a region-witness pair w.r.t.* p, (b) r *is maximal above* p, *and* (c) $p \in \mathsf{rng}(r)$.

2. $\top \triangleq (\mathsf{pr}, \varnothing, \mathsf{pr}(\eth))$;
3. *for any two states* $s_1 \triangleq (r_1, \_, p_1), s_2 \triangleq (r_2, \_, p_2) \in S$, *it holds that* $s_1 \prec s_2$ *iff either* (a) *there exists a priority* $q \in \mathsf{rng}(r_1)$ *with* $q \geq p_1$ *such that* (a.i) $r_1^{(>q)} = r_2^{(>q)}$ *and* (a.ii) $r_2^{-1}(q) \subset r_1 {\restriction} r_1^{-1}(q)$, *or* (b) *both* (b.i) $r_1^{(\geq p_2)} = r_2^{(\geq p_2)}$ *and* (b.ii) $p_1 < p_2$ *hold.*

Condition 1 requires every region $r^{-1}(q)$ with measure $q > p$ to be α-maximal, where $\alpha = q \bmod 2$. This implies that $r^{-1}(q) \subseteq \mathrm{Ps}_{\eth_r^{\leq q}}$. Moreover, the current priority p must be one of the measures recorded in r. Condition 2 specifies the initial state. Finally, Condition 3 defines the ordering relation among states, which the successor operation has to comply with. It asserts that a state s_1 is strictly smaller than another state s_2 if either there is a region recorded in s_1 with some higher measure q that strictly contains the corresponding one in s_2 and all regions with measure grater than q are equal in the two states, or state s_1 is currently processing a lower priority than the one of s_2.

As reported in Definition 2, the compatibility relation describes which regions are compatibles with a state, *i.e.*, which region triples can be returned by the query operator and used by the successor function. A region triple (R, σ, α) is compatible with a state $s \triangleq (r, \tau, p)$ if R is an α-region in the current subgame $\eth_s$. Moreover, if such a region is α-open in that game, it has to be α-maximal and needs to necessarily contain the current region $r^{-1}(p)$ of priority p in r.

Definition 6 (Compatibility Relation). *An open quasi dominion triple* $(R, \sigma, \alpha) \in QD^-$ *is compatible with a state* $s \triangleq (r, \tau, p) \in S$, *in symbols* $s \succ (R, \sigma, \alpha)$, *iff* (1) $(R, \sigma, \alpha) \in \mathrm{Rg}_{\eth_s}$ *and* (2) *if R is α-open in $\eth_s$ then* (2.a) *R is α-maximal in $\eth_s$ and* (2.b) $r^{-1}(p) \subseteq R$.

Algorithm 2 provides a possible implementation for the query function compatible with the region-recovery mechanism. Given the current state $s \triangleq (r, \tau, p)$, Line 1 simply computes the parity α of the priority p to process at s. Line 3, instead, computes the attractor *w.r.t.* player α in subgame $\eth_s$ of the region $R^\star$ contained in r at p, as determined by Line 2. Observe that

---

Algorithm 2: Query Function.

signature $\Re \colon S \to 2^{\mathrm{Ps}} \times \mathrm{Str} \times \{0, 1\}$
function $\Re(s)$

	let $(r, \tau, p) = s$ in
1	$\quad \alpha \leftarrow p \bmod 2$
2	$\quad R^\star \leftarrow r^{-1}(p)$
3	$\quad (R, \sigma) \leftarrow \mathrm{atr}_{\eth_s}^{\alpha}(R^\star, \tau {\restriction} R^\star)$
4	**return** (R, σ, α)

---

here we employ a version of the α-attractor that, given an α-witness core for $R^\star$, also computes the α-witness for R. This can easily be done by first extending $\tau {\restriction} R^\star$ with the attraction strategy on the α-positions in $R \setminus R^\star$ and, then, by choosing, for any α-positions in $R \setminus \mathrm{dom}(\tau {\restriction} R^\star)$ with a successor in $R \setminus R^\star$, any one of those successors. The resulting set R is, according to Proposition 1, an α-maximal α-region of $\eth_s$ containing $r^{-1}(p)$ with α-witness σ.

The promotion operation is based on the notion of best escape priority mentioned above, namely the priority of the lowest α-region in r that has an incident move coming from the α-region, closed in the current subgame, that needs to be promoted. This concept is formally defined as follows. Let $I \triangleq Mv \cap ((R \cap Ps^{\overline{\alpha}}) \times$

Algorithm 3: Successor Function.

signature $\downarrow : \succ \to \Delta \times \text{Str} \times \text{Pr}$
function $s \downarrow (R, \sigma, \alpha)$
    let $(r, \tau, p) = s$ **in**
1   **if** $(R, \sigma, \alpha) \in \text{Rg}_{\partial_s}^{-}$ **then**
2 | **return** $N(r[R \mapsto p], \tau \uplus \sigma, p)$
        else
3           $p^\star \leftarrow \text{bep}^{\overline{\alpha}}(R, r)$
4   **return** $(r[R \mapsto p^\star], \tau \uplus \sigma, p^\star)$

$(\text{dom}(r) \setminus R))$ be the *interface relation* between R and r, *i.e.*, the set of $\overline{\alpha}$-moves exiting from R and reaching some position within a region recorded in r. Then, $\text{bep}^{\overline{\alpha}}(R, r)$ is set to the minimal measure of those regions that contain positions reachable by a move in I. Formally, $\text{bep}^{\overline{\alpha}}(R, r) \triangleq \min(\text{rng}(r \upharpoonright \text{rng}(I)))$. Such a value represents the best priority associated with an α-region contained in r and reachable by $\overline{\alpha}$ when escaping from R. Note that, if R is a closed α-region in ∂_s, then $\text{bep}^{\overline{\alpha}}(R, r)$ is necessarily of parity α and greater than the measure p of R. This property immediately follows from the maximality of r above p. Indeed, no move of an $\overline{\alpha}$-position can lead to a $\overline{\alpha}$-maximal $\overline{\alpha}$-region. For instance, for 1-region $R = \{g, h\}$ with measure 1 in Column 1 of Fig. 3, we have that $I = \{(g, f), (h, b)\}$ and $r \upharpoonright \text{rng}(I) = \{(b, 5), (f, 3)\}$. Hence, $\text{bep}^o(R, r) = 3$.

Algorithm 3 implements the successor function. Given the state $s \triangleq (r, \tau, p)$ and one of its possible compatible region triples (R, σ, α) open in the original game ∂, it produces a successor state $s^\star \prec s$. Line 1 checks if R is open in the subgame ∂_s as well. If this is the case, at Line 2, the next state $s^\star$ is generated by the auxiliary function, called *next state function*, described below, which also applies the required resets. On the other hand, if R is closed in ∂_s, the procedure performs the promotion of R, by exploiting Proposition 2. Indeed, Line 3 computes the best escape priority $p^\star$ to which R needs to be promoted, while Line 4 sets the measure of R to $p^\star$ and merges the strategies contained in τ with the α-witness σ of R. Observe that, unlike in the PP successor function, no reset operation is applied to r at this stage.

Finally, Algorithm 4 reports the pseudo code of the next state function, the essential core of the RR approach. At a state $s \triangleq (r, \sigma, p)$, Line 1 computes the priority $p^\star$ of the successive set of positions $r^{-1}(p^\star)$ occurring in r starting from p in descending order of priority. Then, Line 2 verifies whether this set is actually a region, by computing the truth value of the formula ϕ described below applied to the

Algorithm 4: Next State Function.

signature $N : S \to \Delta \times \text{Str} \times \text{Pr}$
function $N(s)$
    let $(r, \tau, p) = s$ **in**
1         $p^\star \leftarrow \max(\text{rng}(r^{(<p)}))$
2   **if** $\phi(r, \tau, p^\star)$ **then**
3 | **return** $(r, \tau, p^\star)$
        else
4           $r^\star \leftarrow \text{pr} \uplus r^{(\neq p^\star)}$
5           $\tau^\star \leftarrow \sigma \setminus r^{-1}(p^\star)$
6   **return** $N(r^\star, \tau^\star, p)$

triple $(r, \tau, p^\star)$. If this is the case, the successor state $(r, \tau, p^\star)$ of s is returned at Line 3. On the other hand, if the check fails, the algorithm resets, at Line 4, the positions in $r^{-1}(p^\star)$ to their original priority stored in the priority function pr of the game, and deletes, at Line 5, the associated strategy contained in τ. Finally, at Line 6, the next state function is recursively applied to the newly obtained state.

To check whether a set of positions $R \triangleq r^{-1}(p)$ at a certain priority $q < p$ is an α-region with $\alpha \triangleq q \bmod 2$, we make use of the formula $\phi(r, \tau, q) \triangleq \phi_i(r, \tau, q) \wedge \phi_{ii}(r, q)$, which verifies that *(i)* $\sigma \triangleq \tau{\restriction}R$ is a witness core for R and *(ii)* the escape only contains positions of maximal priorities in the subgame. The two predicates are formally defined as follows.

$$\phi_i(r, \tau, q) \triangleq \forall v \in Ps^\alpha_{\eth\star} \cap \mathsf{dom}(\sigma) \,.\, \sigma(v) \in R \qquad \text{with} \quad \begin{cases} \eth^\star \triangleq \eth^{\leq q}_r, \ \alpha \triangleq q \bmod 2, \\ R \triangleq r^{-1}(q), \ \sigma \triangleq \tau{\restriction}R. \end{cases}$$
$$\phi_{ii}(r, q) \triangleq \mathsf{esc}^{\overline{\alpha}}_{\eth\star}(R) \subseteq pr^{-1}_{\eth\star}(pr(\eth^\star))$$

Intuitively, if $\phi_i(r, \tau, q)$ holds, we are sure that $\sigma \in Str^\alpha(R)$. Moreover, due to Item 2 of Definition 4, R is a subset of a quasi α-dominion having a witness containing σ. Therefore, by Lemma 1, we immediately derives that σ is a witness core for R. Additionally, the formula $\phi_{ii}(r, q)$ just checks that the second condition of the definition of region is also met.

The following theorem establishes the correctness of the RR approach.

Theorem 1 (Dominion Space). *For a game $\eth$, the structure $\mathcal{D} \triangleq \langle \eth, \mathcal{S}, \succ, \Re, \downarrow \rangle$, where $\mathcal{S}$ is given in Definition 5, $\succ$ is the relation of Definition 6, and $\Re$ and $\downarrow$ are the functions computed by Algorithms 2 and 3 is a dominion space.*

The RR procedure drastically reduces the number of resets needed to solve a game *w.r.t.* PP. In particular, the exponential worst-case game presented in [2] does not work any more, since the execution depth of the associated RR dominion space is only quadratic in the parameter of game family. Unfortunately, at the present time, we are not able to provide a better asymptotic upper bound for the time complexity *w.r.t.* the PP one.

5   Experimental Evaluation

The technique proposed in the paper has been implemented in the tool PGSOLVER [9], which collects implementations of several parity game solvers proposed in the literature and provides benchmarking tools that can be used to evaluate the solver performances.[1]

---

[1] All the experiments were carried out on a 64-bit 3.1 GHz INTEL®quad-core machine, with i5-2400 processor and 8 GB of RAM, running UBUNTU 12.04 with LINUX kernel version 3.2.0. PGSOLVER was compiled with OCaml version 2.12.1.

Figure 4 compares the running times of the new algorithm RR against the original version PP and the well-known solvers *Rec* and *Str*, implementing the recursive algorithm [23] and the strategy improvement technique [22], respectively. This first pool of benchmarks is taken from [2] and involves 2000 random games of size ranging from 1000 to 20000 positions and 2 outgoing moves per position. Interestingly, random games with very few moves

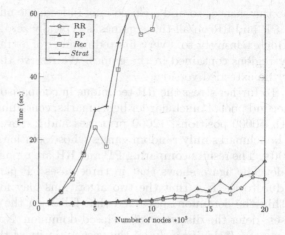

Fig. 4. Comparative results on 2000 random games with up to 20000 positions (from [2]).

prove to be much more challenging for the priority promotion based approaches than those with a higher number of moves per position, and often require a much higher number of promotions. Since the behaviour of the solvers is typically highly variable, even on games of the same size and priorities, to summarise the results we took the average running time on clusters of games.

Therefore, each point in the graph shows the average time over a cluster of 100 different games of the same size: for each size value n, we chose the numbers $k = n \cdot i/10$ of priorities, with $i \in [1, 10]$, and 10 random games were generated for each pair n and k. We set a time-out to 180 s (3 min). The new solver RR shows a significant improvement on all the benchmarks. All the other solvers provided in PGSOLVER, including the Dominion Decomposition [14] and the Big Step [19] algorithms, perform quite poorly on those games, hitting the time-out already for very small instances. Figure 4 shows only the best performing ones on the considered games, namely *Rec* and *Str*.

Similar experiments were also conducted on random games with a higher number of moves per position and up to 100000 positions. The resulting games turn out to be very easy to solve by all the priority promotion based approaches. The reason seems to be that the higher number of moves significantly increases the dimension of the computed regions and, consequently,

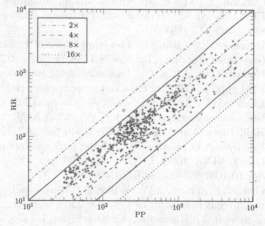

Fig. 5. Comparison between PP and RR on random games with 50000 positions on a logarithmic scale.

also the chances to find a closed one. Indeed, the number of promotions required by PP and RR on all those games is typically zero, and the whole solution time is due exclusively to a very limited number of attractors needed to compute the few regions contained in the games. We reserve the presentation of the results for the extended version.

To further stress the RR technique in comparison with PP, we also generated a second pool of much harder benchmarks, containing more than 500 games, each with 50000 positions, 12000 priorities and 2 moves per positions. We selected as benchmarks only random games whose solution requires PP between 30 and 6000 s. The results comparing PP and RR are reported in Fig. 5 on a logarithmic scale. The figure shows that in three cases PP performs better than RR. This is due to the fact that the two algorithms may follow different solution paths within the dominion space and that following the new technique may, in some cases, defer the discovery of a closed dominion. Nonetheless, the RR algorithm does pay off significantly on the vast majority of the benchmarks, often solving a game between two to sixteen times faster than PP.

In [2] it is shown that PP solves all the known exponential worst cases for the other solvers without promotions and, clearly, the same holds of RR as well. As a consequence, RR only requires polynomial time on those games and the experimental results coincide with the ones for PP.

References

1. Apt, K., Grädel, E.: Lectures in Game Theory for Computer Scientists. Cambridge University Press, Cambridge (2011)
2. Benerecetti, M., Dell'Erba, D., Mogavero, F.: Solving parity games via priority promotion. In: Chaudhuri, S., Farzan, A. (eds.) CAV 2016. LNCS, vol. 9780, pp. 270–290. Springer, Heidelberg (2016). doi:10.1007/978-3-319-41540-6_15
3. Chatterjee, K., Doyen, L., Henzinger, T., Raskin, J.-F.: Generalized mean-payoff and energy games. In: FSTTCS 2010. LIPIcs, vol. 8, pp. 505–516. Leibniz-Zentrum fuer Informatik (2010)
4. Condon, A.: The complexity of stochastic games. IC **96**(2), 203–224 (1992)
5. Ehrenfeucht, A., Mycielski, J.: Positional strategies for mean payoff games. IJGT **8**(2), 109–113 (1979)
6. Emerson, E., Jutla, C.: The complexity of tree automata and logics of programs (extended abstract). In: FOCS 1988, pp. 328–337. IEEE Computer Society (1988)
7. Emerson, E., Jutla, C.: Tree automata, muCalculus, and determinacy. In: FOCS 1991, pp. 368–377. IEEE Computer Society (1991)
8. Emerson, E., Jutla, C., Sistla, A.: On model-checking for fragments of μ-calculus. In: Courcoubetis, C. (ed.) CAV '93. LNCS, vol. 697, pp. 385–396. Springer, Heidelberg (1993). doi:10.1007/3-540-56922-7_32
9. Friedmann, O., Lange, M.: Solving parity games in practice. In: Liu, Z., Ravn, A.P. (eds.) ATVA 2009. LNCS, vol. 5799, pp. 182–196. Springer, Heidelberg (2009). doi:10.1007/978-3-642-04761-9_15
10. Grädel, E., Thomas, W., Wilke, T.: Automata Logics, and Infinite Games: A Guide to Current Research. LNCS, vol. 2500. Springer, Heidelberg (2002)
11. Gurevich, V., Karzanov, A., Khachivan, L.: Cyclic games and an algorithm to find minimax cycle means in directed graphs. USSRCMMP **28**(5), 85–91 (1990)

12. Jurdziński, M.: Deciding the winner in parity games is in UP ∩ co-Up. IPL **68**(3), 119–124 (1998)
13. Jurdziński, M.: Small progress measures for solving parity games. In: Reichel, H., Tison, S. (eds.) STACS 2000. LNCS, vol. 1770, pp. 290–301. Springer, Heidelberg (2000). doi:10.1007/3-540-46541-3_24
14. Jurdziński, M., Paterson, M., Zwick, U.: A deterministic subexponential algorithm for solving parity games. SJM **38**(4), 1519–1532 (2008)
15. Kupferman, O., Vardi, M.: Weak alternating automata and tree automata emptiness. In: STOC 1998, pp. 224–233. Association for Computing Machinery (1998)
16. Kupferman, O., Vardi, M., Wolper, P.: An automata theoretic approach to branching-time model checking. JACM **47**(2), 312–360 (2000)
17. Mostowski, A.W.: Regular expressions for infinite trees and a standard form of automata. In: Skowron, A. (ed.) SCT 1984. LNCS, vol. 208, pp. 157–168. Springer, Heidelberg (1985). doi:10.1007/3-540-16066-3_15
18. Mostowski, A.: Games with forbidden positions. University of Gdańsk, Gdańsk, Poland, Technical report (1991)
19. Schewe, S.: Solving parity games in big steps. In: Arvind, V., Prasad, S. (eds.) FSTTCS 2007. LNCS, vol. 4855, pp. 449–460. Springer, Heidelberg (2007). doi:10.1007/978-3-540-77050-3_37
20. Schewe, S.: An optimal strategy improvement algorithm for solving parity and payoff games. In: Kaminski, M., Martini, S. (eds.) CSL 2008. LNCS, vol. 5213, pp. 369–384. Springer, Heidelberg (2008). doi:10.1007/978-3-540-87531-4_27
21. Schewe, S., Trivedi, A., Varghese, T.: Symmetric strategy improvement. In: Halldórsson, M.M., Iwama, K., Kobayashi, N., Speckmann, B. (eds.) ICALP 2015. LNCS, vol. 9135, pp. 388–400. Springer, Heidelberg (2015). doi:10.1007/978-3-662-47666-6_31
22. Vöge, J., Jurdziński, M.: A discrete strategy improvement algorithm for solving parity games. In: Allen Emerson, E., Sistla, A.P. (eds.) CAV 2000. Lecture Notes in Computer Science, vol. 1855, pp. 202–215. Springer, Heidelberg (2000). doi:10.1007/10722167_18
23. Zielonka, W.: Infinite games on finitely coloured graphs with applications to automata on infinite trees. TCS **200**(1–2), 135–183 (1998)
24. Zwick, U., Paterson, M.: The complexity of mean payoff games on graphs. TCS **158**(1–2), 343–359 (1996)

Synthesis of Admissible Shields

Laura Humphrey[1], Bettina Könighofer[2(✉)], Robert Könighofer[2],
and Ufuk Topcu[3]

[1] Control Science Center of Excellence, AFRL, Wright-Patterson AFB, USA
[2] IAIK, Graz University of Technology, Graz, Austria
bettina.koenighofer@iaik.tugraz.at
[3] University of Texas at Austin, Austin, USA

Abstract. *Shield synthesis* is an approach to enforce a set of safety-critical properties of a reactive system at runtime. A shield monitors the system and corrects any erroneous output values instantaneously. The shield deviates from the given outputs as little as it can and recovers to hand back control to the system as soon as possible. This paper takes its inspiration from a case study on mission planning for unmanned aerial vehicles (UAVs) in which *k-stabilizing* shields, which guarantee recovery in a finite time, could not be constructed. We introduce the notion of *admissible* shields, which improves *k-stabilizing* shields in two ways: (1) whereas *k*-stabilizing shields take an adversarial view on the system, admissible shields take a collaborative view. That is, if there is no shield that guarantees recovery within *k* steps regardless of system behavior, the admissible shield will attempt to work with the system to recover as soon as possible. (2) Admissible shields can handle system failures during the recovery phase. In our experimental results we show that for UAVs, we can generate admissible shields, even when *k*-stabilizing shields do not exist.

1 Introduction

Technological advances enable the development of increasingly sophisticated systems. Smaller and faster microprocessors, wireless networking, and new theoretical results in areas such as machine learning and intelligent control are paving the way for transformative technologies across a variety of domains – self-driving cars that have the potential to reduce accidents, traffic, energy consumption, and pollution; and unmanned systems that can safely and efficiently operate on land, under water, in the air, and in space. However, in each of these domains, concerns about safety are being raised [7,16]. Specifically, there is a concern that due to the complexity of such systems, traditional test and evaluation approaches will not be sufficient for finding errors, and alternative approaches such as those provided by formal methods are needed [17].

This work was supported in part by the Austrian Science Fund (FWF) through the research network RiSE (S11406-N23), and by the European Commission through the project IMMORTAL (644905).

© Springer International Publishing AG 2016
R. Bloem and E. Arbel (Eds.): HVC 2016, LNCS 10028, pp. 134–151, 2016.
DOI: 10.1007/978-3-319-49052-6_9

Formal methods are often used to verify systems at design time, but this is not always realistic. Some systems are simply too large to be fully verified. Others, especially systems that operate in rich dynamic environments or those that continuously adapt their behavior through methods such as machine learning, cannot be fully modeled at design time. Still others may incorporate components that have not been previously verified and cannot be modeled, e.g., proprietary components or pre-compiled code libraries.

Also, even systems that have been fully verified at design time may be subject to external faults such as those introduced by unexpected hardware failures or human inputs. One way to address this issue is to model nondeterministic behaviours (such as faults) as disturbances, and verify the system with respect to this disturbance model [18]. However, it is impossible to model all potential unexpected behavior at design time.

An alternative in such cases is to perform *runtime verification* to detect violations of a set of specified properties while a system is executing [14]. An extension of this idea is to perform *runtime enforcement* of specified properties, in which violations are not only detected but also overwritten in a way that specified properties are maintained.

A general approach for runtime enforcement of specified properties is *shield synthesis*, in which a shield monitors the system and instantaneously overwrites incorrect outputs. A shield must ensure both *correctness*, i.e., it corrects system outputs such that all properties are always satisfied, as well as *minimum deviation*, i.e., it deviates from system outputs only if necessary and as rarely as possible. The latter requirement is important because the system may satisfy additional noncritical properties that are not considered by the shield but should be retained as much as possible.

Bloem et al. [4] proposed the notion of k-stabilizing shields. Since we are given a safety specification, we can identify wrong outputs, that is, outputs after which the specification is violated (more precisely: after which the environment can force the specification to be violated). A wrong trace is then a trace that ends in a wrong output. The idea of shields is that they may modify the outputs so that the specification always holds, but that such deviations last for at most k consecutive steps after a wrong output. If a second violation happens during the k-step recovery phase, the shield enters a mode where it only enforces correctness, but no longer minimizes the deviation. This proposed approach has two limitations with significant impact in practice. (1) The k-stabilizing shield synthesis problem is unrealizable for many safety-critical systems, because a finite number of deviations cannot be guaranteed. (2) k-stabilizing shields make the assumption that there are no further system errors during the recovery phase.

In this paper, we introduce *admissible* shields, which overcome the two issues of k-stabilizing shields. To address shortcoming (1), we guarantee the following: (a) Admissible shields are subgame optimal. That is, for any wrong trace, if there is a finite number k of steps within which the recovery phase can be guaranteed to end, the shield will always achieve this. (b) The shield is *admissible*, that is, if there is no such number k, it always picks a deviation that is optimal in that it ends the recovery phase as soon as possible for some possible future inputs. (This is defined in more detail below.) As a result, admissible shields work well in settings in which finite recovery can not be guaranteed, because they guarantee correctness and may well end the recovery period if the system does not pick adversarial outputs. To address shortcoming (2), admissible shields allow arbitrary failure frequencies and in particular failures that arrive during recovery, without losing the ability to recover.

As a second contribution, we demonstrate the use of admissible shields through a case study involving mission planning for an unmanned aerial vehicle (UAV). Manually creating and executing mission plans that meet mission objectives while addressing all possible contingencies is a complex and error-prone task. Therefore, having a shield that changes the mission only if absolutely necessary to enforce certain safety properties has the potential to lower the burden on human operators, and ensures safety during mission execution. We show that admissible shields are applicable in this setting, whereas k-stabilizing shields are not.

Related Work: Our work builds on synthesis of reactive systems [3,20] and reactive mission plans [9] from formal specifications, and our method is related to synthesis of robust [1] and error-resilient [10] systems. However, our approach differs in that we do not synthesize an entire system, but rather a shield that considers only a small set of properties and corrects the output of the system at runtime. Li et al. [15] focused on the problem of synthesizing a semi-autonomous controller that expects occasional human intervention for correct operation. A human-in-the-loop controller monitors past and current information about the system and its environment. The controller invokes the human operator only when it is necessary, but as soon as a specification is violated ahead of time, such that the human operator has sufficient time to respond. Similarly, our shields monitor the behavior of systems at run time, and interfere as little as possible. Our work relates to more general work on runtime enforcement of properties [12], but shield synthesis [4] is the first appropriative work for reactive systems, since shields act on erroneous system outputs immediately without delay. While [4] focuses on shield synthesis for systems assumed to make no more than one error every k steps, this work assumes only that systems generally have cooperative behavior with respect to the shield, i.e., the shield ensures a finite number of deviations if the system chooses certain outputs. This is similar in concept to cooperative synthesis as considered in [2], in which a synthesized system has to satisfy a set of properties (called guarantees) only if certain environment assumptions hold. The authors present a synthesis procedure that maximizes the cooperation between system and environment for satisfying both guarantees and assumptions as far as possible.

Outline: In what follows, we begin in Sect. 2 by motivating the need for admissible shields through a case study involving mission planning for a UAV. In Sects. 3, 4 and 5, we define preliminary concepts, review the general shield synthesis framework, and describe our approach for synthesizing admissible shields. Section 6 provides experimental results, and Sect. 7 concludes.

2   Motivating Example

In this section, we apply shields on a scenario in which a UAV must maintain certain properties while performing a surveillance mission in a dynamic environment. We show how a shield can be used to enforce the desired properties, where a human operator in conjunction with a lower-level autonomous planner is considered as the reactive system that sends commands to the UAV's autopilot. We discuss how we would intuitively want a shield to behave in such a situation. We show that the *admissible* shields provide the desired behaviors and address the limitations of k-stabilizing shields.

To begin, note that a common UAV control architecture consists of a ground control station that communicates with an autopilot onboard the UAV [5]. The ground control station receives and displays updates from the autopilot on the UAV's state, including position, heading, airspeed, battery level, and sensor imagery. It can also send commands to the UAV's autopilot, such as waypoints to fly to. A human operator can then use the ground control station to plan waypoint-based routes for the UAV, possibly making modifications during mission execution to respond to events observed through the UAV's sensors. However, mission planning and execution can be very workload intensive, especially when operators are expected to control multiple UAVs simultaneously [8]. To address this issue, methods for UAV command and control have been explored in which operators issue high-level commands, and automation carries out low-level execution details.

Several errors can occur in this type of human-automation paradigm [6]. For instance, in issuing high-level commands to the low-level planner, a human operator might neglect required safety properties due to high workload, fatigue, or an incomplete understanding of exactly how the autonomous planner might execute the command. The planner might also neglect these safety properties either because of software errors or by design. Waypoint commands issued by the operator or planner could also be corrupted by software that translates waypoint messages between ground station and autopilot specific formats or during transmission over the communication link.

As the mission unfolds, waypoint commands will be sent periodically to the autopilot. If a waypoint that violates the properties is received, a shield that monitors the system inputs and can overwrite the waypoint outputs to the autopilot would be able to make corrections to ensure the satisfaction of the desired properties.

Consider the mission map in Fig. 1 [13], which contains three tall buildings (illustrated as blue blocks), over which a UAV should not attempt to fly. It also includes two unattended ground sensors (UGS) that provide data on possible nearby targets, one at location loc_1 and one at loc_x, as well as two locations of interest, loc_y and loc_z. The UAV can monitor loc_x, loc_y, and loc_z from several nearby vantage points. The map also contains a restricted operating zone (ROZ), illustrated with a red box, in which flight might be dangerous, and the path of a possible adversary that should be avoided (the pink dashed line). Inside the communication relay region (large green area), communication links are highly reliable. Outside

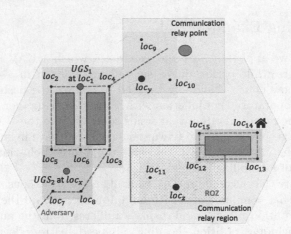

Fig. 1. A map for UAV mission planning. (Color figure online)

this region, communication relies on relay points with lower reliability. Given this scenario, properties of interest include:

1. **Connected waypoints.** The UAV is only allowed to fly to directly connected waypoints.
2. **No communication.** The UAV is not allowed to stay in a location with reduced communication reliability.
3. **Restricted operating zones.** The UAV has to leave a ROZ within 2 time steps.
4. **Detected by an adversary.** Locations on the adversary's path cannot be visited more than once over any window of 3 time steps.
5. **UGS.** If a UGS reports a possible nearby target, the UAV should visit a respective waypoint within 7 steps (for UGS_1 visit loc_1, for UGS_2 visit loc_5, loc_6, loc_7, or loc_8).
6. **Go home.** Once the UAV's battery is low, it should return to a designated landing site at loc_{14} within 10 time steps.

The task of the shield is to ensure these properties during operation. In this setting, the operator in conjunction with a lower-level planner acts as a reactive system that responds to mission-relevant inputs; in this case data from the UGSs and a signal indicating whether the battery is low. In each step, the next waypoint is sent to the autopilot, which is encoded in a bit representation via outputs l_4, l_3, l_2, and l_1. We attach the shield as shown in Fig. 2. The shield monitors mission inputs and waypoint outputs, correcting outputs immediately if a violation of the safety properties becomes unavoidable.

We represent each of the properties by a safety automaton, the product of which serves as the shield specification. Figure 3 models the "connected waypoints" property, where each state represents a waypoint with the same number. Edges are labeled by the values of the variables $l_4 \ldots l_1$. For example, the edge leading from state s_5 to state s_6 is labeled by $\neg l_4 l_3 l_2 \neg l_1$. For clarity, we drop the

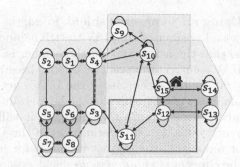

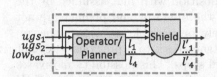

Fig. 2. The interaction between the operator/planner (acting as a reactive system) and the shield.

Fig. 3. Safety automaton of Property 1 over the map in Fig. 1.

labels of edges in Fig. 3. The automaton also includes an error state, which is not shown. Missing edges lead to this error state, denoting forbidden situations.

How should a shield behave in this scenario? If the human operator wants to monitor a location in a ROZ, he or she would like to simply command the UAV to "monitor the location in the ROZ and stay there", with the planner handling the execution details. If the planner cannot do this while meeting all the safety properties, it is appropriate for the shield to revise its outputs. Yet, the operator would still expect his or her commands to be followed to the maximum extent possible, leaving the ROZ when necessary and returning whenever possible. Thus, the shield should minimize deviations from the operator's directives as executed by the planner.

Using a k-stabilizing shield. As a concrete example, assume the UAV is currently at loc_3, and the operator commands it to monitor loc_{12}. The planner then sends commands to fly to loc_{11} then loc_{12}, which are accepted by the shield. The planner then sends a command to loiter at loc_{12}, but the shield must overwrite it to maintain Property 3, which requires the UAV to leave the ROZ within two time steps. The shield instead commands the UAV to go to loc_{15}. Suppose the operator then commands the UAV to fly to loc_{13}, while the planner is still issuing commands as if the UAV is at loc_{12}. The planner then commands the UAV to fly to loc_{13}, but since the actual UAV cannot fly from loc_{15} to loc_{13} directly, the shield directs the UAV to loc_{14} on its way to loc_{15}. The operator might then respond to a change in the mission and command the UAV fly back to loc_{12}, and the shield again deviates from the route assumed by the planner, and directs the UAV back to loc_{15}, and so on. Therefore, a single specification violation can lead to an infinitely long deviation between the UAV's actual position and the UAV's assumed position. A k-stabilizing shield is allowed to deviate from the planner's commands for at most k consecutive time steps. Hence, no k-stabilizing shield exists.

Using an admissible shield. Recall the situation in which the shield caused the actual position of the UAV to "fall behind" the position assumed by the planner, so that the next waypoint the planner issues is two or more steps away from the UAV's current waypoint position. The shield should then implement a best-effort strategy to "synchronize" the UAV's actual position with that assumed by the planner. Though this cannot be guaranteed, the operator and planner are not adversarial towards the shield, so it will likely be possible to achieve this re-synchronization, for instance when the UAV goes back to a previous waypoint or remains at the current waypoint for several steps. This possibility motivates the concept of an *admissible* shield. Assume that the actual position of the UAV is loc_{14} and the its assumed position is loc_{13}. If the operator commands the UAV to loiter at loc_{13}, the shield will be able to catch up with the state assumed by the planner and to end the deviation by the next specification violation.

3   Preliminaries

We denote the Boolean domain by $\mathbb{B} = \{\text{true}, \text{false}\}$, the set of natural numbers by $\mathbb{N}$, and abbreviate $\mathbb{N} \cup \{\infty\}$ by $\mathbb{N}^\infty$. We consider a reactive system with a finite set $I = \{i_1, \ldots, i_m\}$ of Boolean inputs and a finite set $O = \{o_1, \ldots, o_n\}$ of Boolean outputs. The input alphabet is $\Sigma_I = 2^I$, the output alphabet is $\Sigma_O = 2^O$, and $\Sigma = \Sigma_I \times \Sigma_O$. The set of finite (infinite) words over Σ is denoted by Σ^* (Σ^ω), and $\Sigma^\infty = \Sigma^* \cup \Sigma^\omega$. We will also refer to words as *(execution) traces*. We write $|\overline{\sigma}|$ for the length of a trace $\overline{\sigma} \in \Sigma^*$. For $\overline{\sigma_I} = x_0 x_1 \ldots \in \Sigma_I^\infty$ and $\overline{\sigma_O} = y_0 y_1 \ldots \in \Sigma_O^\infty$, we write $\overline{\sigma_I} || \overline{\sigma_O}$ for the composition $(x_0, y_0)(x_1, y_1) \ldots \in \Sigma^\infty$. A set $L \subseteq \Sigma^\infty$ of words is called a *language*. We denote the set of all languages as $\mathcal{L} = 2^{\Sigma^\infty}$.

Reactive Systems. A *Mealy machine* (reactive system, design) is a 6-tuple $\mathcal{D} = (Q, q_0, \Sigma_I, \Sigma_O, \delta, \lambda)$, where Q is a finite set of states, $q_0 \in Q$ is the initial state, $\delta : Q \times \Sigma_I \to Q$ is a complete transition function, and $\lambda : Q \times \Sigma_I \to \Sigma_O$ is a complete output function. Given the input trace $\overline{\sigma_I} = x_0 x_1 \ldots \in \Sigma_I^\infty$, the system $\mathcal{D}$ produces the output trace $\overline{\sigma_O} = \mathcal{D}(\overline{\sigma_I}) = \lambda(q_0, x_0)\lambda(q_1, x_1) \ldots \in \Sigma_O^\infty$, where $q_{i+1} = \delta(q_i, x_i)$ for all $i \geq 0$. The set of words produced by $\mathcal{D}$ is denoted $L(\mathcal{D}) = \{\overline{\sigma_I} || \overline{\sigma_O} \in \Sigma^\infty \mid \mathcal{D}(\overline{\sigma_I}) = \overline{\sigma_O}\}$.

Let $\mathcal{D} = (Q, q_0, \Sigma_I, \Sigma_O, \delta, \lambda)$ and $\mathcal{D}' = (Q', q_0', \Sigma, \Sigma_O, \delta', \lambda')$ be reactive systems. A serial composition of $\mathcal{D}$ and $\mathcal{D}'$ is realized if the input and output of $\mathcal{D}$ are fed to $\mathcal{D}'$. We denote such composition as $\mathcal{D} \circ \mathcal{D}' = (\hat{Q}, \hat{q_0}, \Sigma_I, \Sigma_O, \hat{\delta}, \hat{\lambda})$, where $\hat{Q} = Q \times Q'$, $\hat{q_0} = (q_0, q_0')$, $\hat{\delta}((q, q'), \sigma_I) = (\delta(q, \sigma_I), \delta'(q', (\sigma_I, \lambda(q, \sigma_I))))$, and $\hat{\lambda}((q, q'), \sigma_I) = \lambda'(q', (\sigma_I, \lambda(q, \sigma_I)))$.

Specifications. A *specification* φ is a set $L(\varphi) \subseteq \Sigma^\infty$ of allowed traces. $\mathcal{D}$ *realizes* φ, denoted by $\mathcal{D} \models \varphi$, iff $L(\mathcal{D}) \subseteq L(\varphi)$. A specification φ is *realizable* if there exists a design $\mathcal{D}$ that realizes it. A *safety* specification φ^s is represented by an automaton $\varphi^s = (Q, q_0, \Sigma, \delta, F)$, where $\Sigma = \Sigma_I \cup \Sigma_O$, $\delta : Q \times \Sigma \to Q$, and $F \subseteq Q$ is a set of safe states. The *run* induced by trace $\overline{\sigma} = \sigma_0 \sigma_1 \ldots \in \Sigma^\infty$ is the state sequence $\overline{q} = q_0 q_1 \ldots$ such that $q_{i+1} = \delta(q_i, \sigma_i)$; the run is *accepting* if $\forall i \geq 0 . q_i \in F$. Trace $\overline{\sigma}$ (of a design $\mathcal{D}$) *satisfies* φ^s if the induced run is accepting. The *language* $L(\varphi^s)$ is the set of all traces satisfying φ^s.

Games. A (2-player, alternating) *game* is a tuple $\mathcal{G} = (G, g_0, \Sigma_I, \Sigma_O, \delta, \text{win})$, where G is a finite set of game states, $g_0 \in G$ is the initial state, $\delta : G \times \Sigma_I \times \Sigma_O \rightarrow G$ is a complete transition function, and win $: G^\omega \rightarrow \mathbb{B}$ is a winning condition. The game is played by two players: the system and the environment. In every state $g \in G$ (starting with g_0), the environment first chooses an input letter $\sigma_I \in \Sigma_I$, and then the system chooses some output letter $\sigma_O \in \Sigma_O$. This defines the next state $g' = \delta(g, \sigma_I, \sigma_O)$, and so on. Thus, a (finite or infinite) word over Σ results in a (finite or infinite) *play*, a sequence $\overline{g} = g_0 g_1 \ldots$ of game states. A play is *won* by the system iff $\text{win}(\overline{g})$ is true. A *safety game* defines win via a set $F^s \subseteq G$ of safe states: $\text{win}(g_0 g_1 \ldots)$ is true iff $\forall i \geq 0 . g_i \in F^s$, i.e., if only safe states are visited. Let $\inf(\overline{g})$ denote the states that occur infinitely often in $\overline{g}$. A *Büchi game* defines win via a set $F^b \subseteq G$ of accepting states: $\text{win}(\overline{g})$ is true iff $\inf(\overline{g}) \cap F^b \neq \emptyset$.

It is easy to transform a safety specification into a safety game such that a trace satisfies the specification iff the corresponding play is won. Given a safety specification φ^s. A finite trace $\overline{\sigma} \in \Sigma^*$ is *wrong*, if the corresponding play is not won, i.e., if there is no way for the system to guarantee that any extension of the trace satisfies the specification. An *output* is called *wrong*, if it makes a trace wrong; i.e., given φ^s, a trace $\overline{\sigma} \in \Sigma^*$ an input $\sigma_I \in \Sigma_I$, and an output $\sigma_O \in \Sigma_O$, σ_O is wrong iff $\overline{\sigma}$ is not wrong, but $\overline{\sigma} \cdot (\sigma_I, \sigma_O)$ is.

A deterministic (memoryless) *strategy* for the environment is a function $\rho_e : G \rightarrow \Sigma_I$. A deterministic (memoryless) *strategy* for the system is a function $\rho_s : G \times \Sigma_I \rightarrow \Sigma_O$. A strategy ρ_s is *winning* for the system, if *for all* strategies ρ_e of the environment the play $\overline{g}$ that is constructed when defining the outputs using ρ_e and ρ_s satisfies $\text{win}(\overline{g})$. The *winning region* W is the set of states from which a winning strategy exists. A strategy is *cooperatively winning* if there *exists* a strategy ρ_e and ρ_s, such that the play $\overline{g}$ constructed by ρ_e and ρ_s satisfies $\text{win}(\overline{g})$.

For a Büchi game $\mathcal{G}$ with accepting states F^b, consider a strategy ρ_e of the environment, a strategy ρ_s of the system, and a state $g \in G$. We set the distance $dist(g, \rho_e, \rho_s) = k$, if the play $\overline{g}$ defined by ρ_e and ρ_s reaches from g an accepting state that occurs infinitely often in $\overline{g}$ in k steps. If no such state is visited, we set $dist(g, \rho_e, \rho_s) = \infty$. Given two strategies ρ_s and ρ'_s of the system, we say that ρ'_s *dominates* ρ_s if: (i) for all ρ_e and all $g \in G$, $dist(g, \rho_e, \rho'_s) \leq dist(g, \rho_e, \rho_s)$, and (ii) there exists ρ_e and $g \in G$ such that $dist(g, \rho_e, \rho'_s) < dist(g, \rho_e, \rho_s)$. A strategy is *admissible* if there is no strategy that dominates it.

4 Admissible Shields

Bloem et al. [4] presented the general framework for shield synthesis. A shield has two main properties: (i) For any design, a shield ensures *correctness* with respect to a specification. (ii) A shield ensures *minimal deviation*. We revisit these properties in Sect. 4.1. The definition of minimum deviation is designed to be flexible and different notions of minimum deviation can be realized. k-stabilizing shields represent one concrete realization. In Sect. 4.2, we present a new realization of the minimum deviation property resulting in admissible shields.

4.1 Definition of Shields

A shield reads the input and output of a design as shown in Fig. 2. We then address the two properties, correctness and minimum deviation, to be ensured by a shield.

The Correctness Property. With correctness we refer to the property that the shield corrects any design's output such that a given safety specification is satisfied. Formally, let φ be a safety specification and $\mathcal{S} = (Q', q_0', \Sigma, \Sigma_O, \delta', \lambda')$ be a Mealy machine. We say that $\mathcal{S}$ *ensures correctness* if for any design $\mathcal{D} = (Q, q_0, \Sigma_I, \Sigma_O, \delta, \lambda)$, it holds that $(\mathcal{D} \circ \mathcal{S}) \models \varphi$.

Since a shield must work for any design, the synthesis procedure does not need to consider the design's implementation. This property is crucial because the design may be unknown or too complex to analyze. On the other hand, the design may satisfy additional (noncritical) specifications that are not specified in φ but should be retained as much as possible.

The Minimum Deviation Property. Minimum deviation requires a shield to deviate only if necessary, and as infrequently as possible. To ensure minimum deviation, a shield can only deviate from the design if a property violation becomes unavoidable. Given a safety specification φ, a Mealy machine $\mathcal{S}$ *does not deviate unnecessarily* if for any design $\mathcal{D}$ and any trace $\overline{\sigma_I} || \overline{\sigma_O}$ that is not wrong, we have that $\mathcal{S}(\overline{\sigma_I} || \overline{\sigma_O}) = \overline{\sigma_O}$. In other words, if $\mathcal{D}$ does not violate φ, $\mathcal{S}$ keeps the output of $\mathcal{D}$ intact.

A Mealy machine $\mathcal{S}$ is a *shield* if $\mathcal{S}$ ensures correctness and does not deviate unnecessarily.

Ideally, shields end phases of deviations as soon as possible, recovering quickly. This property leaves room for interpretation. Different types of shields differentiate on how this property is realized.

4.2 Defining Admissible Shields

In this section we define admissible shields using their speed of recovery. We distinguish between two situations. In states of the design in which a finite number k of deviations can be guaranteed, an admissible shield takes an adversarial view on the design: it guarantees recovery within k steps regardless of system behavior, for the smallest k possible. In these states, the strategy of an admissible shield conforms to the strategy of k-stabilizing shield. In all other states, admissible shields take a collaborative view: the admissible shield will attempt to work with the design to recover as soon as possible. In particular, an admissible shield plays an admissible strategy, that is, a strategy that cannot be beaten in recovery speed if the design acts cooperatively.

We will now define admissible shields. For failures of the system that are corrected by the shield, we consider four phases:

1. The *innocent phase* consisting of inputs $\overline{\sigma_I}$ and outputs $\overline{\sigma_O}$, in which no failure occurs; i.e., $(\overline{\sigma_I}||\overline{\sigma_O}) \models \varphi$.
2. The *misstep phase* consisting of a input σ_I and a wrong output $\sigma_O{}^f$; i.e., $(\overline{\sigma_I}||\overline{\sigma_O}) \cdot (\sigma_I, \sigma_O{}^f) \not\models \varphi$.
3. The *deviation phase* consisting of inputs $\overline{\sigma_I}'$ and outputs $\overline{\sigma_O}'$ in which the shield is allowed to deviate, and for a correct output $\sigma_O{}^c$ we have $(\overline{\sigma_I}||\overline{\sigma_O}) \cdot (\sigma_I, \sigma_O{}^c) \cdot (\overline{\sigma_I}'||\overline{\sigma_O}') \models \varphi$.
4. The *final phase* consisting $\overline{\sigma_I}''$ and $\overline{\sigma_O}''$ in which the shield does not deviate, and $(\overline{\sigma_I}||\overline{\sigma_O}) \cdot (\sigma_I, \sigma_O{}^c) \cdot (\overline{\sigma_I}'||\overline{\sigma_O}') \cdot (\overline{\sigma_I}''||\overline{\sigma_O}'') \models \varphi$.

Adversely k-stabilizing shields have a deviation phase of length at most k.

Definition 1. *A shield S adversely k-stabilizes a trace $\overline{\sigma} = \overline{\sigma_I}||\overline{\sigma_O} \in \Sigma^*$, if for any input $\sigma_I \in \Sigma_I$ and any wrong output $\sigma_O{}^f \in \Sigma_O$,* **for any** *correct output $\sigma_O{}^c \in \Sigma_O$ and* **for any** *correct trace $\overline{\sigma_I}'||\overline{\sigma_O}' \in \Sigma^k$ there exists a trace $\sigma_O{}^\#\overline{\sigma_O}{}^\# \in \Sigma_O^{k+1}$ such that for any trace $\overline{\sigma_I}''||\overline{\sigma_O}'' \in \Sigma^\omega$ such that $(\overline{\sigma_I}||\overline{\sigma_O}) \cdot (\sigma_I, \sigma_O{}^c) \cdot (\overline{\sigma_I}'||\overline{\sigma_O}') \cdot (\overline{\sigma_I}''||\overline{\sigma_O}'') \models \varphi$, we have*

$$S(\overline{\sigma} \cdot (\sigma_I, \sigma_O{}^f) \cdot (\overline{\sigma_I}'||\overline{\sigma_O}') \cdot (\overline{\sigma_I}''||\overline{\sigma_O}'')) = \overline{\sigma_O} \cdot \sigma_O{}^\# \cdot \overline{\sigma_O}{}^\# \cdot \overline{\sigma_O}''$$

and

$$(\overline{\sigma_I}||\overline{\sigma_O}) \cdot (\sigma_I, \sigma_O{}^\#) \cdot (\overline{\sigma_I}'||\overline{\sigma_O}{}^\#) \cdot (\overline{\sigma_I}''||\overline{\sigma_O}'') \models \varphi.$$

Note that it is not always possible to adversely k-stabilize a shield for a given k or even for any k.

Definition 2 (Adversely k-Stabilizing Shields [4]). *A shield S is adversely k-stabilizing if it adversely k-stabilies any finite trace.*

An adversely k-stabilizing shield guarantees to end deviations after at most k steps and produces a correct trace under the assumption that the failure of the design consists of a transmission error in the sense that the wrong letter is substituted for a correct one. We use the term *adversely* to emphasize that finitely long deviations are guaranteed for *any* future inputs and outputs of the design.

Definition 3 (Adversely Subgame Optimal Shield). *A shield S is adversely subgame optimal if for any trace $\overline{\sigma} \in \Sigma^*$, S adversely k-stabilizes $\overline{\sigma}$ and there exists no shield that adversely l-stabilizes $\overline{\sigma}$ for any $l < k$.*

An adversely subgame optimal shield S guarantees to deviate in response to an error for at most k time steps, for the smallest k possible.

Definition 4. *A shield S collaboratively k-stabilizes a trace $\overline{\sigma} = \overline{\sigma_I}||\overline{\sigma_O} \in \Sigma^*$, if for any input $\sigma_I \in \Sigma_I$ and any wrong output $\sigma_O{}^f \in \Sigma_O$,* **there exists** *a correct output $\sigma_O{}^c \in \Sigma_O$, a correct trace $\overline{\sigma_I}'||\overline{\sigma_O}' \in \Sigma^k$, and a trace $\sigma_O{}^\#\overline{\sigma_O}{}^\# \in \Sigma_O^{k+1}$*

such that for any trace $\overline{\sigma_I}''||\overline{\sigma_O}'' \in \Sigma^\omega$ such that $(\overline{\sigma_I}||\overline{\sigma_O}) \cdot (\sigma_I, \sigma_O{}^c) \cdot (\overline{\sigma_I}'||\overline{\sigma_O}') \cdot (\overline{\sigma_I}''||\overline{\sigma_O}'') \models \varphi$, we have

$$\mathcal{S}(\overline{\sigma} \cdot (\sigma_I, \sigma_O{}^f) \cdot (\overline{\sigma_I}'||\overline{\sigma_O}') \cdot (\overline{\sigma_I}''||\overline{\sigma_O}'')) = \overline{\sigma_O} \cdot \sigma_O{}^\# \cdot \overline{\sigma_O}{}^\# \cdot \overline{\sigma_O}''$$

and

$$(\overline{\sigma_I}||\overline{\sigma_O}) \cdot (\sigma_I, \sigma_O{}^\#) \cdot (\overline{\sigma_I}'||\overline{\sigma_O}{}^\#) \cdot (\overline{\sigma_I}''||\overline{\sigma_O}'') \models \varphi.$$

Definition 5 (Collaborative k-Stabilizing Shield). *A shield $\mathcal{S}$ is collaboratively k-stabilizing if it collaboratively k-stabilizes any finite trace.*

A collaborative k-stabilizing shield requires that it must be possible to end deviations after k steps, for some future input and output of $\mathcal{D}$. It is not necessary that this is possible for all future behavior of $\mathcal{D}$ allowing infinitely long deviations.

Definition 6 (Collaborative Subgame Optimal Shield). *A shield $\mathcal{S}$ is collaborative subgame optimal if for any trace $\overline{\sigma} \in \Sigma^*$, $\mathcal{S}$ collaboratively $k-$stabilizes $\overline{\sigma}$ and there exists no shield that adversely l-stabilizes $\overline{\sigma}$ for any $l < k$.*

Definition 7 (Admissible Shield). *A shield $\mathcal{S}$ is admissible if for any trace $\overline{\sigma}$, whenever there exists a k and a shield $\mathcal{S}'$ such that $\mathcal{S}'$ adversely k-stabilizes $\overline{\sigma}$, then $\mathcal{S}$ adversely k-stabilizes $\overline{\sigma}$. If such a k does not exist for trace $\overline{\sigma}$, then $\mathcal{S}$ collaboratively k-stabilizes $\overline{\sigma}$ for a minimal k.*

An admissible shield ends deviations whenever possible. In all states of the design $\mathcal{D}$ where a finite number of deviations can be guaranteed, an admissible shield deviates for each violation for at most k steps, for the smallest k possible. In all other states, the shield corrects the output in such a way that there exists design's inputs and outputs such that deviations end after l steps, for the smallest l possible.

5   Synthesizing Admissible Shields

The flow of the synthesis procedure is illustrated in Fig. 4. Starting from a safety specification $\varphi = (Q, q_0, \Sigma, \delta, F)$ with $\Sigma = \Sigma_I \times \Sigma_O$, the admissible shield synthesis procedure consists of five steps.

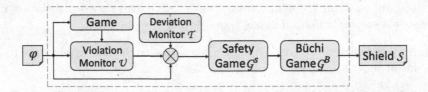

Fig. 4. Outline of our admissible shield synthesis procedure.

Step 1. Constructing the Violation Monitor $\mathcal{U}$. From φ we build the automaton $\mathcal{U} = (U, u_0, \Sigma, \delta^u)$ to monitor property violations by the design. The goal is to identify the latest point in time from which a specification violation can still be corrected with a deviation by the shield. This constitutes the start of the *recovery* period, in which the shield is allowed to deviate from the design. In this phase the shield monitors the design from all states that the design could reach under the current input and a correct output. A second violation occurs only if the next design's output is inconsistent with all states that are currently monitored. In case of a second violation, the shield monitors the set of all input-enabled states that are reachable from the current set of monitored states.

The first phase of the construction of the violation monitor $\mathcal{U}$ considers $\varphi = (Q, q_0, \Sigma, \delta, F)$ as a *safety game* and computes its winning region $W \subseteq F$ so that every reactive system $\mathcal{D} \models \varphi$ must produce outputs such that the next state of φ stays in W. Only in cases in which the next state of φ is outside of W the shield is allowed to interfere.

The second phase expands the state space Q to 2^Q via a subset construction, with the following rationale. If the design makes a mistake (i.e., picks outputs such that φ enters a state $q \notin W$), we have to "guess" what the design actually meant to do and we consider all output letters that would have avoided leaving W and continue monitoring the design from all the corresponding successor states in parallel. Thus, $\mathcal{U}$ is essentially a subset construction of φ, where a state $u \in U$ of $\mathcal{U}$ represents a set of states in φ.

The third phase expands the state space of $\mathcal{U}$ by adding a counter $d \in \{0, 1, 2\}$ and a output variable z. Initially d is 0. Whenever a property is violated d is set to 2. If $d > 0$, the shield is in the recovery phase and can deviate. If $d = 1$ and there is no other violation, d is decremented to 0. In order to decide when to decrement d from 2 to 1, we add an output z to the shield. If this output is set to true and $d = 2$, then d is set to 1.

The final violation monitor is $\mathcal{U} = (U, u_0, \Sigma^u, \delta^u)$, with the set of states $U = (2^Q \times \{0, 1, 2\})$, the initial state $u_0 = (\{q_0\}, 0)$, the input/output alphabet $\Sigma^u = \Sigma_I \times \Sigma_O^u$ with $\Sigma_O^u = \Sigma_O \cup z$, and the next-state function δ^u, which obeys the following rules:

1. $\delta^u((u, d), (\sigma_I, \sigma_O)) = (\{q' \in W \mid \exists q \in u, \sigma_O' \in \Sigma_O^u \,.\, \delta(q, (\sigma_I, \sigma_O')) = q'\}, 2)$
   if $\forall q \in u \,.\, \delta(q, (\sigma_I, \sigma_O)) \notin W$, and
2. $\delta^u((u, d), \sigma) = (\{q' \in W \mid \exists q \in u \,.\, \delta(q, \sigma) = q'\}, \mathsf{dec}(d))$ if $\exists q \in u \,.\, \delta(q, \sigma) \in W$,
   and $\mathsf{dec}(0) = \mathsf{dec}(1) = 0$, and if z is true then $\mathsf{dec}(2) = 1$, else $\mathsf{dec}(2) = 2$.

Our construction sets $d = 2$ whenever the design leaves the winning region, and not when it enters an unsafe state. Hence, the shield $\mathcal{S}$ can take a remedial action as soon as "the crime is committed", before the damage is detected, which would have been too late to correct the erroneous outputs of the design.

Example 1. We illustrate the construction of $\mathcal{U}$ using the specification φ from Fig. 5 over the outputs o_1 and o_2. (Figure 5 represents a safety automaton if we make all missing edges point to an (additional) unsafe state.) The winning region consists of all safe states, i.e., $W = \{F, S, T\}$. The resulting violation monitor

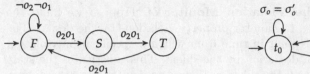

Fig. 5. Safety automaton of Example 1.

Fig. 6. The deviation monitor $\mathcal{T}$.

Table 1. δ^u of $\mathcal{U}$ of Example 1.

	$\neg o_1 \neg o_2$	$\neg o_1 o_2$ or $o_1 \neg o_2$	$o_1 o_2$
{F}	{F}	{F,S}⚡	{S}
{S}	{T}⚡	{T}⚡	{T}
{T}	{F}⚡	{F}⚡	{F}
{F,S}	{F}	{F,S,T}⚡	{S,T}
{S,T}	{F,T}⚡	{F,T}⚡	{F,T}
{F,T}	{F}	{F,S,T}⚡	{F,S}
{F,S,T}	{F}	{F,S,T}⚡	{F,S,T}

is $\mathcal{U} = (\{F, S, T, FS, ST, FT, FST\} \times \{0, 1, 2\}, (F, 0), \Sigma^u, \delta^u)$. The transition relation δ^u is illustrated in Table 1 and lists the next states for all possible present states and outputs. Lightning bolts denote specification violations. The update of counter d, which is not included in Table 1, is as follows: Whenever the design commits a violation d is set to 2. If no violation exists, d is decremented in the following way: if $d = 1$ or $d = 0$, d is set to 0. If $d = 2$ and z is true, d is set to 1, else d remains 2. In this example, z is set to true, whenever we are positive about the current state of the design (i.e. in $(\{F\}, d)$, $(\{S\}, d)$, and $(\{T\}, d)$).

Let us take a closer look at some entries of Table 1. If the current state is $(\{F\}, 0)$ and we observe the output $\neg o_2 o_1$, a specification violation occurs. We assume that $\mathcal{D}$ meant to give an allowed output, either $o_2 o_1$ or $\neg o_2 \neg o_1$. The shield continues to monitor both F and S; thus, $\mathcal{U}$ enters the state $(\{F, S\}, 2)$. If the next observation is $o_2 o_1$, which is allowed from both possible current states, the possible next states are S and T, therefore $\mathcal{U}$ traverses to state $(\{S, T\}, 2)$. However, if the next observation is again $\neg o_2 o_1$, which is neither allowed in F nor in S, we know that a second violation occurs. Therefore, the shield monitors the design from all three states and $\mathcal{U}$ enters the state $(\{F, S, T\}, 2)$.

Step 2. Constructing the Deviation Monitor $\mathcal{T}$. We build $\mathcal{T} = (T, t_0, \Sigma_O \times \Sigma_O, \delta^t)$ to monitor deviations between the shield and design outputs. Here, $T = \{t_0, t_1\}$ and $\delta^t(t, (\sigma_O, \sigma_O')) = t_0$ iff $\sigma_O = \sigma_O'$. That is, if there is a deviation in the current time step, then $\mathcal{T}$ will be in t_1 in the next time step. Otherwise, it will be in t_0. This deviation monitor is shown in Fig. 6.

Step 3. Constructing and Solving the Safety Game $\mathcal{G}^s$. Given the automata $\mathcal{U}$ and $\mathcal{T}$ and the safety automaton φ, we construct a safety game $\mathcal{G}^s = (G^s, g_0^s, \Sigma_I^s, \Sigma_O^s, \delta^s, F^s)$, which is the synchronous product of $\mathcal{U}$, $\mathcal{T}$, and φ, such that $G^s = U \times T \times Q$ is the state space, $g_0^s = (u_0, t_0, q_0)$ is the initial state, $\Sigma_I^s = \Sigma_I \times \Sigma_O$ is the input of the shield, $\Sigma_O^s = \Sigma_O \cup \{z\}$ is the output of the shield, δ^s is the next-state function, and F^s is the set of safe states such that $\delta^s((u, t, q), (\sigma_I, \sigma_O), (\sigma_O', z)) =$

$$(\delta^u[u, (\sigma_I, (\sigma_O, z))], \delta^t[t, (\sigma_O, \sigma_O')], \delta[q, (\sigma_I, \sigma_O')]),$$

and $F^s = \{(u, t, q) \in G^s \mid q \in F \wedge u = (w, 0) \to t = t_0\}$.

We require $q \in F$, which ensures that the output of the shield satisfies φ, and that the shield can only deviate in the recovery period (i.e., if $d = 0$, no deviation is allowed). We use standard algorithms for safety games (cf. [11]) to compute the winning region W^s and the most permissive non-deterministic winning strategy $\rho_s : G \times \Sigma_I \to 2^{\Sigma_O}$ that is not only winning for the system, but also contains all deterministic winning strategies.

Step 4. Constructing the Büchi Game $\mathcal{G}^b$. Implementing the safety game ensures correctness ($\mathcal{D} \circ \mathcal{S} \models \varphi$) and that the shield $\mathcal{S}$ keeps the output of the design $\mathcal{D}$ intact, if $\mathcal{D}$ does not violate φ. The shield still has to keep the number of deviations per violation to a minimum. Therefore, we would like the recovery period to be over infinitely often. This can be formalized as a Büchi winning condition. We construct the Büchi game $\mathcal{G}^b$ by applying the non-deterministic safety strategy ρ^s to the game graph $\mathcal{G}^s$.

Given the safety game $\mathcal{G}^s = (G^s, g_0^s, \Sigma_I^s, \Sigma_O^s, \delta^s, F^s)$ with the non-deterministic winning strategy ρ^s and the winning region W^s, we construct a Büchi game $\mathcal{G}^b = (G^b, g_0^b, \Sigma_I^b, \Sigma_O^b, \delta^b, F^b)$ such that $G^b = W^s$ is the state space, the initial state $g_0^b = g_0^s$ and the input/output alphabet $\Sigma_I^b = \Sigma_I^s$ and $\Sigma_O^b = \Sigma_O^s$ remain unchanged, $\delta^b = \delta^s \cap \rho^s$ is the transition function, and $F^b = \{(u, t, q) \in W^s \mid (u = (w, 0) \vee u = (w, 1))\}$ is the set of accepting states. A play is winning if $d \leq 1$ infinitely often.

Step 5. Solving the Büchi Game $\mathcal{G}^b$. Most likely, the Büchi game $\mathcal{G}^b$ contains reachable states, for which $d \leq 1$ cannot be enforced infinitely often. We implement an admissible strategy that enforces to visit $d \leq 1$ infinitely often whenever possible. This criterion essentially asks for a strategy that is winning with the help of the design.

The admissible strategy ρ^b for a Büchi game $\mathcal{G}^b = (G^b, g_0^b, \Sigma_I^b, \Sigma_O^b, \delta^b, F^b)$ can be computed as follows [11]:

1. Compute the winning region W^b and a winning strategy ρ_w^b for $\mathcal{G}^b$ (cf. [19]).
2. Remove all transitions that start in W^b and do not belong to ρ_w^b from $\mathcal{G}^b$. This results in a new Büchi game $\mathcal{G}_1^b = (G^b, g_0^b, \Sigma_I^b, \Sigma_O^b, \delta_1^b, F^b)$ with $(g, (\sigma_I, \sigma_O), g') \in \delta_1^b$ if $(g, \sigma_I, \sigma_O) \in \rho_w^b$ or if $\forall \sigma_O' \in \Sigma_O^b.(g, \sigma_I, \sigma_O') \notin \rho_w^b \wedge (g, (\sigma_I, \sigma_O), g') \in \delta^b$.
3. In the resulting game $\mathcal{G}_1^b$, compute a cooperatively winning strategy ρ^b. In order to compute ρ^b, one first has to transform all input variables to output

variables. This results in the Büchi game $\mathcal{G}_2^b = (G^b, g_0^b, \emptyset, \Sigma_I^b \times \Sigma_O^b, \delta_1^b, F^b)$. Afterwards, ρ^b can be computed with the standard algorithm for the winning strategy on $\mathcal{G}_2^b$.

The strategy ρ^b is an admissible strategy of the game $\mathcal{G}^b$, since it is winning and cooperatively winning [11]. Whenever the game $\mathcal{G}^b$ starts in a state of the winning region W^b, any play created by ρ_w^b is winning. Since ρ^b coincides with ρ_w^b in all states of the winning region W^b, ρ^b is winning. We know that ρ^b is cooperatively winning in the game $\mathcal{G}_1^b$. A proof that ρ^b is also cooperatively winning in the original game $\mathcal{G}^b$ can be found in [11].

Theorem 1. *A shield that implements the admissible strategy ρ^b in the Büchi game $\mathcal{G}^b = (G^b, g_0^b, \Sigma_I^b, \Sigma_O^b, \delta^b, F^b)$ in a new reactive system $\mathcal{S} = (G^b, g_0^b, \Sigma_I^b, \Sigma_O^b, \delta', \rho^b)$ with $\delta'(g, \sigma_I) = \delta^b(g, \sigma_I, \rho^b(g, \sigma_I))$ is an admissible shield.*

Proof 1. *First, the admissible strategy ρ^b is winning for all winning states of the Büchi game $\mathcal{G}^b$. Since winning strategies for Büchi games are subgame optimal, a shield that implements ρ^b ends deviations after the smallest number of steps possible, for all states of the design in which a finite number of deviations can be guaranteed. Second, ρ^b is cooperatively winning in the Büchi game $\mathcal{G}^b$. Therefore, in all states in which a finite number of deviation cannot be guaranteed, a shield that implements the strategy ρ^b recovers with the help of the design as soon as possible.*

The standard algorithm for solving Büchi games contains the computation of attractors; the i-th attractor for the system contains all states from which the system can "force" a visit of an accepting state in i steps. For all states $g \in G^b$ of the game $\mathcal{G}^b$, the attractor number of g corresponds to the smallest number of steps within which the recovery phase can be guaranteed to end, or can end with the help of the design if a finite number of deviation cannot be guaranteed.

Theorem 2. *Let $\varphi = \{Q, q_0, \Sigma, \delta, F\}$ be a safety specification and $|Q|$ be the cardinality of the state space of φ. An admissible shield with respect to φ can be synthesized in $\mathcal{O}(2^{|Q|})$ time, if it exists.*

Proof 2. *Our safety game $\mathcal{G}^s$ and our Büchi game $\mathcal{G}^b$ have at most $m = (2 \cdot 2^{|Q|} + |Q|) \cdot 2 \cdot |Q|$ states and at most $n = m^2$ edges. Safety games can be solved in $\mathcal{O}(m + n)$ time and Büchi games in $\mathcal{O}(m \cdot n)$ time [19].*

6   Experimental Results

We implemented our admissible shield synthesis procedure in Python, which takes a set of safety automata defined in a textual representation as input. The first step in our synthesis procedure is to build the product of all safety automata and construct the violation monitor 5. This step is performed on an explicit representation. For the remaining steps we use Binary Decision Diagrams (BDDs) for symbolic representation. The synthesized shields are encoded

Table 2. Results of map_8 and map_{31}.

Example	Property	$|Q|$	$|I|$	$|O|$	l	Time [sec]
Map$_8$	1	9	0	3	3	0.52
	1 + 4	12	0	3	3	1.2
	1 + 5a	46	1	3	4	6.2
	1 + 5b	32	1	3	3	7
	1 + 4 + 5a	55	1	3	4	17
	1 + 4 + 5b	36	1	3	3	12
Map$_{31}$	1	32	0	5	6	122
Map$_{31}$	1 + 2	32	0	5	6	143
Map$_{31}$	1 + 2 + 3	34	0	5	6	183
Map$_{31}$	1 + 2 + 3 + 4	38	0	5	6	238

Table 3. Results of map_{15}.

Example	Property	$|Q|$	$|I|$	$|O|$	l	Time [sec]
Map$_{15}$	1	16	0	4	5	12
	1 + 2	16	0	4	5	14
	1 + 2 + 3	19	0	4	5	19
	1 + 2 + 3 + 4	23	0	4	5	28
	1 + 5a	84	1	4	6	173
	1 + 5a + 2	84	1	4	6	205
	1 + 5a + 2 + 3	100	1	4	6	307
	1 + 5b	64	1	4	6	169
	1 + 5b + 2	64	1	4	6	195
	1 + 6	115	1	4	7	690

in Verilog format. To evaluate the performance of our tool, we constructed three sets of experiments, the basis of which is the safety specification of Fig. 1. This example represents a map with 15 waypoints and the six safety properties 1–6. First, we reduced the complexity of the example by only considering 8 out of 15 waypoints. This new example, called Map_8, consists of the waypoints loc_1 to loc_8 with their corresponding properties. The second series of experiments, called Map_{15}, considers the original specification of Fig. 1 over all 15 waypoints. The synthesized shields behave as described in Sect. 2. The third series of experiments, called Map_{31}, considers a map with 31 waypoints, essentially adding a duplicate of the map in Fig. 1. All results are summarized in Table 2 and in Table 3. For both tables, the first columns list the set of specification automata and the number of states, inputs, and outputs of their product automata. The next column lists the smallest number of steps l under which the shield is able to recover with the help of the design. The last column lists the synthesis time in seconds. All computation times are for a computer with a 2.6 GHz Intel i5-3320M CPU with 8 GB RAM running an 64-bit distribution of Linux. Source code, input files, and instructions to reproduce our experiments are available for download[1].

7 Conclusion

We have proposed a new shield synthesis procedure to synthesize *admissible shields*. We have shown that admissible shields overcome the limitations of previously developed k-stabilizing shields. We believe our approach and first experimental results over our case study involving UAV mission planning open several directions for future research. At the moment, shields only attend to safety properties and disregard liveness properties. Integrating liveness is therefore a preferable next step. Furthermore, we plan to further develop our prototype tool and apply shields in other domains such as in the distributed settings or for Safe Reinforcement Learning, in which safety constraints must be enforced during the learning processes. We plan to investigate how a shield might be most beneficial in such settings.

---

[1] http://www.iaik.tugraz.at/content/research/design_verification/others/.

References

1. Bloem, R., Chatterjee, K., Greimel, K., Henzinger, T.A., Hofferek, G., Jobstmann, B., Könighofer, B., Könighofer, R.: Synthesizing robust systems. Acta Informatica **51**(3–4), 193–220 (2014)
2. Bloem, R., Ehlers, E., Könighofer, R.: Cooperative reactive synthesis. In: Finkbeiner, B., Pu, G., Zhang, L. (eds.) ATVA 2015. LNCS, vol. 9364, pp. 394–410. Springer, Heidelberg (2015). doi:10.1007/978-3-319-24953-7_29
3. Bloem, R., Jobstmann, B., Piterman, N., Pnueli, A., Sa'ar, Y.: Synthesis of reactive(1) designs. J. Comput. Syst. Sci. **78**(3), 911–938 (2012)
4. Bloem, R., Könighofer, B., Könighofer, R., Wang, C.: Shield synthesis: - runtime enforcement for reactive systems. In: Baier, C., Tinelli, C. (eds.) TACAS 2015. LNCS, vol. 9035, pp. 533–548. Springer, Heidelberg (2015). doi:10.1007/978-3-662-46681-0_50
5. Chao, H., Cao, Y., Chen, Y.: Autopilots for small unmanned aerial vehicles: a survey. Int. J. Control Autom. Syst. **8**(1), 36–44 (2010)
6. Chen, J., Barnes, M.: Supervisory control of multiple robot: effects of imperfect automation and individual differences. Hum. Fact.: J. Hum. Fact. Ergon. Soc. **54**(2), 157–174 (2012)
7. Dalamagkidis, K., Valavanis, K.P., Piegl, L.A.: On Integrating Unmanned Aircraft Systems into the National Airspace System: Issues, Challenges, Operational Restrictions, Certification, and Recommendations, vol. 54. Springer Science & Business Media, Berlin (2011)
8. Donmez, B., Nehme, C., Cummings, M.L.: Modeling workload impact in multiple unmanned vehicle supervisory control. IEEE Trans. Syst. Man Cybern. A. Syst. Hum. **40**(6), 1180–1190 (2010)
9. Ehlers, R., Könighofer, R., Bloem, R.: Synthesizing cooperative reactive mission plans. In: 2015 IEEE/RSJ International Conference on Intelligent Robots and Systems, IROS 2015, Hamburg, Germany, pp. 3478–3485. IEEE (2015)
10. Ehlers, R., Topcu, U.: Resilience to intermittent assumption violations in reactive synthesis. In: 17th International Conference on Hybrid Systems: Computation and Control, HSCC 2014, Berlin, Germany, 15–17 April 2014, pp. 203–212. ACM (2014)
11. Faella, M.: Admissible strategies in infinite games over graphs. In: Královič, R., Niwiński, D. (eds.) MFCS 2009. LNCS, vol. 5734, pp. 307–318. Springer, Heidelberg (2009). doi:10.1007/978-3-642-03816-7_27
12. Falcone, Y., Fernandez, J.-C., Mounier, L.: What can you verify and enforce at runtime? STTT **14**(3), 349–382 (2012)
13. Feng, L., Wiltsche, C., Humphrey, L., Topcu, U.: Synthesis of human-in-the-loop control protocols for autonomous systems. In: IEEE/RSJ International Conference on Intelligent Robots and Systems (IROS) (2016)
14. Leucker, M., Schallhart, S.: A brief account of runtime verification. J. Log. Algebr. Program. **78**(5), 293–303 (2009)
15. Li, W., Sadigh, D., Sastry, S.S., Seshia, S.A.: Synthesis for human-in-the-loop control systems. In: Ábrahám, E., Havelund, K. (eds.) TACAS 2014. LNCS, vol. 8413, pp. 470–484. Springer, Heidelberg (2014). doi:10.1007/978-3-642-54862-8_40
16. Loh, R., Bian, Y., Roe, T.: UAVs in civil airspace: safety requirements. IEEE Aerosp. Electron. Syst. Mag. **24**(1), 5–17 (2009)
17. Lygeros, J., Godbole, D.N., Sastry, S.: Verified hybrid controllers for automated vehicles. IEEE Trans. Autom. Control **43**, 522–539 (1996)

18. Mancini, T., Mari, F., Massini, A., Melatti, I., Tronci, E.: Anytime system level verification via random exhaustive hardware in the loop simulation. In: 2014 17th Euromicro Conference on Digital System Design (DSD), pp. 236–245, August 2014
19. Mazala, R.: Infinite games. In: Grädel, E., Thomas, W., Wilke, T. (eds.) Automata Logics, and Infinite Games: A Guide to Current Research. LNCS, vol. 2500, pp. 23–38. Springer, Heidelberg (2002). doi:10.1007/3-540-36387-4_2
20. Pnueli, A., Rosner, R.: On the synthesis of an asynchronous reactive module. In: Ausiello, G., Dezani-Ciancaglini, M., Rocca, S.R. (eds.) ICALP 1989. LNCS, vol. 372, pp. 652–671. Springer, Heidelberg (1989). doi:10.1007/BFb0035790

Probabilistic Hybrid Systems Verification via SMT and Monte Carlo Techniques

Fedor Shmarov and Paolo Zuliani[✉]

School of Computing Science, Newcastle University, Newcastle upon Tyne, UK
{f.shmarov,paolo.zuliani}@ncl.ac.uk

Abstract. We develop numerically rigorous Monte Carlo approaches for computing probabilistic reachability in hybrid systems subject to random and nondeterministic parameters. Instead of standard simulation we use δ-complete SMT procedures, which enable formal reasoning for nonlinear systems up to a user-definable numeric precision. Monte Carlo approaches for probability estimation assume that sampling is possible for the real system at hand. However, when using δ-complete simulation one instead samples from an overapproximation of the real random variable. In this paper, we introduce a Monte Carlo-SMT approach for computing probabilistic reachability confidence intervals that are both statistically and numerically rigorous. We apply our technique to hybrid systems involving nonlinear differential equations.

1 Introduction

In this paper we combine statistical (Monte Carlo) techniques and numerically sound decision procedures to reason about hybrid systems with random and nondeterministic parameters. In particular, we devise confidence-interval techniques for *bounded probabilistic reachability*, *i.e.*, we aim at computing statistically valid enclosures for the probability that a hybrid system reaches a given set of states within a given time bound and number of discrete transitions. When nondeterministic parameters are present, a hybrid system will in general feature a range of reachability probabilities, depending on the value of the nondeterministic parameters. Reachability is an important class of behavioural properties, as many verification problems (*e.g.*, proving system safety) can be reduced to reachability questions. A statistical approach to probabilistic reachability is important because statistical techniques trade correctness guarantees with efficiency, and so can scale much better with system size than other rigorous approaches. For example, statistical model checking [15] can be faster than probabilistic model checking, which is based on exhaustive state space search [14]. Also, statistical model checking can handle models for which no efficient verification tools exist, such as cyber-physical systems [2].

Monte Carlo techniques for probability estimation assume that one can sample the random variable representing the true system behaviour. However, while this is possible for certain finite-state systems, for nonlinear systems (*e.g.*, ordinary differential equations (ODEs) with trigonometric functions) it is not.

© Springer International Publishing AG 2016
R. Bloem and E. Arbel (Eds.): HVC 2016, LNCS 10028, pp. 152–168, 2016.
DOI: 10.1007/978-3-319-49052-6_10

In fact, sampling the random variable representing the true system behaviour can be as hard as reachability, which is undecidable even for very simple systems (*e.g.*, linear hybrid automata [1]). Thus, one has to deal with numerical imprecisions that could lead to missing important events in the true system evolution. For example, zero-crossings can be indistinguishable from "safe" trajectories [8].

A novel aspect of our work is that we explicitly take into account undecidability and numerical precision by employing δ-complete decision procedures [4], which enable formal reasoning up to a user-defined numerical precision over bounded domains. In this way it is possible to handle in a sound and safe manner complex dynamical systems, such as nonlinear ODEs [6]. Given any $\delta > 0$ and an arbitrary first-order formula ϕ over the reals, a δ-complete decision procedure returns **unsat** if ϕ is false and δ-**sat** if ϕ^δ (a weaker version of formula ϕ) is true. Note that the latter result does not imply satisfiability of the initial formula. Also, the value of δ affects the precision of the result, and large values of δ can cause *false* alarms (*i.e.*, δ-**sat** is returned for a formula which is in fact false). Statistical techniques must therefore take into account that samples are only approximation of the real random variable corresponding to the system evolution. In particular, we introduce an approach for computing statistically *and* numerically rigorous confidence intervals for probabilistic reachability. We exemplify our techniques to hybrid systems with random and/or nondeterministic parameters. For systems with both random and nondeterministic parameters we estimate the (nondeterministic) parameter values that result in the minimal and maximal reachability probabilities. Our algorithms can in principle be applied to other stochastic models (*e.g.*, continuous-time Markov chains) should the corresponding δ-complete decision procedure be available.

Related Work. We focus on works that combine statistical techniques with SMT procedures, which are the main subject areas of the paper. The tool SReach [13] combines statistical estimation with δ-complete simulation procedures. However, SReach only considers overapproximations of the reachability probability, and thus can offer one-sided confidence intervals only. We instead compute confidence intervals that are *guaranteed* to contain both the under- and overapproximation of the reachability probability. Also, SReach does not handle nondeterministic parameters, while we do. In [3] the authors present a statistical model checking approach combined with SMT decision procedures, but it is restricted to fixed-sample size techniques, while we develop a more efficient sequential Bayesian approach and consider δ-complete decision procedures.

2 Bounded Reachability in Hybrid Systems

Hybrid systems provide a framework for modelling real-world systems that combine continuous and discrete dynamics [1]. We consider parametric hybrid systems as a variant of hybrid systems featuring continuous and discrete parameters whose values are set in the initial state and do not change during the system's evolution. Such parameters can be random when there is a probability measure associated with them, and nondeterministic otherwise. We now formally define the systems we consider in this paper.

Definition 1 (PHS). *A Parametric Hybrid System is a tuple*

$$H = < Q, \Upsilon, X, P, Y, R, \text{jump}, \text{goal} >$$

where

- $Q = \{q_0, \cdots, q_m\}$ *a set of modes (discrete components of the system),*
- $\Upsilon = \{(q, q') : q, q' \in Q\}$ *a set of transitions between modes,*
- $X = [u_1, v_1] \times \cdots \times [u_n, v_n] \subset \mathbb{R}^n$ *a domain of continuous variables,*
- $P = [a_1, b_1] \times \cdots \times [a_k, b_k] \subset \mathbb{R}^k$ *the parameter space of the system,*
- $Y = \{\mathbf{y}_q(\mathbf{p}, t) : q \in Q, \mathbf{p} \in X \times P, t \in [0, T]\}$ *the continuous system dynamics where* $\mathbf{y}_q : X \times P \times [0, T] \to X$,
- $R = \{\mathbf{g}_{(q,q')}(\mathbf{p}, t) : (q, q') \in \Upsilon, \mathbf{p} \in X \times P, t \in [0, T]\}$ *'reset' functions* $\mathbf{g}_{(q,q')} :$ $X \times P \times [0, T] \to X \times P$ *defining the continuous state at time* $t = 0$ *in mode* q' *after taking the transition from mode* q.

and predicates (or relations)

- $\text{jump}_{(q,q')}(\mathbf{x})$ *defines a discrete transition* $(q, q') \in \Upsilon$ *which may (but does not have to) occur upon reaching the jump condition in state* $(\mathbf{x}, q) \in X \times P \times Q$,
- $\text{goal}_q(\mathbf{x})$ *defines the goal state* $\mathbf{x}$ *in mode* q.

The continuous system dynamics Y is represented by initial value problems with Lipschitz-continuous ODEs, which by the well-known Picard-Lindelöf theorem have a unique solution for any given initial condition $\mathbf{p} \in X \times P$ and $t_0 \in [0, T]$. We treat system parameters as any other variable, except that their derivatives are zero. Thus, the parameters are part of the initial conditions.

Bounded reachability in PHSs aims to decide whether, for given initial conditions, the system reaches a goal state in a finite number of discrete transitions. Given a PHS and a reachability depth l we can derive the set $\mathbf{Path}(l)$ of all paths π of length $|\pi| = l + 1$ whose first $(\pi(0))$ and last $(\pi(l))$ elements are the initial and the goal mode, respectively. The *bounded reachability property* for a path $\pi \in \mathbf{Path}(l)$ and initial condition $\mathbf{p}$ can be checked by evaluating the formula:

$$\phi(\pi, \mathbf{p}) := \exists^{[0,T]} t_0, \cdots, \exists^{[0,T]} t_{|\pi|-1} : (\mathbf{x}_{\pi(0)}^t = \mathbf{y}_{\pi(0)}(\mathbf{p}, t_0)) \wedge$$

$$\bigwedge_{i=0}^{|\pi|-2} \left[\text{jump}_{(\pi(i),\pi(i+1))}(\mathbf{x}_{\pi(i)}^t) \wedge \left(\mathbf{x}_{\pi(i+1)}^t = \mathbf{y}_{\pi(i)}(\mathbf{g}_{(\pi(i),\pi(i+1))}(\mathbf{x}_{\pi(i)}^t, t_i), t_{i+1}) \right) \right]$$

$$\wedge \text{goal}_{\pi(|\pi|-1)}(\mathbf{x}_{\pi(|\pi|-1)}^t) \, . \tag{1}$$

where $\exists^{[0,T]} t_i$ is a shorthand for $\exists t_i \in [0, T]$.

Note that the terms $\mathbf{x}_{\pi(i+1)}^t = \mathbf{y}_{\pi(i)}(\mathbf{g}_{(\pi(i),\pi(i+1))}(\mathbf{x}_{\pi(i)}^t, t_i), t_{i+1})$ and $\mathbf{x}_{\pi(0)}^t = \mathbf{y}_{\pi(0)}(\mathbf{p}, t_0)$ are purely syntactic substitutions. Formulas over the reals like (1) are undecidable in general [9], but a relaxed version (δ-weakening [4]) is instead decidable.

Definition 2 (δ-Weakening [4]**).** *Given a bounded Σ_1 sentence and an arbitrarily small positive δ*

$$\exists^X \mathbf{x} : \bigwedge_{i=1}^{m} (\bigvee_{j=1}^{k_i} (f_{i,j}(\mathbf{x}) = 0))$$

(where the $f_{i,j}$ are Type-2 real computable functions) its δ-weakening is

$$\exists^X \mathbf{x} : \bigwedge_{i=1}^{m} (\bigvee_{j=1}^{k_i} (|f_{i,j}(\mathbf{x})| \leq \delta))$$

It is easy to see that the bounded reachability property (1) can be rewritten in the format of Definition 2 (see [4]). A δ-complete decision procedure [4] *correctly* decides whether an arbitrary bounded Σ_1 (existentially quantified) sentence is false (**unsat** answer) or its δ-weakening is true (δ-**sat** answer). Note that with a δ-complete decision procedure **unsat** can always be trusted, while δ-**sat** might in fact be a false alarm due to a coarse overapproximation characterised by δ.

Evaluating (1) by a δ-complete decision procedure returns **unsat** only if for the given parameter value $\mathbf{p}$ the path does not reach a goal state. If δ-**sat** is returned, we may try to sharpen the answer by checking an appropriate formula. For example, an **unsat** answer to formula $\phi^\forall(\pi, \mathbf{p})$ below implies reachability:

$$\phi^\forall(\pi, \mathbf{p}) := \forall^{[0,T]} t_0, \cdots, \forall^{[0,T]} t_{|\pi|-1} : (\mathbf{x}^t_{\pi(0)} \neq \mathbf{y}_{\pi(0)}(\mathbf{p}, t_0)) \vee$$

$$\bigvee_{i=0}^{|\pi|-2} \left[\neg\mathrm{jump}_{(\pi(i),\pi(i+1))}(\mathbf{x}^t_{\pi(i)}) \vee (\mathbf{x}^t_{\pi(i+1)} \neq \mathbf{y}_{\pi(i)}(\mathbf{g}_{(\pi(i),\pi(i+1))}(\mathbf{x}^t_{\pi(i)}, t_i), t_{i+1})) \right]$$

$$\vee \neg\mathrm{goal}_{\pi(|\pi|-1)}(\mathbf{x}^t_{\pi(|\pi|-1)})$$

In the previous formula the time variables are quantified universally. Current implementations of δ-complete decision procedures [5] can only handle formulas where the universal quantification is introduced over a single time variable. The goal predicate in $\phi^\forall(\pi, \mathbf{p})$ depends on $|\pi|$ variables and thus cannot be handled directly. To resolve this issue we instead evaluate a series of formulas ψ_j:

$$\psi_j(\pi, \mathbf{p}) := \exists^{[0,T]} t_0, \cdots, \forall^{[0,T]} t_j : (\mathbf{x}^t_{\pi(0)} = \mathbf{y}_{\pi(0)}(\mathbf{p}, t_0)) \wedge$$

$$\bigwedge_{i=0}^{j-1} \left[\mathbf{x}^t_{\pi(i+1)} = \mathbf{y}_{\pi(i)}(\mathbf{g}_{(\pi(i),\pi(i+1))}(\mathbf{x}^t_{\pi(i)}, t_i), t_{i+1}) \right] \wedge \neg\mathrm{jump}_{(\pi(j),\pi(j+1))}(\mathbf{x}^t_{\pi(j)})$$

$$\tag{2}$$

if $j < |\pi| - 1$ and

$$\psi_j(\pi, \mathbf{p}) := \exists^{[0,T]} t_0, \cdots, \forall^{[0,T]} t_j : (\mathbf{x}^t_{\pi(0)} = \mathbf{y}_{\pi(0)}(\mathbf{p}, t_0)) \wedge$$

$$\bigwedge_{i=0}^{j-1} \left[\mathbf{x}^t_{\pi(i+1)} = \mathbf{y}_{\pi(i)}(\mathbf{g}_{(\pi(i),\pi(i+1))}(\mathbf{x}^t_{\pi(i)}, t_i), t_{i+1}) \right] \wedge \neg\mathrm{goal}_{\pi(j)}(\mathbf{x}^t_{\pi(j)}) \tag{3}$$

if $j = |\pi| - 1$. The next proposition establishes a stronger formula for reachability.

Proposition 1. *With the definitions in (1), (2) and (3) we have*

$$\bigwedge_{j=0}^{|\pi|-1} \neg\psi_j(\pi, \mathbf{p}) \;\Rightarrow\; \phi(\pi, \mathbf{p})$$

Proof. Consider the case $|\pi| = 1$. It can be seen that $\neg\psi_0(\pi, \mathbf{p}) \Leftrightarrow \phi(\pi, \mathbf{p})$ as

$$\neg\psi_0(\pi, \mathbf{p}) := \exists^{[0,T]} t_0 : \text{goal}_{\pi(0)}(\mathbf{x}^t_{\pi(0)}) \Leftrightarrow \phi(\pi, \mathbf{p})$$

Consider now the case $|\pi| > 1$.

$$\bigwedge_{j=0}^{|\pi|-1} \neg\psi_j(\pi, \mathbf{p}) := \bigwedge_{j=0}^{|\pi|-2} \left[\forall^{[0,T]} t_0, \cdots, \forall^{[0,T]} t_{j-1}, \exists^{[0,T]} t_j : (\mathbf{x}^t_{\pi(0)} \neq \mathbf{y}_{\pi(0)}(\mathbf{p}, t_0)) \vee \right.$$

$$\left. \bigvee_{i=0}^{j-1} \left(\mathbf{x}^t_{\pi(i+1)} \neq \mathbf{y}_{\pi(i)}(\mathbf{g}_{(\pi(i),\pi(i+1))}(\mathbf{x}^t_{\pi(i)}, t_i), t_{i+1}) \right) \vee \text{jump}_{(\pi(j),\pi(j+1))}(\mathbf{x}^t_{\pi(i)}) \right] \wedge$$

$$\left[\forall^{[0,T]} t_0, \cdots, \forall^{[0,T]} t_{|\pi|-2}, \exists^{[0,T]} t_{|\pi|-1} : (\mathbf{x}^t_{\pi(0)} \neq \mathbf{y}_{\pi(0)}(\mathbf{p}, t_0)) \vee \right.$$

$$\left. \bigvee_{i=0}^{|\pi|-2} \left(\mathbf{x}^t_{\pi(i+1)} \neq \mathbf{y}_{\pi(i)}(\mathbf{g}_{(\pi(i),\pi(i+1))}(\mathbf{x}^t_{\pi(i)}, t_i), t_{i+1}) \right) \vee \text{goal}_{\pi(|\pi|-1)}(\mathbf{x}^t_{\pi(|\pi|-1)}) \right]$$

We recall that terms $\mathbf{x}^t_{\pi(0)} = \mathbf{y}_{\pi(0)}$ and $\mathbf{x}^t_{\pi(i+1)} = \mathbf{y}_{\pi(i)}(\mathbf{g}_{(\pi(i),\pi(i+1))}(\mathbf{x}^t_{\pi(i)}, t_i), t_{i+1})$ are just a syntactic substitution which cannot be falsified as the system dynamics always exist (by the Picard-Lindelöf theorem). Hence, the formula above implies the following:

$$\bigwedge_{j=0}^{|\pi|-2} \left[\forall^{[0,T]} t_0, \cdots, \forall^{[0,T]} t_{j-1}, \exists^{[0,T]} t_j : (\mathbf{x}^t_{\pi(0)} = \mathbf{y}_{\pi(0)}(\mathbf{p}, t_0)) \wedge \right.$$

$$\left. \bigwedge_{i=0}^{j-1} \left(\mathbf{x}^t_{\pi(i+1)} = \mathbf{y}_{\pi(i)}(\mathbf{g}_{(\pi(i),\pi(i+1),t_i)}(\mathbf{x}^t_{\pi(i)}, t_i), t_{i+1}) \right) \wedge \text{jump}_{(\pi(j),\pi(j+1))}(\mathbf{x}^t_{\pi(i)}) \right] \wedge$$

$$\left[\forall^{[0,T]} t_0, \cdots, \forall^{[0,T]} t_{|\pi|-2}, \exists^{[0,T]} t_{|\pi|-1} : (\mathbf{x}^t_{\pi(0)} = \mathbf{y}_{\pi(0)}(\mathbf{p}, t_0)) \wedge \right.$$

$$\left. \bigwedge_{i=0}^{|\pi|-2} \left(\mathbf{x}^t_{\pi(i+1)} = \mathbf{y}_{\pi(i)}(\mathbf{g}_{(\pi(i),\pi(i+1),t_i)}(\mathbf{x}^t_{\pi(i)}, t_i), t_{i+1}) \right) \wedge \text{goal}_{\pi(|\pi|-1)}(\mathbf{x}^t_{\pi(|\pi|-1)}) \right]$$

The next step can be equivalently derived by moving universal quantifiers from the second part of the formula (square brackets containing the goal predicate) outside the entire formula:

$$\forall^{[0,T]}t_0, \cdots, \forall^{[0,T]}t_{|\pi|-2} : \bigwedge_{j=0}^{|\pi|-2} \left[\exists^{[0,T]}t_j : \left(\mathbf{x}^t_{\pi(0)} = \mathbf{y}_{\pi(0)}(\mathbf{p}, t_0)\right) \wedge \right.$$

$$\left. \bigwedge_{i=0}^{j-1} \left(\mathbf{x}^t_{\pi(i+1)} = \mathbf{y}_{\pi(i)}(\mathbf{g}_{(\pi(i),\pi(i+1))}(\mathbf{x}^t_{\pi(i)}, t_i), t_{i+1})\right) \wedge \mathrm{jump}_{(\pi(j),\pi(j+1))}(\mathbf{x}^t_{\pi(i)}) \right] \wedge$$

$$\left[\exists^{[0,T]}t_{|\pi|-1} : \left(\mathbf{x}^t_{\pi(0)} = \mathbf{y}_{\pi(0)}(\mathbf{p}, t_0)\right) \wedge \right.$$

$$\left. \bigwedge_{i=0}^{|\pi|-2} \left(\mathbf{x}^t_{\pi(i+1)} = \mathbf{y}_{\pi(i)}(\mathbf{g}_{(\pi(i),\pi(i+1))}(\mathbf{x}^t_{\pi(i)}, t_i), t_{i+1})\right) \wedge \mathrm{goal}_{\pi(|\pi|-1)}(\mathbf{x}^t_{\pi(|\pi|-1)}) \right]$$

The existential quantifiers $\exists^{[0,T]}t_j$ can be eliminated as variables t_j are already quantified universally. Also $\exists^{[0,T]}t_{|\pi|-1}$ can be moved in front of the formula as its first part (square brackets containing jump predicates) does not depend of $t_{|\pi|-1}$. Hence, the formula above can be written as:

$$\forall^{[0,T]}t_0, \cdots, \forall^{[0,T]}t_{|\pi|-2}, \exists^{[0,T]}t_{|\pi|-1} : \bigwedge_{j=0}^{|\pi|-2} \left[\left(\mathbf{x}^t_{\pi(0)} = \mathbf{y}_{\pi(0)}(\mathbf{p}, t_0)\right) \wedge \right.$$

$$\left. \bigwedge_{i=0}^{j-1} \left(\mathbf{x}^t_{\pi(i+1)} = \mathbf{y}_{\pi(i)}(\mathbf{g}_{(\pi(i),\pi(i+1))}(\mathbf{x}^t_{\pi(i)}, t_i), t_{i+1})\right) \wedge \mathrm{jump}_{(\pi(j),\pi(j+1))}(\mathbf{x}^t_{\pi(i)}) \right] \wedge$$

$$\left[\left(\mathbf{x}^t_{\pi(0)} = \mathbf{y}_{\pi(0)}(\mathbf{p}, t_0)\right) \wedge \right.$$

$$\left. \bigwedge_{i=0}^{|\pi|-2} \left(\mathbf{x}^t_{\pi(i+1)} = \mathbf{y}_{\pi(i)}(\mathbf{g}_{(\pi(i),\pi(i+1))}(\mathbf{x}^t_{\pi(i)}, t_i), t_{i+1})\right) \wedge \mathrm{goal}_{\pi(|\pi|-1)}(\mathbf{x}^t_{\pi(|\pi|-1)}) \right] \Leftrightarrow$$

By idempotency of conjunction $(A \wedge A = A)$ terms $\mathbf{x}^t_{\pi(0)} = \mathbf{y}_{\pi(0)}$ and $\mathbf{x}^t_{\pi(i+1)} = \mathbf{y}_{\pi(i)}(\mathbf{g}_{(\pi(i),\pi(i+1))}(\mathbf{x}^t_{\pi(i)}, t_i), t_{i+1})$ can be merged:

$$\forall^{[0,T]}t_0, \cdots, \forall^{[0,T]}t_{|\pi|-2}, \exists^{[0,T]}t_{|\pi|-1} : \left(\mathbf{x}^t_{\pi(0)} = \mathbf{y}_{\pi(0)}(\mathbf{p}, t_0)\right) \wedge$$

$$\bigwedge_{j=0}^{|\pi|-2} \left[\left(\mathbf{x}^t_{\pi(j+1)} = \mathbf{y}_{\pi(j)}(\mathbf{g}_{(\pi(j),\pi(j+1))}(\mathbf{x}^t_{\pi(j)}, t_j), t_{j+1})\right) \wedge \mathrm{jump}_{(\pi(j),\pi(j+1))}(\mathbf{x}^t_{\pi(i)}) \right] \wedge$$

$$\mathrm{goal}_{\pi(|\pi|-1)}(\mathbf{x}^t_{\pi(|\pi|-1)})$$

Finally, the following is implied:

$$\exists^{[0,T]}t_0, \cdots, \exists^{[0,T]}t_{|\pi|-2}, \exists^{[0,T]}t_{|\pi|-1} : \left(\mathbf{x}^t_{\pi(0)} = \mathbf{y}_{\pi(0)}(\mathbf{p}, t_0)\right) \wedge$$

$$\bigwedge_{j=0}^{|\pi|-2} \left[\left(\mathbf{x}^t_{\pi(j+1)} = \mathbf{y}_{\pi(j)}(\mathbf{g}_{(\pi(j),\pi(j+1))}(\mathbf{x}^t_{\pi(j)}, t_j), t_{j+1})\right) \wedge \mathrm{jump}_{(\pi(j),\pi(j+1))}(\mathbf{x}^t_{\pi(i)}) \right] \wedge$$

$$\mathrm{goal}_{\pi(|\pi|-1)}(\mathbf{x}^t_{\pi(|\pi|-1)}) \Leftrightarrow \phi(\pi, \mathbf{p})$$

$\square$

Proposition 1 enables us to define an **evaluate** procedure (Algorithm 1) which, given a parametric hybrid system H, reachability depth l, a parameter value $\mathbf{p} \in X \times P$ and a precision δ for the δ-complete decision procedure, returns **sat** if $\exists \pi \in \mathbf{Path}(l) : \phi(\pi, \mathbf{p})$, **unsat** if $\forall \pi \in \mathbf{Path}(l) : \neg\phi(\pi, \mathbf{p})$ and **undet** if neither of the above two can be concluded. In general, the **undet** outcome suggests that either the chosen precision δ is not sufficient to decide the satisfiability of $\phi(\pi, \mathbf{p})$, or that $\phi(\pi, \mathbf{p})$ is undecidable (*i.e.*, non-robust [4]).

The **evaluate** procedure is crucial for building the random variables that under- and over-approximate the true system behaviour on the reachability question, as we show in the next section.

Algorithm 1. evaluate$(H, l, \mathbf{p}, \delta)$

---

1 input: H - PHS, l - reachability depth, $\mathbf{p}$ - parameter value, δ - precision;
2 output: **sat** / **unsat** / **undet**;
3 $\mathbf{Path}(l) = get\_all\_paths(H, l)$;   // compute all paths of length l for H
4 **for** $\pi \in \mathbf{Path}(l)$ **do**
5 $\quad$ **if** $\phi(\pi, \mathbf{p})$ - δ-**sat then**
6 $\quad\quad$ **for** $i \in [0, l]$ **do**
7 $\quad\quad\quad$ **if** $\psi_i(\pi, \mathbf{p})$ - δ-**sat then**
8 $\quad\quad\quad\quad$ **return undet**;
9 $\quad$ **return sat** ;   // all $\psi_i(\pi, \mathbf{p})$ are **unsat** for the current π
10 **return unsat** ;   // all $\phi(\pi, \mathbf{p})$ are **unsat**

---

3 Monte Carlo Probability Estimation

In this section we consider hybrid systems with random parameters only, so that the reachability probability is well-defined. We add nondeterministic parameters in the next section. For any given $\delta > 0$ and any $\mathbf{p}$ from the parameter(s) distribution we introduce the Bernoulli random variables:

$$X = \begin{cases} 1 & \text{if system } H \text{ reaches the goal in } l \text{ steps for a given } \mathbf{p} \\ 0 & \text{otherwise} \end{cases} \tag{4}$$

$$X_{sat} = \begin{cases} 1 & \text{if } \mathbf{evaluate}(H, l, \mathbf{p}, \delta) = \mathbf{sat} \\ 0 & \text{otherwise} \end{cases} \tag{5}$$

$$X_{usat} = \begin{cases} 0 & \text{if } \mathbf{evaluate}(H, l, \mathbf{p}, \delta) = \mathbf{unsat} \\ 1 & \text{otherwise.} \end{cases} \tag{6}$$

Thus, for a given parameter $\mathbf{p}$, X_{sat} is 1 if we can correctly decide that system H reaches the goal, while X_{usat} is 0 if we can correctly decide that H does *not* reach the goal. If no decision can be made (because of the precision δ being used or of the nature of the reachability question), X_{sat} and X_{usat} take 0 and 1, respectively. From the definition of **evaluate** it follows directly that:

$$X_{sat} \leq X \leq X_{usat}. \tag{7}$$

We now introduce a Bayesian technique for calculating confidence intervals for the reachability probability $p = \mathbb{E}[X]$ without sampling X, which is not possible in general, but instead sampling X_{sat} and X_{usat}. For n random variables iid (independent and identically distributed) as X_{sat} and X_{usat}, we define the random variables:

$$\hat{S}_n = \frac{\Sigma_{i=1}^n X_{sat,i}}{n} \qquad \hat{U}_n = \frac{\Sigma_{i=1}^n X_{usat,i}}{n}.$$

The Bayesian approach assumes that the (unknown) reachability probability p is itself a random quantity (here we give a brief overview only, more details can be found in [17]). Bayes' theorem enables computing the *posterior* distribution of the unknown quantity given its *prior* distribution and the likelihood of the data (*i.e.*, samples of X). The posterior distribution of p can be directly used to build confidence (credibility) intervals. In our setting we cannot sample X, so we aim at bounding the posterior of p by the posteriors built from X_{sat} and X_{usat}, as we show below. We use Beta distribution priors since they are conjugate to the Bernoulli likelihood; the cumulative distribution function (CDF) of a Beta with parameters $\alpha, \beta > 0$ is denoted $F_{(\alpha,\beta)}(\cdot)$. We first need a technical lemma about the Beta CDF.

Lemma 1. *For any $n > 0$, $s \leq x \leq u \leq n$, $\alpha, \beta > 0$ ($n, s, x, u \in \mathbb{N}$), $t \in [0,1]$ the following holds:*

$$F_{(u+\alpha,n-u+\beta)}(t) \leq F_{(x+\alpha,n-x+\beta)}(t) \leq F_{(s+\alpha,n-s+\beta)}(t) \tag{8}$$

Proof. We prove the LHS inequality of (8); the proof of the RHS follows similar steps. When $s = x$ the inequality holds trivially.

Consider the case $s < x$. By definition of the Beta distribution function:

$$F_{(s+\alpha,n-s+\beta)}(t) = \int_0^t \frac{v^{s+\alpha-1}(1-v)^{n-s+\beta-1}}{B(s+\alpha, n-s+\beta)} dv \tag{9}$$

In the proof below we refer to the following formulas from [7]:

$$B_y(a,b) = \int_0^y t^{a-1}(1-t)^{b-1} dt \tag{8.17.1}$$

$$I_y(a,b) = \frac{B_y(a,b)}{B(a,b)} \tag{8.17.2}$$

$$I_y(a+1, b-1) = I_y(a,b) - \frac{y^a(1-y)^{b-1}}{aB(a,b)} \tag{8.17.18}$$

By 8.17.1 and 8.17.2 the Beta distribution function (9) can be presented as an *incomplete* Beta function $I_t(s+\alpha, n-s+\beta)$ (the Beta distribution functions for the variables x and u can be written in the same form). Now we show by induction that the following holds:

$$I_t(s+\alpha, n-s+\beta) \geq I_t(x+\alpha, n-x+\beta) \tag{10}$$

As $s < x$, $s, x \in \mathbb{N}$ and $s, x > 0$ the base case is $s = 0$ and $x = 1$. Thus, we need to prove that $I_t(\alpha, n + \beta) \geq I_t(\alpha + 1, (n + \beta) - 1)$. By 8.17.18:

$$I_t((\alpha) + 1, (n + \beta) - 1) = I_t(\alpha, n + \beta) - \frac{t^\alpha (1 - t)^{n+\beta-1}}{\alpha B(\alpha, n + \beta)}$$

It is easy to see that $\frac{t^\alpha (1-t)^{n+\beta-1}}{\alpha B(\alpha, n+\beta)} \geq 0$, and therefore, the base case holds.

Suppose now that $x = s + 1$. By the same formula 8.17.18 [7]:

$$I_t((s + \alpha) + 1, (n - s + \beta) - 1) = I_t(s + \alpha, n - s + \beta) -$$
$$\frac{t^{s+\alpha}(1 - t)^{n-s+\beta-1}}{(s + \alpha) B(s + \alpha, n - s + \beta)}$$

As $\frac{t^{s+\alpha}(1-t)^{n-s+\beta-1}}{(s+\alpha) B(s+\alpha, n-s+\beta)} \geq 0$ the induction step holds as well. Hence, for any $s \leq x$ and $s, x > 0$ (10) holds, and the proof is complete.   □

Now, Proposition 2 below tells us how to bound the posterior distribution of the unknown probability p, by using the posteriors built from X_{sat} and X_{usat}. Given n samples of X_{sat}, X_{usat} and a Beta prior with parameters $\alpha, \beta > 0$ it is easy to show that the posterior means are:

$$\hat{p}_{sat} = \frac{s + \alpha}{n + \alpha + \beta} \qquad \hat{p}_{usat} = \frac{u + \alpha}{n + \alpha + \beta} \qquad (11)$$

where $s = \sum_{i=1}^n X_{sat,i}$ and $u = \sum_{i=1}^n X_{usat,i}$.

Proposition 2. *Given $\xi > 0$, the posterior probability with respect to n samples of X of the interval $[\hat{p}_{sat} - \xi, \hat{p}_{usat} + \xi]$ is bounded below as follows*

$$\mathbf{Pr}(P \in [\hat{p}_{sat} - \xi, \hat{p}_{usat} + \xi] | X_1, \dots, X_n) \geq$$
$$F_{(u+\alpha, n-u+\beta)}(\hat{p}_{usat} + \xi) - F_{(s+\alpha, n-s+\beta)}(\hat{p}_{sat} - \xi)$$

where $X_1, \dots, X_n$ are iid as X, and $\hat{p}_{sat}$ and $\hat{p}_{usat}$ are the posterior means (11).

Proof. By definition of posterior CDF and Lemma 1:

$$\mathbf{Pr}(P \leq \hat{p}_{sat} - \xi | X_1, \dots, X_n) \leq F_{(s+\alpha, n-s+\beta)}(\hat{p}_{sat} - \xi)$$
$$\mathbf{Pr}(P \geq \hat{p}_{usat} + \xi | X_1, \dots, X_n) \leq 1 - F_{(u+\alpha, n-u+\beta)}(\hat{p}_{usat} + \xi)$$

and therefore

$$\mathbf{Pr}(P \in [\hat{p}_{sat} - \xi, \hat{p}_{usat} + \xi] | X_1, \dots, X_n) =$$
$$1 - \mathbf{Pr}(P \leq \hat{p}_{sat} - \xi | X_1, \dots, X_n) - \mathbf{Pr}(P \geq \hat{p}_{usat} + \xi | X_1, \dots, X_n) \geq$$
$$\cdot 1 - F_{(s+\alpha, n-s+\beta)}(\hat{p}_{sat} - \xi) - 1 + F_{(u+\alpha, n-u+\beta)}(\hat{p}_{usat} + \xi) =$$
$$F_{(u+\alpha, n-u+\beta)}(\hat{p}_{usat} + \xi) - F_{(s+\alpha, n-s+\beta)}(\hat{p}_{sat} - \xi)$$

□

Our algorithm is shown in Algorithm 2. Differently from SReach [13], our algorithm first uses procedure **evaluate** to compute under- *and* overapproximations of the system behaviour (line 7), and then builds upper and lower posterior probability estimates (lines 13, 14). The posterior probability of the computed interval (line 15) is guaranteed not to exceed the true posterior by Proposition 2, so when the algorithm terminates we know that the returned interval contains the true probability with the required (or a larger) confidence. Our algorithm is sequential as SReach [13], since it only stops when the desired confidence is achieved. We show its (probabilistic) termination in the next proposition.

Proposition 3. *Algorithm 2 terminates almost surely.*

Proof. Recall that Algorithm 2 generates two sequences of random variables $\{X_{sat,n}\}_{n\in\mathbb{N}}$ and $\{X_{usat,n}\}_{n\in\mathbb{N}}$. From [17, Theorem 1] we get that $X_{sat,n}$ $(X_{usat,n})$ converges a.s., for $n \to \infty$, to the *constant* random variable $\mathbb{E}[X_{sat}]$ $(\mathbb{E}[X_{usat}])$. In particular, the posterior probability of any open interval containing the posterior mean (11) must converge to 1. Therefore, the posterior probability of any interval not including the posterior mean must converge to 0.

Now, the interval $(0, \hat{p}_{usat} + \xi)$ contains the posterior mean $(\hat{p}_{usat})$ of $X_{usat,n}$ and therefore the posterior probability $F_{(u+\alpha, n-u+\beta)}(\hat{p}_{usat} + \xi)$ converges to 1. Also, the interval $(0, \hat{p}_{sat} - \xi)$ does not contain the mean $(\hat{p}_{sat})$ of $X_{sat,n}$, so $F_{(s+\alpha, n-s+\beta)}(\hat{p}_{sat} - \xi)$ tends to 0, and this concludes the proof. □

Algorithm 2. Bayesian Estimation Algorithm

---

1 input: system H, δ - solver precision, l-reachability depth, c - confidence, ξ - accuracy, α, β - Beta distribution parameters;
2 output: confidence interval with posterior probability not smaller than c;
3 $n = 0$; $s = 0$; $u = 0$; $v = 0$;
4 **repeat**
5    $\mathbf{p} = get\_random\_sample()$;   // sample the initial parameters
6    $n = n + 1$;
7   **switch evaluate***(H, l, \mathbf{p}, \delta)* **do**   // δ-complete evaluation
8   **case sat do**
9         $s = s + 1$;
10   **case unsat do**
11         $v = v + 1$;
12    $u = n - v$;
13    $\hat{p}_{sat} = \frac{s+\alpha}{n+\alpha+\beta}$; $\hat{p}_{usat} = \frac{u+\alpha}{n+\alpha+\beta}$;   // posterior means for $X_{sat,n}, X_{usat,n}$
   // calculate confidence
14    $\hat{p}_{sat} = max(\xi, \hat{p}_{sat})$; $\hat{p}_{usat} = min(1 - \xi, \hat{p}_{usat})$;
15    $p = F_{(u+\alpha, n-u+\beta)}(\hat{p}_{usat} + \xi) - F_{(s+\alpha, n-s+\beta)}(\hat{p}_{sat} - \xi)$;
16 **until** $p \geq c$;
17 **return** $[\hat{p}_{sat} - \xi, \hat{p}_{usat} + \xi]$;

In the next section we extend our technique to hybrid systems that feature *both* nondeterministic and random parameters.

4   Cross-Entropy Algorithm

We perform probabilistic reachability analysis for hybrid systems featuring both random and nondeterministic parameters by solving an optimisation problem aimed at finding parameter values for which the system achieves maximum (minimum) reachability probability. We present an algorithm (Algorithm 3) based on the cross-entropy (CE) method [10], a powerful stochastic technique for solving estimation and optimisation problems. The main idea behind the CE method is obtaining the optimal parameter distribution by minimizing the distance between two probability density functions. The cross-entropy (or Kullback-Leibler divergence) between two probability density functions g and f is:

$$\Theta(g, f) = \int g(\boldsymbol{\lambda}) \ln \frac{g(\boldsymbol{\lambda})}{f(\boldsymbol{\lambda})} d\boldsymbol{\lambda}.$$

The CE is nonnegative and $\Theta(g, f) = 0$ iff $g = f$, but it is not symmetric ($\Theta(g, f) \neq \Theta(f, g)$), so it is not a distance in the formal sense.

The optimisation problem solved by the CE method can be formulated as the following: given a family of densities $\{f(\cdot; \mathbf{v})\}_{\mathbf{v} \in V}$ find the value $v^* \in V$ that minimizes $\Theta(g^*, f(\cdot; \mathbf{v}))$ (where g^* is the optimal density). The CE method comprises two general steps: (1) generating random samples from some initial distribution; (2) updating the distribution based on the obtained samples in order to obtain better samples in the next iteration. Note that for solving optimisation problems it is necessary that the family $\{f(\cdot; \mathbf{v})\}_{\mathbf{v} \in V}$ contains distributions that can approximate arbitrarily well single-point distributions.

In Algorithm 3 we use a parametrized family of normal distributions $f(\boldsymbol{\lambda}; \mathbf{v})$ (the first element of $\mathbf{v}$ is the mean and the second element is the standard deviation). Initially the standard deviation should be relatively large in order to sample a larger space on the first iteration of the algorithm. Let D be the definition domain of the nondeterministic parameters (obtained by projecting the hybrid system parameter space P over the nondeterministic parameters only). Starting with $\mathbf{v}_0 = \{\mu_0, \sigma_0\}$ such that μ_0 is the center of D and each element of σ_0 is half-size the corresponding interval from D the algorithm draws s samples from $f(\boldsymbol{\lambda}|\mu_0, \sigma_0)$ and evaluates them using the *sample performance function*:

$$P(\boldsymbol{\lambda}) = \begin{cases} \text{probability that } H(\boldsymbol{\lambda}) \text{ reaches the goal} & \text{if } \boldsymbol{\lambda} \in D \\ -\infty & \text{otherwise.} \end{cases}$$

To compute $P(\cdot)$ we run Algorithm 2 and take the mid point of the returned interval. Note that when solving probability minimization problems the second option in the definition of $P(\cdot)$ should be changed to ∞.

Given a number of samples, it is easy to see that as the number of nondeterministic parameters increases, the more difficult it becomes to draw samples lying inside of D. In fact, given n nondeterministic parameters the probability that a sample $\boldsymbol{\lambda}$ belongs to D is equal to:

$$\mathbf{Pr}(\boldsymbol{\lambda} \in D) = \prod_{j=1}^{n} \int_{D_j} f(\lambda_j | \mu_j, \sigma_j) d\lambda_j \tag{12}$$

where D_j is the domain of the j-th parameter, and we assumed that the parameters are sampled independently. Hence, in order to increase the likelihood that s samples lie in D it is sufficient to generate $s^* = \lceil \frac{s}{\eta} \rceil$ samples, where $\eta = \mathbf{Pr}(\boldsymbol{\lambda} \in D)$ is obtained using (12). The performance of each sample is then evaluated, and the samples are sorted in descending order (ascending in the case of probability minimization) according to their performance value. We label a number $k = \lceil \rho s^* \rceil$ of them as *elite* samples, where $\rho \in [10^{-2}, 10^{-1}]$ is a positive constant chosen by the user. The set of elite samples E is then used for updating the distribution parameters μ_i and σ_i on the i-th iteration of the algorithm using the formulas from [10, Chapter 8.7]:

$$
\mu_i = \frac{\sum_{j \in [1,k]} E_j}{k}
$$
$$
\sigma_i = \sqrt{\frac{\sum_{j \in [1,k]} (E_j - \mu_i)^2}{k}}
$$

(13)

The algorithm terminates when the largest element of vector σ reaches a user-defined precision $\hat{\sigma}$, and it outputs the estimated maximum reachability probability $\mathbf{P}$ and a (nondeterministic) parameter value $\boldsymbol{\lambda}$ for which $P(\boldsymbol{\lambda}) = \mathbf{P}$.

5   Experiments

We apply our algorithms to three models (two of which are hybrid), a model of irradiation therapy for psoriasis [16], a car collision scenario and a model of human starvation [12]. The algorithms have been implemented in C++, and the experiments have been carried out on a 32-core (2.9 GHz) Linux machine.

UVB Irradiation Therapy. We consider a simplified version of a hybrid UVB irradiation therapy model [16] used for treating psoriasis, an immune system-mediated chronic skin condition which is characterised by overproduction of keratinocytes. The simplified model comprises of three (six in the original model) categories of normal and three (five in the original model) categories of psoriatic keratinocytes whose dynamics is presented by nonlinear ODEs. The therapy consists of several episodes of UVB irradiation, which is simulated in the model by increasing the apoptosis rate constants (β_1 and β_2) for stem cells (SC) and transit amplifying (TA) cells by In_A times. Every such episode lasts for 48 h and is followed by 8 h of rest ($In_A = 1$) before starting the next irradiation. The efficiency of the therapy depends on the number of alternations between the irradiation and rest stages. An insufficient number of treatment episodes can result into early psoriasis relapse: The deterministic version of this model predicts psoriasis relapse for the number of therapy episodes less than seven [16]. We consider the parameter In_A characterising the therapy strength to be normally distributed with mean value $6 \cdot 10^4$ and standard deviation 10^4 and $\lambda \in [0.2, 0.5]$ characterising the strength of psoriatic stem cells to be nondeterministic, and we calculate the maximum and the minimum probabilities of psoriasis relapse within

Table 1. UVB irradiation therapy: results with $\xi = 10^{-1}$, $c = 0.99$, $\delta = 10^{-3}$, $\rho = 10^{-1}$, $s = 10$ and $\hat{\sigma} = 10^{-2}$, where λ – estimated value of nondeterministic parameter, μ_λ and σ_λ – mean and standard deviation of the resulting distribution, CI – confidence interval returned, s_R – total number of random samples used during s_N^* executions of Algorithm 2, s_N – total number of nondeterministic samples, s_N^* – number of nondeterministic samples drawn from D, i – number of iterations of Algorithm 3, **Time** – CPU time in seconds.

λ	μ_λ	σ_λ	CI	s_R	$s_N(s_N^*)$	Time
0.4953	0.4878	0.0089	[0.8268,1]	3,118	26(24)	13,492
0.1303	0.1347	0.0079	[0,0.1086]	2,880	26(23)	12,550

2,000 days after the last therapy episode for nine alternations ($l = 9$) between the 'on' and 'off' therapy modes (five therapy cycles). The results (Table 1) show that the estimated maximum probability lies in the interval [0.8268, 1] for $\lambda = 0.4953$ and the minimum probability is in the interval [0, 0.1086] for $\lambda = 0.1303$. Algorithm 3 required two iterations in both cases and generated 24 (out of total 26) and 23 (out of 26) samples from the domain of nondeterministic parameters D.

Cars Collision Scenario. We consider a taking over and deceleration scenario modelled as a hybrid system. Initially two cars are moving with speed $v_{A0} = v_{B0} = 11.12$ m/s at a distance $v_A \cdot \tau_{safe}$ from each other, where $\tau_{safe} \in [1, 2]$ s is nondeterministic. In the initial mode $CarA$ changes the lane and starts accelerating until it gets ahead of $CarB$ by $v_B \cdot \tau_{safe}$ meters. After that $CarA$ changes the lane back and starts decelerating with normally-distributed acceleration $a_{dA} \sim N(-2, 0.2)$. The driver in $CarB$ reacts within $\tau_{react} \in [0.5, 1.5]$ s and starts decelerating with acceleration $a_{dB} \sim N(-1.35, 0.1)$ until both cars stop completely.

The model contains three modes: $CarA$ overtakes $CarB$, $CarA$ decelerates while $CarB$ keeps moving for τ_{react} second, and both cars decelerate until they stop. There are two nondeterministic (τ_{safe} and τ_{react}) and two random (a_{d1} and a_{d2}) parameters in the system. We aim at determining whether there is a non-zero probability of the cars colliding ($l = 2$).

We apply Algorithm 3 to this model with different values of s, the CE sample size. The obtained results (Table 2) confirm that choosing smaller values of τ_{react} and larger values of τ_{safe} decreases the probability value. Also, choosing a larger s increases the accuracy of the obtained result from $P(0.609, 1.791) = [0.0252, 0.0352]$ for $s = 10$ to $P(0.522, 1.953) = [0.0121, 0.0221]$ for $s = 20$. The execution of the algorithm took three iterations in both cases drawing 32 (out of 43) and 57 (out of 90) samples lying in D for $s = 10$ and $s = 20$ respectively.

Human Starvation. The human starvation model [12] tracks the amount of fat (F), protein in muscle mass (M), and ketone bodies (K) in the human body after glucose reserves have been depleted from three to four days of fasting. These three variables are modelled using material and energy balances to ensure that the behaviour of the model tracks what is observed in actual experiments

---

Algorithm 3. Cross-Entropy Algorithm

---

1 input: hybrid system H, δ - solver precision, l - reachability depth, α, β - Beta
    distribution parameters, c - confidence, ξ - accuracy, s - sample size, ρ - elite
    samples ratio, $\hat{\sigma}$ - maximum variance ;

2 output: (parameter value, maximum probability) ;

3 $\mu = \{ \frac{\min(D_1) + \max(D_1)}{2}, \ldots, \frac{\min(D_n) + \max(D_n)}{2} \}$;

4 $\sigma = \{ \frac{|D_1|}{2}, \ldots, \frac{|D_n|}{2} \}$; $\sigma' = \sigma$;

5 **while** $(\max_{1 \le j \le n} \sigma'_j) > \hat{\sigma}$ **do**

6      $\eta = \prod_{j=1}^{n} \int_{D_j} f(x_j | \mu_j, \sigma_j) dx_j$;

7      $m = \lceil \frac{s}{\eta} \rceil$; $k = \lceil \rho \frac{s}{\eta} \rceil$;   // adjusting sample size

8   **for** $i = 1 : m$ **do**

9          $\lambda = get\_random\_normal\_sample()$;

10   **if** $\lambda \notin D$ **then**

11             $\mathbf{P} = [-\infty, -\infty]$;

12   **else**

13             $\mathbf{P} = \text{mid}(\mathbf{bayes}(H(\lambda), \delta, l, \alpha, \beta, \xi, c))$;   // applying Algorithm 2

14         $Q.push(\lambda, \mathbf{P})$;

15     $\text{sort}(Q)$;   // sorting in descending order by the probability value

16     $res = Q[1]$;   // updating the result

17     $\mu = \frac{\sum_{i \in [1,k]} Q[i]}{k}$;   // updating the mean

18     $\sigma' = \sigma$;   // saving current value of standard deviation

19     $\sigma = \sqrt{\frac{\sum_{i \in [1,k]} (Q[i] - \mu)^2}{k}}$;   // updating the standard deviation

20     $\text{clear}(Q)$;

21 **return** res;

Table 2. The minimum probability for the cars collision scenario with $\xi = 5 \cdot 10^{-3}$, $c = 0.99$, $\delta = 10^{-3}$, $\rho = 10^{-1}$ and $\hat{\sigma} = 10^{-1}$, where τ_{react} – $CarB$ driver reaction time, τ_{safe} – time interval between the cars, $\mu_{\tau_{react}}$ and $\sigma_{\tau_{react}}$ – mean and standard deviation of the resulting distribution for τ_{react}, $\mu_{\tau_{safe}}$ and $\sigma_{\tau_{safe}}$ – mean and standard deviation of the resulting distribution for τ_{safe}, CI – confidence interval returned, s_R – total number of random samples used during s_N^* executions of Algorithm 2, s_N – total number of nondeterministic samples, s_N^* – number of nondeterministic samples drawn from D, **Time** – CPU time in seconds.

τ_{react}	$\mu_{\tau_{react}}$	$\sigma_{\tau_{react}}$	τ_{safe}	$\mu_{\tau_{safe}}$	$\sigma_{\tau_{safe}}$	CI	s_R	s	$s_N(s_N^*)$	Time
0.609	0.619	0.011	1.791	1.753	0.019	[0.0252,0.0352]	658,528	10	43(32)	18,005
0.522	0.583	0.077	1.953	1.795	0.079	[0.0121,0.0221]	952,057	20	90(57)	27,126

involving fasting. Randomising two model parameters we evaluate the probability of a 40 % decrease in the muscle mass by the τ_g's day of fasting where $\tau_g \in [20, 27]$ is a nondeterministic parameter. The reachability depth value l is 0. The results (Table 3) demonstrate that the maximum probability of losing 40 % of the muscle mass is within the interval $[0.99131, 1]$ for $\tau_g = 26.47$ and the minimum probability is inside $[0, 0.0057]$ for $\tau_g = 20.22$. The execution of

Table 3. The minimum and the maximum reachability probabilities for the human starvation model with $\xi = 5 \cdot 10^{-3}$, $c = 0.99$, $\delta = 10^{-3}$, $\rho = 10^{-1}$, $s = 10$ and $\hat{\sigma} = 10^{-1}$, where τ_g – time (days) from the beginning of fasting, μ_{τ_g} and σ_{τ_g} – mean and standard deviation of the resulting distribution, CI – confidence interval returned, s_R – total number of random samples used during s_N^* executions of Algorithm 2, s_N – total number of nondeterministic samples, s_N^* – number of nondeterministic samples drawn from D, **Time** – CPU time in seconds.

τ_g	μ_{τ_g}	σ_{τ_g}	CI	s_R	$s_N(s_N^*)$	Time
20.2264	20.2125	0.068	[0,0.0057]	408,061	37(31)	2,703
26.4713	26.5146	0.033	[0.99131,1]	485,721	36(34)	4,360

the algorithm took three iterations in both cases drawing 31 (out of 37) and 34 (out of 36) samples from D for calculating the minimum and the maximum probabilities respectively.

Discussion. From our results we see that the chosen value of δ did not affect the length (2ξ) of the returned confidence intervals in any experiment. Also choosing a larger number of samples per iteration (s) in Algorithm 3 and a higher precision (ξ) for Algorithm 2 increases the accuracy of the obtained result. The sample size adjustment in Algorithm 3 increases the likelihood of drawing the desired number of samples from the domain of nondeterministic parameters. For example, in the cars collision scenario featuring two nondeterministic parameters almost a third of all drawn samples were outliers. However, the desired number of samples belonging to the domain of nondeterministic parameters was still provided. Finally, the performance of Algorithms 2 and 3 significantly depends of the complexity of the system's dynamics. For example, the UVB irradiation therapy model is more complex in comparison to other two models. As a result, Algorithm 1 required more CPU time for evaluating each pair (random and nondeterministic) of samples.

Implementation. All algorithms presented in this paper were implemented in our tool `ProbReach` [11], which can be downloaded from https://github.com/dreal/probreach. We also used `dReal` [5] as an SMT solver (δ-complete decision procedure). The models used in this section can be found at https://github.com/dreal/probreach/tree/master/model/hvc2016.

6   Conclusions and Future Work

We introduce novel Monte Carlo (*i.e.*, statistical) techniques for computing both numerically *and* statistically rigorous confidence intervals for bounded reachability probability in hybrid systems with random and nondeterministic parameters. To enable formal numerical reasoning we employ δ-complete SMT decision procedures, and we combine them with sequential Bayesian estimation and the cross-entropy method. We exploit δ-complete procedures to build under- and over-approximations of the reachability probability. We prove the correctness of such approximations, the statistical validity of our techniques, and termination of our Bayesian algorithm. Our techniques compute confidence intervals that are formally and statistically correct *independently* of the numeric precision (δ) used. This offers users the choice of trading accuracy of the returned interval for computational cost, thereby enabling faster verification. Our experiments with highly nonlinear hybrid systems show that our techniques are useful in practice.

For future work, understanding the relation between the numerical precision (δ) and the returned interval size is an important avenue of research. Also, we plan to extend the range of models analysable (*e.g.*, probabilistic jumps and stochastic differential equations).

Acknowledgements. F.S. was supported by award N00014-13-1-0090 of the US Office of Naval Research; P.Z. was supported by EPSRC grant EP/N031962/1.

References

1. Alur, R., Courcoubetis, C., Henzinger, T.A., Ho, P.-H.: Hybrid automata: an algorithmic approach to the specification and verification of hybrid systems. In: Grossman, R.L., Nerode, A., Ravn, A.P., Rischel, H. (eds.) HS 1991-1992. LNCS, vol. 736, pp. 209–229. Springer, Heidelberg (1993). doi:10.1007/3-540-57318-6_30
2. Clarke, E.M., Zuliani, P.: Statistical model checking for cyber-physical systems. In: Bultan, T., Hsiung, P.-A. (eds.) ATVA 2011. LNCS, vol. 6996, pp. 1–12. Springer, Heidelberg (2011). doi:10.1007/978-3-642-24372-1_1
3. Ellen, C., Gerwinn, S., Fränzle, M.: Statistical model checking for stochastic hybrid systems involving nondeterminism over continuous domains. Int. J. Softw. Tools Technol. Transf. (STTT) **17**(4), 485–504 (2015)
4. Gao, S., Avigad, J., Clarke, E.M.: Delta-decidability over the reals. In: LICS, pp. 305–314 (2012)
5. Gao, S., Kong, S., Clarke, E.M.: dReal: an SMT solver for nonlinear theories over the reals. In: Bonacina, M.P. (ed.) CADE 2013. LNCS (LNAI), vol. 7898, pp. 208–214. Springer, Heidelberg (2013). doi:10.1007/978-3-642-38574-2_14
6. Gao, S., Kong, S., Clarke, E.M.: Satisfiability modulo ODEs. In: FMCAD, pp. 105–112 (2013)
7. Olver, F.W., Lozier, D.W., Boisvert, R.F., Clark, C.W.: NIST Handbook of Mathematical Functions, 1st edn. Cambridge University Press, Cambridge (2010)
8. Platzer, A., Clarke, E.M.: The image computation problem in hybrid systems model checking. In: Bemporad, A., Bicchi, A., Buttazzo, G. (eds.) HSCC 2007. LNCS, vol. 4416, pp. 473–486. Springer, Heidelberg (2007). doi:10.1007/978-3-540-71493-4_37
9. Richardson, D.: Some undecidable problems involving elementary functions of a real variable. J. Symb. Log. **33**(4), 514–520 (1968)
10. Rubinstein, R.Y., Kroese, D.: Simulation and the Monte Carlo Method. Wiley, Hoboken (2008)
11. Shmarov, F., Zuliani, P.: ProbReach: verified probabilistic δ-reachability for stochastic hybrid systems. In: HSCC, pp. 134–139. ACM (2015)
12. Song, B., Thomas, D.: Dynamics of starvation in humans. J. Math. Biol. **54**(1), 27–43 (2007)

13. Wang, Q., Zuliani, P., Kong, S., Gao, S., Clarke, E.M.: SReach: a probabilistic bounded delta-reachability analyzer for stochastic hybrid systems. In: Roux, O., Bourdon, J. (eds.) CMSB 2015. LNCS, vol. 9308, pp. 15–27. Springer, Heidelberg (2015). doi:10.1007/978-3-319-23401-4_3
14. Younes, H.L.S., Kwiatkowska, M.Z., Norman, G., Parker, D.: Numerical vs. statistical probabilistic model checking. STTT **8**(3), 216–228 (2006)
15. Younes, H.L.S., Simmons, R.G.: Statistical probabilistic model checking with a focus on time-bounded properties. Inf. Comput. **204**(9), 1368–1409 (2006)
16. Zhang, H., Hou, W., Henrot, L., Schnebert, S., Dumas, M., Heusèle, C., Yang, J.: Modelling epidermis homoeostasis and psoriasis pathogenesis. J. R. Soc. Interface **12**(103), 20141071 (2015)
17. Zuliani, P., Platzer, A., Clarke, E.M.: Bayesian statistical model checking with application to Stateflow/Simulink verification. Formal Methods Syst. Des. **43**(2), 338–367 (2013)

Formula Slicing: Inductive Invariants from Preconditions

Egor George Karpenkov[1,2]([⊠]) and David Monniaux[1,2]

[1] Univ. Grenoble Alpes, VERIMAG, 38000 Grenoble, France
george@metaworld.me
[2] CNRS, VERIMAG, 38000 Grenoble, France

Abstract. We propose a "formula slicing" method for finding inductive invariants. It is based on the observation that many loops in the program affect only a small part of the memory, and many invariants which were valid before a loop are still valid after.

Given a precondition of the loop, obtained from the preceding program fragment, we weaken it until it becomes inductive. The weakening procedure is guided by counterexamples-to-induction given by an SMT solver. Our algorithm applies to programs with arbitrary loop structure, and it computes the strongest invariant in an abstract domain of weakenings of preconditions. We call this algorithm "formula slicing", as it effectively performs "slicing" on formulas derived from symbolic execution.

We evaluate our algorithm on the device driver benchmarks from the International Competition on Software Verification (SV-COMP), and we show that it is competitive with the state-of-the-art verification techniques.

1 Introduction

In automated program verification, one crucial task is establishing *inductive invariants* for loops: properties that hold initially, and also by induction for any number of execution steps.

Abstract-interpretation-based approaches restrict the class of expressible invariants to a predefined *abstract domain*, such as intervals, octagons, or convex polyhedra. Any *candidate invariants* which can not be expressed in the chosen abstract domain get over-approximated. Traditionally, this restriction applies at all program locations, but approaches such as *path focusing* [1] limit the precision loss only to loop heads, representing program executions between the loop-heads *precisely* using first-order formulas.

This is still a severe restriction: if a property flows from the beginning of the program to a loop head, and holds inductively after, but is not representable

---

The research leading to these results has received funding from the http://erc.europa.int/European Research Council under the European Union's Seventh Framework Programme (FP/2007-2013)/ERC Grant Agreement nr. 306595 http://stator.imag.fr/"STATOR".

R. Bloem and E. Arbel (Eds.): HVC 2016, LNCS 10028, pp. 169–185, 2016.
DOI: 10.1007/978-3-319-49052-6_11

```
int x = input(), p = input();
if (p)
    assume(x >= 0);
else
    assume(x < 0);
for (int i=0; i < input(); i++) x *= 2;
```

Fig. 1. Motivating example for finding inductive weakenings.

within the chosen abstract domain, it is discarded. In contrast, our idea exploits the insight that many loops in the program affect only a small part of the memory, and many invariants which were valid before the loop are still valid.

Consider finding an inductive invariant for the motivating example in Fig. 1. Symbolic execution up to the loop-head can precisely express all reachable states:

$$i = 0 \land (p \neq 0 \implies x \geq 0) \land (p = 0 \implies x < 0) \tag{1}$$

Yet abstraction in a numeric convex domain at the loop head yields $i = 0$, completely losing the information that x is positive iff $p \neq 0$. Observe that this information loss is not *necessary*, as the sign of x stays invariant under the multiplication by a positive constant (assuming mathematical integers for the simplicity of exposition). To avoid this loss of precision, we develop a "formula slicing" algorithm which computes inductive *weakenings* of propagated formulas, allowing to propagate the formulas representing inductive invariants *across* loop heads. In the motivating example, formula slicing computes an inductive weakening of the initial condition in Eq. 1), which is $(p \neq 0 \implies x \geq 0) \land (p = 0 \implies x < 0)$, and is thus true at every iteration of the loop. The computation of inductive weakenings is performed by iteratively filtering out conjuncts falsified by *counterexamples-to-induction*, derived using an SMT solver. In the motivating example, transition $i = 1$ from $i = 0$ falsifies the constraint $i = 0$, and the rest of the conjuncts are inductive.

The formula slicing fixpoint computation algorithm is based on performing abstract interpretation on the lattice of conjunctions over a finite set of predicates. The computation starts with a seed invariant which *necessarily* holds at the given location on the first time the control reaches it, and during the computation it is iteratively weakened until inductiveness. The algorithm terminates within a polynomial number of SMT calls with the *smallest* invariant which can be expressed in the chosen lattice.

Contributions. We present a novel insight for generating inductive invariants, and a method for creating a lattice of weakenings from an arbitrary formula describing the loop precondition using a *relaxed conjunctive normal form* (Definition 2) and best-effort quantifier elimination (Sect. 4).

We evaluate (Sect. 7) our implementation of the formula slicing algorithm on the "Device Drivers" benchmarks from the International Competition on Software Verification [2], and we demonstrate that it can successfully verify large, real-world programs which can not be handled with traditional numeric abstract interpretation, and that it is competitive with state of the art techniques.

Related Work. The *Houdini* [3] algorithm mines the program for a set of predicates, and then finds the largest inductive subset, dropping the candidate non-inductive lemmas until the overall inductiveness is achieved. The optimality proof for *Houdini* is present in the companion paper [4]. A very similar algorithm is used by Bradley et al. [5] to generate the inductive invariants from negations of the counter-examples to induction.

Inductive weakening based on counterexamples-to-induction can be seen as an algorithm for performing predicate abstraction [6]. Generalizing inductive weakening to *best abstract postcondition computation* Reps et al. [7] use the weakening approach for computing the best abstract transformer for any finite-height domain, which we also perform in Sect. 3.1.

Generating inductive invariants from a number of heuristically generated lemmas is a recurrent theme in the verification field. In *automatic abstraction* [8] a set of predicates is found for the simplified program with a capped number of loop iterations, and is filtered until the remaining invariants are inductive for the original, unmodified program. A similar approach is used for synthesizing bit-precise invariants by Gurfinkel et al. [9].

The complexity of the inductive weakening and that of the related template abstraction problem are analyzed by Lahiri and Qadeer [10].

2   Background

2.1   Logic Preliminaries

We operate over first-order, existentially quantified logic formulas within an efficiently decidable theory. A set of all such formulas over free variables in X is denoted by $\mathcal{F}(X)$. Checking such formulas for satisfiability is NP-hard, but with modern SMT (*satisfiability modulo theories*) solvers these checks can often be performed very fast.

A formula is said to be an *atom* if it does not contain logical connectives (e.g. it is a comparison $x \leq y$ between integer variables), a *literal* if it is an atom or its negation, and a *clause* if it is a disjunction of literals. A formula is in *negation normal form* (NNF) if negations are applied only to atoms, and it is in *conjunctive normal form* (CNF) if it is a conjunction of clauses. For a set of variables X, we denote by X' a set where the prime symbol was added to all the elements of X. With $\phi[a_1/a_2]$ we denote the formula ϕ after all free occurrences of the variable a_1 have been replaced by a_2. This notation is extended to sets of variables: $\phi[X/X']$ denotes the formula ϕ after all occurrences of the free variables from X were replaced with corresponding free variables from X'. For brevity, a formula $\phi[X/X']$ may be denoted by ϕ'. We use the brackets notation to indicate what free variables can occur in a formula: e.g. $\phi(X)$ can only contain free variables in X. The brackets can be dropped if the context is obvious.

A formula $\phi(X)$, representing a set of program states, is said to be *inductive* with respect to a formula $\tau(X \cup X')$, representing a *transition*, if Eq. 2 is valid:

$$\phi(X) \wedge \tau(X \cup X') \implies \phi'(X') \tag{2}$$

That is, all transitions originating in ϕ end up in ϕ'. We can query an SMT solver for the inductiveness of $\phi(X)$ with respect to $\tau(X \cup X')$ using the constraint in Eq. 3, which is unsatisfiable iff $\phi(X)$ is inductive.

$$\phi(X) \wedge \tau(X \cup X') \wedge \neg\phi'(X') \tag{3}$$

For a quantifier-free formula ϕ inductiveness checking is co-NP-complete. However, if ϕ is existentially quantified, the problem becomes Π_2^p-complete. For efficiency, we shall thus restrict inductiveness checks to quantifier-free formulas.

2.2   Program Semantics and Verification Task

Definition 1 (CFA). A control flow automaton is a tuple $(nodes, edges, n_0, X)$, where $nodes$ is a set of program control states, modelling the program counter, $n_0 \in nodes$ is a program starting point, and X is a set of program variables. Each edge $e \in edges$ is a tuple $(a, \tau(X \cup X'), b)$, modelling a possible transition, where $\{a, b\} \subseteq nodes$, and $\tau(X \cup X')$ is a formula defining the semantics of a transition over the sets of input variables X and output variables X'.

A non-recursive program in a C-like programming language can be trivially converted to a CFA by inlining functions, replacing loops and conditionals with guarded `goto`s, and converting guards and assignments to constraints over input variables X and output variables X'.

A *concrete data state* m of a CFA is a variable assignment $X \to \mathbb{Z}$ which assigns each variable an integral value.[1] The set of all concrete data states is denoted by $\mathcal{C}$. A set $r \subseteq \mathcal{C}$ is called a *region*. A formula $\phi(X)$ defines a region S of all states which it models ($S \equiv \{c \mid c \models \phi\}$). A set of all formulas over X is denoted by $\mathcal{F}(X)$. A *concrete state* c is a tuple (m, n) where m is a concrete data state, and $n \in nodes$ is a control state. A *program path* is a sequence of concrete states $\langle c_0, \ldots, c_n \rangle$ such that for any two consecutive states $c_i = (m_i, n_i)$ and $c_{i+1} = (m_{i+1}, n_{i+1})$ there exists an edge (n_i, τ, n_{i+1}) such that $m_i(X) \cup m_{i+1}(X') \models \tau(X \cup X')$. A concrete state $s_i = (m, n)$, and the contained node n, are both called *reachable* iff there exists a program path which contains s_i.

A *verification task* is a pair (P, n_e) where P is a CFA and $n_e \in nodes$ is an *error node*. A verification task is *safe* if n_e is not reachable. Safety is traditionally decided by finding a *separating* inductive invariant: a mapping from program locations to regions which is closed under the transition relation and does not contain the error state.

2.3   Invariant and Inductive Invariant

A set of concrete states is called a *state-space*, and is defined using a mapping from nodes to regions. A mapping $I : nodes \to \mathcal{F}(X)$ is an *invariant* if it contains

---

[1] The restriction to integers is for the simplicity of exposition, and is not present in the implementation.

all reachable states, and an *inductive invariant* if it is closed under the transition relation: that is, it satisfies the conditions for *initiation* and *consecution*:

$$\text{Initiation: } I(n_0) = \top$$

$$\text{Consecution: for all edges } (a, \tau, b) \in edges, \text{ for all } X, X' \qquad (4)$$
$$I(a)(X) \wedge \tau(X \cup X') \implies (I(b))'(X')$$

Intuitively, the initiation condition dictates that the initial program state at n_0 (arbitrary contents of memory) is covered by I, and the consecution condition dictates that under all transitions I should map into itself. Similarly to Eq. 3, the consecution condition in Eq. 4 can be verified by checking one constraint for unsatisfiability using SMT for each edge in a CFA. This constraint is given in Eq. 5, which is unsatisfiable for each edge $(a, \tau, b) \in edges$ iff the consecution condition holds for I.

$$I(a)(X) \wedge \tau(X \cup X') \wedge \neg(I(b))'(X') \qquad (5)$$

2.4 Abstract Interpretation over Formulas

Program analysis by abstract interpretation [11] searches for inductive invariants in a given *abstract domain*: the class of properties considered by the analysis (e.g. upper and lower bounds on each numeric variable). The run of abstract interpretation effectively *interprets* the program in the given *abstract domain*, performing operations on the elements of an abstract domain instead of concrete values (e.g. the interval $x \in [1, 2]$ under the transition x += 1 becomes $x \in [2, 3]$).

We define the abstract domain $\mathcal{D} \equiv 2^{\mathcal{L}} \cup \{\bot\}$ to be a powerset of the set of formulas $\mathcal{L} \subseteq \mathcal{F}(X)$ with an extra element $\bot$ attached. A *concretization* of an element $d \in \mathcal{D}$ is a conjunction over all elements of d, or a formula *false* for $\bot$.

Observe that $\mathcal{D}$ forms a complete lattice by using set operations of intersection and union as meet and join operators respectively, and using *syntactical* equality for comparing individual formulas. The syntactic comparison is an over-approximation as it does not take the formula semantics into account. However, this comparison generates a complete lattice of height $\|\mathcal{L}\| + 2$.

2.5 Large Block Encoding

The approach of large block encoding [12] for model checking, and the approach of path focusing [1] for abstract interpretation are based on the observation that by *compacting* a control flow and reducing a number of abstraction points, analysis precision and sometimes even analysis performance can be greatly improved. Both approaches utilize SMT solvers for performing abstraction afterwards.

A simplified version of compaction is possible by applying the following two rules to a CFA until a fixed point is reached:

- Two consecutive edges (a, s_1, b) and (b, s_2, c) with no other existing edge entering or leaving b get replaced by a new edge $(a, \exists \hat{X}. \, s_1[X'/\hat{X}] \wedge s_2[X/\hat{X}], c)$.
- Two parallel edges (a, s_1, b) and (a, s_2, b) get replaced by $(a, s_1 \vee s_2, c)$.

In our approach, this pre-processing is used on the CFA obtained from the analyzed program.

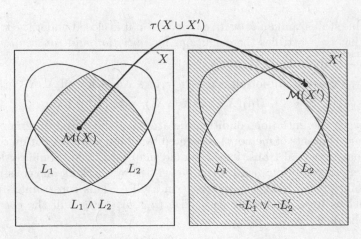

Fig. 2. Formula $\phi(X) \equiv L_1(X) \wedge L_2(X)$ is tested for inductiveness under $\tau(X \cup X')$. Model $\mathcal{M}$ identifies a counter-example to induction. From $\mathcal{M} \models \neg L_2'(X')$ we know that the lemma L_2 has to be dropped. As weakening progresses, the shaded region in the left box is growing, while the shaded region in the right box is shrinking, until there are no more counterexamples to induction.

3   Counterexample-to-Induction Weakening Algorithm

The approaches [3,5,8,9] mentioned in Sect. 1 are all based on using counterexamples to induction for filtering the input set of candidate lemmas. For completeness, we restate this approach in Algorithm 1.

In order to perform the weakening without syntactically modifying ϕ during the intermediate queries, we perform *selector variables* annotation: we replace each lemma $l_i \in \phi$ with a disjunction $s_i \vee l_i$, using a fresh boolean variable s_i. Observe that if all selector variables are assumed to be false the annotated formula $\phi_{\text{annotated}}$ is equivalent to ϕ, and that assuming any individual selector s_i is equivalent to removing (replacing with $\top$) the corresponding lemma l_i from ϕ. Such an annotation allows us to make use of *incrementality* support by SMT solvers, by using the *solving with assumptions* feature.

Algorithm 1 iteratively checks input formula ϕ for inductiveness using Eq. 3 (line 13). The solver will either report that the constraint is unsatisfiable, in which case ϕ is inductive, or provide a counterexample-to-induction represented by a model $\mathcal{M}(X \cup X')$ (line 14). The counterexample-driven algorithm uses $\mathcal{M}$ to find the set of lemmas which should be removed from ϕ, by removing the lemmas modelled by $\mathcal{M}$ in $\neg \phi'$ (line 20). The visualization of such a filtering step for a formula ϕ consisting of two lemmas is given in Fig. 2.

As shown in related literature [4], Algorithm 1 terminates with the *strongest* possible weakening within the linear number of SMT calls with respect to $\|\phi_{\text{annotated}}\|$.

Algorithm 1. Counterexample-Driven Weakening.

1: **Input:** Formula $\phi(X)$ to weaken in RCNF, transition relation $\tau(X \cup X')$
2: **Output:** Inductive $\hat{\phi} \subseteq \phi$

3: ▷ Annotate lemmas with selectors, S is a mapping from selectors to lemmas they annotate.
4: $S, \phi_{\text{annotated}} \leftarrow$ Annotate(ϕ)
5: $T \leftarrow$ SMT solver instance
6: $query \leftarrow \phi_{\text{annotated}} \wedge \tau \wedge \neg\phi'_{\text{annotated}}$
7: Add $query$ to constraints in T
8: $assumptions \leftarrow \emptyset$
9: $removed \leftarrow \emptyset$

10: ▷ In the beginning, all of the lemmas are present
11: **for all** $(selector, lemma) \in S$ **do**
12:      $assumptions \leftarrow assumptions \cup \{\neg selector\}$
13: **while** T is satisfiable with $assumptions$ **do**
14:      $\mathcal{M} \leftarrow$ model of T
15:      $assumptions \leftarrow \emptyset$
16:      **for all** $(selector, lemma) \in S$ **do**
17:           **if** $\mathcal{M} \models \neg lemma'$ or $lemma'$ is *irrelevant* to satisfiability **then**
18:                ▷ *lemma* has to be removed.
19:                $assumptions \leftarrow assumptions \cup \{selector\}$
20:                $removed \leftarrow removed \cup \{lemma\}$
21:           **else**
22:                $assumptions \leftarrow assumptions \cup \{\neg selector\}$

23: ▷ Remove all lemmas which were filtered out
24: **return** $\phi[removed/\top]$

3.1 From Weakenings to Abstract Postconditions

As shown by Reps et al. [7], the inductive weakening algorithm can be generalized for the abstract postcondition computation for any finite-height lattice.

For given formulas $\psi(X)$, $\tau(X \cup X')$, and $\phi(X)$ consider the problem of finding a weakening $\hat{\phi} \subseteq \phi$, such that all feasible transitions from ψ through τ end up in $\hat{\phi}$. This is an abstract postcondition of ψ under τ in the lattice of all weakenings of ϕ (Sect. 2.4). The problem of finding it is very similar to the problem of finding an inductive weakening, as similarly to Eq. 3, we can check whether a given weakening of ϕ is a postcondition of ψ under τ using Eq. 6,

$$\psi(X) \wedge \tau(X \cup X') \wedge \neg\phi'_{\text{annotated}}(X') \tag{6}$$

Algorithm 1 can be adapted for finding the *strongest* postcondition in the abstract domain of weakenings of the input formula with very minor modifications. The required changes are accepting an extra parameter ψ, and changing the queried constraint (line 6) to Eq. 6. The found postcondition is indeed strongest [7].

4   The Space of All Possible Weakenings

We wish to find a *weakening* of a set of states represented by $\phi(X)$, such that it is inductive under a given transition $\tau(X \cup X')$. For a single-node CFA defined by initial condition ϕ and a loop transition τ such a weakening would constitute an *inductive invariant* as by definition of weakening it satisfies the initial condition and is inductive.

We start with an observation that for a formula in NNF replacing any subset of literals with $\top$ results in an over-approximation, as both conjunction and disjunction are monotone operators. E.g. for a formula $\phi \equiv (l_a \wedge l_b) \vee l_c$ such possible weakenings are $\top$, $l_b \vee l_c$, and $l_a \vee l_c$.

The set of weakenings defined in the previous paragraph is redundant, as it does not take the formula structure into account — e.g. in the given example if l_c is replaced with $\top$ it is irrelevant what other literals are replaced, as the entire formula simplifies to $\top$. The most obvious way to address this redundancy is to convert ϕ to CNF and to define the set of all possible weakenings as conjunctions over the subsets of clauses in ϕ_{CNF}. E.g. for the formula $\phi \equiv l_a \wedge l_b \wedge l_c$ possible weakenings are $l_a \wedge l_b$, $l_b \wedge l_c$, and $l_a \wedge l_c$. This method is appealing due to the fact that for a set of lemmas the *strongest* (implying all other possible inductive weakenings) inductive subset can be found using a linear number of SMT checks [5]. However (Sect. 2.1) polynomial-sized CNF conversion (e.g. Tseitin encoding) requires introducing existentially quantified boolean variables which make inductiveness checking Π_2^p-hard.

The arising complexity of finding inductive weakenings is inherent to the problem: in fact, the problem of finding *any* non-trivial ($\neq \top$) weakening within the search space described above is Σ_2^p-hard.

Thus instead we use an over-approximating set of weakenings, defined by all possible subsets of lemmas present in ϕ after the conversion to *relaxed conjunctive normal form*.

Definition 2 (Relaxed Conjunctive Normal Form (RCNF)). A formula $\phi(X)$ is in relaxed conjunctive normal form if it is a conjunction of quantifier-free formulas (lemmas).

For example, the formula $\phi \equiv l_a \wedge (l_b \vee (l_c \wedge l_d))$ is in RCNF. The over-approximation comes from the fact that non-atomic parts of the formula are grouped together: the only possible non-trivial weakenings for ϕ are l_a and $l_b \vee (l_c \wedge l_d)$, and it is impossible to express $l_a \wedge (l_b \vee l_c)$ within the search space.

We may abuse the notation by treating ϕ in RCNF as a set of its conjuncts, and writing $l \in \phi$ for a lemma l which is an argument of the parent conjunction of ϕ, or $\phi_1 \subseteq \phi_2$ to indicate that all lemmas in ϕ_1 are contained in ϕ_2, or $\|\phi\|$ for the number of lemmas in ϕ. For ϕ in RCNF we define a set of all possible *weakenings* as conjunctions over all sets of lemmas contained in ϕ. We use an existing, optimal counter-example based algorithm in order to find the *strongest* weakening of ϕ with respect to τ in the next section.

A trivially correct conversion to a relaxed conjunctive normal is to convert an input formula ϕ to a conjunction $\bigwedge \{\phi\}$. However, this conversion is not very interesting, as it gives rise to a very small set of weakenings: ϕ and $\top$. Consequently, with such a conversion, if ϕ is not inductive with respect to the transition of interest, no non-trivial weakening can be found. On the other extreme, ϕ can be converted to CNF explicitly using associativity and distributivity laws, giving rise to a very large set of possible weakenings. Yet the output of such a conversion is exponentially large.

We present an algorithm which converts ϕ into a polynomially-sized conjunction of lemmas. The following rules are applied recursively until a fixpoint is reached:

Flattening. All nested conjunctions are flattened. E.g. $a \wedge (b \wedge c) \mapsto a \wedge b \wedge c$.

Factorization. When processing a disjunction over multiple conjunctions we find and extract a common factor. E.g. $(a \wedge b) \vee (b \wedge c) \mapsto b \wedge (a \vee c)$.

Explicit expansion with size limit. A disjunction $\bigvee L$, where each $l \in L$ is a conjunction, can be converted to a conjunction over disjunctions over all elements in the cross product over L. E.g. $(a \wedge b) \vee (c \wedge d)$ can be converted $(a \vee c) \wedge (a \vee d) \wedge (b \vee c) \wedge (b \vee d)$.

Applying such an expansion results in an exponential blow-up, but we only perform it if the resulting formula size is smaller than a fixed constant, and we limit the expansion depth to one.

Eliminating Existentially Quantified Variables. The formulas resulting form large block encoding (Sect. 2.5) may have intermediate (neither input nor output), existentially bound variables. In general, existential quantifier elimination (with e.g. Fourier-Motzkin) is exponential. However, for many cases such as simple deterministic assignments, existential quantifier elimination is easy: e.g. $\exists t . x' = t + 3 \wedge t = x + 2$ can be trivially replaced by $x' = x + 5$ using substitution.

We use a two-step method to remove the quantified variables: we run a best-effort pattern-matching approach, removing the bound variables which can be eliminated in polynomial time, and in the second step we drop all the lemmas which still contain the existentially bound variables. The resulting formula is an over-approximation of the original one.

5 Formula Slicing: Overall Algorithm

We develop the *formula slicing* algorithm in order to apply the inductive weakening approach for generating inductive invariants in large, potentially non-reducible programs with nested loops.

"Classical" Houdini-based algorithms consist of two steps: *candidate* lemmas generation, followed by counterexample-to-induction-based filtering. However, in our case candidate lemmas representing postconditions depend on previous filtering steps, and careful consideration is required in order to generate *unique* candidate lemmas which do not depend on the chosen iteration order.

Abstract Reachability Tree. In order to solve this problem we use abstract reachability tree [13] (ART) as a main datastructure for our algorithm. For the simplicity of notation we introduce the projection function π_i, which projects the ith element of the tuple. An ART describes the current invariant candidate processed by the analysis for a fixed CFA ($nodes, edges, n_0, X$), and is defined by a set of nodes T. Each node $t \in T$ is a triple, consisting of a CFA node $n \in nodes$, defining which location t corresponds to, an abstract domain element $d \in \mathcal{D}$, defining the reachable state space at t, and an optional backpointer $b \in (T \cup \{\emptyset\})$, defining the tree structure. The tree topology has to be consistent with the structure of the underlying CFA: node $a \in T$ can have a backpointer to the node $b \in T$ only if there exists an edge $(\pi_1(a), \_, \pi_1(b))$ in the CFA. The starting tree node t_0 is $(n_0, \top, \emptyset)$.

An ART is *sound* if the output of each transition over-approximates the strongest postcondition: that is, for each node $t \in T$ with non-empty backpointer $b = \pi_3(t)$, an edge $e = (\pi_1(b), \tau, \pi_1(t))$ must exist in *edges*, and the abstract domain element associated with t must over-approximate the strongest postcondition of b under τ. Formally, the following must hold: $\exists X. [\![\pi_2(b)]\!] \wedge \tau \implies [\![\pi_2(t)]\!]'$ (recall that priming is a renaming operation $[X/X']$). A node $b \in T$ is *fully expanded* if for all edges $(\pi_1(t), \tau, n) \subseteq edges$ there exists a node $t \in T$, where $\pi_1(t) = n$, and $\pi_2(t)$ over-approximates the strongest post-condition of $\pi_2(b)$ under τ. A node $(a, d_1, \_)$ *covers* another node $(a, d_2, \_)$ iff $[\![d_2]\!] \implies [\![d_1]\!]$. A sound labelled ART where all nodes are either fully expanded or covered represents an inductive invariant.

The transfer relation for the formula slicing is given in Algorithm 3. In order to generate a successor for an element (n_a, d, b), and an edge (n_a, τ, n_b) we first traverse the chain of backpointers up the tree. If we can find a "sibling" element s where $\pi_1(s) = n_a$[2] by following the backpointers, we weaken s until inductiveness (line 4) relative to the new incoming transition τ, and return that as a postcondition. Such an operation effectively performs widening [11] to enforce convergence. Alternatively, if no such sibling exists, we convert $\exists X. \wedge \tau$ to RCNF form (line 6), and this becomes a new element of the abstract domain.

The main fixpoint loop performs the following calculation: for every leaf in the tree which is not yet expanded or covered, all successors are found using the transfer relation defined in Algorithm 3, and for each newly created element, coverage relation is checked against all elements in the same partition. A simplified version of this standard fixpoint iteration on ART is given in Algorithm 2.

Observe that our algorithm has a number of positive features. Firstly, because our main datastructure is an ART, in case of a counterexample we get a *path* to a property violation (though due to abstraction used, not all taken transitions are necessarily feasible, similarly to the *leaping counterexamples* of LoopFrog [14]). Secondly, our approach for generating initial candidate invariants ensures uniqueness, even in the case of a non-reducible CFA.

As a downside, tree representation may lead to the exponential state-space explosion (as a single node in a CFA may correspond to many nodes in an ART). However, from our experience in the evaluation (Sect. 7), with a good iteration order (stabilizing inner components first [15]) this problem does not occur in practice.

---

[2] In the implementation, the *sibling* is defined by a combination of callstack, CFA node and loopstack.

Algorithm 2. Formula Slicing: Overall Algorithm

1: **Input:** CFA $(nodes, edges, n_0, X)$

2: ▷ Expanded.
3: $E \leftarrow \emptyset$

4: ▷ Covered.
5: $C \leftarrow \emptyset$
6: $t_0 \leftarrow (n_0, \top, \emptyset)$
7: $T \leftarrow \{t_0\}$
8: **while** $\exists t \in (T \setminus E \setminus C)$ **do**

9:     ▷ Expand.
10:     **for all** edge $e \in edges$ where $\pi_1(e) = \pi_1(t)$ **do**
11:         $T \leftarrow T \cup \{ \text{TRANSFERRELATION}(e, t) \}$
12:     $E \leftarrow E \cup \{t\}$

13:     ▷ Check Coverage.
14:     **for all** $t_1 \in (T \setminus C)$ where $\pi_1(t_1) = \pi_1(t)$ **do**
15:         **if** $[\![\pi_2(t_1)]\!] \implies [\![\pi_2(t)]\!]$ **then**
16:             $C \leftarrow C \cup \{t_1\}$
17:         **if** $[\![\pi_2(t)]\!] \implies [\![\pi_2(t_1)]\!]$ **then**
18:             $C \leftarrow C \cup \{t\}$

Algorithm 3. Formula Slicing: Postcondition Computation.

1: **function** TRANSFERRELATION(edge $e \equiv (n_a, \tau, n_b)$, state $t \equiv (n_a, d, b)$)
2:     sibling $s \leftarrow$ FINDSIBLING(b, n_0)
3:     **if** $s \neq \emptyset$ **then**

4:         ▷ Abstract postcondition of d under τ in weakenings of s (Sect. 3.1).
5:         $e \leftarrow$ WEAKEN$(d, \tau \wedge n_b, s)$
6:     **else**

7:         ▷ Convert the current invariant candidate to RCNF.
8:         $e \leftarrow$ TORCNF$([\![d]\!] \wedge \tau)$
9:     **return** (n_b, e, t)
10: **function** FINDSIBLING(state b, CFA node n)
11:     **if** $\pi_1(b) = n$ **then**
12:         **return** b
13:     **else if** $\pi_3(b) = \emptyset$ **then**
14:         **return** $\emptyset$
15:     **else**
16:         **return** FINDSIBLING$(\pi_3(b), n)$

5.1 Example Formula Slicing Run

Consider running formula slicing on the program in Fig. 3, which contains two nested loops. The corresponding edge encoding is given in Eq. 7:

```
int p, c, s=nondet(), x = 0, y = 0;
p = s ? 1 : 2;
while (nondet()) { // A(X)
    x++;
    c = 100;
    while (nondet()) { // B(X)
        if (p != 1 && p != 2) {
            c = 0;
        }
        y++;
    }
    assert(c == 100);
}
assert((s && p == 1) || (!s && p == 2));
```

Fig. 3. Example program with nested loops: listing and CFA.

$$\tau_1 \equiv x' = 0 \wedge y' = 0 \wedge (p' = 1 \wedge s' \vee p' = 2 \wedge \neg s')$$
$$\tau_2 \equiv x' = x + 1 \wedge c' = 100$$
$$\tau_3 \equiv (\neg(p \neq 1 \wedge p \neq 2) \vee (p \neq 1 \wedge p \neq 2 \wedge c' = 0)) \qquad (7)$$
$$\wedge\, y' = y + 1 \wedge p' = p$$
$$\tau_4 \equiv x' = x \wedge y' = y \wedge p' = p \wedge c' = c$$

Similarly to Eq. 3, we can check candidate invariants $A(X), B(X)$ for inductiveness by posing an SMT query shown in Eq. 8. The constraint in Eq. 8 is unsatisfiable iff $\{A : A(X), B : B(X)\}$ is an inductive invariant (Sect. 2.3).

$$\exists X \cup X' \bigvee \begin{array}{l} \tau_1(X') \wedge \neg A(X') \\ A(X) \wedge \tau_2(X \cup X') \wedge \neg B(X') \\ B(X) \wedge \tau_3(X \cup X') \wedge \neg B(X') \\ B(X) \wedge \tau_4(X \cup X') \wedge \neg A(X') \end{array} \qquad (8)$$

Equation 8 is unsatisfiable iff *all* of the disjunction arguments are unsatisfiable, and hence the checking can be split into multiple steps, one per analyzed edge. Each postcondition computation (Algorithm 3) either generates an initial seed invariant candidate, or picks one argument of Eq. 8, and weakens the right hand side until the constraint becomes unsatisfiable. Run of the formula slicing algorithm on the example is given below:

- Traversing τ_1, we get the initial candidate invariant
  $I(A) \leftarrow \bigwedge \{x = 0, y = 0, p = 1 \vee p = 2, s \implies p = 1\}$.
- Traversing τ_2, the candidate invariant for B becomes
  $I(B) \leftarrow \bigwedge \{x = 1, y = 0, p = 1 \vee p = 2, s \implies p = 1, c = 100\}$.
- After traversing τ_3, we weaken the candidate invariant $I(B)$ by dropping the lemma $y = 0$ which gives rise to the counterexample to induction (y gets incremented). The result is $\bigwedge \{x = 1, p = 1 \vee p = 2, s \implies p = 1, c = 100\}$, which is inductive under τ_3.

- The edge τ_4 is an identity, and the postcondition computation results in lemmas $x = 0$ and $y = 0$ dropped from $I(A)$, resulting in $\bigwedge\{y = 0, p = 1 \vee p = 2, s \implies p = 1\}$.
- After traversing τ_2, we obtain the weakening of $I(A)$ by dropping the lemma $x = 1$ from $I(B)$, resulting in $\bigwedge\{p = 1 \vee p = 2, s \implies p = 1, c = 100\}$.
- Finally, the iteration converges, as all further postconditions are already covered by existing invariant candidates. Observe that the computed invariant is sufficient for proving the asserted property.

6 Implementation

We have developed the SLICER tool, which runs the formula slicing algorithm on an input C program. SLICER performs inductive weakenings using the Z3 [16] SMT solver, and best-effort quantifier elimination using the `qe-light` Z3 tactic. The source code is integrated inside the open-source verification framework CPAchecker [17], and the usage details are available at http://slicer.metaworld. me. Our tool can analyze a verification task (Sect. 2.2) by finding an inductive invariant and reporting `true` if the found invariant *separates* the initial state from the error property, and `unknown` otherwise.

We have implemented the following optimizations:

Live Variables. We precompute live variables, and the candidate lemmas generated during RCNF conversion (Algorithm 3, line 6) which do not contain live variables are discarded.

Non-Nested Loops. When performing the inductive weakening (Algorithm 3, line 4) on the edge (N, τ, N) we annotate and weaken the candidate invariants on both sides (without modifications described in Sect. 3.1), and we cache the fact that the resulting weakening is inductive under τ.

CFA Reduction. We pre-process the input CFA and we remove all nodes from which there exists no path to an error state.

6.1 Syntactic Weakening Algorithm

A syntactic-based approach is possible as a faster and less precise alternative which does not require SMT queries. For an input formula $\phi(X)$ in RCNF, and a transition $\tau(X \cup X')$, syntactic weakening returns a subset of lemmas in ϕ, which are not *syntactically modified* by τ: that is, none of the variables are modified or have their address taken. For example, the lemma $x > 0$ is not syntactically modified by the transition $y' = y + 1 \wedge x \geq 1$, but it is modified by $x' = x + 1$.

7 Experiments and Evaluation

We have evaluated the formula slicing algorithm on the "Device Drivers" category from the International Competition on Software Verification (SV-COMP) [2]. The dataset consists of 2120 verification tasks, of which 1857 are designated as *correct* (the error property is unreachable), and the rest admit a counter-example. All the experiments were performed on Intel Xeon E5-2650 at 2.00 GHz, and limits of 8 GB RAM, 2 cores, and 600 s CPU time per program. We compare the following three approaches:

Slicer-CEX (rev 21098). Formula slicing algorithm running counterexample-based weakening (Sect. 3).

Slicer-Syntactic. Same, with syntactic weakening (Sect. 6.1).

Predicate Analysis (rev 21098). Predicate abstraction with interpolants [18], as implemented inside CPAchecker [19]. We have chosen this approach for comparison as it represents state-of-the-art in model checking, and was found especially suitable for analyzing device drivers.

PAGAI [20] (git hash e44910). Abstract interpretation-based tool, which implements the path focusing [1] approach.

Unabridged experimental results are available at http://slicer.metaworld.me.

In Table 1 we show overall precision and performance of the four compared approaches. As formula slicing is over-approximating, it is not capable of finding counterexamples, and we only compare the number of produced safety proofs.

From the data in the table we can see that predicate analysis produces the most correct proofs. This is expected since it can generate new predicates, and it is *driven* by the target property. However, formula slicing and abstract interpretation have much less timeouts, and they do not require target property annotation, making them more suitable for use in domains where a single error property is not available (advanced compiler optimizations, multi-property verification, and boosting another analysis by providing an inductive invariant). The programs verified by different approaches are also different, and formula slicing verifies 22 programs predicate analysis could not.

The performance of the four analyzed approaches is shown in the quantile plot in Fig. 4a. The plot shows that predicate analysis is considerably more time consuming than other analyzed approaches. Initially, PAGAI is much faster than other tools, but around 15 s it gets overtaken by both slicing approaches. Though the graph seems to indicate that PAGAI overtakes slicing again around 100 s, in fact the bend is due to out of memory errors.

The quantile plot also shows that the time taken to perform inductive weakening does not dominate the overall analysis time for formula slicing. This can be seen from the small timing difference between the syntactic and counterexample-based approaches, as the syntactic approach does not require querying the SMT solver in order to produce a weakening.

Finally, we present data on the number of SMT calls required for computing inductive weakenings in Fig. 4b. The distribution shows that the overwhelming majority of weakenings can be found within just a few SMT queries.

Table 1. Evaluation results. The "# incorrect" column shows the number of safety proofs the tool has produced where the analyzed program admitted a counterexample.

Tool	# proofs	# incorrect	# timeouts	# memory outs
Slicer-CEX	1253	0	475	0
Slicer-Syntactic	1166	0	407	0
Predicate analysis	1301	0	657	0
PAGAI	1214	3	409	240

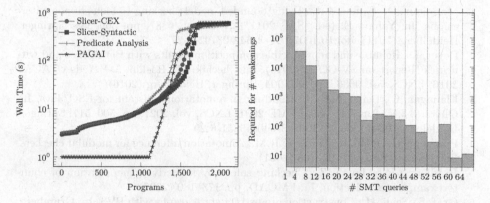

(a) Quantile plot showing performance of the compared approaches. Shows analysis time for each benchmark, where the data series are sorted by time separately for each tool. For readability, the dot is drawn for every 20th program, and the time is rounded up to one second.

(b) Distribution of the number of iterations of inductive weakening (Sec. 3) required for convergence across all benchmarks. Horizontal axis represents the number of SMT calls required for convergence of each weakening, and vertical axis represents the count of the number of such weakenings.

Fig. 4. Evaluation results: timing data.

8   Conclusion and Future Work

We have proposed a "formula slicing" algorithm for efficiently finding potentially disjunctive inductive invariants in programs, which performs abstract interpretation in the space of weakenings over the formulas representing the "initial" state. We have demonstrated that it could verify many programs other approaches could not, and that the algorithm can be run on real programs.

The motivation for our approach is addressing the limitation of abstract interpretation which forces it to perform abstraction after each analysis step, which often results in a very rough over-approximation. Thus we believe our method is well-suited for augmenting numeric abstract interpretation.

As with any new inductive invariant generation technique, a possible future work is investigating whether formula slicing can be used for increasing the performance and precision of other program analysis techniques, such as k-induction, predicate abstraction or property-directed reachability. An obvious approach would be feeding the invariants generated by formula slicing to a convex analysis running abstract interpretation or policy iteration [21].

Acknowledgements. The authors wish to thank Grigory Fedyukovich and Alexey Bakhirkin for proof-reading and providing valuable feedback, and the anonymous reviewers for their helpful suggestions.

References

1. Monniaux, D., Gonnord, L.: Using bounded model checking to focus fixpoint iterations. In: Yahav, E. (ed.) SAS 2011. LNCS, vol. 6887, pp. 369–385. Springer, Heidelberg (2011). doi:10.1007/978-3-642-23702-7_27
2. Beyer, D.: Reliable and reproducible competition results with BenchExec and witnesses (Report on SV-COMP 2016). In: Chechik, M., Raskin, J.-F. (eds.) TACAS 2016. LNCS, vol. 9636, pp. 887–904. Springer, Heidelberg (2016)
3. Flanagan, C., Leino, K.R.M.: Houdini, an annotation assistant for ESC/Java. In: Oliveira, J.N., Zave, P. (eds.) FME 2001. LNCS, vol. 2021, pp. 500–517. Springer, Heidelberg (2001). doi:10.1007/3-540-45251-6_29
4. Flanagan, C., Joshi, R., Leino, K.R.M.: Annotation inference for modular checkers. Inf. Process. Lett. **77**, 97–108 (2001)
5. Bradley, A.R., Manna, Z.: Checking safety by inductive generalization of counterexamples to induction. In: FMCAD, pp. 173–180 (2007)
6. Graf, S., Saidi, H.: Construction of abstract state graphs with PVS. In: Grumberg, O. (ed.) CAV 1997. LNCS, vol. 1254, pp. 72–83. Springer, Heidelberg (1997). doi:10.1007/3-540-63166-6_10
7. Reps, T., Sagiv, M., Yorsh, G.: Symbolic implementation of the best transformer. In: Steffen, B., Levi, G. (eds.) VMCAI 2004. LNCS, vol. 2937, pp. 252–266. Springer, Heidelberg (2004)
8. Komuravelli, A., Gurfinkel, A., Chaki, S., Clarke, E.M.: Automatic abstraction in SMT-based unbounded software model checking. In: Sharygina, N., Veith, H. (eds.) CAV 2013. LNCS, vol. 8044, pp. 846–862. Springer, Heidelberg (2013). doi:10.1007/978-3-642-39799-8_59
9. Gurfinkel, A., Belov, A., Marques-Silva, J.: Synthesizing safe bit-precise invariants. In: Ábrahám, E., Havelund, K. (eds.) TACAS 2014. LNCS, vol. 8413, pp. 93–108. Springer, Heidelberg (2014). doi:10.1007/978-3-642-54862-8_7
10. Lahiri, S.K., Qadeer, S.: Complexity and algorithms for monomial and clausal predicate abstraction. In: Schmidt, R.A. (ed.) CADE 2009. LNCS (LNAI), vol. 5663, pp. 214–229. Springer, Heidelberg (2009). doi:10.1007/978-3-642-02959-2_18
11. Cousot, P., Cousot, R.: Abstract interpretation: a unified lattice model for static analysis of programs by construction or approximation of fixpoints. In: POPL, pp. 238–252 (1977)
12. Beyer, D., Cimatti, A., Griggio, A., Keremoglu, M.E., Sebastiani, R.: Software model checking via large-block encoding. In: FMCAD, pp. 25–32 (2009)
13. Beyer, D., Henzinger, T.A., Jhala, R., Majumdar, R.: The software model checker Blast. STTT **9**(5–6), 505–525 (2007)
14. Kroening, D., Sharygina, N., Tonetta, S., Tsitovich, A., Wintersteiger, C.M.: Loop summarization using abstract transformers. In: Cha, S.S., Choi, J.-Y., Kim, M., Lee, I., Viswanathan, M. (eds.) ATVA 2008. LNCS, vol. 5311, pp. 111–125. Springer, Heidelberg (2008). doi:10.1007/978-3-540-88387-6_10

15. Bourdoncle, F.: Efficient chaotic iteration strategies with widenings. In: Bjørner, D., Broy, M., Pottosin, I.V. (eds.) Formal Methods in Programming and Their Applications. LNCS, vol. 735, pp. 128–141. Springer, Heidelberg (1993)
16. Moura, L., Bjørner, N.: Z3: an efficient SMT solver. In: Ramakrishnan, C.R., Rehof, J. (eds.) TACAS 2008. LNCS, vol. 4963, pp. 337–340. Springer, Heidelberg (2008). doi:10.1007/978-3-540-78800-3_24
17. Beyer, D., Keremoglu, M.E.: CPACHECKER: a tool for configurable software verification. In: Gopalakrishnan, G., Qadeer, S. (eds.) CAV 2011. LNCS, vol. 6806, pp. 184–190. Springer, Heidelberg (2011). doi:10.1007/978-3-642-22110-1_16
18. McMillan, K.L.: Lazy abstraction with interpolants. In: Ball, T., Jones, R.B. (eds.) CAV 2006. LNCS, vol. 4144, pp. 123–136. Springer, Heidelberg (2006). doi:10.1007/11817963_14
19. Beyer, D., Keremoglu, M.E., Wendler, P.: Predicate abstraction with adjustable-block encoding. In: FMCAD, pp. 189–197 (2010)
20. Henry, J., Monniaux, D., Moy, M.: PAGAI: a path sensitive static analyser. Electr. Notes Theor. Comput. Sci. **289**, 15–25 (2012)
21. Karpenkov, E.G., Monniaux, D., Wendler, P.: Program analysis with local policy iteration. In: Jobstmann, B., Leino, K.R.M. (eds.) VMCAI 2016. LNCS, vol. 9583, pp. 127–146. Springer, Heidelberg (2016). doi:10.1007/978-3-662-49122-5_6

Advancing Software Model Checking Beyond Linear Arithmetic Theories

Ahmed Mahdi[1]([✉]), Karsten Scheibler[2], Felix Neubauer[2], Martin Fränzle[1],
and Bernd Becker[2]

[1] Carl von Ossietzky Universität Oldenburg, Oldenburg, Germany
{mahdi,fraenzle}@informatik.uni-oldenburg.de
[2] Albert-Ludwigs-Universität Freiburg, Freiburg im Breisgau, Germany
{scheibler,neubauef,becker}@informatik.uni-freiburg.de

Abstract. Motivated by the practical need for verifying embedded control programs involving linear, polynomial, and transcendental arithmetics, we demonstrate in this paper a CEGAR technique addressing reachability checking over that rich fragment of arithmetics. In contrast to previous approaches, it is neither based on bit-blasting of floating-point implementations nor confined to decidable fragments of real arithmetic, namely linear or polynomial arithmetic. Its CEGAR loop is based on Craig interpolation within the iSAT3 SMT solver, which employs (abstract) conflict-driven clause learning (CDCL) over interval domains together with interval constraint propagation. As usual, the interpolants thus obtained on spurious counterexamples are used to subsequently refine the abstraction, yet in contrast to manipulating and refining the state set of a discrete-state abstraction, we propose a novel technique for refining the abstraction, where we annotate the abstract model's transitions with side-conditions summarizing their effect. We exploit this for implementing case-based reasoning based on assumption-commitment predicates extracted from the stepwise interpolants in a lazy abstraction mechanism. We implemented our approach within iSAT3 and demonstrate its effectiveness by verifying several benchmarks.

1 Introduction

The wide-spread use of embedded control programs involving linear, polynomial, and transcendental arithmetic provokes a quest for corresponding verification methods. A crucial technique here is the automatic verification of reachability properties in such programs, as many problems can be reduced to it and as it in particular provides a method for detecting unreachable code fragments, a.k.a. *dead code*, in such programs. The latter is an industrial requirement, as various pertinent standards for embedded system development either demand adequate handling of dead code during testing or even bar it altogether, like DO-178C, DO-278A, or ISO/IEC PDTR 24772.

This work was supported by the German Research Council (DFG) as part of SFB/TR 14 AVACS (http://www.avacs.org).

R. Bloem and E. Arbel (Eds.): HVC 2016, LNCS 10028, pp. 186–201, 2016.
DOI: 10.1007/978-3-319-49052-6_12

The set of verification tools being able to address reachability properties in arithmetic programs involving such a rich fragment of arithmetic is confined. Tools manipulating real-valued rather than machine arithmetic tend to be limited to linear or at most polynomial arithmetic due to the obvious decidability issues arising in richer fragments of real arithmetic; tools resorting to bit-blasting, like C Bounded Model Checking (CBMC) [1], tend to adopt the very same restrictions for complexity reasons. Abstract interpretation [2] could in principle easily go beyond, but then suffers from inexactness since the geometry of sets of numbers representable by its usual lattices and the graphs of the monotonic functions over these can only provide coarse overapproximations.

Our Contributions: Within this paper, **(1)** we are trying to overcome this deficiency by a combination of techniques forming a viable counterexample guided abstraction refinement (CEGAR) loop: we exploit Craig interpolation [3] in the interval constraint-propagation based satisfiability modulo theory (SMT) solving algorithm iSAT [4,5] in order to extract reasons for an abstract counterexample being spurious, leading to goal-directed abstraction refinement as in CEGAR [6]. **(2)** In contrast to the usual scheme manipulating and refining the state set of a discrete-state abstraction by splitting cases [7,8] or splitting paths depending on automata [9], we annotate the abstract model's transitions with side-conditions summarizing their effect. Due to a tight integration of checking the abstraction into the SMT solver iSAT3, we can exploit these annotations for implementing case-based reasoning based on assumption-commitment predicates extracted from the stepwise interpolants in a lazy abstraction mechanism, thereby eliminating all spurious counterexamples that share a local reason of being spurious at one transition by using *one predicative expression*.

We implemented our approach within iSAT3 and demonstrate its effectiveness by verifying several benchmarks. We do in particular compare our approach to a model-checking technique exploiting Craig interpolants over the same fragment of arithmetics as an overapproximation of reachable state sets [5], as originally suggested for the finite-state case by McMillan [10], i.e., implementing approximate reach-set computation rather than CEGAR. The benchmarks indicate superior performance of the new CEGAR approach on non-linear benchmarks.

Related Work: To the authors' best knowledge, this is the first attempt to verify programs which may involve transcendental functions by using CEGAR. Most previous work is confined only to linear arithmetics or polynomials [8,11–15], where our work supports richer arithmetic theories, namely transcendental functions. Although our approach is similar with IMPACT [8], WHALE [16] and Ultimate Automizer [17] solvers regarding the usage of interpolants as necessary predicates in refining the abstraction, there are fundamental differences in the learning procedure. While IMPACT and WHALE explicitly split the states after each learning, Ultimate Automizer which is based on ω−automata in learning reasons of spurious counterexamples [18], applies trace abstraction where interpolants are used to construct an automaton that accepts a whole set of infeasible traces and on the same time overapproximates the set of possible traces of the safe program. In contrast to that, our refinement procedure adds neither transitions nor states to the abstraction, but we do annotate the abstract program transitions with necessary assumption-commitment conditions that eliminate the spurious counterexamples.

2   Preliminaries

We use and suitably adapt several existing concepts. A *control flow graph* (CFG) is a cyclic graph representation of all paths that might be traversed during program execution. In our context, we attach code effect to edges rather than nodes of the CFG. i.e., each edge comes with a set of constraints and assignments pertaining to execution of the edge. Formally, constraints and assignments are defined as follows:

Definition 1 (Assignments and constraints). *Let V be a set of integer and real variables, with typical element v, B be a set of boolean variables, with typical element b, and C be a set of constants over rationals, with typical element c.*

- *The set $\Psi(V, B)$ of assignments over integer, real, and boolean variables with typical element ψ is defined by the following syntax:*

$$\psi ::= v := aterm \mid b := bterm$$
$$aterm ::= uaop\ v \mid v\ baop\ v \mid v\ baop\ c \mid c \mid v$$
$$bterm ::= ubop\ b \mid b\ bbop\ b \mid b$$
$$uaop ::= - \mid sin \mid cos \mid exp \mid abs \mid ...$$
$$baop ::= + \mid - \mid \cdot \mid ...$$
$$ubop ::= \neg$$
$$bbop ::= \wedge \mid \vee \mid \oplus \mid ...$$

By ψ we denote a finite list of assignments on integer, real, and boolean variables, $\psi = \langle \psi_1, ..., \psi_n \rangle$ where $n \in \mathbb{N}_{\geq 0}$. We use $\Psi(V, B)^*$ to denote the set of lists of assignments and $\langle\ \rangle$ to denote the empty list of assignments.
- *The set $\Phi(V, B)$ of constraints over integer, real, and boolean variables with typical element ϕ is defined by the following syntax:*

$$\phi ::= atom \mid ubop\ atom \mid atom\ bbop\ atom$$
$$atom ::= theory\_atom \mid bool$$
$$theory\_atom ::= comp \mid simple\_bound$$
$$comp ::= term\ lop\ c \mid term\ lop\ v$$
$$simple\_bound ::= v\ lop\ c$$
$$bool ::= b \mid ubop\ b \mid b\ bbop\ b$$
$$term ::= uaop\ v \mid v\ baop\ v \mid v\ baop\ c$$
$$lop ::= < \mid \leq \mid = \mid > \mid \geq$$

where uaop, baop, ubop and bbop are defined above.

We assume that there is a well-defined valuation mapping $\nu : V \cup B \rightarrow \mathcal{D}(V) \cup \mathcal{D}(B)$ that assigns to each assigned variable a value from its associated domain. Also, we assume that there is a satisfaction relation $\models \subseteq (V \cup B \rightarrow \mathcal{D}(V) \cup \mathcal{D}(B)) \times \Phi(V, B)$ and in case of arithmetic or boolean variables we write $\nu \models \phi$ iff $\nu|_{V \cup B} \models \phi$. The modification of a valuation ν under a finite list of assignment $\psi = \langle \psi_1, ..., \psi_n \rangle$ denoted by $\nu[\psi] = \nu[\psi_1]...\nu[\psi_n]$, where $\nu[v := aterm](v') = \nu[aterm]$ if $v' = v$, otherwise $\nu[v := aterm](v') = \nu(v')$. The same concept of modification is applied in case of boolean assignments.

Definition 2 (Control Flow Graph (CFG)). *A control flow graph $\gamma = (N, E, i)$ consists of a finite set of nodes N, a set $E \subseteq N \times \Phi \times \Psi \times N$ of directed edges, and an initial node $i \in N$ which has no incoming edges. Each edge $(n, \phi, \psi, n') \in E$ has a source node n, a constraint ϕ, a list ψ of assignments and a destination node n'.*

CFG's operational semantics interprets the edge constraints and assignments:

Definition 3 (Operational Semantics). *The operational semantics $\mathcal{T}$ assigns to each control flow graph $\gamma = (N, E, i)$ a labelled transition system $\mathcal{T}(\gamma) = (Conf(\gamma), \{\xrightarrow{e} \mid e \in E\}, C_{init})$ where $Conf(\gamma) = \{\langle n, \nu \rangle \mid n \in N \wedge \nu : V \cup B \rightarrow \mathcal{D}(V) \cup \mathcal{D}(B)\}$ is the set of configurations of γ, $\xrightarrow{e} \subseteq Conf(\gamma) \times Conf(\gamma)$ are transition relations where $\langle n, \nu \rangle \xrightarrow{e} \langle n', \nu' \rangle$ occurs if there is an edge $e = (n, \phi, \psi, n')$, $\nu \models \phi$ and $\nu' = \nu[\psi]$, and $C_{init} = \{\langle i, \nu_{init} \rangle\} \cap Conf(\gamma)$ is the set of initial configurations of γ.*

A path σ of control flow graph γ is an infinite or finite sequence $\langle n_0, \nu_0 \rangle \xrightarrow{e_1} \langle n_1, \nu_1 \rangle \xrightarrow{e_2} \langle n_2, \nu_2 \rangle \ldots$ of consecutive transitions in the transition system $\mathcal{T}(\gamma)$, which furthermore has to be anchored in the sense of starting in an initial state $\langle n_0, \nu_0 \rangle \in C_{init}$. We denote by $\Sigma(\gamma)$ the set of paths of γ and by $\downarrow \sigma$ the set $\{\langle n_0, \nu_0 \rangle, \langle n_1, \nu_1 \rangle, ...\}$ of configurations visited along a path σ.

As we are interested in determining reachability in control flow graphs, we formally define reachability properties as follows:

Definition 4 (Reachability Property(RP)). *The set $\Theta(N, \Phi)$ of reachability properties (RP) over a control flow graph $\gamma = (N, E, i)$ is given by the syntax*

$$\theta ::= n$$

Given an RP θ and a path σ, we say that σ satisfies θ and write $\sigma \models \theta$ iff σ traverses a configuration $\langle n, \nu \rangle$ that satisfies θ, i.e., $\sigma \models \theta$ iff $\exists \nu : \langle n, \nu \rangle \in \downarrow \sigma$. We say that γ satisfies a reachability property θ iff some path $\sigma \in \Sigma(\gamma)$ satisfies θ. By $\Sigma(\gamma, \theta)$, we denote the set of all paths of γ that satisfy θ.

We analyze CFGs by a counterexample-guided abstraction refinement (CEGAR) scheme [6] employing *lazy abstraction* [11]. As usual, that refinement is based on identifying reasons for an abstract counterexample by means of constructing a *Craig interpolant* [3].

Definition 5 (Craig Interpolation). *Given two propositional logic formulae A and B in an interpreted logics $\mathcal{L}$ such that $\models_{\mathcal{L}} A \rightarrow \neg B$, a Craig interpolant for (A, B) is a quantifier-free $\mathcal{L}$-formula $\mathcal{I}$ such that $\models_{\mathcal{L}} A \rightarrow \mathcal{I}$, $\models_{\mathcal{L}} \mathcal{I} \rightarrow \neg B$, and the set of variables of $\mathcal{I}$ is a subset of the set of the free variables shared between A and B, i.e., $Var(\mathcal{I}) \subseteq Var(A) \cap Var(B)$.*

Depending on the logics $\mathcal{L}$, such a Craig interpolant can be computed by various mechanisms. If $\mathcal{L}$ admits quantifier elimination then this can in principle be used; various more efficient schemes have been devised for propositional logic and SAT-modulo theory by exploiting the connection between resolution and variable elimination [13,19].

3   Description of the SMT Solver iSAT3

We build our CEGAR loop on the iSAT3 solver, which is an SMT solver accepting formulas containing arbitrary boolean combinations of theory atoms involving linear, polynomial and transcendental functions (as explained in Definition 1). In classical SMT solving a given SMT formula is split into a boolean skeleton and a set of theory atoms. The boolean skeleton (which represents the truth values of the theory atoms) is processed by a SAT solver in order to search for a satisfying assignment. If such an assignment is found, a separate theory solver is used to check the consistency of the theory atoms under the truth values determined by the SAT solver. In case of an inconsistency the theory solver determines an infeasible sub-set of the theory-atoms which is then encoded into a clause and added to the boolean skeleton. This scheme is called CDCL(T).

In contrast to CDCL(T), there is no such separation between the SAT and the theory part in the family of iSAT solvers [4]; instead interval constraint propagation (ICP) [20] is tightly integrated into the CDCL framework in order to dynamically build the boolean abstraction by deriving new facts from theory atoms. Similarly to SAT solvers, which usually operate on a *conjunctive normal form* (CNF), iSAT3 operates on a CNF as well, but a CNF additionally containing the decomposed theory atoms (so-called *primitive constraints*). We apply a definitional translation akin to the Tseitin-transformation [21] in order to rewrite a given formula into a CNF with primitive constraints.

iSAT3 solves the resulting CNF through a tight integration of the Davis-Putnam-Logemann-Loveland (DPLL) algorithm [22] in its conflict-driven clause learning (CDCL) variant and interval constraint propagation [20]. Details of the algorithm, which operates on interval valuations for both the boolean and the numeric variables and alternates between choice steps splitting such intervals and deduction steps narrowing them based on logical deductions computed through ICP or boolean constraint propagation (BCP), can be found in [4]. Implementing branch-and-prune search in interval lattices and conflict-driven clause learning of clauses comprising irreducible atoms in those lattices, it can be classified as an early implementation of abstract conflict-driven clause learning (ACDCL) [15].

iSAT3 is also able to generate Craig interpolants. Here we exploit the similarities between iSAT3 and a CDCL SAT solver with respect to the conflict resolution. As atoms occurring as pivot variables in resolution steps are always simple bounds mentioning a single variable only, we are able to straightforwardly generalize the technique employed in propositional SAT solvers to generate partial interpolants [5].

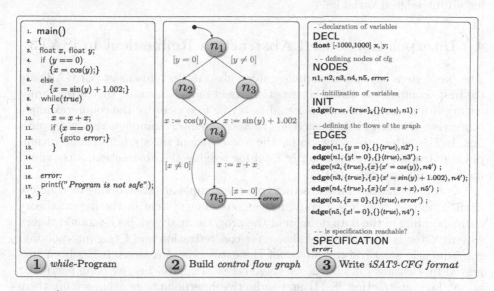

Fig. 1. Left: an arithmetic program, middle: corresponding control flow graph, right: encoding in iSAT3 CFG format.

3.1 Encoding Control Flow Graphs in iSAT3

In order to encode control flow graphs in the iSAT3 input language, we extend the syntax of iSAT3 as shown in Fig. 1. A control flow graph file in iSAT3 (iSAT3-CFG) contains five parts, namely the *declaration, nodes, initialization, edges*, and *specification* sections, which are all started by the respective keywords.

As in iSAT3, the declaration part defines all variables and constants to be used subsequently. Non-boolean variables must have an assigned initial range over which a solution is sought. The second part is the newly introduced nodes part, which defines the set of control flow graph nodes to be used as *source* or *destination* locations of transitions. The initialization part then defines both the initial edge of the CFG and the permissible initial values of all program variables. The latter is achieved by stating a predicate confining the possible values. Its counterpart is the reachability specification, which may name the destination node or define a set of variable valuations to be reached.

The edges part, introduced by the keyword EDGES, represents the control flows in the graph. This part contains a list of edges as defined in Definition 2, each defined by a source node, a list of guards, a list of assigned variables that are changed, a list of assignments where the assigned variable has to be primed, and a destination node which has to be primed as well. In case that the list of assigned variables is empty, it means all previous values of variables are propagated. In contrast to the iSAT3 tradition, a framing rule is applied such that all unspecified assignments and behaviors during unrolling are not considered to be nondeterministic choices, but values are maintained by implicit equations $x' = x$ for all unassigned variables.

4   Interpolation-Based Abstraction Refinement in iSAT3

The basic steps in counterexample guided abstraction refinement (CEGAR) are to, first, compute an initial abstraction, then model-check it, thereafter terminating if no counterexample is found or trying to concretize the counterexample otherwise. If concretization succeeds then the counterexample is real, else spurious. In the latter case, a reason for the occurrence of the spurious counterexample is extracted and subsequently used for refining the abstraction, after which model checking is repeated.

As concretization of the abstract counterexample involves solving its concrete path condition, which is a conjunctive constraint system in the logical theory corresponding to the data domain of the program analyzed, SAT-modulo-theory solving often is the method of choice for concretization and Craig interpolation consequently a natural candidate for the extraction of reasons. It has been suggested by Henzinger et al. [12]. Of these classical approaches, we do in particular adopt lazy abstraction [8,11] and inductive interpolants in [14], yet lift them to the analysis of programs featuring arithmetic beyond decidable fragments. While CEGAR on such rich fragments of arithmetic has been pursued within the field of hybrid-system verification, in particular by Ratschan et al. [23], refinement there has not been directed by Craig interpolation and, using explicit-state techniques, the targets where relatively small control skeletons rather possibly unwieldy CFGs. By a tight integration of checking the abstraction and SMT including CI, we are trying to overcome such limitations.

4.1   The Algorithm

This section presents the four main steps of CEGAR in iSAT3; namely abstraction, abstract model verification, predicate extraction during counterexample validation, and refinement.

Initial Abstraction. The first step of applying CEGAR is to extract an initial abstraction from the concrete model by a well-defined abstraction function. The first abstraction represents just the graph structure of the CFG without considering edge interpretations by assignments and guards. It is introduced as follows:

Definition 6 (Initial Abstraction Function). *Given a control flow graph* $\gamma = (N, E, i) \in \Gamma$, *its initial abstraction mediated by the abstraction function* α *is the CFG* $\alpha(\gamma) = (N, E', i)$, *where* $E' = \{(n, true, \langle\rangle, n') \mid (n, \phi, \psi, n') \in E\}$.

Verifying the Abstraction. In the model checking community it is common to verify reachability problems in the abstract model by using finite-state model-checkers, like BDD-based approaches [24]. In this work, we verify reachability properties in the abstract models by SMT solving together with interpolation [10] in order to verify reachability for unbounded depths. The individual runs of thus unbounded SMT-based model-checking are bound to terminate, as the initial abstraction is equivalent to a finite-state problem and as the predicates that are added to enrich the abstraction during refinement are just logical formula over simple bounds $x \sim c$ which are bounds on boolean propositions; i.e., *literals*, thus keeping the model finite-state. By this idea, we can pursue model-checking of the abstraction and the concretizability test of abstract counterexamples within the same tool, thus avoiding back and forth translation between different tools and checking technologies.

Path-Condition Generation and Extraction of Reasons. Given that the abstract model $\alpha(\gamma)$ is a CFG, it induces a set of paths. We call any path $\sigma_{abs} \in \Sigma(\alpha(\gamma))$ an *abstract path*. As the abstraction function just relaxes edge conditions, we can build a corresponding concrete path—if existent—by just reintroducing the missing constraints and assignments as follows.

Definition 7 (Path-Conditions Generation Function). *Given a control flow graph $\gamma = (N, E, i)$ and its abstraction $\alpha(\gamma) = (N, E', i) \in \Gamma$ and a finite abstract path $\sigma_{abs} : \langle i, \nu'_{init} \rangle \xrightarrow{e'_1} \langle n_1, \nu'_1 \rangle \xrightarrow{e'_2} ... \xrightarrow{e'_m} \langle n_m, \nu'_m \rangle \in \Sigma(\alpha(\gamma))$, the path-conditions generation function $\kappa : \Gamma \times \Sigma \to \Sigma$ that builds a concrete path semantically by completing its conditions, is defined as follows:*

$$\kappa(\gamma, \sigma_{abs}) = \sigma \text{ where, } \sigma : \langle i, \nu_{init} \rangle \xrightarrow{e_1} \langle n_1, \nu_1 \rangle \xrightarrow{e_2} ... \xrightarrow{e_m} \langle n_m, \nu_m \rangle,$$

$$\{e_1, ..., e_m\} \subseteq E \text{ and } \{n_1, ..., n_m\} \subseteq N$$

We say that σ is a real path if and only if its generated path condition, i.e., $\nu_{ini} \wedge \bigwedge_{i=1}^{m} \phi_i \wedge \psi_i$ is satisfiable, else it is spurious.

The crucial step in the CEGAR loop is to extract a reason for counterexamples being spurious such that case splitting on that reason would exclude the particular (and similar) counterexamples. Several previous works used different approaches and schemes to capture such reasons, like state splitting [23], word matching by using ω-automata [18], or interpolants [8,11–14]. In our work, we exploit stepwise interpolants as in [13,14] in order to obtain predicates capturing the reasons, where the first and last interpolants during refining any spurious counterexample are always *true* and *false* respectively [13]. This can be carried out as follows: When encountering a spurious counterexample $\sigma_{sp} = \langle i, \nu'_{init} \rangle \xrightarrow{e'_1} ... \xrightarrow{e'_m} \langle n_m, \nu'_m \rangle \in \Sigma(\gamma')$, where γ' is an abstraction, $\{e'_1, .., e'_m\} \subseteq E'$ – primed edges denote abstract ones –, $m > 0$ and $\theta = n_m$ is the goal to be reached,

- we complete the abstract path σ_{sp} in the original model γ semantically by using the path-conditions generation function κ as in Definition 7.

- as σ_{sp} is spurious, we obtain an unsatisfiable path formula $\kappa(\gamma, \sigma_{sp}) \notin \Sigma(\gamma)$, i.e., $\nu_{init} \wedge \bigwedge_{i=1}^{m} \phi_i \wedge \psi_i \models \mathsf{False}$.
- by using CI in order to extract reasonable predicates as in lazy abstraction [12], one computes a reason of unsatisfiability at each control point (node) of γ. For example, consider that $\kappa(\gamma, \sigma_{sp}) = A \wedge B$, where $A = \nu_{init} \wedge \bigwedge_{j=1}^{k} \phi_j \wedge \psi_j$, $B = \bigwedge_{j=k+1}^{m} \phi_j \wedge \psi_j$ and $0 \leq k \leq m$. If we run the iSAT3 solver iteratively for all possible values of k, we obtain $m+1$ interpolants, where interpolant I_k is an adequate reason at edge e_k justifying the spuriousness of σ_{sp}.
- in case of using *inductive interpolants*, one uses the interpolant of iteration k, i.e., $\mathcal{I}_k$ as A-formula while interpolating against the above formula B in order to obtain interpolant $\mathcal{I}_{k+1}$. As $\mathcal{I}_k$ overapproximates the prefix path formula till k, we compute the next interpolant $\mathcal{I}_{k+1}$ that overapproximates $\mathcal{I}_k \wedge \phi_{k+1} \wedge \psi_{k+1}$. This step assures that the interpolant at step k implies the interpolant at step $k+1$.

This guarantees that the interpolants at the different locations achieve the goal of providing a reason eliminating the infeasible error path from further exploration.

Abstraction Refinement. After finding a spurious counterexample and extracting adequate predicates from the path, we need to refine the abstract model in a way such that at least this counterexample is excluded from the abstract model behavior. This refinement step can be performed in different ways. The first way is a global refinement procedure which is the earliest traditional approach, where the whole abstract model is refined after adding a new predicate [25]. The second way is a *lazy abstraction* [8,11,26] where instead of iteratively refining an abstraction, it refines the abstract model on demand, as it is constructed. This refinement has been based on predicate abstraction [11] or on interpolants derived from refuting program paths [8]. The common theme, however, has been to refine and thus generally enlarge the discrete state-space of the abstraction on demand such that the abstract transition relation could locally disambiguate post-states (or pre-states) in a way eliminating the spurious counterexample.

Our approach of checking the abstraction within an SMT solver (by using interpolation based model checking) rather than a finite-state model-checker facilitates a subtly different solution. **Instead of explicitly splitting states in the abstraction**, i.e., refining the nodes of the initial abstraction, we stay with the initial abstraction **and just add adequate pre-post-relations to its edges**. These pre-post-relations are akin to the ones analyzed when locally determining the transitions in a classical abstraction refinement, yet play a different role here in that they are not mapped to transition arcs in a state-enriched finite-state model, but rather added merely syntactically to the existing edges, whereby they only refine the transition effect on an unaltered state space. It is only during path search on the (refined) abstraction that the SMT solver may actually pursue an implicit state refinement by means of case splitting; being a tool for proof search, it would, however, only do so on demand, i.e., only when the particular case distinction happens to be instrumental to reasoning.

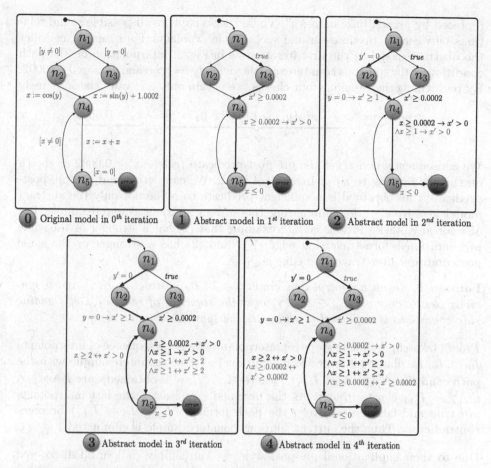

Fig. 2. CEGAR iterations where bold **paths** and cyan predicates represent the current counterexample and added constraints in each iteration after refinement. (Color figure online)

We support this implicit refinement technique for both lazy abstraction (with inductive interpolants as optional configuration) and global refinement.

In the following we concisely state how the (novel) implicit refinement is performed by attaching pre-post-conditions to edges. Given a spurious counterexample $\sigma_{sp} = \langle i, \nu_{init} \rangle \xrightarrow{e_1'} \ldots \xrightarrow{e_m'} \langle n_m, \nu_m \rangle \in \Sigma(\gamma')$ with $\theta = n_m$ as shown in the previous subsection, we obtain $m + 1$ (optionally inductive) interpolants, where I_k and I_{k+1} are consecutive interpolants at edges e_k and e_{k+1}, respectively, and $0 < k < m$. We continue as follows:

1. if $I_k \wedge \phi_{k+1} \wedge \psi_{k+1} \rightarrow I_{k+1}$ holds, then we add $I \rightarrow I'$ to e_{k+1}',
2. if $I_k \wedge \phi_{k+1} \wedge \psi_{k+1} \rightarrow \neg I_{k+1}$ holds, then we add $I \rightarrow \neg I'$ to e_{k+1}',
3. if $\neg I_k \wedge \phi_{k+1} \wedge \psi_{k+1} \rightarrow \neg I_{k+1}$ holds, then we add $\neg I \rightarrow \neg I'$ to e_{k+1}',
4. if $\neg I_k \wedge \phi_{k+1} \wedge \psi_{k+1} \rightarrow I_{k+1}$ holds, then we add $\neg I \rightarrow I'$ to e_{k+1}',

where I is I_k with all its indexed variable instances x_k replaced by undecorated base names x and I' is I_{k+1} with all its indexed variable instances x_{k+1}

replaced by primed base names x'. These checks capture all possible sound relations between the predecessor and successor interpolants. For example, consider the abstract model in the first iteration as in Fig. 2. Interpolation on the path condition of the spurious counterexample yields $I_1 := true$ and $I_2 := x \geq 0.0002$. By performing the previous four checks, we obtain only one valid check, namely

$$\underbrace{true}_{I_1} \wedge \underbrace{true}_{\phi_1} \wedge \underbrace{x_2 = sin(y_1) + 1.0002 \wedge y_2 = y_1}_{\psi_1} \rightarrow \underbrace{x_2 \geq 0.0002}_{I_2}$$

We consequently construct the pre-post-predicate $true \rightarrow x' \geq 0.0002$ as shown on the arc from n_3 to n_4 of Image 1 of Fig. 2. We can derive that the pre-post-predicate thus obtained is a sufficient predicate to refine not only the abstract model at edge e'_{k+1} for eliminating the current spurious counterexample, but also for any other spurious counterexample that (1) has a stronger or the same precondition before traversing edge e'_{k+1} and (2) has a stronger or the same postcondition after traversing edge e'_{k+1}.

Lemma 1. *Given a control flow graph $\gamma \in \Gamma$, its abstraction $\alpha(\gamma)$ and a spurious counterexample $\sigma_{sp} \in \Sigma(\alpha(\gamma)$ over the sequence of edges $e_1, ... e_m$, adding side-conditions is sufficient to eliminate the spurious counterexample.*

Proof. (sketch): by using stepwise interpolants, we get a sequence of interpolants $I_0, ..., I_m$ attributing the previous (spurious) abstract counterexample with the path condition $\bigwedge_{i=0}^{m-1}(I_i \rightarrow I_{i+1})$,[1] where "$I_i \rightarrow I_{i+1}$" is obtained since $I_i \wedge \phi_{i+1} \wedge \psi_{i+1} \rightarrow I_{i+1}$ is a tautology. As the first and – at least – the last interpolants are true and false respectively, the path formula $(\bigwedge_{i=0}^{m-1} I_i \rightarrow I_{i+1})$ becomes contradictory. Thus the current spurious counterexample is eliminated.   □

Due to their implicational pre-post-style, we can simply conjoin all discovered predicates at an edge, regardless on which path and after how many refinement steps they are discovered. Such incremental refinement of the symbolically represented pre-post-relation attached to edges by means of successively conjoining new cases proceeds until finally we can prove the safety of the model by proving that the bad state is disconnected from all reachable states of the abstract model, or until an eventual counterexample gets real in the sense of its concretization succeeding. To prove unreachability of a node in the new abstraction, we use Craig interpolation for computing a safe overapproximation of the reachable state space as proposed by McMillan [10]. The computation of the overapproximating CI exploits the pre-post conditions added.

In the following, we illustrate how the program in Fig. 1 is proven to be safe; i.e., that location error is unreachable. The arithmetic program, the corresponding control flow graph, and the encoding of the control flow graph in iSAT3 are stated in the Fig. 1. In the first iteration, we get the initial coarse abstraction according to Definition 6. In case of finding spurious counterexample, which is the case in the first four iterations, we refine the model as shown in Fig. 2. After

---

[1] The proof considers the first type of implication check, the others hold analogously.

that, the solver proves that the error is not reachable in the abstract model. Additionally, the third and fourth counterexamples have a common suffix, but differ in the prefix formula, therefore both are needed for refining the abstraction in the third and fourth iterations. However, as all following paths from loop unwinding share the prefix formula with the previous two counterexamples, yet have stronger suffix formulas, the already added pre-post predicates are sufficient to eliminate all further counterexamples.

5   Experiments

We have implemented our approach, in particular the control flow graph encoding and the interpolation-based CEGAR verification, within the iSAT3 solver. We verified reachability in several linear and non-linear arithmetic programs and CFG encodings of hybrid systems. The following tests are mostly C-programs modified from [25] or hybrid models discussed in [5,27]. As automatic translation into CFG format is not yet implemented, the C benchmarks are currently mostly of moderate size (as encoding of problems is done manually), but challenging; e.g., hénon map and logistic map [5]. We compared our approach with interpolant-based model checking implemented in both CPAchecker [28] (IMPACT configuration [8]), version 1.6.1, and iSAT3,[2] where the interpolants are used as overapproximations of reachable state sets [5]. Also, we compared with CBMC [1] as it can verify linear and polynomial arithmetic programs. Comparison on programs involving transcendental functions could, however, only be performed with interpolant-based model checking in iSAT3 as CBMC does not support these functions and CPAchecker treats them as uninterpreted functions.

CBMC, version 4.9, was used in its native bounded model-checking mode with an adequate unwinding depth, which represents a logically simpler problem, as the k-inductor [34] built on top of CBMC requires different parameters to be given in advance for each benchmark, in particular for loops, such that it offers a different level of automation. We limited solving time for each problem to five minutes and memory to 4 GB. The benchmarks were run on an Intel(R) Core(TM) i7 M 620@2.67GHz with 8 GB RAM.

5.1   Verifying Reachability in Arithmetic Programs

Table 1 summaries the results of our experimental evaluation. It comprises five groups of columns. The first includes the name of the benchmark, type of the problem (whether it includes non-linear constraints or loops), number of control points, and number of edges. The second group shows the result of verifying the benchmarks when using iSAT3 CEGAR (lazy abstraction), thereby stating the verification time in seconds, memory usage in kilobytes, number of abstraction refinements, and the final verdict. The third group has the same structure, yet

---

[2] Although we contacted the authors of *dReal* [29] which supports unbounded model checking for non-linear constraints [30], they referred us to the latest version which does not support unbounded model checking, thus it is excluded.

Table 1. Verification results of linear/non-linear hybrid models. Bold lines refer to best results w.r.t. best verification time.

No	Name	Non-linear	Loops	#Nodes	#Edges	iSAT3 CEGAR, lazy abstraction Time(s)	Memory(KB)	Iteration	Result	iSAT3 Interpolation-based MC Time(s)	Memory(KB)	Depth	Result	CBMC maximum depth 250 Time(s)	Memory(KB)	unwinding loop	Result	CPAchecker ITP + lazy abstraction Time(s)	Memory(KB)	#Refinements	Result
1	cfa_test0001 [25]	✗	✓	11	13	1.962	17256	14	SAFE	TO	6038428	20	UNKNOWN	98.396	151028	56	SAFE	2.782	150984	2	SAFE
2	cfa_test0002 [25]	✗	✓	11	13	0.173	6352	5	SAFE	TO	168240	801	UNKNOWN	9.406	141152	56	SAFE	2.242	143948	1	SAFE
3	cfa_test0003 [25]	✗	✓	11	13	0.127	5716	5	SAFE	TO	169072	800	UNKNOWN	8.160	140996	56	SAFE	2.202	128216	1	SAFE
4	cfa_test0004 [25]	✗	✓	11	13	0.174	6568	8	UNSAFE	55.653	5883156	15	UNSAFE	3.801	140936	56	UNSAFE	2.818	149652	2	UNSAFE
5	cfa_test0005 [25]	✓	✓	15	18	0.455	8812	9	CAND.	1.657	30840	16	CAND.	**0.150**	**22972**	**6**	**UNSAFE**	3.690	158588	3	UNSAFE
6	cfa_test0006 [25]	✓	✗	13	17	0.043	5196	2	SAFE	0.070	6500	7	SAFE	0.137	22320	0	SAFE	2.561	141876	2	SAFE
7	cfa_test0007 [25]	✓	✗	7	8	0.047	4856	2	SAFE	TO	4541444	3	UNKNOWN	unsupported functions				2.424	127384	1	SAFE
8	cfa_test0008 [25]	✗	✗	3	3	0.017	4180	1	UNSAFE	0.023	4112	1	UNSAFE	0.140	22600	0	UNSAFE	2.456	145936	2	UNSAFE
9	cfa_test0009 [31]	✗	✓	6	8	0.054	5048	3	SAFE	TO	157748	864	UNKNOWN	7.702	50248	56	SAFE	2.510	145684	1	SAFE
10	cfa_test0010 [27]	✗	✓	6	8	0.075	5268	3	SAFE	TO	775032	2	UNKNOWN	unsupported functions				2.229	128328	1	SAFE
11	control flow [5]	✗	✗	7	8	0.035	4904	1	SAFE	0.039	4716	5	SAFE	0.303	26820	116	SAFE	2.330	127968	1	SAFE
12	cruise control [5]	✓	✓	8	15	0.103	5724	8	SAFE	TO	3196492	130	UNKNOWN	0.147	22528	18	SAFE	2.819	146284	3	UNSAFE
13	frontier_01 [32]	✓	✓	3	4	0.050	4744	1	CAND.	0.056	4824	2	CAND.	3.367	101844	32	UNSAFE	2.650	145524	2	UNSAFE
14	frontier_02 [32]	✓	✓	3	4	0.173	6148	3	SAFE	TO	94200	721	UNKNOWN	1.276	102124	32	SAFE	3.046	149128	2	UNSAFE
15	frontier_03 [32]	✓	✓	3	4	0.141	5332	3	SAFE	TO	97580	796	UNKNOWN	1.284	102056	32	SAFE	2.868	148964	2	UNSAFE
16	hénon map [5]	✓	✓	3	4	0.033	4628	3	CAND.	0.041	4628	3	CAND.	0.694	24496	25	SAFE	2.216	129908	1	UNSAFE
17	logistic map [5]	✓	✓	3	4	0.149	7380	3	SAFE	0.205	5932	12	CAND	4.759	188928	38	SAFE	2.142	124620	1	UNSAFE
18	two circles_01	✓	✓	6	7	0.067	4608	1	SAFE	48.938	13848	8	SAFE	0.163	22452	54	SAFE	2.359	145832	1	UNSAFE
19	two circles_02	✓	✓	6	7	0.033	4584	1	SAFE	0.144	5260	8	SAFE	0.155	22204	55	SAFE	2.383	145204	1	UNSAFE
20	tank_controller [27]	✗	✓	5	13	7.822	159708	24	SAFE	0.107	6784	20	SAFE	0.149	22344	69	SAFE	2.446	143688	1	UNSAFE
21	gas_burner [27]	✗	✓	4	8	3.776	12720	42	SAFE	0.361	7260	33	SAFE	27.843	43580	1282	SAFE	4.511	151460	3	UNSAFE
22	cfa_test0022 [33]	✗	✓	8	19	2.264	18468	23	SAFE	0.845	126680	6	SAFE	**0.151**	**22312**	**25**	**SAFE**	5.358	202840	2	SAFE
23	cfa_test0023 [33]	✗	✓	3	4	8.189	42620	21	SAFE	0.143	6716	22	SAFE	0.264	26880	56	SAFE	3.025	145360	2	UNSAFE

reports results for using iSAT3 with interpolation-based reach-set overapproximation used for model checking.

The fourth part provides figures for CBMC with a maximum unwinding depth of 250. CBMC could not address the benchmarks 7 and 10 as they contain unsupported transcendental functions. The fifth part provides the figures for CPAchecker while using the default IMPACT configuration where the red lines refer to false alarms (*for comparison, CPAchecker was run with different configurations, yet this didn't affect the presence of false alarms.*)

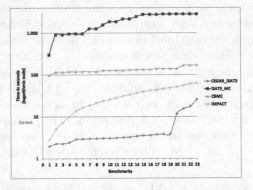

Fig. 3. Accumulated verification times for the first n benchmarks

reported by IMPACT due to non-linearity or non-deterministic behaviour of the program. For each benchmark, we mark in boldface the best results in terms of time. iSAT3-based CEGAR outperforms the others in 18 cases, interpolation-based MC in iSAT3 outperforms the others in 2 cases, and CBMC outperforms the others in 3 cases. Figures 3 and 4 summarize the main findings. The tests demonstrate the efficacy of the new CEGAR approach in comparison to other competitor tools. Concerning verification time, we observe that iSAT3 with CEGAR scores the best results. Namely, iSAT3-based CEGAR needs about 27 s for processing the full set of benchmarks, equivalent to an average verification time of 1.2 s, iSAT3 with the interpolation-based approach needs 2809 s total and 122 s on average, CBMC needs 168 s total and 8 s on average, and IMPACT needs 64 s total and 2.7 s on average.

Concerning memory, we observe that iSAT3 with CEGAR needs about 15 MB on average, iSAT3 with interpolation 906 MB on average, CBMC needs 66 MB on average, and IMPACT needs 141 MB on average. The findings confirm that at least on the current set of benchmarks, the CEGAR approach is by a fair margin the most efficient one.

The only weakness of both iSAT3-based approaches is that they sometimes report a *candidate solution*, i.e., a very narrow interval box that is hull consistent, rather than a firm satisfia-

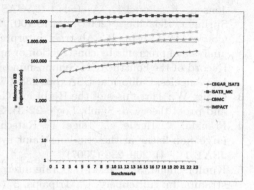

Fig. 4. Memory usage (#benchmarks processed within given memory limit)

bility verdict. This effect is due to the incompleteness of interval reasoning, which here is employed in its outward rounding variant providing safe overapproximation of real arithmetic rather than floating-point arithmetic. It is expected that these deficiencies vanish once floating-point support in iSAT3 is complete, which currently is under development as an alternative theory to real arithmetic. It should, however, be noted that CEGAR with its preoccupation to generating conjunctive constraint systems (the path conditions) already alleviates most of the incompleteness, which arises particularly upon disjunctive reasoning.

6   Conclusion and Future Work

In this paper, we tightly integrated interpolation-based CEGAR with SMT solving based on interval constraint propagation. The use of the very same tool, namely iSAT3, for verifying the abstraction and for concretizing abstract error paths facilitated a novel implicit abstraction-refinement scheme based on attaching symbolic pre-post relations to edges in a structurally fixed abstraction. The resulting tool is able to verify reachability properties in arithmetic programs which may involve transcendental functions, like *sin*, *cos*, and *exp*. With our prototype implementation, we verified several benchmarks and demonstrated the feasibility of interpolation-based CEGAR for non-linear arithmetic programs well beyond the polynomial fragment.

Minimizing the size of interpolants (and thus pre-post relations generated) and finding adequate summaries of loops in case of monotonic functions will be subject of future work.

References

1. Clarke, E., Kroening, D., Lerda, F.: A tool for checking ANSI-C programs. In: Jensen, K., Podelski, A. (eds.) TACAS 2004. LNCS, vol. 2988, pp. 168–176. Springer, Heidelberg (2004). doi:10.1007/978-3-540-24730-2_15

2. Cousot, P., Cousot, R.: Abstract interpretation: a unified lattice model for static analysis of programs by construction or approximation of fixpoints. In: Conference Record of the Fourth ACM Symposium on Principles of Programming Languages, Los Angeles, California, USA, pp. 238–252 (1977)

3. Craig, W.: Three uses of the Herbrand-Gentzen theorem in relating model theory and proof theory. J. Symb. Logic **22**(3), 269–285 (1957)

4. Fränzle, M., Herde, C., Teige, T., Ratschan, S., Schubert, T.: Efficient solving of large non-linear arithmetic constraint systems with complex Boolean structure. JSAT **1**(3–4), 209–236 (2007)

5. Kupferschmid, S., Becker, B.: Craig interpolation in the presence of non-linear constraints. In: Fahrenberg, U., Tripakis, S. (eds.) FORMATS 2011. LNCS, vol. 6919, pp. 240–255. Springer, Heidelberg (2011). doi:10.1007/978-3-642-24310-3_17

6. Clarke, E., Grumberg, O., Jha, S., Lu, Y., Veith, H.: Counterexample-guided abstraction refinement. In: Emerson, E.A., Sistla, A.P. (eds.) CAV 2000. LNCS, vol. 1855, pp. 154–169. Springer, Heidelberg (2000). doi:10.1007/10722167_15

7. Clarke, E.M.: SAT-based counterexample guided abstraction refinement in model checking. In: Baader, F. (ed.) CADE 2003. LNCS (LNAI), vol. 2741, pp. 1–1. Springer, Heidelberg (2003). doi:10.1007/978-3-540-45085-6_1

8. McMillan, K.L.: Lazy abstraction with interpolants. In: Ball, T., Jones, R.B. (eds.) CAV 2006. LNCS, vol. 4144, pp. 123–136. Springer, Heidelberg (2006). doi:10.1007/11817963_14

9. Heizmann, M., Hoenicke, J., Podelski, A.: Refinement of trace abstraction. In: Palsberg, J., Su, Z. (eds.) SAS 2009. LNCS, vol. 5673, pp. 69–85. Springer, Heidelberg (2009). doi:10.1007/978-3-642-03237-0_7

10. McMillan, K.L.: Interpolation and SAT-based model checking. In: Hunt, W.A., Somenzi, F. (eds.) CAV 2003. LNCS, vol. 2725, pp. 1–13. Springer, Heidelberg (2003). doi:10.1007/978-3-540-45069-6_1

11. Henzinger, T.A., Jhala, R., Majumdar, R., Sutre, G.: Lazy abstraction. In: Conference Record of POPL 2002: The 29th SIGPLAN-SIGACT Symposium on Principles of Programming Languages, Portland, OR, USA, January 16–18, pp. 58–70 (2002)

12. Henzinger, T.A., Jhala, R., Majumdar, R., McMillan, K.L.: Abstractions from proofs. In: POPL, pp. 232–244 (2004)

13. Esparza, J., Kiefer, S., Schwoon, S.: Abstraction refinement with Craig interpolation and symbolic pushdown systems. JSAT **5**(1–4), 27–56 (2008)

14. Beyer, D., Löwe, S.: Explicit-value analysis based on CEGAR and interpolation. CoRR abs/1212.6542 (2012)

15. Brain, M., D'Silva, V., Griggio, A., Haller, L., Kroening, D.: Interpolation-based verification of floating-point programs with abstract CDCL. In: Logozzo, F., Fähndrich, M. (eds.) SAS 2013. LNCS, vol. 7935, pp. 412–432. Springer, Heidelberg (2013). doi:10.1007/978-3-642-38856-9_22

16. Albarghouthi, A., Gurfinkel, A., Chechik, M.: WHALE: an interpolation-based algorithm for inter-procedural verification. In: Kuncak, V., Rybalchenko, A. (eds.) VMCAI 2012. LNCS, vol. 7148, pp. 39–55. Springer, Heidelberg (2012). doi:10.1007/978-3-642-27940-9_4

17. Heizmann, M., Hoenicke, J., Podelski, A.: Software model checking for people who love automata. In: Sharygina, N., Veith, H. (eds.) CAV 2013. LNCS, vol. 8044, pp. 36–52. Springer, Heidelberg (2013). doi:10.1007/978-3-642-39799-8_2

18. Segelken, M.: Abstraction and counterexample-guided construction of ω-automata for model checking of step-discrete linear hybrid models. In: Damm, W., Hermanns, H. (eds.) CAV 2007. LNCS, vol. 4590, pp. 433–448. Springer, Heidelberg (2007). doi:10.1007/978-3-540-73368-3_46

19. Pudlák, P.: Lower bounds for resolution and cutting plane proofs and monotone computations. J. Symb. Logic 62(3), 981–998 (1997)

20. Benhamou, F., Granvilliers, L.: Combining local consistency, symbolic rewriting and interval methods. In: Calmet, J., Campbell, J.A., Pfalzgraf, J. (eds.) AISMC 1996. LNCS, vol. 1138, pp. 144–159. Springer, Heidelberg (1996). doi:10.1007/3-540-61732-9_55

21. Tseitin, G.S.: On the complexity of derivations in the propositional calculus. Stud. Math. Math. Logic Part II, 115–125 (1968)

22. Davis, M., Logemann, G., Loveland, D.W.: A machine program for theorem-proving. Commun. ACM 5(7), 394–397 (1962)

23. Ratschan, S., She, Z.: Safety verification of hybrid systems by constraint propagation-based abstraction refinement. ACM Trans. Embedded Comput. Syst. 6(1), 8 (2007)

24. Ball, T., Rajamani, S.K.: Bebop: a symbolic model checker for boolean programs. In: Havelund, K., Penix, J., Visser, W. (eds.) SPIN 2000. LNCS, vol. 1885, pp. 113–130. Springer, Heidelberg (2000). doi:10.1007/10722468_7

25. Dinh, N.T.: Dead code analysis using satisfiability checking. Master's thesis, Carl von Ossietzky Universität Oldenburg (2013)

26. Jha, S.K.: Numerical simulation guided lazy abstraction refinement for nonlinear hybrid automata. CoRR abs/cs/0611051 (2006)

27. Alur, R., Courcoubetis, C., Halbwachs, N., Henzinger, T.A., Ho, P., Nicollin, X., Olivero, A., Sifakis, J., Yovine, S.: The algorithmic analysis of hybrid systems. Theor. Comput. Sci. 138(1), 3–34 (1995)

28. Beyer, D., Henzinger, T.A., Théoduloz, G.: Configurable software verification: concretizing the convergence of model checking and program analysis. In: Damm, W., Hermanns, H. (eds.) CAV 2007. LNCS, vol. 4590, pp. 504–518. Springer, Heidelberg (2007). doi:10.1007/978-3-540-73368-3_51

29. Gao, S., Kong, S., Clarke, E.M.: dReal: an SMT solver for nonlinear theories over the reals. In: Bonacina, M.P. (ed.) CADE 2013. LNCS (LNAI), vol. 7898, pp. 208–214. Springer, Heidelberg (2013). doi:10.1007/978-3-642-38574-2_14

30. Gao, S., Zufferey, D.: Interpolants in nonlinear theories over the reals. In: Chechik, M., Raskin, J.-F. (eds.) TACAS 2016. LNCS, vol. 9636, pp. 625–641. Springer, Heidelberg (2016). doi:10.1007/978-3-662-49674-9_41

31. D'Silva, V., Haller, L., Kroening, D., Tautschnig, M.: Numeric bounds analysis with conflict-driven learning. In: Flanagan, C., König, B. (eds.) TACAS 2012. LNCS, vol. 7214, pp. 48–63. Springer, Heidelberg (2012). doi:10.1007/978-3-642-28756-5_5

32. Kupferschmid, S.: Über Craigsche Interpolation und deren Anwendung in der formalen Modellprüfung. Ph.D. thesis, Albert-Ludwigs-Universität Freiburg im Breisgau (2013)

33. Seghir, M.N.: Abstraction refinement techniques for software model checking. Ph.D. thesis, Albert-Ludwigs-Universität Freiburg im Breisgau (2010)

34. Donaldson, A.F., Haller, L., Kroening, D., Rümmer, P.: Software verification using k-induction. In: Yahav, E. (ed.) SAS 2011. LNCS, vol. 6887, pp. 351–368. Springer, Heidelberg (2011). doi:10.1007/978-3-642-23702-7_26

Predator Shape Analysis Tool Suite

Lukáš Holík, Michal Kotoun, Petr Peringer, Veronika Šoková,
Marek Trtík, and Tomáš Vojnar[✉]

FIT, IT4Innovations Centre of Excellence,
Brno University of Technology, Brno, Czech Republic
vojnar@fit.vutbr.cz

Abstract. The paper presents a tool suite centered around the Predator
shape analyzer for low-level C code based on the notion of symbolic memory graphs. Its architecture, optimizations, extensions, inputs, options,
and outputs are covered.

1 Introduction

Analysing programs with *dynamic pointer-linked data structures* is one of the
most difficult tasks in program analysis. The reason is that one has to deal
with infinite sets of program configurations having the form of complex graphs
representing the contents of the program heap. The task becomes even more
complicated when considering low-level pointer manipulating programs where
one has to deal with operations such as pointer arithmetic, address alignment,
or block operations.

Many different formalisms have been proposed for finitely representing infinite sets of heap configurations. One of them is the formalism of *symbolic memory graphs* (SMGs) [6]. In particular, SMGs specialise—at least for the time
being—in representing sets of configurations of programs manipulating various
kinds of lists, which can be singly- or doubly-linked, hierarchically nested, cyclic,
shared, and have various additional links (head pointers, tail pointers, data pointers, etc.). SMGs were originally inspired by the notion of separation logic with
higher-order list predicates, but they were given a graph form to allow for an as
efficient fully-automated shape analysis based on abstract interpretation as possible. Moreover, SMGs turned out to be a suitable basis for extensions allowing
one to capture various low-level memory features.

SMGs are used as the underlying formalism of the Predator shape analyser for
low-level pointer programs written in C. The first version of Predator, based on
a notion of SMGs significantly simpler than that of [6], appeared in [5]. Predator
is capable of checking *memory safety* (no dereferencing of invalid pointers, no
memory leaks, no double free operations, etc.), it can check *assertions* present
in the code, and it can also print out the computed shape invariants. Since its
first version, Predator was extended to support low-level memory operations in

Supported by the Czech Science Foundation project 14-11384S, the IT4IXS:
IT4Innovations Excellence in Science project (LQ1602), and the internal BUT
project FIT-S-14-2486.

the way proposed in [6] and optimized in various ways (e.g., by using function summaries, elimination of dead variables, etc.).

Later on, a parallelized layer, called *Predator Hunting Party* (Predator HP), was built on top of the basic Predator analyzer [8]. Predator HP runs the original analyzer in parallel with several bounded versions of the analysis in order to speed up error discovery and reduce the number of false alarms. The efficiency of SMGs together with all the optimizations allowed Predator to win 6 gold medals, 3 silver medals, and 1 bronze medal at the International Software Verification Competition SV-COMP'12–16 organised within TACAS'12–16 as well as the Gödel medal at FLoC'14 Olympic Games.

Apart from optimizations, Predator has also been extended with various further outputs, such as error traces required at SV-COMP. Moreover, recently, another (experimental) extension of Predator has been implemented [3] which uses (slightly extended) shape invariants computed by Predator to automatically convert pointer programs manipulating lists to higher-level *container programs*.

In this paper, we describe the architecture of Predator and the entire tool suite formed around it, its various optimizations, as well as its different inputs, options, and possible outputs. This should make it significantly easier for anybody interested in Predator to start using it, join its further development, and/or get inspiration applicable in development of other program analyzers. Moreover, we believe that one can also directly re-use some of the modules of the architecture, such as the Predator's connection to both gcc and (recently added) LLVM. Indeed, all components of the tool suite are open source and freely available[1] together with an extensive set of use cases.

Related work. There are, of course, many other shape analysers, such as TVLA [10], Invader [11], SLAyer [1], Xisa [2], or Forester [7]. These tools differ in the underlying formalisms, generality, scalability, and/or degree of automation. Predator is distinguished by its high efficiency, degree of automation, and coverage of low-level features for analysing list-manipulating programs.

2   Abstract Domain of Symbolic Memory Graphs

Predator is based on the SMG abstract domain [6]. We now shortly highlight its main features. For an illustration of SMGs, see Fig. 1 which provides an SMG describing a cyclic Linux-style doubly-linked list with nodes linked by pointers pointing into the middle of the nodes (requiring pointer arithmetic to get access to the data stored in the list). SMGs

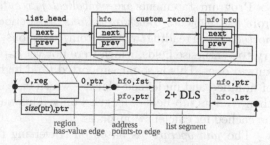

Fig. 1. An example of a Linux-style cyclic DLL (top) and its SMG representation (bottom)

---

[1] http://www.fit.vutbr.cz/research/groups/verifit/tools/predator.

are directed graphs consisting of two kinds of nodes and two kinds of edges. The nodes include *objects* representing allocated space and *values* representing addresses and non-pointer data (mainly, integers). The edges have the form of *has-value* and *points-to* edges.

Objects are further divided into *regions* representing individual blocks of memory, *doubly-* and *singly-linked list segments* (DLSs/SLSs) representing doubly- and singly-linked sequences of nodes uninterrupted by any external incoming pointer, respectively, and *optional objects* that can but need not be present. Each object has some constant *size* in bytes (with a so far preliminary extension to interval-sized objects), a *validity flag* (deleted objects are kept till they are pointed to), and a *placement tag* distinguishing objects stored in the heap, stack, and statically allocated memory.

Each DLS is given by the `hfo` offset of the *head structure* of its nodes, storing the next and previous ("prev") pointers, which is the offset to which linking fields usually point in low-level list implementations, and the `nfo/pfo` offsets of the *next* and *prev fields* themselves. DLSs are tagged by a length constraint of the form $N+$ for $N \geq 0$, meaning that the DLS abstractly represents all concrete list segments of length N or bigger, or by a constraint of the form 0-1 representing segments of length zero or one. Nodes of DLSs can point to objects that are *shared* (each node points to the same object) or *nested* (each node points to a separate copy of the object). The nesting is implemented by tagging objects by their *nesting level*. For SLSs, the situation is similar.

Has-value edges lead from objects to values and are labelled by the *field offset* at which the given value is stored and the *type of the value* (like the simplified pointer type `ptr` in Fig. 1). Points-to edges lead from values encoding addresses to the objects they point to. They are labelled by a *target offset* and a *target specifier*. For a DLS, the latter specifies whether a points-to edge encodes a pointer to its *first* or *last node* (`fst/lst` in Fig. 1), or even a *set* of pointers (one for each node abstracted by the DLS) incoming into the DLS from *"below"*. This way, back-links from nested objects to their parent DLS are encoded. Predator supports even offsets with constant *interval bounds*, which is crucial to support pointers obtained by *address alignment* wrt an unknown base pointer. In addition, SMGs can also contain *inequality constraints* between values.

Program statements are *symbolically executed* on regions, possibly concretised from list segments. *Block operations*, like `memcopy`, `memset`, or `memmove`, are supported. When reading/writing from/to regions, Predator uses *re-interpretation* to try to synthesise fields, which were not yet explicitly defined, from the currently known ones. This is so far supported (and highly needed) for low-level handling of nullified and undefined blocks—which can, e.g., nullify a field of 32 bytes and then read its sub-field of length 4 only. This way, overlapping fields can arise and be cached for efficiency purposes.

The *join operator* is based on traversing two SMGs from the same pointer variables and joining simultaneously encountered objects, sometimes replacing some more concrete objects with more abstract ones and/or inserting 0+ or 0-1 list segments when some list segment is found missing in one of the SMGs.

Entailment checking is based on the join operator: Predator checks whether the two given SMGs can be joined while always encountering more general objects in the same SMG out of the two given. *Abstraction* collapses uninterrupted sequences of compatible regions and list segments into a single list segment, using the join operator to join sub-heaps nested below the nodes being collapsed. Predator tries to collapse first the longest sequence of objects with the lowest loss of precision (with configurable thresholds on the minimum such length). The abstraction loop is repeated till some collapsing can be done.

3   Predator Front End

The architecture of the Predator tool suite is shown in Fig. 2. Its *front end* is based on the *Code Listener* (CL) infrastructure [4] that can accept input from both the gcc and Clang/LLVM compilers. CL is connected to both gcc and Clang as their plug-in.

When used with *gcc*, CL reads in the GIMPLE intermediate representation (IR) from gcc and transforms it into its own *Code Listener IR* (CL IR), based on simplified GIMPLE. The resulting CL IR can be *filtered*—currently there is a filter that replaces `switch` instructions by simple conditions—and stored into the code storage. When used with *Clang/LLVM*, CL reads in the LLVM IR and (optionally) simplifies it through a number of *filters* in the form of LLVM optimization passes, both LLVM native and newly added. These filters can in-line functions, split composed initialization of global variables, remove usage of `memcpy` and `memset` added by LLVM, change memory references to register references (removing unnecessary `alloca` instructions), and/or remove LLVM `switch` instructions. These transformations can be used independently of Predator to simplify the LLVM IR to have a simpler starting point for developing new analyzers. Moreover, CL offers a *listeners architecture* that can be used to further process CL IR. Currently, there are listeners that can print out the CL IR or produce a graphical form of the control flow graphs (CFGs) present in it.

The *code storage* stores the obtained CL IR and makes it available to the Predator verifier kernel through a special API. This API allows one to easily iterate over the types, global variables, and functions defined in the code. For each function, one can then iterate over its parameters, local variables, and its CFG. Of course, other verifier kernels than the one of Predator can be linked to the code storage. Currently, it is also used by the Forester shape analyzer [7], and, as a demo example, a simple static analyzer for finding null pointer dereferences (`fwnull`) is implemented over it too.

4   The Predator Kernel

The kernel of Predator (written in C++ like its front end) implements an abstract interpretation loop over the SMG domain. An inter-procedural approach based on *function summaries*, in the form of pairs of input/output sub-SMGs encoding parts of the heap visible to a given function call, is used. As a further

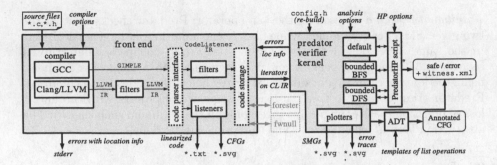

Fig. 2. Architecture of the Predator tool suite

optimization, *copy-on write* is used when creating new SMGs by modifying the already existing ones.

Predator's support of *non-pointer data* is currently limited. Predator can track integer data precisely up to a given bound and can—optionally—use intervals with constant bounds (which may be widened to infinity). Arrays are handled as allocated memory blocks with their entries accessible via field offsets. Reinterpretation is used to handle unions. Predator also supports function pointers. String and float constants can be assigned, but any operations on these data types conservatively yield an undefined value.

The kernel supports many *options*. Some of them can be set in the `config.h` file and some when starting the analysis. Apart from various debugging options and some options mentioned already above, one can, e.g., decide whether the abstraction and join should be performed after every basic block or at loop points only (abstraction can also be performed when returning from function calls). One can specify the maximum call depth, choose between various search orders, switch on/off the use of function summaries and destruction of dead local variables, control error recovery, or control re-ordering and pruning of the lists of SMGs kept for program locations.

5   Outputs and Extensions

Predator automatically looks for *memory safety errors*: illegal pointer dereferences (i.e., dereferences of uninitialised, deleted, null, or out-of-bound pointers), memory leaks, and/or double-free errors. It also looks for violations of *assertions* written in the code. Predator reports discovered errors together with their location in the code in the standard gcc format, and so they can be displayed in standard editors or IDEs. Predator can also produce error traces in a textual or graphical format or in the XML format of SV-COMP.

5.1   Predator Hunting Party

Predator Hunting Party is an extension of the Predator analyzer implemented in Python. It runs in parallel several instances of Predator with different options.

One Predator instance, called *verifier*, runs the standard sound SMG-based analysis. Then there are several (by default two) Predator instances—called *DFS hunters*—running bounded depth first searches over the CL IR of the program (with different bounds on the number of CL IR instructions to perform in one branch of the search). Finally, there is also a single Predator instance, a *BFS hunter*, running a timeout-bounded breadth-first search. The hunters use SMGs but without any heap abstraction, just non-pointer data get abstracted as usual. The verifier is allowed to claim a program safe, but it cannot report errors (to avoid false alarms stemming from heap abstraction). The hunters can report errors but cannot report a program safe (unless they exhaust the state space without reaching any bound). This strategy significantly increases the speed of the tool as well as its precision.

5.2   Transformation from Low-Level Lists to Containers

The latest (experimental) extension of Predator—denoted as ADT in Fig. 2— leverages the sound shape analysis of Predator to provide a sound recognition of implementation of *list-based containers* in low-level pointer code [3]. Moreover, it also implements a fully automated (and sound) replacement of the low-level implementation of the containers by calls of standard container operations (such as push_back, pop_front, etc.). Currently, (non-hierarchical) NULL-terminated doubly-linked lists (DLLs), cyclic DLLs, as well as DLLs with head/tail pointers are supported.

At the input, Predator ADT expects a specification of destructive container operations (such as push_back or pop_front) to look for. The operations are specified by pairs of input/output SMGs whose objects are linked to show which object is transformed into which. A fixed set of non-destructive operations (i.e., iterators, tests, etc.) is also supported. Predator ADT takes from Predator the program CFG labelled by the computed shape invariants (i.e., sets of SMGs per location), slightly extended by links showing which objects are transformed into which between the locations. It then looks in the SMGs for *container shapes* (i.e., sub-SMGs representing the supported container types) and sub-sequently tries to match the way the containers change along the CFG with the provided templates of container operations. While doing so, safe reordering of program statements is done. If all operations with some part of memory are covered this way, Predator replaces the original operations by calls of standard library functions (so far in the CFG labels only).

The recognition of container operations and their transformation to library calls can be used in a number of ways, ranging from program understanding and optimization to simplification of verification. The last possibility is due to a split of concerns: first, low-level pointer manipulation is resolved, then data-related properties can be checked [3].

6   Experiments

Predator was successfully tested on a quite high number of test cases that are all freely available. Among them, there are over 250 test cases specially created to test capabilities of Predator. They, however, reflect typical patterns of dealing with various kinds of lists (creating, traversing, searching, destructing, or sorting) with a stress on the way lists are used in system code (such as the Linux kernel). Predator was also successfully tested on the driver code snippets available with SLAyer [1]. Next, Predator found a bug in the cdrom.c test case of Invader [11] caused by the test harness used (unfound by Invader itself as it was not designed to track the size of allocated memory blocks)[2].

Further, Predator successfully verified several aspects of the *Netscape Portable Runtime* (NSPR). Memory safety and built-in asserts during repeated allocation and deallocation of differently sized blocks in arena pools (lists of arenas) and lists of arena pools (lists of lists of arenas) were checked (for one arena size and without allocations exceeding it). Further, some aspects of the *Logical Volume Manager (lvm2)* were checked, so far with a restricted test harness using doubly-linked lists instead of hash tables.

Predator was quite successful on memory-related tasks of the *SV-COMP competition* as noted already in the introduction. Up to SV-COMP'16, if Predator was beaten on such tasks, it was by unsound bounded checkers only. In the competition, in line with its stress on soundness, Predator has never produced a false negative.

Finally, the extension of Predator for *transforming pointers to containers* was successfully tested on more than 20 programs using typical list operations (insertion, removal, iteration, tests) on null-terminated DLLs, cyclic DLLs, and DLLs with head/tail pointers. Moreover, various SLAyer's test cases on null-terminated DLLs were handled too. Verification of data-related properties (not handled by Predator) on the resulting container programs (transformed to Java) was tested by verifying several programs (such as insertion into sorted lists) by a combination of Predator and J2BP [9].

7   Future Directions

In the future, the kernel of Predator should be partially re-engineered to allow for easier extensions. Next, a better support for non-pointer data, a support for non-list dynamic data structures, and for open programs are planned to be added.

References

1. Berdine, J., Cook, B., Ishtiaq, S.: SLAYER: memory safety for systems-level code. In: Gopalakrishnan, G., Qadeer, S. (eds.) CAV 2011. LNCS, vol. 6806, pp. 178–183. Springer, Heidelberg (2011). doi:10.1007/978-3-642-22110-1_15

---

[2] Other test cases of Invader were not handled due to problems with compiling them.

2. Laviron, V., Chang, B.-Y.E., Rival, X.: Separating shape graphs. In: Gordon, A.D. (ed.) ESOP 2010. LNCS, vol. 6012, pp. 387–406. Springer, Heidelberg (2010). doi:10.1007/978-3-642-11957-6_21

3. Dudka, K., Holík, L., Peringer, P., Trtík, M., Vojnar, T.: From low-level pointers to high-level containers. In: Jobstmann, B., Leino, K.R.M. (eds.) VMCAI 2016. LNCS, vol. 9583, pp. 431–452. Springer, Heidelberg (2016). doi:10.1007/978-3-662-49122-5_21

4. Dudka, K., Peringer, P., Vojnar, T.: An easy to use infrastructure for building static analysis tools. In: Moreno-Díaz, R., Pichler, F., Quesada-Arencibia, A. (eds.) EUROCAST 2011. LNCS, vol. 6927, pp. 527–534. Springer, Heidelberg (2012). doi:10.1007/978-3-642-27549-4_68

5. Dudka, K., Peringer, P., Vojnar, T.: Predator: a practical tool for checking manipulation of dynamic data structures using separation logic. In: Gopalakrishnan, G., Qadeer, S. (eds.) CAV 2011. LNCS, vol. 6806, pp. 372–378. Springer, Heidelberg (2011). doi:10.1007/978-3-642-22110-1_29

6. Dudka, K., Peringer, P., Vojnar, T.: Byte-precise verification of low-level list manipulation. In: Logozzo, F., Fähndrich, M. (eds.) SAS 2013. LNCS, vol. 7935, pp. 215–237. Springer, Heidelberg (2013). doi:10.1007/978-3-642-38856-9_13

7. Holík, L., Lengál, O., Rogalewicz, A., Šimáček, J., Vojnar, T.: Fully automated shape analysis based on forest automata. In: Sharygina, N., Veith, H. (eds.) CAV 2013. LNCS, vol. 8044, pp. 740–755. Springer, Heidelberg (2013). doi:10.1007/978-3-642-39799-8_52

8. Muller, P., Peringer, P., Vojnar, T.: Predator hunting party (competition contribution). In: Baier, C., Tinelli, C. (eds.) TACAS 2015. LNCS, vol. 9035, pp. 443–446. Springer, Heidelberg (2015). doi:10.1007/978-3-662-46681-0_40

9. Parízek, P., Lhoták, O.: Predicate abstraction of Java programs with collections. In: Proceedings of OOPSLA 2012. ACM Press (2012)

10. Sagiv, M., Reps, T.W., Wilhelm, R.: Parametric shape analysis via 3-valued logic. ACM Trans. Program. Lang. Syst. (TOPLAS) 24(3), 217–298 (2002). ACM

11. Yang, H., Lee, O., Berdine, J., Calcagno, C., Cook, B., Distefano, D., O'Hearn, P.: Scalable Shape Analysis for Systems Code. In: Gupta, A., Malik, S. (eds.) CAV 2008. LNCS, vol. 5123, pp. 385–398. Springer, Heidelberg (2008). doi:10.1007/978-3-540-70545-1_36

Author Index

Printed in the United States
By Bookmasters